THE IDEA OF HISTORY

IN THE ANCIENT NEAR EAST

LECTURES OF THE DEPARTMENT OF

NEAR EASTERN LANGUAGES AND LITERATURES

AT YALE UNIVERSITY

EDITED BY ROBERT C. DENTAN

WITH A PREFACE BY JULIAN OBERMANN

THE IDEA OF HISTORY in the ANCIENT NEAR EAST

by ROLAND H. BAINTON
LUDLOW BULL
MILLAR BURROWS
GEORGE G. CAMERON
ERICH DINKLER
JULIAN OBERMANN
PAUL SCHUBERT
E. A. SPEISER
C. BRADFORD WELLES

AMERICAN ORIENTAL SOCIETY
New Haven

Second Reissue

ISBN Number 0-940490-38-2

PREFACE

THE PLAN of the present volume has grown out of the realization that the field it concerns is greatly in need of a new approach. Owing to far-flung archaeological exploration, coupled with an ever growing multitude of new epigraphic and literary finds, the study of each of the leading areas of the Ancient Near East has in recent times developed into an independent philological discipline, with a highly specialized apparatus and a technique and methodology of its own. As a result, it is no longer possible for a single scholar to master the several disciplines involved with equal authority, while attempts made by individual writers to deal with the Near Eastern field in general, or merely to go beyond the realm of their particular specialization, are all but certain to prove unable to stand the test of critical scrutiny.

At the same time, however, the need for a comprehensive study of certain aspects of Near Eastern civilization as a whole—such as religion, law, society, history, literature, the arts and sciences—has now become more urgent than ever before. The fact is that the more fully any one of the major regions of the Ancient Near East gradually came to light, the more clearly it could be recognized as having helped to prepare the ground for the emergence of future civilizations, in particular as having provided some of the roots and seeds for the development of the medieval-Mediterranean culture and even of modern Western culture itself. At present, it is a commonplace to say that awareness of the civilization of the Ancient Near East has become indispensable for any student of the humanities and especially of culture history. But to be of critical validity, such awareness must depend on close collaboration of all the distinctive philological disciplines bearing on that civilization.

In the years past, members of the Department of Near Eastern Languages and Literatures at Yale have engaged in sporadic informal discussions on questions of the kind just indicated and, specifically, on their possible implications for the work of the department. One concrete outcome of those discussions was the clear recognition that an effort should be made to provide for a series of extracurricular symposia, each centered around a single topic characteristic of the cultural quest of Near Eastern antiquity, and pursuing that topic through all the main areas of the field, from Egypt and Mesopotamia down to Islam. Each such symposium, it was felt, would widen the outlook and, in a way, supplement the specialized training of students in the department; in addition, it would afford opportunity to students in other departments of the humanities to gain an authentic insight into the Ancient Near East, at least in terms of the given topic. Following a suggestion of Professor Paul Schubert, it was agreed that the first such symposium be given to the topic of the " idea of history "; and with the approval of the Semitic and Biblical Club it was agreed that the monthly meetings of that venerable club would in 1952-53 be held under the aegis of " The Idea of History in the Ancient Near East," the individual meetings to be dedicated to lectures on Egypt, Mesopotamia, Persia, Israel, the Hellenistic Orient, Apostolic Christianity, Patristic Christianity, and Islam, in that succession.

In a strictly methodological sense, too, the need of a new approach made itself felt during the exploratory discussions of the project. The source material for some of the leading areas of the field, it was realized, might be found primarily or indeed exclusively in synoptic compilations and more or less canonized collections put forward in an advanced age. Hence the actual source material might have been tinted by the compiler or collector in favor of a conventionalized theory, in the interest of an influential school, in deference to a ruling dynasty, or simply in the spirit of the new age. To some extent, this may well be the case in all areas of the Ancient Near East, but it is demonstrably the case in those of Ancient Israel, Primitive Christianity, and

Early Islam. Of course, the meaning of religion, the conception of law and authority, the force of social consciousness, the notion of truth and knowledge, or—in the instance before us—the idea of history, as evidenced in the developed age of a given culture of antiquity, is of primary importance in itself. This, however, does not diminish, let alone solve, the problem of that culture, and therefore should not be allowed to forestall the critical effort of penetrating into its anticipatory stages, of laying bare the rungs and strata of its making.

In the nature of things, it was assumed that the several scholars who would contribute to the planned symposium, while undoubtedly aware of the necessity of critical treatment of ancient source material, might hold diverse views as regards the approach to the particular topic proposed. In order, therefore, to insure a maximum of unity as to purpose and procedure, the following directives were drawn up and, eventually, submitted to the contributors for their consideration and approval.

" What we have in mind is an attempt to define such concepts of the past as may be found to be expressed or implied in the monuments or inscriptions of a given culture, as well as in its legends, songs, proverbs, liturgies, epics, and the like. We feel that even such areas of the Ancient Near East as did produce historiography proper should first be considered for their representations of the past without regard to the work of their historians in the conventional sense of the word.

" While it is understood that each area presents data and problems peculiar to itself, we venture to propose that all contributors to our ' symposium ' consider such questions as the following.

" What popular conceptions and ideas of the past, if any, may be found expressed or implied in the earliest manifestations of a given religious or cultural area? What is the meaning of the past for those who preserve, modify, or create the early stories and records? What interests and motives are perceptible in the telling and retelling of stories of the past?

" Are early conceptions and ideas found to prevail in the further development of the area? To what extent do they undergo modification, or do they meet with challenge or opposition of any kind? May early conceptions of the past in a given cultural sphere be said to have been replaced or superseded by a different set of conceptions? What attempts, if any, have been made to harmonize early attitudes toward the past with later, more advanced ones?

" To what extent is the sum total of historical trends recognizable in the conventional works of chroniclers, apologists, historians, and theologians after a given cultural epoch has reached its prime and has achieved its full expression in literary manifestations? Finally, does historiography of a given area ever reflect or produce critical awareness of the idea or ideas of history that attended its growth and development? "

Whether and to what extent the individual lectures have followed the above directives—and, accordingly, what measure of unity, in approach and results, they may be seen to have established when taken together—is a question that may be left for others to examine. When considered separately, however, there can be no question that, " present company excepted," each lecture will be found to offer in and by itself a distinct and indeed novel contribution to Near Eastern research. To some, no doubt, the particular import of the volume will be found in that, although it deals with a single topic and with the same over-all milieu as to time and space, each lecture is unmistakably stamped with the scholarly personality of the lecturer. This in itself, quite apart from the sustained interest the lectures aroused in the academic community which attended the monthly meetings, has seemed sufficient to justify making the lectures available for publication.

The project was conceived of as an experiment to be carried out in its entirety by members of the Yale faculty. It was, therefore, a disappointment when some of our close associates found it impossible to take active part in this work. We were then all the more appreciative of the ready response to our invitation to join in the symposium given us by two distinguished outside scholars,

Professor George G. Cameron of the University of Michigan and Professor E. A. Speiser of the University of Pennsylvania.

Ludlow Bull's contribution to this volume was destined to be the last essay from his pen, based on the last public lecture he gave at his alma mater. As the first of his works to be published posthumously, it would seem especially designed to keep alive the memory of his genial personality among his colleagues and pupils and the many devoted friends he has left in all schools and divisions of Yale University. His associate of many years at the Metropolitan Museum of Art, William C. Hayes, has cleared the proofs of " Ancient Egypt " for publication.

JULIAN OBERMANN

New Haven
December, 1954

CONTENTS

ANCIENT EGYPT

Ludlow Bull

I. NATURE OF THE EVIDENCE FOR AN IDEA OF HISTORY[1]

There is no ancient Egyptian word known to the writer which closely corresponds to the English word history as used in the general title of these essays,[2] nor is there any Egyptian text known to him which can be said to express an " idea of history " held by an ancient Egyptian author. It is clear, however, that the Egyptians were intensely interested in the origin of the universe, in their gods, in life after death, and in making and preserving records of their past as a nation. Their kings carefully recorded what may be called the facts of public history, and private individuals took great pains to preserve those facts of personal history which would reflect credit upon them. In the circumstances the Egyptian view of history must be sought in the surviving records of events that were considered by those in authority worthy of report for the information of their contemporaries and for posterity. Such records go well back into the predynastic period. And when one considers the calendrical records of primitive peoples of modern times, peoples who are without any system of writing, it seems certain that some kind of record keeping must have existed in Egypt as well as in other ancient nations, long before the time of any surviving examples.

II. HISTORICAL RECORDS

It is interesting that the oldest surviving record of the earliest historical data set down as such by the Egyptians is very far from

1. The writer wishes to express his thanks to his colleague, Dr. William C. Hayes, for valuable suggestions.

2. The nearest approach to such a word is probably *gn.wt* (pl.), generally translated " annals." It seems to refer to historical records as physical documents.

being contemporary with the earliest events recorded. At some time, apparently in the 5th Dynasty[3] (ca. 2550 B.C.) and on grounds of style certainly not later than the 6th Dynasty, there was set up, presumably at Memphis, the capital, a large slab of stone almost seven feet long and something over two feet high, inscribed on both sides in horizontal registers. The dimensions of this stone cannot be given with any exactness. All that we have of it is six fragments. One of these is the celebrated Palermo Stone, which has been in Sicily since about 1859 and in the Palermo Museum since 1877. Four fragments are in the Cairo Museum; three of these were bought by the authorities of the Egyptian Antiquities Service in 1910, and the fourth was found later by a guardian of the service on the site of ancient Memphis. The sixth fragment, which Sir Flinders Petrie bought from a dealer in Egypt about the time of the purchase of three of the Cairo fragments, is in University College, London. It is possible though not certain that the six fragments (all, I believe, of the same type of diorite) belong to the same monument; if more than one monument is involved their inscriptions were much the same. There might of course have been more than one example of this stele of annals. A study of the fragments shows that the annals began with a register which included a list of kings of the two separate predynastic kingdoms of Upper and Lower Egypt, the names being arranged horizontally and each name being determined below by a squatting royal figure wearing the distinctive crown of the kingdom over which he ruled.[4] There may have been 140 or

3. This numbering of the dynasties is not the invention of modern historians but goes back at least to the Egyptian historian Manetho who lived in the time of Ptolemy II (3d century B.C.); fragments of his history of Egypt survive in the works of classical writers, pagan, Jewish, and Christian. He transmitted the numbering which has been followed ever since; and in the main it seems to be perfectly valid.

4. Upper Egypt, the general reader may be reminded, is not the northern kingdom, but comprises the Nile Valley between the First Cataract, near modern Aswān, and the Delta. It is the southern kingdom. The northern kingdom is the Delta. The southern crown is a tall white crown and that of

more of these kings in the first register. Several of the kings shown in the first line of the principal Cairo fragment appear to be wearing the double crown of Upper and Lower Egypt, for at the time of union the two crowns were combined.[5] The fact that there were kings in the first line of the Palermo Stone wearing the double crown was first noticed, I think, by Sir Alan Gardiner[6] in his examination of the photographs in Gauthier's publication of the Cairo fragments in 1915. The fact was confirmed by J. H. Breasted, the American Egyptologist, from an inspection of the original.[7] The existence of kings of united Egypt at some time before the dynasties bears out the theory of an early union of the two lands resulting from a conquest of the south by the north, followed by a reseparation of the two kingdoms. P. E. Newberry, the British Egyptologist, as early as 1906,[8] had called attention to the superiority of the early Delta civilization before he was aware of the evidence supplied by the largest Cairo fragment of the Old Kingdom annals; and in 1922[9] the German, Kurt Sethe, had suggested the likelihood of an early victory by the Delta people over the south.

At this point mention should be made of the Egyptian belief that the long line of kings of the two separate kingdoms was preceded by certain of the great gods who reigned on earth successively, presumably over the whole of Egypt. In some of their king lists the Egyptians named the gods who had thus reigned on earth before departing to the sky or to the underworld. In the famous Turin Papyrus of Kings, almost certainly written

the Delta a low red crown with a flat piece projecting upward at the back and a slender antenna-like coil in front.

5. The tall white crown is somewhat in the shape of a bottle, and it fits into the low red crown.

6. *Journal of Egyptian Archaeology, 3* (London, 1916), 145.

7. *Bulletin de l'Institut Français d'Archéologie Orientale au Caire, 30* (Cairo, 1931), 709 ff.

8. *Proceedings of the Society of Biblical Archaeology, 28* (London, 1906), 69.

9. *Nachrichten der Königliche Gesellschaft der Wissenschaften zu Göttingen* (1922), pp. 197–252.

down in the 19th Dynasty (13th century B. C.),[10] the supposed lengths of the gods' reigns are noted after their names. The Turin papyrus is a truly remarkable document. It was found in the early 19th century by the Italian explorer Drovetti at Memphis, and he brought it to Italy and deposited it in the Turin Museum of Archeology. It contained the names, when it was originally written, of more than three hundred kings of Egypt, beginning with the gods and extending down to the end of the Second Intermediate Period, in the early 16th century B. C., just before the 18th Dynasty, including the invading Hyksos kings. It is said to have been in very bad condition when found,[11] and many fragments are missing, but the document has been largely restored through the work of many scholars over a long period of years. The most remarkable recent work was done by the German expert, Hugo Ibscher, who died in 1943. He was a specialist in the restoration of fragmentary papyri through a study of their fibers, and he made some important additional placings of fragments of the Turin papyrus. The papyrus as restored by Ibscher was published by the Italian Egyptologist, Giulio Farina, in 1938.[12] Many scholars have quoted from this document and have used it in their researches. Again in the 3d century B. C. under Ptolemy II, as we have said, the history of Egypt composed in Greek by the priest Manetho also listed the same gods as appear in the Turin papyrus, and it is from Manetho's king list alone that we have the complete thirty dynasties which bring us down to the time of Alexander the Great, in the late 4th century B. C. Both the Turin list and Manetho place between the gods and the kings, just preceding

10. The papyrus may be a copy of a list of kings compiled from ancient records in the early 18th Dynasty after the expulsion of the Hyksos.

11. G. Farina, *Il papiro dei re restaurato*, Publicazioni egittologiche del R. Museo di Torino, Rome, 1938. Farina denies (p. 7) the story that the papyrus was badly damaged in transport.

12. See note 5. Since the appearance of Farina's work Sir Alan Gardiner and Professor Jaroslav Černý of Oxford have made a new collation of the papyrus and a new transcription into hieroglyphic. This has been privately circulated in a photostat edition as *The Turin Canon of Kings* (1952).

the dynasties, a list of " glorified ones " (Egyptian *akhu*), called by Manetho " demigods." In view of the arrangement of the later lists, it is possible that the Old Kingdom stele of annals also named the gods and the glorified ones at the beginning of its first register, but the part that has survived does not contain them. The predynastic kings, whether of the separate and independent kingdoms of Upper and Lower Egypt or of the first and later dissolved union of the Two Lands, are the personages referred to in later times as the " Followers of Horus." The rulers of both the northern and the southern kingdoms worshiped Horus, the last of the god-kings, and traced their descent from him, each king being considered a reincarnation of Horus himself. The earliest historical data in the royal annals must thus have belonged to a time perhaps as much as a thousand years earlier than the date of the stele of annals or several centuries back into the 4th millennium B. C.

Beside the Old Kingdom annals, the Turin papyrus, and Manetho's history, there are four other shorter king lists. These all date from the New Kingdom. The earliest of these is a selective list recorded by Thut-mosĕ III (earlier half of the 15th century B. C.) in a small chamber adjoining his festival hall in the temple of Karnak at Thebes. The inscribed stones from the walls of this room were taken to France by Prisse d'Avennes in 1844 and are now in the Louvre. This list contained sixty-one names of certain kings of the 4th, 5th, 6th, 11th, 12th, 13th, 14th, and 17th dynasties. Since the names are not all in correct order and some of them are partly or wholly destroyed, the list is not of great value. The first name in the list is destroyed. The next is that of Snefru, first king of the 4th Dynasty (27th century B. C.), followed by several kings of the 5th Dynasty. The reason for the selection of names is not clear. This is especially true of a dozen names of rather obscure rulers belonging to the 13th or 14th Dynasty in the Second Intermediate Period (18th and 17th centuries B. C.). Thut-mosĕ may have had reason to believe that he was directly descended from these particular kings.

The next document in order is much more interesting and valuable. It is the list of seventy-six kings placed on a wall of his mortuary temple at Abydos by Sethy I, second king of the 19th Dynasty (ca. 1300 B. C.).[13] It begins with eight of the nine known names of 1st Dynasty kings, followed by seven of the ten names assignable to the 2d Dynasty, four of the five given to the 3d Dynasty, six of nine possible kings of the 4th Dynasty, and eight of the nine names given to the 5th Dynasty in one or more lists. Then follow all the known kings of the 6th Dynasty. For the First Intermediate Period the Abydos list gives fifteen names, some of which occur only here. The Herakleopolitans (9th and 10th dynasties) are not mentioned. The list moves on to the Middle Kingdom, naming two of the more important kings of the 11th Dynasty (ca. 2000 B. C.), and all but one of the eight monarchs of the 12th Dynasty. The one missing ruler is the last, Sobk-nefru, a queen regnant.[14] The Second Intermediate Period is passed over, including the Hyksos, who are ignored as foreign invaders. The list continues with the New Kingdom (beginning 1580 B. C.), naming all the kings of the 18th Dynasty except Akh-en-Aton and his followers, including Tut-ʿankh-Amūn, who were omitted because of their connection with the Atonist heresy. Hor-em-ḥāb ends the dynasty. Queen Ḥat-shepsūt was not included, probably on the ground that legally she was never more than regent during the minority of Thut-mosĕ III. The list ends with Sethy's two predecessors in the 19th Dynasty and his own name.

The third of the shorter king lists is that found in a private tomb of the reign of Ramesses II at Saqqārah (ancient Memphis) and now in the Cairo Museum. It originally contained the names of fifty-eight kings ending with Ramesses II (13th century B. C.). The first name is that of Manetho's Miebis (*Mr-bꜣ-p*), probably the sixth king of the 1st Dynasty, which it has been suggested,

13. For the Abydos and Saqqārah lists, see E. Meyer, *Aegyptische Chronologie* (Berlin, 1904), Tafel I.

14. On this name, see P. E. Newberry in *Journal of Egyptian Archaeology*, *29* (1943), 74–5.

may mean that this king was the first of the so-called Thinites to take up regular residence at the new capital of Memphis. Two more 1st Dynasty kings are listed, eight of the ten generally assigned to the 2d Dynasty, and four of the five 3d Dynasty rulers. There seem to have been nine names for the 4th Dynasty, probably a full roster of this group. It is unfortunate that the last four of these names have been destroyed, for there are no examples of three of them in hieroglyphic writing. One of the missing names was almost certainly that of Shepses-kuf. Eight of the nine 5th Dynasty kings are included, but only the four most prominent rulers of the 6th. The First Intermediate Period is passed over, and to begin the Middle Kingdom the same two kings of the 11th Dynasty who were selected for the Abydos list are recorded at Saqqārah. All seven kings of the 12th Dynasty are listed, and Queen Sobk-nefru appears under her throne name, Sobk-ku-Rē‘.[15] The Second Intermediate Period, including the Hyksos, is disregarded as at Abydos. For the New Kingdom the arrangement is the same as at Abydos, Ḥat-shepsūt and the heretical ‘Amārneh group being omitted in the 18th Dynasty. The list ends with the first three kings of the 19th Dynasty.

A fourth list was placed by Ramesses II in his temple at Abydos. Remains of it are in the British Museum.[16]

There is another type of historical record which might be cited to illustrate the importance which the Egyptians attached to such records, whether public or private, and their ability to keep them from loss or destruction. This is represented by a number of long genealogical lists which have been preserved.[17] Several of these cover many generations and involve periods ranging from 300 to 750 years. While there are short genealogies from all

15. *Ibid.*

16. See Bertha Porter and R. L. B. Moss, *Topographical Bibliography of Ancient Egyptian Hieroglyphic Texts, Reliefs, and Paintings, 6,* No. 27, 35.

17. For genealogies see Ludwig Borchardt, *Mittel zur zeitlichen Festlegung von Punkten der aegyptischen Geschichte und ihre Anwendung* (Cairo, 1935), pp. 92–114.

periods, the specially long ones date from the Late Dynastic Period, a time of gradual decay and a time also of archaism and particular interest in tracing descent from the great days of old. One of these genealogies can be proved incorrect in the exalted titles it gives to the ancestors,[18] but for the most part, especially where they can be checked by references to some of the individuals from contemporary sources, the lists are probably fairly accurate. By far the most remarkable of these genealogies, both because of its length and because originally it named more than twenty of the kings in whose reigns certain of the listed individuals lived, is the genealogy of Memphite priests,[19] carved on a white limestone slab which is, or was, in the Egyptian Department of the State Museum of Berlin (No. 23.673). This extraordinary list originally gave the names of sixty men, each of whom is said to be the son of his predecessor in the list. Only six of the names have become illegible through injuries to the stone. These sixty generations extend from near the end of the 22d or Libyan Dynasty (ca. 750 B. C.) back at least to the earlier part of the 11th Dynasty (ca. 2100 B. C.) or over a period of not less than 1,350 years. This would be the equivalent of a modern genealogy naming a continuous line of direct ancestors going back to about A. D. 600. The general correctness of this remarkable genealogy is supported here and there by the evidence of other dated monuments on which some of the individuals of the Berlin list are mentioned; moreover the sixty generations cited accord well with the number of years that can reasonably be assigned to the whole period involved. The monument may be presumed to have been erected at Memphis by the first personage named in the list, a priest of Ptaḥ of Memphis and of his consort Sakhmet, whose name was ʿAnkhef-en-Sakhmet. Names of kings probably occurred with those of about half of the men named in the list. In these cases the titles and name of the individual are followed by the formula: "in the time (*m rk*) of King X." Kings' names seem not to be inserted according to any recognizable plan. The earliest

18. See *ibid.*, p. 95, n. 5.
19. *Ibid.*, pp. 96–112.

two names of priests in the list, chronologically speaking, are lost with the whole of their inscriptions, which may have included one or even two kings' names. The third personage is said to have lived " in the time of King Neb-ḥepet-Rēʿ [Montu-ḥotpe]," the most famous ruler of the 11th Dynasty. Seven generations later the name of Amun-em-ḥēt I, first king of the 12th Dynasty, appears. The lapse of time here, so far as it can be estimated, seems too short for so many generations. Three more kings of the 12th Dynasty are named. Three priests seem to have served under Seʿn-Wosret III, which is reasonable in a reign of thirty-five or more years. After two lost ancestors come the names in adjoining generations of a King Iby and an elsewhere unknown King ʿO-qen (ʿ3-qn), both from the Second Intermediate Period. Possibly the latter name is a misplaced and miswritten rendering of the name of ʿO-qen-en-Rēʿ, a Hyksos king. Six generations later there are in adjoining places a King *Š3rk*[20] and an Apophis, evidently two Hyksos kings, followed immediately by Aʿḥ-mosĕ I of the 18th Dynasty. Two generations later Amun-ḥotpe I appears, and after two more, Tḥut-mosĕ III. In the second and third places for Tḥut-mosĕ III are two priests, both serving Amun-ḥotpe III. Next comes " the King, the God's Father Ay." It is interesting that although he is given the title of king (*Ny-Św.t*), the name of this representative of the ʿAmārneh heresy is not honored with a cartouche. Next to Ay appears Ḥor-em-ḥāb, and immediately following this generation come two priests both serving under Seṯhy I of the 19th Dynasty. During the following very long reign of Ramesses II four generations served, the representative of the earliest being the well-known high priest of Ptaḥ, Nofer-ronpet. The second ancestor after the last priest of the time of Ramesses II is represented as belonging to the reign of Manetho's Amenophthis of the 21st Dynasty some two hundred years later. It is obvious that in the course of centuries certain of the royal names have become associated incorrectly with particular priests, but such errors do not necessarily throw suspicion on the general reliability of the Memphite genealogy.

20. *Ibid.*, pp. 106–7. Borchard suggests that King *S3rk* may just possibly be Mantheo's Salatis.

Let us now turn to records of public history other than lists of kings or commoners. The Old Kingdom stele of annals gives us no details about the predynastic kings. But one of the last kings of Upper Egypt before the final union of the two lands, perhaps the very last, has left monuments which have a bearing on his view of what should be recorded for posterity. In 1898 at Hierakonpolis, the ancient Upper Egyptian capital of the followers of Horus, the British excavator, J. E. Quibell, found an enormous pear-shaped ceremonial macehead of limestone with scenes in relief.[21] This macehead is about a foot high and was made presumably as a votive offering; but it is also an historical monument. Maceheads of this shape used as actual weapons were only about three inches in height, that is, about the size of an actual pear. The macehead was made for the king whose name was written with the representation of a scorpion, and he is known to Egyptologists simply as " King Scorpion," since the reading of the sign as used in this name is not certain. The decoration is in three registers. At the top are a number of poles surmounted by emblems of deities of Upper Egyptian provinces. To some of these poles are bound dead birds representing a word for a section of the Egyptian people (*rekhyet*),[22] and to others are attached bows, representing probably the so-called Nine Bows, the aboriginal tribes of the Nile Valley that had been conquered by the historic Egyptians and still dwelt on the outskirts of the country. This register seems to symbolize the conquest of Egyptian foes (probably the forces of the northern kingdom) and of disaffected outlying tribes, perhaps in alliance with the northerners. The second register shows a large figure of King Scorpion wearing the tall white crown of Upper Egypt. He bears a hoe and is about to break ground, perhaps for the annual planting of grain or a new system of irrigation canals. The third register shows the Nile with islands on which men are working and palm trees grow.

It is probably the Scorpion King's successor, whose name on

21. J. E. Quibell, *Hierakonpolis*, Pt. I (London, 1900), pp. 9–10 and pls. 25 and 26C; and Pt. II (London, 1902), p. 41.

22. A. H. Gardiner, *Ancient Egyptian Onomastica* (Oxford, 1947), *1*, 100–8.

his monuments is generally read Naʿr-mer, who is the southern ruler to be considered as having completed the conquest of the Delta and reunited the Two Lands into one kingdom, which endured with only a few short interruptions until the Persian conquest in 525 B.C., some 2,500 years later. The view which seems to be best supported by such evidence as we have is that which holds that Naʿr-mer is the person known to the compilers of the king lists of 1500-1200 B.C. (the lists of the New Kingdom) and to Manetho as Menes, the traditional unifier of Egypt. The name Men or Meni from the later dynastic lists (from which the Greek form Menes derives) is not found with certainty on any monument before the New Kingdom, and the known fragments of the 5th Dynasty stele of annals do not help us here. We can only hope that further fragments of the annals or other monuments may some day come to light to prove or disprove this identification.

The most important monument of Naʿr-mer is the great palette of dark-green slate, two feet long, found by Quibell in the temple at Hierakonpolis.[23] Small palettes for ordinary use, perhaps four or five inches long and of the same shape, were very common, and this royal palette is simply a magnification of the common form for ceremonial purposes. This is the type of slate palette made in various forms on which malachite was ground for the green eye paint used throughout Egypt for centuries before Naʿr-mer's time. Even the circular depression where the grinding was done is carved into one side of this purely ornamental piece. The decoration of this hollowed side is in three registers. Apparently it was considered the obverse of the palette, but from the modern historian's point of view the opposite face seems to come first. On the latter side we see a large figure of the king, whose name appears at the top of both sides of the palette. He wears the tall white crown of the south, his native land. His upraised arm bears a mace with which he is about to brain a kneeling captive (Bedawi), who has the heavy hair and beard of the northerner, and whose name or that of his place of origin appears

23. Quibell, Pt. I, p. 10 and pl. 29.

beside his head. This scene is repeated over and over again throughout Egyptian history to record victories of Egyptian arms. Above the head of the hapless prisoner on this palette is a composition indicating very clearly the nationality of the defeated enemy. A human head is shown projecting from a sign representing a body of land in which are growing papyrus plants, the symbol of the Delta. Upon the papyrus plants and facing the king stands Horus, the victorious falcon of Upper Egypt. In his talons he holds a cord attached to the nose of the head, symbolizing the people of Lower Egypt, and thus presents to the king the defeated country. If there were any doubt about the meaning of this scene it would be resolved by looking at the three registers on the hollowed side of the palette. At the top Naʿr-mer, his name beside his head, wears the peculiar red crown of the north, showing that he has seized the throne of the Delta kingdom. He is accompanied by retainers, and before him are the decapitated bodies of defeated enemies. In the center two lions with impossibly long, giraffe-like necks, comparable to the contemporary or slightly earlier balanced animals of southwest Asiatic art, seem to symbolize the new fraternization of the Two Lands, despite the efforts of two northern personages to part them.[24] At the bottom the king is shown as a bull trampling a northerner and knocking down a hostile fortress with his horns. The king's name is repeated here, near his head, to emphasize the fact that this man wearing the northern crown is the same man from Upper Egypt depicted above and on the opposite face.

Naʿr-mer, too, had made for him a handsome macehead between seven and eight inches in height, also found at Hierakonpolis,[25] which was another record of his victory over the north. Here the king wearing the captured northern crown is shown enthroned and surrounded by his court in the act of receiving the submission of northern or Libyan prisoners, who are stated to number 120,000. Large and small cattle taken from the enemy are num-

24. H. Senk, *Chronique d'Egypte* (Brussels), No. 53 (Jan., 1952), pp. 23–30.

25. Quibell, Pt. I, pp. 8–9 and pl. 26B; Pt. II, pp. 40–1.

bered at 1,822,000. It is interesting that the system of numerals has already been perfected at this early time. The signs used for these large figures were exactly the same signs used in later times throughout the dynastic period. These figures are not necessarily fantastic, since they may represent an approximation of the total military man power of the Delta and may have included, so far as the cattle are concerned, many animals not removed from Lower Egypt but considered as surrendered.

For a consideration of the matters thought worthy of record by the early dynastic kings we may return to the Old Kingdom stele of royal annals. Beginning with the 1st Dynasty a much more detailed system is used than a mere list of kings. Each ruler is alloted a rectangular space for each calendar year of his reign, and in this space are recorded important events of the year. The end of each reign is given in terms of months and days of the calendar year. The events recorded include rites associated with the accession of the new king, annual feasts of certain gods, the dedication of statues of the gods, the census of cattle, which occurred at first every other year and later every year, the founding and dedication of temples, and the creation of reservoirs and canals. One of the 2d Dynasty kings records the destruction of two towns with apparently Egyptian names, suggesting a revolt in the Delta (Palermo Stone, year 13 of King *Ny-ntr* or *Ntry-mw*). Finally, in the great majority of the yearly rectangles on the surviving fragments of the annals, the height of the Nile inundation above an arbitrary zero is recorded in cubits, palms, and fingerbreadths, data which must have been of great value over a period of years. This shows that there must have been graded Nilometers from predynastic times.

Besides the Old Kingdom royal annals there are a considerable number of monuments of kings of the 1st and 2d dynasties. Many of these give us little more than their names, but there are a few which show us some of the facts they thought worthy of remembrance. These are the kings whose capital was at Tiny (Greek *Thinis*) near Abydos and who are known as the protodynastic rulers or Thinite kings. There are also a number of small tablets of ivory and wood recording the observation of feasts, the founding of temples, and the taking of prisoners.

Mining and quarrying expeditions outside the Nile Valley were matters of importance to Egyptians even in much later times, because of the extensive preparations involved and the problems to be solved in what is called logistics in modern American military parlance. Therefore it is not surprising that King Wadjy of the 1st Dynasty should have recorded his name forty miles out in the eastern desert on the ancient route between the town of Edfu and the Red Sea, or that King Sekhem-ẖet, of the 3d Dynasty, should have depicted himself three times on a rock stele in the mining region of the Wadi Maghāreh in the far-away Sinai peninsula. This, like many similar records in the Sinai peninsula, shows that the Egyptians frequently had to smite the local Bedawīn before they could carry on their mining operations for copper and malachite. Sekhem-ẖet raises his mace in one representation, just as Na'r-mer is represented on his palettes as doing, to brain the Bedawi, whom he holds by the hair. He wears the white crown in two of the scenes, the red crown in the other. The double crown is not often shown in these very early carvings. The king is accompanied by his general, whose title, " overseer of the army," is clearly to be read. This suggests that a considerable force was necessary on these early expeditions. By the time of the Middle Kingdom, eight centuries later, when a temple of the goddess Ḥat-Ḥor was built at Sarabīt el Khādim in Sinai, perhaps to replace an Old Kingdom shrine, conditions had changed, and the region was under constant Egyptian control.

Most of the records to which reference has been made are carved in stone. The number of these records greatly increased as Egypt emerged, with the accession of Manetho's 3d Dynasty, into the great period known to modern historians as the Old Kingdom. There were also records on ivory, wood, and papyrus, and to a lesser extent, on leather. The early Egyptian kings were conscious that they were making history, and they wished the story to last forever. Thus far it has lasted for more than five thousand years.

Stone architecture began to flourish under Djoser, first king of the 3d Dynasty. His tomb was under the famous step pyramid built by his architect, Im-ḥotep, at Saqqārah, near Cairo. This official's name was known at first to modern students from the late references to him in Ptolemaic times rather than from periods more nearly contemporaneous with him. It is only since 1918 that contemporary occurrence of his name has been found in the complex of buildings around the step pyramid which he designed. Stone pavements exist in some of the 1st or 2d Dynasty tombs, and even stone door frames, but nothing more than that. Then suddenly in the 3d Dynasty appeared a tremendous monument of stone two hundred feet high, a pyramid which is not a true pyramid but seems to consist of several rectangular masses, posed one on another, each smaller than the one below. It is because of this arrangement that the modern appellation step pyramid is applied to Djoser's monument. The model for each of the steps of this pyramid may have been the so-called *masṭabah* tomb—a structure with sloping sides and a flat top which resembles the Arab masṭabah, a bench generally made of mud bricks—but the inner structure of the pyramid does not support this theory.

This first stone architecture is an experimental science. An interesting fact is that the stones of which this monument was built are extraordinarily small, approximating in size the adobes [26] of Nile mud which had been the standard building unit. Later, the Great Pyramids of the 4th Dynasty were built of enormous blocks of stone. Im-ḥotep included in the complex of buildings surrounding the step pyramid a festival courtyard for the celebration of the king's jubilee. In it he erected stone reproductions of the light wood and wattle buildings that were used by the kings for these celebrations. However, no similar stone structures were built again, and it is evident that the royal festival continued to be celebrated for more than two thousand years with the old wood and wattle buildings that had already been consecrated

26. This Spanish word descends from the ancient Egyptian *djōbe* through the Arabic *ṭūb*.

by centuries of usage. Several kings did build large stone halls as a setting for their jubilee rites, and Tḥut-mosĕ III, in his hall at Karnak, used columns whose form suggests the tent poles of the ancient jubilee structures. Djoser's architect was able to reproduce the very slender, freestanding columns of the wooden buildings by engaging them into the façade of the building before which they formed a colonnade. These same buildings contain a different type of column, which Im-ḥotep used to make a colonnade down the center of a hall. These columns were made up of stone drums carved to look like the reed bundles that formed the columns of the predynastic buildings. They have quite a respectable diameter, a foot or more; but again Im-ḥotep did not feel that they would stand without support, so he provided each column with a light wall running out from the side wall of the building to support it, although this actually would not have been necessary.

The pyramid was built as a great mountain of stone to prevent anyone from carrying off the king's corpse or in any way desecrating his burial. It has not been successful in this regard, but it has fulfilled its second purpose, that of perpetuating the memory of the king. The same is true of the other types of tombs which were built or excavated by kings or private persons. All pyramids had a public and a private part. The subterranean burial chamber was supposed to be inacessible, but on the east side a temple was built in which offering could be made for the well-being of the king's soul. In all the private tombs, whether rock tombs or masṭabahs built on the surface of the ground, there was the same dual arrangement. The burial chamber was always excavated in the solid rock, but there was a chapel in the outer part of the rock tomb or in the superstructure of the masṭabahs, so that at least the inscriptions in these tomb chapels served their purpose of handing down to posterity the name, titles, and deeds of the deceased, whether he were king or commoner. In these inscriptions we have autobiographical data which showed the appreciation of the people for private as well as public history. We also find references to kings of a very much earlier period.

The Egyptians knew their history; they remembered the great figures of the past. It is a striking fact that we have detailed lists of kings giving the lengths of their reigns over a period of two thousand years, during which occurred civil wars and invasions. In spite of all disturbances those records were somehow maintained to the end. Among the early kings who have been mentioned many centuries after their times in inscriptions were Snefru, first king of the 4th Dynasty, and Khufu, another king of the 4th Dynasty and the builder of the Great Pyramid at Gīzeh. The mortuary cults of the Old Kingdom and Middle Kingdom kings carried on into the New Kingdom. At times of serious revolution or invasion, the ceremonies of these funerary cults must have ceased. There were no priests to conduct the services or make the offerings. However, with the return of peace, the royal cults were revived.

Another indication of the Egyptians' regard for history is their commemoration of great personages other than kings. Im-ḥotep, the great minister and royal architect of the beginning of the 3d Dynasty, was such a personage. As has been mentioned, he is now known to have built the tomb of King Djoser. But he was also remembered throughout Egyptian history as a great sage. A song of Middle Kingdom origin, preserved in two New Kingdom copies, refers to him as a famous wise man, along with Prince Ḥor-ded-ef, a son of King Khufu of the 4th Dynasty.[27] In Ptolemaic times Im-ḥotep was actually deified and had temples of his own. He was declared to be a son of Ptaḥ, chief god of Memphis, and the " temple of Asklepios " there, which is referred to by classical writers, was undoubtedly the temple of Im-ḥotep. Another man of similar reputation was Amun-ḥotpe, son of Ḥapu, a man of the New Kingdom who lived under the 18th Dynasty in the reign of King Amun-ḥotpe III. So great was the king's affection for him that he erected a funerary temple for him. After Amun-ḥotpe's death his cult began to grow, and in the end he became a full-fledged member of the pantheon, worshiped in many temples throughout the country.

27. Adolph, Erman, *Literature of the Ancient Egyptians*, p. 133.

The great kings of the New Kingdom, when they came back from their campaigns in Asia or Africa, mentioned in their inscriptions the countries they had conquered and described their battles in such detail that actions like those of Megiddo (Tḥut-mosĕ III) and Kadesh (Ramesses II) can be reconstructed. These military adventures were very much to the fore, but occasionally such things as treaties were recorded. We have also the celebrated treaty that Ramesses II made with the Hittite king, Hattušili, about 1280 B. C. There are two long-known copies of this treaty in hieroglyphic inscriptions on the walls of temples in Egypt, and when the files of the Hittite foreign office at Bogazköy in central Asia Minor were excavated in the present century, the Hittite copy of that same treaty was found.[28] Sometimes, too, the great kings recorded other things. Tḥut-mosĕ III, one of the greatest of the 18th Dynasty kings, a man who conquered the whole of Palestine and Syria up to the Euphrates, was somewhat interested in plants. In one of his additions to the great temple of Karnak he illustrated the strange plants he found in Palestine and Syria, placing a great number of them on the walls of one of the rooms.

Another indication of the Egyptians' love of history and their appreciation of the past is shown in the archaism in architecture and art that appears in the New Kingdom and later. At the beginning of the New Kingdom, in the 18th Dynasty, we find a very distinct tendency to imitate the art of the Old Kingdom, and in the 26th Dynasty, which brings us down into the 6th century B. C., we have several direct copies of specific reliefs of the Old Kingdom two thousand years earlier and of the 18th Dynasty a thousand years earlier.

The Egyptians were appreciative of history, but we cannot say that they were great historiographers, for no histories have survived from the dynastic period. We are not particularly concerned with historiography here, but it should be recalled that the only historical work of any great importance known to us

28. Stephen Langdon and A. H. Gardiner, *Journal of Egyptian Archaeology*, *6* (1920), 179 ff.

is the lost history of Manetho of which we have spoken already. It may well be thought of as inspired by the Greek view of history.

As we have stated, one of the most important sources for the Egyptians' view of what should be recorded as history is the great body of inscriptions of nonroyal personages existing on stelae of stone and on the stone walls of tombs. The practice of erecting inscribed tombs for a commoner who had become an important official began with the 3d Dynasty. In such a tomb the official often told, rather boastfully it must be said, of the services that he had performed for his king in peace or war. If his tomb were not extensively inscribed he might at least erect a stele at his grave or at the holy city of Abydos. The stone chapel in the masṭabah or rock tomb, like the king's mortuary temple, was for eternity and open for public visitation, even though the funerary offerings might cease because the family fell into disfavor or failed to keep it up or because of wars or invasions. The tomb itself remained, and we have much autobiographical material that is from something over two thousand to nearly five thousand years old. In addition to autobiography copies of important legal documents were sometimes inscribed in tombs in order that their terms might still be preserved if other records failed. Several examples of wills and deeds of trust in the Old and Middle kingdoms exist, known only from copies on the walls of tombs.

Throughout the 2,500 years of dynastic history, it does not seem to the writer that the Egyptians' view of history changed greatly. They traded by land and sea with Syria and Palestine, voyaged down the Red Sea to the Indian Ocean and to the mysterious land of Punt, traded with the lower Nubians in central Africa, suffered collapse, and recovered under the leadership of the Theban rulers of the 11th and 12th dynasties that formed the Middle Kingdom. In the 17th century B.C. they succumbed to the Hyksos invasion. Rescued by the 17th and 18th dynasties they developed great military power, and the Thutmosids conquered Syria up to the Euphrates. In the latter part of the 18th Dynasty we have the short-lived religious revolution of Akh-en-Aton and the subsequent return to orthodoxy. This was followed by the Libyan and Ethiopian dynasties, then a renaissance under the 26th Dynasty, and eventually, the conquest by Persia in 525 B.C. There was certainly a kind of static quality in the Egyptians' view of history. The old days were good days in general. Individuals might boast in their tomb inscriptions of unusual feats of arms or organization or engineering, and they would sometimes say that such a thing had never been done before or had never been done since the time of the gods; but sometimes also a deed would be compared by an autobiographer to a similar deed done centuries before in the time of an ancient king. The Egyptians were vividly conscious of their past, while at least on the material side they attempted to build for the future.

III. CREATION AND OTHER MYTHS

Like other peoples the Egyptians speculated about the beginning of things, and various hypotheses about this were developed independently in various centers of culture in the Nile Valley. These hypotheses, or syntheses of a number of them, came to be regarded by the Egyptians as part of their history. The more popular of these had their origin, as might be expected, in the more powerful city-states of prehistoric Egypt, which were able to absorb a number of neighboring provinces and impose their cultures upon the conquered towns.[29] Among the earliest of these cultural centers was undoubtedly Ōn, a Lower Egyptian town near the southern point of the Nile Delta, known to the Greeks of the last pre-Christian centuries as Heliopolis. The theology of Ōn believed that at the beginning of time there was nothing but the primordial ocean, the Nuu or Nūn (Egyptian *Nw.w* or *Nwn*). How this ocean came into being we are not told. In it the sun-god Atūm created himself. Then from his spittle or semen (there are two version of the story) he created Shu,

29. Drioton and Vandier, pp. 80–2 and references cited p. 115.

god of the atmosphere, and the goddess Tefēnet, the consort of Shu. To this pair were born Gēb, the earth-god, and Nūt, the goddess of the sky. Gēb and Nūt in their turn became the parents of the gods Osiris and Seth̲ and the goddesses Isis and Nephthys. Atūm and his eight descendants were adored as the Great Ennead of Heliopolis.

Another early and well-known theology was that of Khmūn, 180 miles up the Nile from the Delta. This was the city of the great god Tḥōt,[30] whom the Greeks later identified with Hermes, calling the place Hermopolis. Here everything began with Tḥōt, who, apparently self-created, called into existence by his word, upon the primeval mound, four divinities whose names show that they represent 1) the primeval water, 2) perhaps spatial infinity, 3) darkness, and 4) a being who is called " obscurity " and also " lack " or " loss." Each of these male beings had a female counterpart. These divinities together were called the Eight, and this is reflected in the name of their town Khmūn, the Egyptian word for the number eight. The males of the group are represented as frogs, and the females as serpents or human forms with the heads of serpents.[31] Tḥōt and his Ogdoad thus came into being before the sun, and it was the Eight who created the egg from which the sun emerged.

Later, but already in the protodynastic period (the 1st and 2d dynasties before 3000 B.C.), when Memphis had been the official capital of reunited Egypt since the time of Menes, the priesthood of Ptaḥ, the ancient deity of the place, wished to give their god the highest position in the pantheon. They promulgated dogmas designed to make Ptaḥ supreme among the gods. It is probable that he had long been considered the creator of the universe in his own locality and was always held to be the patron

30. Tḥōt is the ibis god, probably of Delta origin but very early adored at Khmūn. An old baboon god of Upper Egypt (Hedj-wer) was also worshiped at Khmūn and became identified with Tḥōt. See Bonnet, *Reallexikon der aegyptischen Religionsgeschichte*, *s.v.* " Affe," " Hermopolis," " Thot."

31. From the New Kingdom on, the Ogdoad were sometimes represented as baboons.

of sculptors and workers in metal. In the new Memphite theology, in which certain features were borrowed from both Heliopolis and Hermopolis, Ptaḥ, under the name of To-tenen (" the emerged land "), was himself the primeval mound of earth. He created the primeval ocean Nuu and his consort Nūwet (sometimes called Nūnet). They in turn produced the lotus (the god Nefer-tēm), from which came forth the sun (Atūm). Through Atūm, Ptaḥ created Horus, Tḥōt, and the other great gods that formed with him an Ennead. In the Memphite theology the other gods were merely functions of Ptaḥ (heart, tongue, etc), used by him in creating and ruling the universe. Our primary source for the Ptaḥ-centered theology is a remarkable document which will be referred to again in the following section of this essay.

Another theological system was that of Amūn of Thebes. Originally the " hidden " or " obscure one " of the Hermopolitan creation myth, Amūn had been given a cult at Thebes, 280 miles to the south, some time before the 11th Dynasty (ca. 2150 B. C.), when he is first mentioned as a Theban god. There, however, he had an appearance resembling that of Mīn, ancient deity of the neighboring nome of Gubtiu, Koptos of the Greeks. Since the 11th Dynasty arose at Thebes this town became the capital of the kingdom, and Amūn tended to replace the ancient local falcon god Montu as the chief dynastic deity. Amūn was soon identified with Rēʻ, the sun-god, and as such became the head of the Heliopolitan Ennead and also of the Ogdoad of Hermopolis, to which latter he had originally belonged.

The Egyptians seem not to have been particularly interested in the details of the creation of man. There is no story of an ancestral human pair. Children were thought to be shaped by the power of the god Ḫnūm, patron of potters, but that applied to all children. It is true that an old legend states, almost incidentally, that the eye of Rēʻ on an occasion shed tears of rage which turned into men, thus creating the human race. This statement, found only in one source, a papyrus of the early part of the Greek period (shortly before 300 B.C.),[32] was probably invented largely because of the opportunity it presented for one of those plays on words of which the Egyptians were fond. The word for tear is *rmy.t*, that for mankind is *rmṯ*.

Another legend purports to record an event in the early history of man. It is known to Egyptologists as the story of the Deliverance of Mankind, and its earliest version is found in the tomb of Seṯhy I at Thebes (ca. 1300 B.C.).[33] However, the legend itself must go back to the Old Kingdom, for there seems to be an allusion to it in a text whose content dates from the 10th Dynasty (ca. 2100 B.C.), although the surviving copy was written in the 18th Dynasty.[34] According to this legend, when Rēʿ, the sun-god, was " king over men and gods together," mankind devised against him a plot, the details of which are not given. Rēʿ " discerned the things that were planned against him " and summoned the Ennead in council, requesting also the presence of Nuu, the primeval water in which Rēʿ had originally appeared. When the gods are assembled Rēʿ with great respect addresses Nuu, asking counsel of him. Nuu graciously responds, referring to Rēʿ as " one mightier than he that created him." He urges Rēʿ not to be troubled but merely to turn his eye upon the rebels and blasphemers. When Rēʿ says that mankind has fled into the desert in fear of him the gods join in advising him to send down his eye in the form of the goddess Ḥat-Ḥor.[35] This is done, and Ḥat-Ḥor slays many of the conspirators, desisting only to report to Rēʿ and presumably to take repose. It is evident, although the text is corrupt at this point, that Rēʿ no longer wished to

32. The Papyrus Bremner-Rhind in the British Museum. See R. O. Faulkner, *Journal of Egyptian Archaeology, 23* (1937), 172 (p. 27, ll. 2 and 3 of the original) and *24* (1938), 41 (p. 29, ll. 3 and 4 of the original).

33. Erman, pp. 47 ff.

34. The Instruction for King Mery-ku-Rēʿ. A. H. Gardiner, *Journal of Egyptian Archaeology, 1* (1914), 22. Erman, p. 75. Alexander Scharff, *Der historische Abschnitt der Lehre für König Merikarê*, Munich, 1936. Aksel Volten, *Zwei altägyptische politische Schriften*, Copenhagen, 1945.

35. Several of the principal Egyptian goddesses often are given the epithet " Eye of Rēʿ."

destroy the whole of mankind. He sent messengers to procure a substance called *dedy*, evidently a mineral that makes a red stain. Under cover of night this was ground to powder, and seven thousand jars of fresh beer were impregnated with it. The beer, turned red as blood, was poured out over the fields where Ḥat-Ḥor was to continue her slaughter the following morning. We are told that the blood-red beer lay four palms deep over the fields. When Ḥat-Ḥor appeared she imagined this to be the blood of those she had slaughtered. She tasted it, found it good, and drank so copiously of it that she became drunken and forgot forever the mission on which she had been sent. Thus mankind was saved from total destruction.

IV. LATE COPIES OF EARLIER TEXTS

The importance which the Egyptians attached to the records they considered a part of their history is shown by their ability to preserve texts, written presumably on papyrus rolls, over many centuries and through periods of civil strife and hostile invasion. Evidence of this care of records has been alluded to above in referring to the Turin Papyrus of Kings and to the sources of Manetho's history. Other examples are not lacking. We have spoken in the third section of this essay of the Memphite theology in which Ptaḥ, the ancient local god of Memphis, was raised to the apex of the pantheon by his votaries as a result of the promotion of his town to the position of official capital of united Egypt. Our only important source for this theology is a monument of the reign of King Shabako of the 25th or Ethiopian Dynasty, who ruled from 716 to 701 B. C.[36] It is a thick slab of

36. J. H. Breasted, "The Philosophy of a Memphite Priest," *Zeitschrift für aegyptische Sprache, 39* (Leipzig, 1901), 39–54. K. H. Sethe, *Dramatische Texte zu altaegyptischen Mysterienspielen* (Leipzig, 1928), pp. 1–80. H. J. B. Junker, *Die Götterlehre von Memphis* (Berlin, 1940) and *Die politische Lehre von Memphis* (Berlin, 1941) = *Abhandl. der Preuss. Akad. v. Wissenschaften, Phil.-hist. Klasse* (1939), No. 23 and (1941), No. 6, and references cited. Wilson, pp. 58–60.

black granite about 54¼ inches long and 36¼ inches high. It was presented to the British Museum in 1805 by Earl Spencer, and nothing is known of its provenience. It is assumed that the stone was erected by Shabako at the temple of Ptaḥ at Memphis. Along the top of the face of the stone are two horizontal lines of inscription which serve as a heading for the long texts in sixty-two vertical columns that follow. The first line contains the titualry of King Shabako. The second line reads:

> His majesty wrote this document anew in the house of his father Ptaḥ. His majesty had discovered it as a work of the forefathers which had been eaten of worms and was not [completely] legible from beginning to end. Therefore his majesty wrote it anew, so that it is more beautiful than it was before, in order that his name might endure and his monument be fixed in the house of his father Ptaḥ forever.

The language and orthography of the texts in vertical columns make it clear that the document copied by Shabako's scribes dates from the Old Kingdom, perhaps the 5th Dynasty, or from a period perhaps 1,800 years before Shabako's time. Moreover, the content of the texts and such knowledge as we possess of early Egyptian history and religion suggest that the Old Kingdom version must have been a copy of a document of the protodynastic period, near the end of the 4th millennium B. C., and that it was composed not long after the establishment of Memphis as the official capital of united Egypt. It is remarkable that a perishable document (a slender roll of papyrus kept in a pottery jar or perhaps a wooden writing board) should have survived for so many centuries in the library or sacristy of the temple of Ptaḥ at Memphis. We are indebted to Shabako, and doubtless also to the contemporaneous high priest of Ptaḥ, for the preservation of one of the most important documents that has come down us from ancient Egypt. Unfortunately, through the use of the stone, presumably during some part of the Christian Era, as a nether millstone, about a third of the inscribed area has been so abraded that nothing can be recovered of the texts. Enough remains, however, to reveal the remarkable religious philosophy of this early theological statement. It was evidently thought necessary to accept the well-established and neighboring Heliopolitan Ennead with Atūm at its head. However, for the Memphite theologians, Ptaḥ was above all and behind and beyond all. He was the heart (i. e., the mind), which conceived creation and the tongue which called it into being. Atūm himself is made to say that Ptaḥ was the self-creating ultimate cause which produced the Ennead. This ancient Memphite theology has often been compared with the Logos doctrine of Christian philosophy.[37]

In the third year of his reign (ca. 1965 B. C) Seʿn-Wosret I, second king of the 12th Dynasty and one of the great rulers of the Middle Kingdom, laid the foundations at Heliopolis of either a new temple of the sun-god or an important addition to the temple existing in his time. There had been a temple of the sun-god there since prehistoric times, and undoubtedly a stone temple had been there for five hundred years or more. We have no contemporary record of this foundation. Fortunately, however, more than five hundred years later a scribe in the reign of Amunḥotpe II of the 18th Dynasty copied in ink on a leather roll in the hieratic script [38] part of the text that had been carved on a stone stele at the direction of Sesostris I. This stele must have been set up in the temple, but both temple and stele have disappeared. Nothing remains but a few stones on the ground and one of a pair of obelisks erected by Seʿn-wosret I before his temple. The date on the leather roll appears among some half-erased notes on the verso of the piece, but it is said to be in the same hand as that of the copy of the 12th Dynasty building inscription. This latter text was evidently copied as a model of literary excellence. In it, following the date in the third year of Seʿn-wosret I, it is stated that the king summoned his court and announced that he

37. Breasted, p. 54, and Wilson, p. 59.

38. The roll is or was preserved in the State Museum of Berlin (P 3029). For translations see Breasted, *Ancient Records of Egypt, 1,* 240–5; Erman, pp. 49–52; Adriaan de Buck, " The Building Inscriptions of the Berlin Leather Roll," *Studia aegyptiaca* (Rome, 1938), *1,* 48–57.

had determined to build a new temple to the sun-god, here called Ḥor-akhity, but referred to later on in the speech as Atūm. In a long poetic address the king expresses his adoration of the god who had formed him and trained him for the kingship from babyhood. He declares that he will maintain the offerings of the god, " sacrificing to him who made me and satisfying the god with that which he [the god] gave." He goes on to say that he will preserve his own memory by the splendor of his monument to the god. The courtiers then praise the king for his wisdom and look forward with joy to the completion of the temple under his direction. The king now addresses the chief treasurer and, expressing confidence in him, bids him make plans for the building of the temple. At this point the scene shifts to the actual foundation ceremony. Whereas the king had worn the double crown at the assembly of the court, for the rite of " stretching the cord " for the plan of the new building he dons a narrow diadem with two tall plumes. Before a throng of onlookers—the text reads, " all his subjects "—the proper officials stretched the cord and placed something, perhaps the foundation deposits, in the earth. Soon after this point the copy comes to an end.

Mention has been made above of Amun-ḥotpe, son of Ḥapu, who was one of the most outstanding nonroyal personalities to emerge from the long history of dynastic Egypt. He was born in the provincial town of Athribis in the Delta, the son of a man who apparently possessed no title or office, yet he was proud of his birthplace and of his father, for both are frequently mentioned in his inscriptions, and he persuaded his royal master to adorn and beautify his native town. He also often mentioned his own honorific titles of chief of his nome, which in his time was no longer a functional post, and overseer of the priests of its god Ḥor-khent-eḫtoy. Amun-ḥotpe, son of Ḥapu, was already middle-aged when King Amun-ḥotpe III came to the throne. Perhaps the king had known him before. In any case we know little of his earlier life, but his advancement was rapid under Amun-ḥotpe III. He first served in a military capacity and probably saw service in Nubia, but he spent most of his later life as the chief architect of the most magnificent of Egypt's sovereigns. He probably was responsible for most of the king's great buildings, including those at Thebes; the king's mortuary temple on the west side of the Nile, the largest such temple in Egypt, of which almost nothing now remains; the palace nearby; and the new temple of Amūn at Luxor. He also saw to the quarrying, probably at Gebel el Aḥmar near modern Cairo, of enormous single blocks of quartzite for the two huge seated figures of the king before his mortuary temple which still tower over the western plain of Thebes and are popularly known as the Colossi of Memnon. They are about sixty-four feet in height. The extraction of such blocks from the quarry and their transport more than four hundred miles up the Nile to Thebes were feats of which Amun-ḥotpe, son of Ḥapu, may well have been proud. He also undoubtedly built elsewhere for the king, whose architectual enterprises stretch from the Delta to the northern Sūdān. In the latter region at Soleb a figure of the architect appears in the temple. Presumably he designed his own mortuary temple, a magnificent structure larger than those of many kings, being more than one hundred meters in length and about forty-five meters wide. It was probably completed before his death at the age of about eighty, presumably in or soon after the thirty-fourth regnal year of his king.[39] It was in his thirty-first regnal year, if we may rely on the document described below, that the king issued a decree to insure the maintenance of offerings in the mortuary temple of his great minister. The decree was probably carved on a stele set up in the now-ruined temple. This has not survived, but an apparent copy in hieratic, which scholars agree may be dated to the 21st Dynasty, exists in the British Museum.[40] Nothing is known of its provenience, nor is it certain when it came into the possession of the museum. It was first mentioned in 1838. The monument is a roughly rectangular limestone slab

39. His name appears on a jar label of this year. See W. C. Hayes, *Journal of Near Eastern Studies, 10* (1951), 105, fig. 17.

40. Robichon and Varille, *Le Temple du scribe royal Amenhotep fils de Hapou* (Cairo, 1936), pp. 1–24 and pl. 1.

about 32 inches high and about 24½ inches wide. The stone is not of very good quality, and no attempt was made to make its surface perfectly smooth. Instead it was covered with a layer of plaster on which the nineteen horizontal lines of the inscription were cut. Oddly enough the text is not in hieroglyphic. The scribe has used the hieratic script, the cursive hand developed originally for writing with pen or brush and ink. Moreover, since the signs were not written in ink but were scratched into the plaster with a sharp instrument, the result is somewhat inelegant. But at least most of the signs are clear. The strokes of the signs were filled with coloring matter, now of a greenish-blue tone. This is a very common technique in the case of incised hieroglyphs, but hieratic inscriptions cut in stone or plaster are not common and in general would be brief graffiti not worthy of adornment with color.[41] A few hieratic stelae are known from shortly after the 21st Dynasty, and these, together with the orthography of this text, have made it possible to date the monument to that dynasty. At the same time the evidence has raised the question of whether the stele is not a forgery created in the 21st Dynasty by the mortuary priests serving the temple of Amun-ḥotpe, son of Ḥapu, at that time in order to maintain the endowments of the shrine in a period when corruption had invaded the Theban necropolis, as is suggested by the well-known records of the trials of tomb robbers near the end of the 20th Dynasty.[42] In these records four men attached to the service of this temple are mentioned, two of them as robbers.

It is clear from its language that the stele cannot be a literal copy of an 18th Dynasty document; but it seems equally clear that it quotes from the decree whereby King Amun-ḥotpe III had established the funerary endowment of his great minister three hundred years before the stele was incribed. At that time the king summoned two men well-known as being prominent at

41. The reader should note that hieratic inscriptions on stone are among the commonest of ancient Egyptian documents, but these are written in ink on flakes of white limestone, the so-called *ostraka*.

42. Robichon and Varille, pp. 19–21.

his court, his vizier Amun-ḥotpe and his treasurer Mery-Ptaḥ, to accompany him to the new temple, together with courtiers and scribes. Here the king caused his edict to be read. It provided for the mortuary endowment, with workers of both sexes to cultivate the lands set apart for the endowment and to serve the temple and make the daily offerings therein. The workers are to hand on their duties to their children from generation to generation under the protection of Amun Rēʿ, king of the gods. At this point the text becomes an utterance by the great beneficiary of the decree. Any persons who force any of the personnel of the lands of the endowment into other employment, even for the king's service, shall be accursed and eventually destroyed. Their bodies shall be burned. They shall receive no mortuary offerings after death; their children shall not inherit their property; their wives shall be violated. The king warns all officials, from the vizier down, that if they do not carry out the necessary services of the foundation they will become liable to the fate mentioned above. Then the son of Ḥapu speaks, promising that all future generations of officials who do not interfere with the operations of the endowment but foster them shall be favored by the kings reigning in their time. They shall live to a ripe old age and come to rest in the necropolis provided with suitable mortuary offerings. So ends the document.

V. CONCLUSION

In the writer's view it seems fair to say that the ancient Egyptians cannot have had an " idea of history " in any sense resembling what the phrase means to thinkers of the present age or perhaps of the last 2,400 years. They do not seem to have developed a philosophy of history so far as can be observed in the surviving fragments of their literature. They do not seem to have thought in terms of cause and effect or of trends that were observable in their own story or in those of neighboring peoples in the ancient world. As we said earlier there was a definitely static quality about the Egyptians' view of life and of their past.

This was in part due to their comparative isolation geographically. Above the Delta the inhabitants of Egypt lived on the floor of a canyon five hundred miles long and never more than thirty miles wide, hemmed in by deserts to east and west and the " great green sea " to the north. But the most important element in their view of life was their belief that the conditions of their existence as a people had always been, and always would be, governed by the gods, whose will and purposes were utterly inscrutable.

BIBLIOGRAPHY

General works only are given here and most of them are cited in the notes.

Architecture

E. Baldwin Smith, *Egyptian Architecture*, New York, 1938.

History

James Henry Breasted, *Ancient Records of Egypt*, 5 vols. Chicago, 1906.
———, *A History of Egypt*, New York, 1905 (or later reprints).
Etienne Drioton and Jacques Vandier, *L'Egypte*, New York, 1952.
W. C. Hayes, *The Scepter of Egypt*, New York, 1953.
J. A. Wilson, *The Burden of Egypt*, Chicago, 1951.

Literature

Adolph Erman, *The Literature of the Ancient Egyptians*, trans. A. M. Blackman, London, 1927.

Religion

Hans Bonnet, *Reallexikon der aegyptischen Religionsgeschichte*, Berlin, 1952.
Adolph, Erman, *Die Religion der Aegypter*, Berlin and Leipzig, 1934. French trans. by H. Wilde, *La Religion des Egyptiens*, Paris, 1937.
H. Frankfort, *Ancient Egyptian Religion: an Interpretation*, New York, 1948.
Jacques Vandier, *La Religion égyptienne*, 2d ed., Paris, 1949.

ANCIENT MESOPOTAMIA

E. A. Speiser

I. NATURE OF THE PROBLEM

IN the intellectual world of the Sumerians no concepts would seem to be more distinctive and fundamental than the associated ideas of n a m and m e. The first has the approximate force of our " essence " and " destiny " combined. The other has no suitable analogue in the world of ideas with which we are familiar, for m e appears to be the activating feature appropriate to each n a m and required for its proper functioning.[1] Every essential element of nature and society has its individual m e.[2] Cosmic rule and kingship on earth, qualities and emotions noble as well as base, arts and crafts—these and many others become dormant when their special m e is absent.[3]

No rendering of such an intimate cultural term can be more than a rough approximation. We may choose " norm " or " decree," " dynamic force " or the like.[4] We may go on to point out that the m e was endowed with esoteric and enduring properties. Yet, for all our efforts, we find ourselves unable to evoke the meaning inherent in the native term. It is in the nature of distinctive civilizations that their distinguishing features cannot be lifted intact out of their context. Neither can their original designations be translated into words stemming from a foreign source and based on alien experiences.

1. Cf. B. Landsberger, *Archiv für Keilschriftforschung*, *2* (1924–25), 64–8; *Islamica*, *2* (1926), 369; *Fakültesi Dergisi*, *3*, 154.

2. See Kramer, *Sumerian Mythology*, pp. 64–7.

3. When the Zû bird stole the Tablets of Destinies from Enlil every m e became inoperative; cf. *ANET*, pp. 111 ff. Does this myth imply that the Tablets of Destinies controlled each and every m e or that they constituted the individual m e of the universe on which all others depended?

4. For a recent discussion see T. Jacobsen, *JNES*, *5* (1946), 139, n. 20, where " *modus operandi* " is proposed as a reasonable approximation.

Ideas of history peculiar to a given society are likely to constitute some of that society's most meaningful features. Because they reflect, however, basic societal values, they are difficult for outsiders to apprehend. To appreciate the Mesopotamian idea of history in all its ramifications we should need to know in effect what the Sumerians, who played a major role in the evolution of the civilization of Mesopotamia, conceived as the n a m and the m e of history in general and their own history in particular. This we cannot determine. The two characteristic concepts, which are elusive for us in the first place,[5] are never applied by the sources to an institution or an abstraction which we could confidently equate with " history." All of this is a fair measure of the complexity of the problem that now confronts us.

Does this absence of a native term corresponding to our " history " imply that Mesopotamia, in its long career as an integral civilization, failed to evolve a particular idea of history? Hardly. The historic Mesopotamian was keenly aware of his past; he was forever busy recording its details; and he was intent on drawing from the past certain practical lessons. All this can readily be demonstrated. What is less obvious is the over-all system resulting from the sum of such interests and activities. The sense of history varies from place to place and from period to period. In the ancient Near East that sense was highly developed in Palestine [6] but very little, apparently, in Egypt. To

5. It is significant in this connection that Frankfort, *The Birth of Civilization*, p. 16, in analyzing the nature of civilization, concludes that its two primary aspects are " form " and " dynamics." Now " form," or " the elusive identity " of a given civilization or of any of its distinctive components, is for all practical purposes very close to the Sumerian n a m; and " dynamics " would be as good a rendering of m e as has yet been suggested. Frankfort does not adduce our terms for a possible comparison, but he might easily have done so. It would thus seem that the Sumerians had already anticipated this particular—and altogether convincing—result.

6. Cf. Meyer, *2*, 285: " So hat die Blütezeit des judaeischen Königtums eine wirkliche Geschichtsschreibung geschaffen." Contrast, however, Collingwood, *The Idea of History*, p. 12: " two forms of quasi-history, theocratic history and myth, dominated the whole of the Near East until the rise of

the Mesopotamian, history was something involved in the larger issues of life and destiny as manifested in the past, tied up with the present, and projected into the future. But it was also something to be lived, not dissected. Accordingly, the Mesopotamian's awareness of the process was reflected in numerous ways, but it did not lead to a direct statement of principles.

Our conception then, of the idea of history in ancient Mesopotamia has to be pieced together from the incidental reflections of that idea in sundry phases of the underlying civilization. We can thus expect here only a reflection of a reflection or, to paraphrase a distinguished student of historiosophy, a reflection of the second degree [7]—our analysis of the analysis of the ancients indirectly conveyed. To attempt this we have to approach the subject with the fragmentary data of our own age, two millennia and more after the history in question had come to a close at long last. Yet the results need not be unduly speculative, for the themes involved pervade large areas of Mesopotamian civilization and are thus capable of repeated control. The question is whether we can reassemble the component motifs into a self-consistent pattern.

Most of the pertinent source material has been treated in separate investigations by eminently competent authorities.[8] Larger portions of the total design have also been subjected to

Greece." This is not the place to demonstrate in detail that Meyer's statement rests on a sounder foundation than Collingwood's. But in justice to Collingwood's provocative study it should be added that its author had not had the opportunity to acquaint himself with much essential information on the progress of historiography among "our forerunners in civilization."

7. *Ibid.*, p. 3.

8. See Olmstead, *Assyrian Historiography*, which although antiquated and rather tangential to the present topic, being primarily a textual comparison of late annals, is still useful; Güterbock, *ZA*, *42*, Pt. I, 1–91, a penetrating and pioneering discussion; Jacobsen, *The Sumerian King List*, which is no less important, although limited to the earliest phase of the problem. Note also Mowinckel, *Gunkel Festschrift*, pp. 278–322, and W. A. Irwin, "The Orientalist as Historian," *JNES*, *8* (1949), 298–309.

penetrating analysis.[9] All such results loom large in the presentation that follows. Yet no study to date has focused directly on the whole topic before us; although some of the territory has been well explored, large stretches of it remain untouched. To that extent therefore our argument must carry with it some of the risks and hazards of an initial effort. This is not, to be sure, a case of a writer rushing in but an instance of his having been persuaded to take the plunge. Nevertheless, the wisdom of a venture must be open to doubt when the field is one where angels have not been known to tarry.

II. THE GENERAL CULTURAL SETTING

Our task, then, is first, to seek out the principal elements which enter in one way or another into the concept of history in ancient Mesopotamia; and second, to inquire whether these sundry elements yield anything resembling a harmonious design. Before we survey the separate motifs we must touch briefly on three broader themes which furnish the essential background. These themes are civilization, religion, and government. It goes without saying that only the roughest kind of outline is possible at this time; no more than is necessary to suggest how each of these factors might affect the superimposed idea of history.

1. CIVILIZATION

Mesopotamian civilization reaches back to remote prehistoric times—an indeterminate number of centuries prior to 3,000 B. C. —and it survives as an active force until Hellenistic times. The prehistoric age, although brilliantly illuminated in some respects,

9. Cf. e. g., these major studies on the connection between religion and the state in Mesopotamia, a subject that has a pronounced bearing on the question before us: Labat, *Le Caractère religieux de la royauté assyro-babylonienne*; Gadd, *Ideas of Divine Rule in the Ancient Near East*; Frankfort, *Kingship and the Gods*. See also Jacobsen, *Intellectual Adventure*, pp. 125–222, and Albright, *From the Stone Age to Christianity*. Other references will be given in the course of the discussion.

must forever remain dim and inarticulate in others, notably in the social and intellectual fields.[10] This is precisely why it is prehistoric. The long historic span, however, is richly documented thanks to the presence of writing. The picture that emerges is clear enough in its main contours, although innumerable details remain obscure.

Perhaps clearest of all is the fact that the underlying civilization enjoyed substantial uniformity throughout its long career. This is not to imply that it was a static civilization; its dynamic character is constantly in evidence. But the statement can be made and upheld that certain basic values present from the start retain their vitality to the very end. Dominant beliefs and practices which we notice under the Sargonids of Akkad, in the third millennium, are still in vogue in the first millennium, under the Sargonids of Nineveh. The changes that the passing centuries bring with them do not affect the main framework. For purposes of our over-all appraisal, therefore, the cultural constants outweigh the chronological variables.[11]

It is particularly noteworthy that this essential uniformity of Mesopotamian civilization throughout its historic course was maintained in spite of a great diversity of participants. For Mesopotamia, unlike Egypt or Palestine, was not the home of a single dominant ethnic group in the period under discussion. On the contrary, several significant groups pass in review, usually more than one at a time. The Sumerians, the Babylonians, and the Assyrians are the best known, but there are others. The Sumerians, moreover, inject into the scene the potentially disruptive feature of a language apart. The common civilization, then,

10. Cf., in general, Frankfort, *The Birth of Civilization*, pp. 32 ff.; Speiser, *JAOS*, *59*, suppl. *4*, 17–31.

11. It should be stressed in passing that over its long course Mesopotamian civilization confronts us with abundant evidence for discontinuity as well as continuity and that opinions differ in regard to the interpretation of these contrasting phenomena; cf. Speiser, *Hebrew Union College Annual*, *23*, Pt. I, 339–56. Yet such differences of opinion center primarily about sundry details. The over-all structure remains uniform and self-consistent.

was uniquely cosmopolitan. It transcended ethnic, linguistic, and political boundaries, achieving cultural unity where disparity would be the normal outcome.

This unusual attainment of unity through disparity must be credited to the Sumerians. It is wholly immaterial in this connection what position one takes in regard to the question of ultimate Sumerian priority.[12] The long prehistoric stage lacked the means to leave to posterity definite ethnolinguistic criteria. All it could do was strew the area with material remains of several distinctive cultures.[13] Eventually, however, the survivors are drawn within a single orbit. They come to reflect the same kind of cultural content and direction in religion and literature, law and government, arts and sciences.[14] By that time the normative features are unmistakably Sumerian. These features appear early in the historic age. And whether the Sumerians had been on the scene from the very beginning or had arrived recently—which the present writer regards as an inescapable conclusion—it is they who made history beyond all dispute.

The fact, however, that the Sumerians were not alone in building up the civilization of Mesopotamia had this important consequence. For all cultural purposes, the land was bilingual: for the last two thousand years of its history the literate elements had to make use not alone of the Semitic Akkadian but also of the unrelated Sumerian.[15] Recourse to two languages was a broadening experience in many ways. It implied a victory over parochial-

12. *Ibid.*

13. Cf. Perkins, *The Comparative Archeology of Early Mesopotamia.*

14. Political differences, notably between Babylonia and Assyria, could not offset the underlying cultural unity. Thus, Shamshi-Adad I of Assyria, whose concluding years dovetailed with the beginning of Hammurabi's reign, caused his own inscriptions to be couched in the style and spirit of Babylonia. His lead was followed by all Assyrian rulers after 1350 B.C.; cf. Landsberger and Balkan, *14*, 220. Analogous instances could be adduced for various other phases of the intellectual life of Assyria.

15. Hence when the combined Sumero-Akkadian vehicle proved its usefulness farther afield, as it did with the Hittites, the ultimate tool became trilingual to some extent, as any student of Hittite will feelingly confirm.

ism, some capacity for toleration, and a certain universality of outlook. And the eventual bearer of this heritage, in the strict cultural sense, was not properly a Sumerian, a Babylonian, or an Assyrian. He was essentially a Mesopotamian.

2. RELIGION

The tendency toward universalism just mentioned is most clearly evident in religion. And since the religion of Mesopotamia was in all essentials a contribution of the Sumerians, we may speak this time specifically of the Sumerian religion. Perhaps its two outstanding features are the human attributes of its gods and their identification with the powers of nature and the cosmos. It is on this last count that we have here a universalistic, and certainly a supranational, conception of religion.

Furthermore, the Sumerians saw in the society of the gods the prototype of human society. The two interpenetrated. Man took his cue from the gods at the same time that the gods were being drawn closer to mankind.[16] No one god was the sole source of power and authority. All the leading figures of the pantheon had themselves been created. None was fully secure in his status, none really omnipotent. Authority resided in the community of the gods. As a community, the gods required organization. This organization took the form of a state. The state, in turn, was a self-governing body and, as such, a safeguard against absolutism.

But the lack of absolute authority on the part of any one god led to uncertainty about the actions of the divine powers combined. Nothing was settled for all time, nothing could be taken for granted; hence the anxiety and the insecurity of the mortals, who must forever be intent on propitiating the gods in order to obtain a favorable decision. The view that nothing was permanent and that the gods were unpredictable brought with it a fitful and dramatic conception of the universe, one that called

16. Cf. the literature cited in n. 9; also Landsberger, *Fakültesi Dergisi, 3*, 151.

for constant watchfulness and elaborate ritual.[17] By the same token, however, there was always room for hope rather than apathy and resignation.

3. GOVERNMENT

Since the cosmos was conceived as a state, and since government on earth was a replica of divine government, the Mesopotamian state must correspond to the cosmic state. This principle remains valid throughout the entire history of Mesopotamia. It follows that the authority of the mortal ruler was severely circumscribed by two factors. First, his mandate stemmed from the gods to whom he was responsible for his every move. Second, the head of the pantheon lacked absolute power, in that the cosmic state subscribed to the principle of government by assembly.[18] Hence so it must be also with government on earth.

The normative place of the assembly in the sociopolitical structure of Mesopotamia has only recently come in for proper appreciation.[19] It is a feature that combines with the overriding importance of the law to impose effective checks on unilateral authority. No major societal undertaking can be sanctioned without the prior approval of the appropriate assembly. This applies to the choice of the head of the pantheon [20] or to the grant of immortality to a mortal,[21] just as it does to political moves by human rulers,[22] whether these be legendary or histori-

17. See Frankfort, *Intellectual Adventure*, ch. 1, and *Kingship and the Gods*, Bk. II. The fundamental fact is the limited authority of any one god, no matter how high his position in the pantheon.

18. Cf. Jacobsen, *Intellectual Adventure*, pp. 125 ff., and *JNES*, *2*, 159 ff. For similar results arrived at from a different starting point cf. Speiser, *Studies in the History of Science* (Philadelphia, 1941), pp. 1–13, and *Waldo Leland Volume*, pp. 51–62.

19. In addition to the references in n. 18, cf. also, Oppenheim, *5*, 224 ff.

20. "The Creation Epic," Tab. 3, ll. 130 ff. (*ANET*, p. 64 f.).

21. "Epic of Gilgamesh," Tab. 11, ll. 197–8.

22. An Old Assyrian text expresses this in a succinct formula: "Ashur is the king; Irishum is [but] the toparch [*iššakku*] for Ashur"; cf. Landsberger and Balkan, *14*, 231. Similarly, in the Cappadocian tablets *Šarrum-kên*

cal. In this all-pervasive safeguard against autocracy lies perhaps the key to the appeal and the magnetism which Mesopotamian civilization exercised upon many neighboring cultures.

So much for the general cultural setting against which we must now endeavor to trace the idea of history in Mesopotamia. To some extent the background has already determined the scale and disclosed the outlines of the design that we seek to recover. But the whole cannot be placed in focus without due attention to the component parts.

III. NATURE OF THE SOURCE MATERIAL

Before there can be any systematic thought about history there must be sufficient interest in the past. For such preoccupation in Mesopotamia there is manifold and extensive evidence. Much of it consists of direct historical references: regnal lists, chronicles, annals. In addition to these there are literary compositions in which bare historical facts have been woven into a richer fabric of myth and legend; historical tales, in short, as opposed to straight history. That literature should go to the past for its most popular motifs is in itself significant. But echoes of remote days are not confined to literature. They are clearly audible also in a field that has no room for fancy, the deadly serious field of omens. Another form of awareness of the past is attested in certain architectural practices. And lastly, a number of Mesopotamian rulers have left us concrete evidence of their antiquarian pursuits, with an occasional hint as to motivation. These, then, are the main types of sources where we must look for the fugitive idea of history in Mesopotamia. The clue these sources furnish will be followed up later in the so-called wisdom

(Sargon) I of Ashur is only a *rubā'um*, or "prince," whereas the ruler of Hattum boasts the title of *šarrum*, or "king"; cf. *ibid.*, p. 231 and *Orientalia, 20* (1951), 483. Thus, far from being despotic, as has often been alleged, the Assyrian rulers were careful to emphasize their subsidiary role in affairs of state, for even there the leading parts were reserved for the gods.

literature. First, however, let us isolate that clue. We shall begin with the rulers whose antiquarian leanings are noted in the records.

Royal inquiries into the past are connected as a rule with religious matters. They may revolve, for instance, about the building history of major temples. Thus we are told by Shalmaneser I, an Assyrian ruler of the 13th century, that a temple at Ashur originally built by Ushpia had been rebuilt by Irishum I (i. e., Erishu), restored 159 years later by Shamshi-Adad, and reconstructed by Shalmaneser himself after a lapse of 580 years.[23] The same temple required urgent attention under Esarhaddon, who counts another 580 years between Shalmaneser's reconstruction and his own.[24] The fact that the various computations reveal some discrepancies need not concern us here. It is the detailed record of the successive restorations that is alone important in the present instance.

Of similar import is the statement by Ashurbanipal that, on capturing Susa, he was able to recover the image of the goddess Nana which the Elamite Kudur-Naḫundi had carried off from Uruk 1,635 years before.[25] Likewise related is the observation by Nabonidus, a frustrated archeologist turned king, that 3,200 years had elapsed between the burial of Naram-Sin's foundation inscription in the Shamash temple at Sippar and his own recovery of that inscription.[26] Once again the chronology does not stand up to modern audits, but the research behind such data cannot be ignored.[27]

How is this form of interest in the past to be explained? The answer is hinted at by the Old Assyrian king Irishum I, the same ruler who is cited first by Shalmaneser I, and later, by Esarhaddon. In writing about the Ashur temple, Irishum says: " Should

23. *KAH, 1,* 13, col. 3, ll. 32 ff.

24. A. Poebel, *JNES, 1* (1942), 290 ff.; E. Weidner, *AFO, 15* (1945–51), 89.

25. Cf. L. W. King, *Chronicles Concerning Early Babylonian Kings* (1907), *1,* 12, n. 1.

26. *Ibid.*, p. 11, n. 2.

27. For other ancient retrospects of this kind cf. Meissner, *Babylonien und Assyrien, 2,* 363.

the building grow weak with age, and a king like me wishes to rebuild the structure, he shall not displace the nail that I have driven in, but shall restore it to its place."[28] The nail or peg (*sikkatum*), as has recently been demonstrated, is here—and in many instances elsewhere—a symbol of the completion and dedication of a solemn project for which the protection of the appropriate deity is being invoked. It is in a sense the outward sign of a pact between the devout builder and his deity. The usage can be traced back, independently, well into the 3d millennium.[29]

We may assume, then, that temples were viewed in Mesopotamia, from early days on, as the embodiment of a covenant between a god and his community. It was vitally important for succeeding generations that the covenant, and the good will which it betokened, be maintained. Hence the original foundations must not be disregarded in later repairs and alterations. Nor must the symbol of relationship with the deity, the peg that literally nailed down the agreement, be moved from its original spot.

It thus follows that here was one practical and vital reason for the constant and exacting study for the past. That reason was the urgent need for not upsetting the friendly relations with the cosmic powers that had been established in the past. A distant echo of this policy is reflected in II Kings 17:24 ff. The people whom the Assyrians had transplanted to Israel after the fall of Samaria are instructed by the conqueror to make their peace with the god of the vanquished in order to obviate his wrath.

The principle that the past must be studied so that the present may learn how to get along is evidenced also in the process of assembling great libraries of ancient records, notably the library of Ashurbanipal.[30] There was a utilitarian purpose to that king's intellectual pretensions. He spells it out for us himself. In an itemized order for texts to be procured—looted might be a better

28. Landsberger and Balkan, *14*, 224 ff., ll. 19–23.

29. *Ibid.*, pp. 252 ff.

30. In the process of accumulating this library inferior copies were withdrawn to be replaced by better and earlier texts. For a specific reference to a Hammurabi original thus utilized cf. Olmstead, *History of Assyria*, pp. 490–1.

term—in the city of Borsippa, there is included a blanket request for " rituals, prayers, inscriptions on stone, and whatever may be good for kingship," as well as " any tablet or ritual . . . that is good for my palace."[31] The phrases " good for kingship " and " good for my palace " go a long way toward defining the meaning of the past as viewed by Mesopotamian royalty. It was a case of self-interest, even enlightened self-interest, in a sense. The past was significant because it could inform the present in regard to the future. But what was the information thus gathered and the lesson obtained from it?

Before we take up this question, there still are some general points to be made in passing. The preceding remarks have stressed the fact that the Mesopotamian view of history, once it had been formulated, remained substantially unchanged through the ages. To be sure, events of the passing centuries must have left their mark on historical thinking. Yet the underlying civilization, as we have seen, continued intact in terms of basic values. In a history as long as Mesopotamia's this outstanding fact cannot be stressed too strongly. It's not surprising, therefore, that Ashurbanipal's astrologers should consult the same manuals that had been used by Hammurabi's diviners more than a thousand years earlier or that historical tradition in the 1st millenium should dwell on themes that had won popularity as early as the turn of the 3d millennium. The living past was an abiding reality.

The presence of such a stock of common themes makes it easier for us to choose a particular segment of the past for closer scrutiny. History can be apprehended only in retrospect from a fixed point in time. The whole history of Mesopotamia would be too vast a span for a brief yet fruitful survey. If it is true, however, that the normative concepts of the civilization of Mesopotamia had crystallized already by the end of the 3d millennium, a convenient vantage point early in the 2d millennium should afford us all the necessary perspective. Although later periods will not be left out of account, we shall concentrate on the earlier as the basis for ideas about history.

31. See *CT*, *22*, 1, and R. H. Pfeiffer, *State Letters of Assyria* (1935), No. 256.

The modern student breaks up the old sources of historical tradition into such categories as folklore, history or quasi history, theology, magic, and the like. This is a logical procedure from our standpoint. Yet we should not lose sight of the fact that to the originating civilization such categories differed from one another in emphasis and purpose but scarcely in validity. All made use of the same data of past experience. A given episode or motif is often utilized simultaneously by each. It is as if the main themes of historical tradition, before they were released to the separate disciplines of the day, had been screened and distilled by a central school of thought. The thinking of that school, and not our thoughts about the same data, must be our ideal objective. The point has been well made by R. G. Collingwood that "the historian who studies a civilization other than his own can apprehend the mental life of that civilization only by re-enacting that experience for himself."[32] We should try, then, to put ourselves in the position of a native student of history of long ago—it is a synthetic and ideal abstraction, of course—and look back on the past as he saw it. In so doing, we have to take over the student's personal failures of knowledge and sympathy. Yet no stage of historiosophy, including our own, can be said to have shaken off completely the shackles of its particular environment.

IV. THE PAST AS SEEN BY THE MESOPOTAMIANS

Let us suppose, then, that a promising young scholar, say in the year 1750 B. C., desiring recognition at Ur, Nippur, or Babylon as Doctor of the Past, has been asked by his examiners to name five epochal junctures in the history of his culture. If he was thoughtful and learned beyond his years, these are the stages that he might have singled out: 1) The beginning of civilization; 2) the Deluge; 3) the crisis under Etana, the shepherd; 4) the rivalry between Kish and Uruk, culminating in the clash of Agga and Gilgamesh; and 5) the period of Sargon and Naram-Sin.

32. *The Idea of History*, p. 163; cf. also, pp. 282 ff.

Local traditions could cause some changes in such a list; [33] the accession of the given reigning dynasty would not be overlooked. But the culture as a whole would probably have agreed on these five epochs. What was the consensus about them?

1) Civilization was a gift from the gods who vouchsafed it to mankind as a full-grown product. It was abroad from the day that " kingship had been lowered from heaven." [34] The primeval kings learned the necessary details through the Seven Sages.[35] But it was the presence of kingship as such that marked the difference between order on the one hand and anarchy and barbarism on the other.

2) After a hazy period of enormous length the gods saw fit to regret their gift to mankind. They sent down the Deluge, which all but swept away the last vestige of life on earth. For a number of anxious days the future of life and civilization hinged on the fate of the precarious craft that bore the hero of the cataclysm; his ark contained, providentially, " the seed of all living creatures," including " all the craftsmen." [36] Thus was culture saved from the elements.

3) The fresh start marked the beginning of an unbroken chain in which the present was but the latest link. (It meant much the same thing to the ancients that the dawn of history means to us.) Shadowy outlines of postdiluvian rulers appear on the distant horizon. The first realm to become manifest is the city-state of Kish. And the first of the new rulers to be featured by historic tradition is the shepherd Etana.

Etana's place in the traditional lore of Mesopotamia is attested in several ways. He is recognized in art,[37] figures in an omen, is

33. Thus the Chronicle Weidner (see the next section, cf. n. 42) assigns prominence to Marduk and Babylon at a time when neither had as yet risen above the level of mediocrity; see rev. ll. 11 ff.

34. This is the introductory phrase in the Sumerian king list; cf. Jacobsen, *The Sumerian King List*, pp. 58 f.; 64, n. 119; 70.

35. Landsberger, *Fakültesi Dergisi*, *2*, 431; O. R. Gurney, *JRAS* (1936), 459–66.

36. " Gilgamesh Epic," Tab. 11, ll. 83, 85.

37. Frankfort, *Cylinder Seals*, pp. 138, 139.

prominent in a bilingual text dealing with the Seven Sages, and receives more than passing notice from the Sumerian king list.[38] Above all, however, Etana is known as the hero of a celebrated epic which was to live on in at least three recensions: the Old Babylonian, the Middle Assyrian, and the Neo-Assyrian.[39] There can thus be no doubt about Etana's enduring place in the culture of his land.

What does that lasting impression signify? The popular answer is given in this repeated phrase: "Etana, a shepherd who ascended to heaven."[40] But what had caused that extraordinary journey? The epic traces the reason to a crisis in the hero's family, but it is doubtful whether learned circles were satisfied with that account. Our imaginary candidate, for instance, might be expected to refer to the proemium of the tale, which gives a different setting. Mankind, as the Old Babylonian poet informs us, had as yet to have a king. All the characteristic norms of kingship lay inactive before Anu in heaven, "there being no consultation (*mitluku*) for the people."[41] In other words, government by assembly had not yet come into being.

38. For the epigraphic material on Etana cf. Güterbock, *ZA*, *42*, *22*; Jacobsen, *The Sumerian King List*, p. 80, n. 67.

39. Speiser in *ANET*, pp. 114 ff.

40. Cf. Jacobsen, *The Sumerian King List*, p. 80, n. 67.

41. Speiser, *ANET*, pp. 114, A–1, ll. 11–14. The norms (i. e., m e symbols) in question are virtually the same that are cited in the Sumerian m e myth discussed by Kramer, *Sumerian Mythology*, pp. 64 ff.; the pertinent lines are given in transliteration, *ibid.*, p. 116.

The myth just referred to has a further and broader significance for our present purposes. In the divine hierarchy which this myth reflects first place is held by e n, with the as yet obscure s i coming next; both are accompanied by the abstract element n a m mentioned earlier. The list continues with "godship, the tiara exalted and enduring, the throne of kingship . . . the exalted scepter, staffs[?], the exalted shrine, shepherdship, kingship" (cf. Kramer, *op. cit.*, p. 66). In other words, "god" is third in the list, whereas "king" is considerably farther down and is preceded by "shepherd." It follows that here and in related instances e n cannot simply be rendered "high priest," as is often done, nor can the derived Akkadian abstract *enūtu* (e. g., "Creation Epic," Tab. 6, l. 97) be analogously translated. The term

If this explanation is valid—and all signs would seem to show that it is—then the crisis under Etana was social and cultural rather than personal. It is to that juncture that historical tradition would appear to date the introduction of representative government in Mesopotamia as a basic factor in civilization. The shepherd in Etana would thus be a symbol of the king's limited authority and the source of a cultural stereotype featured in all subsequent history.

4) For further literary support of this early dating of representative government we need not go further than the end of the dynasty to which Etana himself has been assigned. According to the king list, the last ruler of the 1st Dynasty of Kish was one Agga.[42] What saves this king from being just another name in a tedious list is the fact that we know him independently from a Sumerian epic which describes his contest with Gilgamesh, lord of Uruk. Perhaps the most important thing about this particular poem is the insight which it affords into the role of the assembly in vital matters of state. Before he can embark on his perilous venture against the dominant power of Kish, Gilgamesh seeks the sanction of two separate bodies: first, the assembly of the elders, and next, the assembly of the warriors.[43] It is there that ultimate authority was evidently vested, as early as the period when history can be apprehended only through the spyglass of legend.

obviously stands for " master of the universe " and is thus an exact equivalent of the West Semitic *Ba'al*. For a slightly different view see now, Jacobsen, *JNES*, *12* (1953), 180 ff.

In human government the above hierarchy is reduced at the top to three positions: e n/*bêlu* "sovereign," l u g a l/*šarru* "king," and e n s i (-a k)/ *iššakku* " local chief " or " toparch," the last being the representative of some higher authority, either divine or human. The mortal king was no more than a steward under orders from his god, a shepherd tending his master's flock.

42. This is the Sumerian form. The Semitic pronunciation was evidently *Ak* (*k*) *a*. Cf. Chronicle Weidner, *ZA*, *42*, 48, ll. 31, see Jacobsen, *The Sumerian King List*, p. 84, n. 99. Note that the name is Sumerian although the dominant local element would seem to be Semitic; cf. below n. 62.

43. Cf. Jacobsen, *JNES*, *2*, 165–6; S. N. Kramer, *ANET*, pp. 44–5.

And lest one think that the assembly was little more than a hollow form, we have now the unimpeachable testimony of an Old Babylonian omen, which shows that approval in such cases was by no means automatic. The verdict of the assembly was sometimes *puḫrum ul imtagar* "the assembly will fail to reach an agreement." [44]

The poem about Agga and Gilgamesh—to dwell on it for another moment—lends color to the assumption that the hero of the cycle of Gilgamesh legends was originally an historical figure. It follows that Lugalbanda and Enmerkar,[45] two predecessors of Gilgamesh who are likewise no strangers to legend, can no longer be dismissed outright as fictional. The possibility has to be reckoned with—direct proof, of course, is not to be expected—that these three rulers of Uruk had played memorable parts in the penumbral stage of the history of Sumer. The victory of Gilgamesh over Agga, which appears to have terminated the supremacy of Kish, may well have heralded the emergence of the Sumerians as the political masters of Sumer and Akkad.[46] To the Sumerians the event was history. To us it comes through only as a weak and indistinct echo. We are not in a position, therefore, to decide how much of the outcome may have been due to the ethnic factor—if Kish had been substantially non-Sumerian—and how much to political and cultural influences

44. *YOS*, Vol. 10, No. 31, col. 10, ll. 43–4; cf. also, *Orientalia*, *5* (1935), 225 f.

45. For a recently published epic about this hero see Kramer, *Enmerkar and the Lord of Aratta*.

46. It may therefore be significant in this connection that the king list gives Mes-kiag-gasher, the legendary founder of this royal house—the 1st Dynasty of Uruk—the title e n as well as that of l u g a l (col. 3, ll. 1–3); the translation of the first as "high priest" is not appropriate (see above, n. 41). What this titulary would seem to imply is transition from city-state to empire. The dynasty is continued by Enmerkar, Lugalbanda, and Gilgamesh—in the order cited—each a celebrated figure in the legendary lore of Sumer, with Gilgamesh obviously regarded as the greatest of them. This is indeed an Heroic Age, as Kramer has emphasized (cf. *Proceedings of the American Philosophical Society*, *90*, 120–30), not only of Sumer but also, and more particularly, of the Sumerians as such.

alone. We can appreciate, however, the unparalleled impact of Gilgamesh on later ages. If his historical prototype was really the founder of Sumerian supremacy, the unique vigor of the Gilgamesh motif would receive a convincing explanation.

5) The last major juncture in the early history of Mesopotamia, as listed by our imaginary informant, is the age of Akkad. To us, at a remove of over four millennia, the period of Sargon and Naram-Sin easily outweighs in importance any of the preceding eras. This is so mainly because the Akkad age is at last under the full light of history. The contemporary rulers left us original accounts of their achievements as well as various monuments which enable us to check these accounts. Claims of conquests ranging from Elam to Anatolia are substantiated by statues, stelae, and temples from the places conquered: Susa, Ashur, Nineveh, Diyarbekir, and others.[47] We can thus start out for the first time with a hard factual core.

The ancients were just as impressed with the Sargonids as we are, although not for quite the same reasons. We welcome that age because of the material it provides for concrete research. The ancients seized on it because it stirred their imagination, even though the underlying history may still have been vivid in memory and tradition had not yet strayed far from reality. The times of Sargon and Naram-Sin soon become the favorite themes of epics and folk tales, poetry and prose, admonitions and omens. And the leading figures of the age are not merely local celebrities. Their fame spreads to other lands and cultures; it is reflected, for instance, in the literature of the Hurrians and the Hittites.[48] The civilization that had long been nurtured in southern Mespotamia becomes an international factor, transcending ethnic, geographic, and political boundaries.

Much of this, however, is primarily source material for history. In order to appreciate the impact of the events on the idea of history we must concentrate on the secondary sources, the edi-

47. Cf. Speiser, *JAOS*, *72*, 97–101.

48. See Güterbock, *Kumarbi*, and *JCS*, *5*, 135–61; *6*, 8–42.

torials and the columns and the sermons, so to speak, rather than the direct news accounts. Because the Sargonid era had been so rich in events, it gave rise also to a corresponding amount of reflection; hence its central place in the pattern which we are seeking to recapture. Other historical milestones should not, of course, be ignored. But it will simplify matters if, in common with the ancients, we allow the Akkad age to dominate the design of historical thought, while reserving other stages in the long career of Mesopotamia for purposes of control and elaboration.

V. TRADITIONAL VIEWS ON THE MEANING OF THE PAST

To the succeeding ages, then, the century of Sargon and Naram-Sin stood out as a period of unprecedented achievement. But it was no less memorable a fact that the power of Akkad collapsed eventually. The history of that dynasty was thus a vivid example of ebb and flow in the fortunes of an empire. It brought into sharper relief the rise and decline of other dynasties. There was an almost rhythmic regularity to this unvarying alternation. Regularity was suggestive of cosmic laws. In short, here was a ready basis on which to found a system for the interpretation of history.[49]

In its main outlines the scheme in question may have been as old as the emergence of the characteristic civilization of Mesopotamia; but the details must have been long in taking shape. Things on earth were directed from heaven, therefore history was necessarily theocratic history.[50] The victorious king was the

49. See Güterbock, *ZA*, *42*, 13 ff.

50. It should be stressed, however, that Collingwood's strictures against theocratic history—in that it is not history proper—(*op. cit.*, pp. 14 ff.) apply in this instance only in part. The fundamental thing is that the supreme god of Mesopotamia is not an omnipotent being. His authority can be affected not only by the divine assembly but also by such extraneous circumstances as the theft of the Tablets of Destinies. Under the resulting system, therefore, the object of historical thinking cannot be "single and infinite," to cite Collingwood's description of theocratic thought (*ibid.*, p. 5). To some extent,

recipient of divine favors, whereas disaster was brought upon the land by ill-fated rulers. Sargon, as the founder of Akkad's might, was obviously destiny's favorite. By the same token, Naram-Sin must have been marked for ill fortune, since the waning years of his reign were disastrous for Akkad. Similarly, the end of any dynasty was the direct result of the gods' displeasure.[51]

Given the theocratic premise and the long succession of dynasties that had come and gone by the end of the 3d millennium, the social philosopher of the Old Babylonian period had every reason to see the past in terms of recurring cycles. But did he apply such findings to the future? Was Marduk certain to do to Babylon as Nidaba had done to Lagash or Enlil to the Guti? Would the timeless cure-all which spells "It cannot happen to me" have stood in the way of a tidal school of historiosophy? The question is of considerable interest, but the available data do not add up to a conclusive answer.

The past, at any rate, was high-lighted by alternating periods of bliss and disaster. As a rule, each succeeding dynasty was the instrument whereby the gods displaced the given incumbent. Occasionally, however, the gods might send a strange new people as a scourge, as happened in the case of the Ummān Manda who broke the power of the Sargonids. In other words, sequence was construed as consequence.

There had to be, of course, a reason for the dynastic changes consistent with the theocratic principle of state. The gods would forsake a mortal ruler and turn against him because he had offended them in some way (the technical Akkadian term is

at least, past events must have appeared to the traditional Mesoptamian as "final and plural," thus fulfilling some of Collingwood's criteria of historicity (*ibid.*). It would surely not be going too far to assert that in Mesopotamia history ruled the gods more than the gods ruled history. Theocratic government, in short, was to the Mesopotamian merely human government one stage removed. The local theocracy, in other words, did not of itself constitute an insuperable barrier to research and inquiry. And research and inquiry amount to a convenient paraphrase for "history."

51. Güterbock, *ZA*, *42*, 75 f.; Speiser, *JAOS*, *72*, 97 ff.

qullulu). The offender is said to have transgressed his solemn oath of office (*mamīta etēqu*) or overstepped the bounds set for him by his god (*itê ili etēqu*).[52]

The classic illustration is the well-known case of Lugalzaggesi of Umma and Urukagina of Lagash. Rivalry between these two remarkable rulers—in a prodigal generation which was to see both eclipsed by the matchless Sargon—brought about the destruction of Lagash. To the Lagash chronicler of the event the destruction of his city was "an offense against Ningirsu, its god." No blame attaches to Urukagina, on whose part "there is no offense." Both Lugalzaggesi and his goddess Nidaba shall bear the consequences. Thus a political clash resolves itself into a contest between the respective patron deities, much as a dispute between shepherds might have to be settled by their masters. In practice, might was right. In theory, right was invoked to account for might.

This motif of theological offense as grounds for historic change confronts us throughout Mesopotamian history. I shall cite only two further instances, which may be less familiar than most. In a unique document from Mari, which will interest us again later on, Yasmaḫ-Addu, a contemporary of Hammurabi, solemnly affirms that no member of his family had ever "committed an offense against his god" (*ša ana ilim uqallilu ul ibašši*).[53] None had violated his oath to the deity or broken international agreements which the gods had witnessed. On the other hand, the very opposite was true of the rival rulers.[54] For their part, no doubt, the accused hastened to reverse the charges.

The same attitude animates a poetic work of the Middle Assyrian period, wherein Tukulti-Ninurta I contrasts the perfidy of Babylon with the unfailing righteousness of Ashur.[55] The Kassite

52. See *Belleten, 14*, 263.

53. *ARM*, Vol. 1, No. 3, l. 6. The king of Eshnunna is alleged to be planning a similar offense, cf. *ibid.*, No. 26, ll. 32 ff.

54. Their guilt is termed *qullultum* (l. 18).

55. The text has been presented in transliteration and translation by Ebeling, *MAOG*, Vol. 12, fasc. 2.

king of Babylon is branded as " transgressor of the oath " (*ētiq mamīti*),[56] who admits at length that " most grievous have been the offenses of my land, numerous its sins " (*qellēt mātiya šupšuqā imīdū arnū*).[57] Echoes of similar sentiments are common in the inscriptions of the 1st millennium.[58]

With so much stress on formal features, the idea of history developed against this kind of background could not readily free itself from stereotypes. To be sure, with Urukagina or Yasmaḫ-Addu or Tukulti-Ninurta I the theocratic concept of state was modified by practical needs, except that expediency sought retroactive moral sanction. With theologians, however, unsobered by

56. *Ibid.*, col. 4, l. 20.

57. *Ibid.*, l. 27. Ebeling's translation of this passage cannot be right. In the first place the feminine (pl.) *šupšuqā* is not co-ordinate with the masculine *imīdū*; it modifies the preceding *qellēt*, construct plural to *qillatu*. Accordingly, the initial *inanna abrā* cannot be rendered with Ebeling's translation in a transitive sense: " Jetzt (aber) habe ich die Schlechtigkeit meines Landes gesehen " (p. 17); the phrase means " Now I looked about." Cf. *ZA*, *43*, 64, l. 243: *ina adnāti abrēma šitnā idātu*, which Landsberger translates " As I looked about among the habitations, the signs were contradictory." Secondly, Ebeling himself renders the parallel passage in col. 6, l. 33 in the way just advocated: " [Seine Vergehen] sind drückend, viel sind (seine) Sünden." Even in the latter passage, however, the supplemented form should be [*šu*]-*up-šu-q*[*at*], as required by the original (*Archaeologia*, Vol. 69, pl. 52), and not [*šu*]-*up-šu-q*[*u*]; the missing noun was evidently [*qillassu*] " his offense."

58. It is not impossible that we may have the approximate wording of the king's oath on assuming his obligations under a treaty. The Etana epic, as has already been pointed out, reflects a considerable measure of interest in social philosophy. It is very suggestive, therefore, that its three extant versions—the Old Babylonian, the Middle Assyrian, and the Late Assyrian—give us the same basic oath: " He who oversteps the bounds of Shamash [note the motif of *itê ili etēqu*], may Shamash surrender him for evil to the executioner! He who oversteps the bounds of Shamash, may the mountain withhold from him its passage! May the darting weapon of Shamash, overthrow him and catch him! " Cf. *ANET*, p. 114, A–2, ll. 1–3; p. 115, B, ll. 4–7; p. 116, C–2, ll. 11–16. It is clear from the context that this solemn oath was meant to evoke a picture well known to the audience. [The view just expressed has been confirmed in the meantime by an Old Babylonian text, D. J. Wiseman, *The Alalakh Tablets* (1953), No. *1*, l. 18.]

every-day burdens of state, history could reduce itself under particular circumstances to a mechanism of utmost simplicity. It was all a matter of either honoring or ignoring elementary orders from on high. Everything else was incidental.

This monolithic approach is especially pronounced in the so-called Chronicle Weidner.[59] The text has an Old Babylonian setting and an incurable Babylonian bias. What makes it significant, for all its stilted features, is that the chronicle is, in fact, the first Mesopotamian textbook on the idea of history; partisan, doctrinaire, and obviously below the level of the best thought of the time, but a historiosophy of a sort nonetheless.

The beginning is lost save for a few disconnected phrases,[60] just enough to indicate that the writer had started out with an exposition of general principles: " which you have commanded I have noted, and for the life of distant days . . ." (21′); " he who offends against the gods (*šá a-na i-li^{pl} . . . ú-qal-la-lu*)[61] of this city, his star shall not be stable in heaven . . ." (27′); " the conduct of a [?] former king that I have heard much about . . ." (30′). In other words, the purpose of the work was didactic. The past had a lesson which should be heeded for the sake of the future.

The chronicle then proceeds to a schematized survey of important stages in human history, including the time of Akka[62] of Kish and Enme(r)kar of Uruk, representatives of the first two dynasties after the Flood.[63] But the bulk of the account concerns

59. For the publication of this text and invaluable spade work on it see Güterbock, *ZA*, *42*, 47 ff.

60. *Ibid.*, p. 50.

61. Note the telltale technical term.

62. The corresponding form in Sumerian contexts is the aforementioned A(g)ga which need not, however, indicate any real difference in pronunciation, since the Sumerian stops do not appear to have been distinctive as to voice. Incidentally, the name itself appears to be Sumerian, whereas the earlier kings of that dynasty bear Semitic names. Does this circumstance reflect a gradual Sumerianization of Akkad?

63. See above, Pt. IV, sec. 4 of this article. It is clear from this and other occurrences that these early Sumerian heroes maintained their hold on tradition even after the decline of Sumerian political authority.

itself with the Dynasty of Sargon and the events before and after that period. Sargon was punctilious about the cult and so he prospered. But Naram-Sin was hostile to the people of Babylon,[64] thereby inviting divine retribution through the medium of the Gutian barbarians. Nothing could be simpler than this temple view of history; cult and ritual were the most significant factors in the affairs of state. We know, however, from the instances already cited, and from many others that can be adduced, that this was by no means the prevailing view. The gods could be arbitrary, but scarcely to such a degree. When Nabonidus, about a millennium later, refers to the destruction of Babylon by Sennacherib, he stresses Marduk's wrath against that god's favorite city, with the implication that the city got what it deserved.[65] The Chronicle Weidner is a long way behind the spirit of even that stock interpretation, not to mention the Deuteronomic formulation in such passages as Judg. 2: 6 ff.

VI. OMENS AND LETTERS TO THE GODS

As we have seen, Mesopotamia developed a twofold check on the authority of her rulers. One was societal: it was inherent in the role of the assembly. The other was religious: divine bounds must not be transgressed. By extension, any major undertaking on the part of the ruler required divine sanction, in addition to approval by the assembly. How was such sanction ascertained?

The attitude of the gods was signified in the form of directions or oracles (*tērētu*) obtained through the medium of omens. These could be contrived with the aid of sacrifies (*tērēt nīqī*), the organs of slaughtered animals, for instance, furnishing the signs that the seer (*bārū*) went on to interpret; or they were based on observations of natural phenomena which the diviner (*mašmašu*) was

64. The mention of Babylon in this context is an obvious anachronism which serves to circumscribe the time and place of the composition.

65. Nabonidus Stele, col. 16, l. 36. For an instructive Hittite parallel, in a "Pestgebet" of Mursilis, cf. Götze, *Kleinasien*, Vol. 91.

trained to decipher.[66] Since the need to know what lay in store was imperative and constant, particularly in regard to the state, divination become a vital factor in the civilization of Mesopotamia and one of its outstanding characteristics. No step of any consequence could be risked without proper word from the bārū or the mašmašu.

These priests did not arrive at their decisions arbitrarily. They were guided by detailed and elaborate manuals in which virtually every possible contingency had been systematically recorded. The basis of the discipline was circumstantial association. Let us suppose that some memorable event (E) had been observed originally under a particular set of extraneous circumstances (C). Since coincidence is not admitted, any time in the future that C comes up again, E is anticipated. C is of course capable of infinite variety. These innumerable variations must be filed away for reference, not unlike our fingerprints. Now when a client calls upon his seer, that analyst identifies the problem from the omen, checks the omen readings against the file, and comes up with the answer.

The omen material is worthless as science but invaluable as raw source material. It utilizes a mass of plain facts as the basis for peculiar constructions. Stripped of these constructions, the facts stand out in stark simplicity. And since some of the events thus treated are taken from history—recent history in the first instance—the omens give us an independent version of the given historical happenings and personalities.[67] They are especially useful as a check on results obtained elsewhere.

We know now that the recording of omens for future reference was an established practice by the end of the 3d millennium. The Sargonid age and the individual members of that dynasty were fully exploited. The volume of Old Babylonian omens in the Yale collection published by A. Goetze a few years ago shows how intensively the field was cultivated in that relatively early

66. Cf. Ungnad, *AFO, 14* (1941–44), 251 ff.; Oppenheim, *Orientalia, 5* (1936), 199 ff.

67. See especially, Goetze, *JCS, 1* (1947), 253 ff.

period.[68] The use to which such compendia were put may be illustrated by an example from Mari. Among the Mari letters there is one which contains a rather detailed reading of an omen on behalf of the viceroy Yasmaḫ-Addu.[69] If the bārū who performed the service (ca. 1700 B. C.) had been unable to consult his own reference library, he might have got almost the same results by borrowing one of Dr. Goetze's copies.[70]

There are two points about the omens that need to be stressed in the present connection. One is the fundamental fact of the ruler's abject dependence in all matters on the will of the gods. This fact, which the omens point up to an overwhelming extent, would be sufficient in itself to refute the assumption that Mesopotamia, in common with Egypt, viewed her kings as divine. A god incarnate does not take his cue from the liver of a sheep. The other point to be emphasized is this: it is a fact that some of the kings of the Dynasty of Akkad, the 3d Dynasty of Ur, and certain other places and periods have their names written with the determinative for god and appear to enjoy other prerogatives of divinity. Yet the omens single out precisely these same rulers as human to a fault [71]—in the way they died or in the manner in which they brought disaster upon their land. Their claim to divinity is thus found to rest on superficial attributes. We

68. *YOS*, Vol. 10.

69. *ARM*, *4*, 54; cf. also, *ibid.*, *5*, 65, and the comment of W. von Soden, *Orientalia*, *22* (1933), 209.

70. Some parallels to *ARM*, *5*, 65, have been cited by von Soden, *loc. cit.* In commenting on *ARM*, *4*, 54, von Soden (*op. cit.*, p. 204) would change the editor's translation of *tarik* from "est [de couleur] sombre" to "ist geschlagen." This is not quite adequate. The term means primarily "pinched," or "jammed," hence "bruised," or "blood-shot," and hence in a specific sense "dark" as opposed to "clear" (*nawer*).

71. This applies to rulers of the Dynasty of Akkad and of Ur III—kings who are elsewhere represented as deified. As for Naram-Sin, who is likewise included in the deified group, there is ample independent information to the effect that he, above all others, was the very archetype of the ill-fated ruler, the "Unheilsherrscher" of Güterbock's penetrating analysis (cf. *ZA*, *42*, 75). For a recent refutation of the deification theory, see Fish, *34*, 37 ff. On the question in general, cf. the references given in n. 9, above.

cannot be sure what the attributes may have signified in those scattered instances, but we know that the practice was not widespread and that it could not have been far-reaching in scope.[72] Above all, the mere concept of a deified ruler is incompatible with the basic features of Mesopotamia's civilization and out of keeping with its over-all character.

The problem of the ruler's divinity has an obvious bearing on the local idea of history. For history will be viewed one way if the ruler is a mere mortal, and another way if he is accepted as a god. Where government is in human hands throughout, but the state is ultimately theocratic, much will depend on the power attributed to the immortal sovereign. Because no individual god in the Mesopotamian pantheon was really omnipotent, the purposes of the cosmic society were difficult to fathom. The mortal ruler was forever intent on pleasing the cosmic powers. Often he found himself obliged to appease them. There were times when the need was urgent to establish direct contact with the distant gods. In a literate society distances can be neutralized through writing. It is logical, therefore, in these circumstances that the kings of historic Mesopotamia should write to their gods, even as they were themselves petitioned by their own subjects. Such letters to the gods add a significant touch to the underlying idea of history.[73]

Let us first cite, once again, some instances from the recently published Mari archives. In one of these, Ishme-Dagan of Ashur relates that his campaigns in hostile lands had caused concern to his personal god, or *lamassu*. Accordingly, he had written his lamassu to tell him not to worry.[74] It is noteworthy that it is

72. There is, for instance, not the slightest hint of such a practice in Assyria, where we would normally be inclined to look for it first.

73. Cf. Gadd, *Ideas of Divine Rule*, pp. 61 f.

74. *ARM* Vol. 4, No. 68, ll. 17 ff. It should be pointed out, however, that in the opinion of von Soden (*Orientalia, 22*, 205), the *La-ma-sí* of this passage can only be a proper name. Von Soden does not give his reasons for this conclusion, but it must be admitted that the form presents certain technical difficulties no matter which way it is interpreted. But the eventual solution

the god who is being reassured, although it may be merely a case of a writer whistling in the dark. The converse is naturally more common and orthodox, as witness our second instance, which is a letter from Ishme-Dagan's brother, Yasmaḫ-Addu, a young prince whom we have met before.[75] Obviously in trouble, Yasmaḫ-Addu reviews for his god the last three generations in the history of Mari. In all that time, his family has proved righteous and god-fearing, whereas the competing dynasty violated the rules of god and man. Parenthetically, the opponents whom Yasmaḫ-Addu accuses had a prior right to the throne of Mari and were eventually restored to power despite our writer's appeal to heaven. Presently, however—and this is our third instance—the successor, in turn, has to address a message to his own protector, the river god.[76] We happen to know that this last appeal, like the one before it, proved of no avail, inasmuch as Hammurabi took over Mari in due time. Under the circumstances, it would have been impossible to disabuse Hammurabi of the conviction that his particular brand of piety was the most efficacious of all.

The first two of the three instances just cited may throw a new light on Assyrian historiography. The writers in question were sons of Shamshi-Adad, one of the most influential kings in the early career of Ashur. The question now arises whether the practice of Shamshi-Adad's family to address the gods sporadically, in times of special need,[77] did not lead eventually to routine reports addressed to the gods at regular intervals.

The annals left us by later Assyrian rulers, from the 14th century on, were periodic accounts by definition. It has always been assumed that they were intended for posterity in general.

would not affect our argument in that the Mari evidence for letters to the gods is sufficient even if this particular text is left out of account altogether.

75. *ARM*, *2*, 3. The document was recognized as a letter to a god by B. Landsberger; cf. *JNES*, *11* (1952), 130.

76. See G. Dossin, *Syria*, *19* (1938), 126.

77. In turn, that practice has older Sumerian antecedents; cf. A. Falkenstein, *ZA*, *49* (1939), 1 ff.

Perhaps their most striking feature is the boastful, even bombastic, tone which the kings, writing in the first person, invariably employ. These royal writers are egocentric in the extreme.[78] Yet there is something about the whole pattern that does not ring true. The normal attitude of the Mesopotamian ruler when facing his gods was one of modesty and humility. The annals were certainly not meant to be concealed from the gods. Why do they display, then, so much seeming arrogance?

I believe that by establishing a link between the annals and the letters to the gods—there is, of course, the further and long-known connection with building inscriptions[79]—we may be in a position to revise the common estimate of the Assyrian royal accounts. In point of fact, there is a concrete link between the annals and the letters to the gods. The parade example is the detailed report by Sargon II about his eighth campaign.[80] Al-

78. Cf. e.g., Mowinckel, *Gunkel Festschrift*, p. 287; D. D. Luckenbill, *The Annals of Sennacherib* (1924), pp. 1 ff.

79. See Olmstead, *Assyrian Historiography*, pp. 2, 64. Yet the building inscription is not of itself a logical forerunner of the annalistic account. Since the annals are first found among the Hittites, and since the Assyrian annals follow shortly thereafter, Güterbock has made out a good case in favor of deriving the Assyrian practice from the Hittites; cf. *ZA*, *44*, 98 f. Goetze, *Hethiter, Churriter und Assyrer*, pp. 181 f., has contributed the further observation that the Assyrian annals incorporate mythical-epic motifs which are foreign to Hittite historical writings, but might ultimately be traced to the Hurrians. Furthermore, Goetze (*ibid.*) and others, especially Laqueur, pp. 489–506, have realized that the Assyrian and the Hittite annals show an awareness of the need for giving the deity an account of the ruler's conduct. Specific connection with the letters to the gods, however, has not been suggested so far. If the present suggestion proves valid, then the characteristic tone of the annals would have owed nothing to outside influences, although the form of the accounts might have been borrowed. But even this last supposition would now seem doubtful. We cannot, accordingly, discount the possibility that all the basic features were Mesopotamian after all, although their full potential could not be realized without Hurrian or Hittite assistance.

80. F. Thureau-Dangin, *Une relation de la huitième campagne de Sargon*, 1912. After this paper had been presented at Yale, in the form in which it is here given, I came upon the statement by A. Moortgat (Moortgat and

though addressed to the gods, this is not the petition of a man in trouble but a proud account of successes achieved. Later on this report is entered, in condensed form and without the epistolary trimmings, in the composite edition of Sargon's annals.

Is there any reason to assume that this expedition alone required exceptional treatment? The facts related in this case do not depart from the pattern of other Assyrian expeditions. Furthermore, Shamshi-Adad V, a century earlier, had addressed a report about one of his campaigns to an unnamed deity, receiving this time an itemized acknowledgment from his divine addressee.[81] In other words, this kind of reporting was by no means unusual. Is it possible that the kings of Assyria, when annual reports had become customary, first composed these reports in the form of letters to their acknowledged sovereign, to be abridged in due course for purposes of a year-by-year edition?

On further examination it will be found, I think, that there is nothing inconsistent with such an assumption, whereas additional arguments can be adduced in its favor. This interesting question cannot be pursued in detail at present. This much, however, is worth noting: if the annals link up ultimately with letters to the gods, their egocentrism can no longer be ascribed to mere conceit. The missions recorded were the god's missions. They

Scharff, pp. 429 f.), which voices independently conclusions very similar to mine. Moortgat, too, would see in the Assyrian annals not so much the boasts by vainglorious rulers as the glorification of the might of the god Ashur. And although the letters to the gods are mentioned in passing, the conclusions which Moortgat offers are based primarily on the testimony of art. Our two modes of approach thus complement each other. The letters to the gods, however, suggest the ultimate form of the annals in addition to accounting for their characteristic tone.

81. E. F. Weidner, *AFO*, *9* (1933-34), 102 f. For these and other examples cf. Gadd, *Ideas of Divine Rule*, pp. 61 f., and Labat, *Le Caractère religieux*, pp. 273 f. One of the most striking instances of this genre has come down to us from Ashurbanipal; see *CT*, Vol. 35, Nos. 44–5 and T. Bauer, *Das Inschriftenwerk Assurbanipals* (1933), Pt. II, pp. 83 f. (Der Gottesbrief). The colophon is highly instructive, for it reads (rev. ll. 23–6): "Message of Ashur[banipal . . .] to Ashur who dwells in E[ḫursaggalkurkurra], that he may accept [his] prayer, strike down his foe, slay [. . .]."

could not be undertaken except with divine sanction as signified by the omens. The words which the king used to report them were the words of the god's original mandate. The tone was exaggerated because, in phrasing the utterances of a god, man is tempted to resort to superlatives. It was boastful because the authority and valor of a god were involved in the last analysis, and not the achievements of his worshipful servant.

Thus, if the foregoing hypothesis is valid, Assyrian historiography suffered not so much from the conceit of the ruler as from his excessive piety. The material is voluminous, the language picturesque, the detail abundant—yet the coefficient of reliability is low. By the same token, Babylonia, which never had formal annals, let alone annals stylized into letters to the gods, was in a position to render a more objective performance. This is true certainly of the so-called Babylonian Chronicle. It is jejune history, to be sure, but history nevertheless in "its sobriety of presentation and its coldly impartial statement of fact." [82] That even this superior work does not approach the high level of biblical historiography is a fact too obvious to need special emphasis.

VII. THE IDEA OF HISTORY IN THE WISDOM LITERATURE

Before this rapid survey is completed there is still one last witness to be heard from. The idea of history is not likely to have been ignored by the branch of literature that deals largely with ideas. Ancient Near Eastern sources devoted to speculative or didactic matters are commonly classified as wisdom literature. Extant wisdom material from Mesopotamia includes some independent works and a number of incidental passages which bear in one way or another on the problem before us. What does this testimony add up to, and how does it compare with the circumstantial evidence that has been abstracted so far?

We have seen that the ancient Mesopotamian was forever

82. Olmstead, *Historiography*, p. 62.

uneasy about the relation of his society to nature.[83] Because he endowed the powers of nature with most of the failings of mankind, he lacked full confidence in his gods.[84] They were unpredictable, hence mankind was doomed to be restless and insecure. The one thing that the past revealed above all others was the impermanence of all things. This note is struck with singular clarity in the Epic of Gilgamesh:

Since the days of yore there has been no [permanence];
The resting and the dead, how alike they are!
Do they not compose a picture of death,
The commoner and the noble,
Once they have drawn near to [their fate]?
The Anunnaki, the great gods, foregather;
Mammetum, authoress of destiny, with them the fates decrees:
Death and life they determine;
Yet of death the days are not revealed.[85]

All is thus ephemeral and uncertain. Everything is in the hands of the gods, but man is kept in ignorance of their plans.

The king, as a faithful shepherd, must strive to maintain the existing equilibrium at all costs. Any misadventure may be proof that the gods have been offended. Normally, the balance can be restored through elaborate efforts at purification and expiation. At times, it may even be expedient to set up a substitute king in order to divert the divine wrath from the established ruler.[86] There are occasions, however, when none of the known remedies will produce the desired effect. Although the king appears blameless, his land remains afflicted. The wisdom sources deal with this subject under the theme of the Righteous Sufferer.

We now know this motif from three major recensions. One of

83. This point is properly stressed by Frankfort, *Kingship and the Gods* and introduction to *Intellectual Adventure*; also by Jacobsen, *ibid.*

84. The Babylonian Theodicy expresses this thought by the phrase *nesī milik* [*ilim*] " impenetrable is the resolve [of the god]," *ZA*, *43*, 50, 58.

85. Tab. 10, col. 6, pp. 32 ff.; cf. *ANET*, p. 93.

86. Cf. Frankfort, *Kingship and the Gods*, pp. 263 f.

these, "I shall praise the god of wisdom," is extant only in copies of the 1st millennium B. C.[87] Another, the so-called Acrostic Dialogue or Babylonian Theodicy [88] may perhaps go back to the end of the 2d millennium. The third, which has just been published, takes us back to Old Babylonian times.[89] The three together serve to demonstrate that the problem of unjust suffering was forever alive in Mesopotamia.

For all their differences in form, approach, and phraseology, all three compositions have this conclusion in common: although the blameless may be exposed to suffering, deliverance is sure to come to him in the end. The ways of the gods are indeed inscrutable, but the truly meritorious need never despair of ultimate salvation. The emphasis, in short, is not so much on the trials of the sufferer as on the miracle of final deliverance.[90] Our three versions of the Mesopotamian counterpart of Job, spread though they are over a total span of more than a millenium, are in full agreement on this significant affirmation.

Is there a connection between the theme of Job and the idea of history? The established popularity of this subject in the literature of Mesopotamia, not to speak for the moment of outside echoes, suggests that the protagonist may have had an historical prototype.[91] At all events, the story of a Job is one of the strongest arguments why history should be studied. There have been kings in the past whom the gods deserted. Some never recovered, but others were eventually restored to grace. The Dynasty of Akkad was highly instructive in this respect. Old Sargon,[92] as the omens

87. The Akkadian title is *Ludlul bêl nêmeqi*; for this work, see especially S. Langdon in *Babyloniaca*, *7* (1923), 163 ff. See also, O. R. Gurney, *AFO*, *11* (1936-37), 367; R. J. Williams, *JCS*, *6* (1952), 4–7.

88. We owe to Landsberger, *ZA*, *43*, 32–76, the fundamental treatment of this composition.

89. See Nougayrol, pp. 239–50.

90. *Ibid.*, p. 250.

91. *Ibid.*

92. The fact that Sargon was a usurper (originally cupbearer of Ur-Zababa, cf. Jacobsen, *Sumerian King List*, p. 107, n. 217) detracts in no way from his traditional stature. He was not, however, a legitimate king in the accepted

epitomize him, was "one who encountered darkness, but the light emerged for him."[93] On the other hand, the remaining rulers of that dynasty were either assassinated or lived to see their power extinguished.[94] A study of the past may help one to emulate the successful and avoid the mistakes of the ill-fated. The main purpose, then, of such a study is to master the formula of deliverance, for one never knows when such knowledge may prove vital.

The symbol of Job was not the only one that was held up as a source of solace. The hero of the Flood was another comforting example, for no one in the entire history of mankind had ever emerged triumphant from greater peril. In this case, however, the Mesopotamian wisdom literature goes back a step to the father of Utnapishtim, the local Noah. For it was apparently parental wisdom that had stood Utnapishtim in such good stead. And so it is Shuruppak, the eponymous hero of the Flood city, substituting for Utnapishtim's father, who figures as the fountainhead of proverbial wisdom in Sumerian and Akkadian literature alike.[95]

The links between the heroes of the Flood and proverbial literature on the one hand, and between the Job image and the theme of deliverance on the other, combine to give a new meaning to

sense of the term, which is no doubt the reason for his assuming the name *Šarru* (*m*) *-kên*, "the king is legitimate." What his real name may have been we do not know any more than we know the name of the northern neighbor of Sumer before Sargon had made "Akkad" famous. Incidentally, another known usurper is familiar to us by the name of Sargon II of Assyria. The question arises, therefore, whether Sargon I of Assyria bore that name from the start in honor of the most celebrated of Mesopotamian rulers (note that his grandson's name was Naram-Sin), or whether he assumed it later on in his life for some specific purpose; say, to break away from the more humble title of *rubā'um* (see above, n. 22) and to have himself honored as *šarrum* "king," as many of his lesser contemporaries were doing.

93. See Goetze, *JCS*, *1*, 255 f.

94. *Ibid.*, pp. 256 ff.

95. For this specific figure in the Sumerian wisdom material cf. Kramer, *JCS*, *1*, 33, n. 208; the same name appears in an introduction to Akkadian proverbs in *KAR*, No. 27 obv (marked rev.[?] in the copy), 1.

the famous verse in Ezek. 14:14. According to that statement, Noah, Dan (i) el, and Job were the only men to emerge unscathed, because of their righteousness, from universal upheavals. Noah and Job, in Mesopotamian garb, are now known to us as celebrated wisdom personalities. Daniel's counterpart in Sumerian or Akkadian sources has yet to be identified. But the prominence of this particular theme is independently attested in Ugaritic.[96] Moreover, the biblical Book of Daniel has a Babylonian setting, quite aside from the fact that Ezekiel, who cites all three names in the same breath, knew his Babylonian culture at first hand. In other words, the Mesopotamian origin of the three heroes of Ezekiel is assured beyond all doubt. The prophet's statement merely testifies to the great popularity of the underlying tradition.

How each of these heroes had proved worthy of his extraordinary distinction is not made clear. The popular explanation may perhaps be indicated in an old omen which says: " If he has abhorred sin, his god will walk with him." [97] In any case, the use of these themes in the wisdom literature suggests that they had come to symbolize the lesson of the past at the intellectual level. That lesson may be summed up as follows: the history of the heroes of old who survived great trials and disasters could, at best, help to safeguard against recurrences. At worst, it might bring a measure of comfort in the disclosure that, even in a capricious cosmos, someone is likely to be singled out to save civilization.[98]

96. See Spiegel, pp. 305–55. On the location of *Hrnm*, the traditional home of the Ugaritic Danel, see now Albright, *BASOR*, *130* (1953), 28 f. The prominence of the biblical Daniel in the apocalyptic literature, notably the Book of Enoch, is brought out by Spiegel, *op. cit.*, pp. 336 ff. All in all, it appears certain that the Mesopotamian original of Daniel must be disguised under some other name. I would suggest with due reserve that the person in question was Adapa, who appears as an *apkallu* (" sage ") in the Chronicle Weidner and has otherwise some claim to being the patron of history.

97. *ZA*, *43*, 98, l. 31: *šumma ḫaṭītam izīr ilšu ittišu ittanallak.* Note the close parallel between this saying and the biblical statement about Enoch (Gen. 5:23), where a virtually identical verbal form is used.

98. This thought lends added force to the Ezekiel passage just cited. It

Yet, circumscribed as such views may be, they were obviously looked upon as much too broad for official purposes. The average king, at least in late Assyrian times, was too chauvinistic for philosophic appraisals.[99] This is well illustrated by the concluding paragraph of the so-called Synchronistic History: " The scholar who apprehends all that is written, may he ponder it and sing the praises of the land of Ashur for all time. But as for the land of Sumer and Akkad, may he expose its wickedness to all the quarters." It is not a case of " my country right or wrong." It is rather an instance of " my country is always right and the other country always wrong." [100]

In summary, Mesopotamian civilization was faced with the same two major problems that each civilization must solve for itself. One was the relation of the individual to society, and the other was the relation of society to nature.[101] The Mesopotamian solution of the first problem proved most successful and productive. The solution of the other problem, however, was a less constructive achievement. Since the gods were unsure of themselves, no values were really enduring. The need to avoid harm gave a negative meaning to the pursuit of happiness. Ritual rather than ethics, form far more than content, promised the best protection against the schemes of heaven. Because the king and the priest alike were slaves to the mistrust and fear of nature, they were jointly the captives of the forms calculated to protect mankind from nature. In the end, this emphasis on form became

should be stressed again in this connection that the three sages cited by Ezekiel were ancient Babylonian heroes of the magnitude of Noah himself, each of whom was qualified, by reason of his own extraordinary experience, to bring mankind a measure of comfort in times of cosmic distress.

99. That such appraisals, however, were not lacking in intellectual circles is attested by a composition universally misnamed the " Babylonian Dialogue of Pessimism "; cf. Langdon, *Babyloniaca*, 7, 195 ff. I expect to show elsewhere that this work is instead a splendid parody exposing weak leaders who seek to explain their inefficiency by recourse to threadbare clichés. See *JCS*, Vol. 8, No. 3 (1954).

100. The Assyrian Chronicle, *CT*, *34*, 41, col. 4, ll. 23 ff.

101. See above, n. 83.

a barrier to further progress. The collapse of Nineveh and of Babylon was due not so much to the heavy blows on the part of the Scythians, the Medes, and the Persians as to the crushing weight of the internal structure.

The Mesopotamian idea of history cannot but mirror the uneven advance of the major components of the parent civilization. It suffers from the limitations of its constituent elements. Other cultures, enriched and forwarned by the Mesopotamian experience, were to carry the study of history many strides forward. Along that course, however, the contribution of Mespotamia marks a significant early milestone; a milestone in the progress of the idea of history as well as of the history of ideas.

BIBLIOGRAPHY

AFO: Archiv für Orientforschung.

W. F. Albright, *From the Stone Age to Christianity*, 1940.

ANET: Ancient Near Eastern Texts Relating to the Old Testament, ed. J. B. Pritchard, 1950.

ARM: Archives royales de Mari: Texts, *TCL*, Vols. 22 ff.; Transliterations, Translations, and Notes, Vols. 1 ff.

BASOR: Bulletin Amer. Schools of Oriental Research.

Belleten: Türk Tarih Kurumu Basimevi, Ankara.

R. G. Collingwood, *The Idea of History*, 1946.

CT: Cuneiform Texts from the Babylonian Tablets . . . in the British Museum, London.

E. Ebeling, *Bruchstücke eines politischen Propaganda-Gedichtes aus einer assyrischen Kanzlei*, *MAOG*, Vol. 12, fasc. 2 1938.

Fakültesi Dergisi: Ankara Üniversitesi, Dil ve Tarih-Coğrafya Fakültesi Dergisi, 1943 ff.

T. Fish, " Some Aspects of Kingship in the Sumerian City and Kingdom of Ur," *Bulletin of the John Rylands Library*, *34* (1951), 37 ff.

H. Frankfort., *The Birth of Civilization in the Near East*, 1951.

——— *Cylinder Seals*, 1939.

——— *Kingship and the Gods*, 1949.

——— *et al.*, *The Intellectual Adventure of Ancient Man*, 1946.

C. J. Gadd, *Ideas of Divine Rule in the Ancient Near East*, 1947.

A. Goetze (Götze), *Hethiter, Churriter und Assyrer*, 1936.

——— *Kleinasien*, 1933.

——— *Old Babylonian Omen Texts, YOS*, (1947), Vol. 10.

——— " Historical Allusions in Old Babylonian Omen Texts," *JCS*, *1* (1947), 253 ff.

Gunkel Festschrift: Eucharisteion, 1923.

H. G. Güterbock, *Kumarbi*, 1946.

——— " Die historische Tradition und ihre literarische Gestaltung bei Babyloniern und Hethitern: Part I," *ZA*, *42* (1934), 1–91.

——— " The Song of Ullikummi," *JCS*, *5* (1951), 135–61; *6* (1952), 8–42.

T. Jacobsen, *The Sumerian King List*, Oriental Institute Assyriological Studies (1939), Vol. 11.

——— "Mesopotamia," *Intellectual Adventure of Ancient Man*, ed. H. Frankfort *et al.*, 1946.

——— "Primitive Democracy in Ancient Mesopotamia," *JNES, 2* (1943), 159 ff.

JAOS: Journal of the American Oriental Society.

JCS: Journal of Cuneiform Studies.

JNES: Journal of Near Eastern Studies.

JRAS: Journal of the Royal Asiatic Society.

KAH: Keilschrifttexte aus Assur historischen Inhalts.

KAR: Keilschrifttexte aus Assur religiösen Inhalts, Berlin.

S. N. Kramer, *Enmerkar and the Lord of Aratta*, University of Pennsylvania Museum Monographs, 1952.

——— *Sumerian Mythology, Memoirs of the American Philosophical Society* (1944), Vol. 21.

——— "Heroes of Sumer: a New Heroic Age in World History and Literature," Proceedings of the American Philosophical Society, *90* (1946), 120–30.

R. Labat, *Le Caractère religieux de la royauté assyro-babylonienne*, 1939.

B. Landsberger, "Die babylonische Theodizee," *ZA, 43* (1936), 32–76.

——— "Die Sumerer," *Fakültesi Dergisi, 1* (1943), 97–102.

——— "Die Anfaenge der Zivilization in Mesopotamien," *ibid., 2* (1944), 431–8.

——— "Die geistigen Leistungen der Sumerer," *ibid., 3* (1945), 150–9.

——— and K. Balkan, "Die Inschrift des assyrischen Könings Irișum, gefunden in Kültepe 1948," *Belleten, 14* (1950), 219–68, pls. 1–11.

R. Laqueur, "Formen geschichtlichen Denkens im alten Orient und Okzident," *Neue Jahrbücher für Wissenschaft und Jugendbildung, 7* (1931), 489–506.

MAOG: Mitteilungen der alten Orientgesellschaft.

B. Meissner, *Babylonien und Assyrien*, 1920–25, 2 vols.

E. Meyer, *Geschichte des Altertums*, 2d ed., 1928 ff.

A. Moortgat, and A. Scharff, *Ägypten und Vorderasien im Altertum* (1950), pp. 429–31.

S. Mowinckel, "Die vorderasiatischen Königs-und Fürsteninschriften," *Gunkel Festschrift*, 1923.

J. Nougayrol, "Une version ancienne du 'Juste Souffrant,'" *RB, 59* (1952), 239–50.

A. T. Olmstead, *Assyrian Historiography: a Source Study*, University of Missouri Studies in Social Science, Ser. III, Vol. 1, 1916.

——— *History of Assyria*, 1923.

A. L. Oppenheim, "Zur keilschriftlichen Omen-Literatur," *Orientalia, 5* (1936), 199 ff.

Orientalia, N. S.

A. L. Perkins, *The Comparative Archaeology of Early Mesopotamia*, Oriental Institute Studies in Ancient Civilization (1949), Vol. 25.

RB: Revue Biblique.

E. A. Speiser, " The Beginnings of Civilization in Mesopotamia," *JAOS*, *59*, suppl. 4 (1939), 17–31.

——— " Some Factors in the Collapse of Akkad," *JAOS*, *72* (1952), 97–101.

——— " Some Sources of Intellectual Progress in the Ancient Near East," *Waldo Leland Volume* (1942), pp. 51–62.

——— " The Sumerian Problem Reviewed," *Hebrew Union College Annual*, *23*, Pt. I (1950–51), 339–56.

S. Spiegel, " Noah, Danel, and Job," *Ginzberg Jubilee Volume* (1945), pp. 305–55.

TCL: Textes cunéiformes du Louvre.

A. Ungnad, " Besprechungskunst und Astrologie in Babylonien," *AFO*, *14* 1941–44), 251 ff.

YOS: Yale Oriental Series, Babylonian Texts.

ZA: Zeitschrift für Assyriologie.

[The following two papers appeared too late for inclusion in this discussion:

Burr C. Brundage, " The Birth of Clio: A Résumé and Interpretation of Ancient Near Eastern Historiography," *Teachers of History* (ed. by H. Stuart Hughes, 1954), pp. 199–230.

S. N. Kramer, " Sumerian Historiography," *Israel Exploration Journal*, *3* (1953), 217–32.]

ANCIENT PERSIA

George G. Cameron

I. PROLOGUE

To the historian concerned with the ideas and ideals of men, the beginnings of history among the Persians of Iran are seen but dimly through scanty and mostly non-Persian sources, varied languages and systems of writing, and sorely inadequate materials provided by archeological excavations. In sharp relief against this background stand the developments within Iran under the Achaemenids (550–332 B. C.), under Alexander the Great and his successors, under the Parthians, and under the Sassanids, who witnessed the advent of Arab rule. Ideally, each of these periods should be assessed.

The present essay is devoted exclusively to a portion of the history of the Achaemenids. This is not because new ideas of history failed to make their appearance subsequently, but chiefly because this is the only period of Persian history in which the writer even begins to feel competent and also because he believes that with the Achaemenids there came into being a new concept regarding the past that was not later so fully expressed. How and why this concept originated, then, is the topic of this essay.

II. THE SETTING

The Persians ride into civilization out of the dim mists of the past, almost literally out of obscurity. Late in the 9th century before the Christian Era they and their close relatives, the Medes, impinge but lightly on the "civilized" Assyrian Empire. Two centuries later they have already begun to be the dominant factor in the Near East. What of their earlier history? We do not know it, and there is little evidence that they themselves were familiar with it.

That their life was prosaic may be judged from the nature of the terrain where they are first encountered; that it was prosaic *movement*, from the vigorous efforts of Assyria to stem what threatened to be an awesome, compelling flood of Mede and Persian invaders.

From time immemorial the inhabitants of Mesopotamia had sought entry into the mountains to the east and northeast which cut them off from the plateau of Iran. Here was oak needed for building purposes in place of the weak home-grown palm tree; here were sandstone and enduring limestone to fill the void left in the stone-free alluvium. Here trade routes led to sources of lapis lazuli, the prized blue stone of all antiquity. Here were the highland-lowland nomads who in early fall brought their flocks of sheep and goats down to feed on the lush grass produced by the first rains of the Assyrian winter, and who in early spring, when the vegetation was already becoming parched by the sun's heat, began the annual migration leading them back up to the rich, terraced pastures at the very top of the mountain rim. These are rugged mountains, and the migration breeds rugged people. Beyond the mountain rim to the east lies steppe land; by Assyrian times when empire, to be effective, demanded the rapid movement of cavalry, this steppe was the unwilling source of fine thoroughbred horses.

In this region, in what is today known as Kurdistan or the country of the Kurds, Medes and Persians made contact with Assyria. That contact made them aware of a civilization more advanced technologically, if not also spiritually, than their own. By that contact they discovered also that the world was old and that the world knew its own antiquity. Contrast their backgrounds! The Assyrian could point with pride to teeming, wealthy cities, each built on earlier foundations of still earlier man. He could refer to lists of Assyrian kings reaching back a thousand years or more and to lists of Babylonian dynasts whose reigns extended uninterruptedly from the current day to those aeons long since gone when kingship descended from heaven after the Flood. Still earlier were other monarchs, sons of gods and so themselves demigods. In substantiation of these claims to antiquity were the monuments: temple towers, the temples themselves, colossal figures of protecting deities and genii, freestanding stones or stelae—all inscribed or made of inscribed bricks. In substantiation also were written epics, legends, laws, prayers to gods and boasts of men, even lowly business contracts.

Could the Medes and Persians, untutored, often rude, almost barbaric, hope to vie with this? In contrast with the known and learned past of their adversaries, the Medes and Persians could place only unwritten sagas and stories sung by wandering minstrels like those who, to this day, entertain Kurdish chiefs and tribesmen. Could they, to whom even writing—the use of written symbols to record or communicate ideas—was a complete novelty, fail to be impressed by the intellectual giants of Ashur and Babylon, even though the timid cavalry of those giants could so easily be put to flight and shame? Did they not long for an equivalent, but an equivalent which was at the same time a reality, the word made flesh? Did they not seek some way to balance their own vague, dim knowledge of the past against their opponents' concrete evidence of antiquity? History demonstrates that they not only sought but found a way; and the method they evolved led to a new idea in history writing. Simply stated, it involved balancing—with a propagandistic, almost proselytizing flavor—their own justice against the rank injustice of their predecessors and adversaries. Aimed at their contemporaries, it was also persuasive to succeeding generations.

III. "FATHER" CYRUS AND HISTORY REWRITTEN

While Persian tribesmen were filtering through the steppes east of the Zagros rim and finding a heartland in that area of Iran, Parsa, where subsequently they were to build Pasargadae and Persepolis,[1] Medes were breaking the protective shell of hollow

1. Described in George G. Cameron, *History of Early Iran* (1936), pp. 143 ff.; F. W. Koenig, "Aelteste Geschichte der Meder und Perser," *Der Alte*

Ashur and joining Babylonia in successful assault on once-proud Nineveh. The political history which followed is not wholly clear, for details are sadly lacking. We know only that an uneasy peace prevailed between the two conquerors,[2] and that the Medes added a part of old Assyria and the cold uplands of Armenia to their domains and empire. Forces more subtle than arms and armies, and yet more powerful, were at work, and here it might be said that Ashur, already the intellectual captive of great Babylon, took captive her subsequent conqueror.

Official Median royal titles, subsequently borrowed by the Persians in the Median dialect form, are those of Ashur; thus "———, great king, king of kings, king of lands." This simple fact betrays the alacrity with which the Medes and their kinsmen Persians embraced the outward form, the external formulae, of the giants whom they were replacing. With the Persian victory over the Medes and, eleven years later, the conquest of Babylon by Cyrus in 539 B. C., the opportunity to rewrite history in terms of justice versus injustice could not be denied.

Promptly there swung into action a magnificent propaganda machine. First, we are told that the last king of Babylon, Nabunaid, was unjust even to the established gods of his own land: " [In] rituals not worthy of them . . . . daily he blabbered; fiendishly he interrupted the regular offerings . . . his hands defiled [even] the worship of Marduk, king of the gods." [3] Second, at

Orient, 33, Heft 3/4 (Leipzig, 1934), 8; Sidney Smith, *Isaiah, Chapters XL–LV*, The Schweich Lectures of the British Academy, 1940 (London, 1944), pp. 27 ff.; F. H. Weissbach in Pauly and Wissowa, eds., *Real-Encyclopaedie*, suppl., *4* (1924), 1132 ff., *s. v.* " Kyros."

The evidence is meager and is based primarily on acceptance of the somewhat dubious equation of peoples inhabiting lands called Parsua, Parsuash, Parsamash, and Parsa.

2. At which time captive Jews in Babylonia, by literary productions now embedded in Isa. 13–14 and Jer. 50–1, hoped for alleviation of their woes.

3. Cyrus Cylinder, ll. 6 f., text: H. C. Rawlinson, *Cuneiform Inscriptions of Western Asia*, Vol. 5 (2d. ed. 1910), pl. 35; translation: L. Oppenheim in James B. Pritchard, ed., *Ancient Near Eastern Texts Relating to the Old Testament* (Princeton, 1950), pp. 315 ff.

Nabunaid's command the established institutions, built up over thousands of years of recorded history, were desecrated, for he introduced things never before seen in the land,[4] omitted all festivals, and brought an end even to the sacred New Year's ceremony.[5] Finally, Nabunaid was unjust even to his own Babylonian subjects: " To his people he used to do evil . . . . in yokes without relief he ruined them all.[6] Their faces became changed, They no longer paraded in the squares, One saw happiness no more." [7] With what satisfaction must the unlettered Cyrus, himself respecting the learning of Babylon, have listened to the accusations made about Nabunaid, who is said to have declared: " I am wise, I know, I have seen what is hidden, [even] if I do not know how to write with the stylus." [8]

By contrast, the newcomer Cyrus is presented as a just and righteous savior, whose good deeds and upright mind captured the heart of Babylon's chief deity, Marduk, who had brought him into being. The very titles given Cyrus are those reiterated down through the centuries: " king of totality, great king, mighty king, king of Babylon, king of Sumer and Akkad, king of the four world quarters." The inference here is that Cyrus is no alien king of far-off Parsa; instead, he is the legitimate sovereign of " the enduring seed of royalty, whose rule Bel and Nabu loved and whose kingship they desired." [9]

Unquestionably these texts were written by native Babylonian priests irked by Nabunaid's former lack of attention to local affairs and local deities. What did it matter to them that in his

4. Persian Verse Account, col. 1: 21, text: Sidney Smith, *Babylonian Historical Texts* (London, 1924), pls. 5 ff.; translation: Oppenheim in Pritchard, pp. 312 ff.

5. Verse Account, col. 2: 11.

6. Cyrus Cylinder, l. 8; cf. also l. 11: " The peoples of Sumer and Akkad were like corpses." Cf. also, the Nabunaid-Cyrus Chronicle, col. 3: 13–14; text: Smith, *Babylonian Historical Texts*, pls. 11 ff.; translation: Oppenheim in Pritchard, pp. 305 ff.

7. Verse Account, col. 1: 14 ff.

8. *Ibid.*, col. 5: 9 f.

9. Cyrus Cylinder, l. 22.

last hectic months and pursuant to the almost universal belief that " a captured city is forsaken, deserted by its gods " Nabunaid sought desperately to protect the deities and the temple paraphernalia by bringing them within the ring of Babylon's defenses? [10] For this, too, could later be turned against him, and they could declare that " The gods forsook their mansions in anger because he [Nabunaid] had made them enter Babylon." [11] But disregarding the question of specific authorship of these documents, there is no doubt that they rightly portrayed the attitude of the new sovereign toward the people in this recently acquired land. His first acts demonstrate conclusively that he felt he had a mission to accomplish, a mission involving both the substitution of new and just deeds for existing and previous practices and the simultaneous acquisition for himself and his regime of that renown which should accrue, in current and succeeding generations, for such substitution.

In solemn procession Cyrus returned to their former homes the many deities who had forcibly been incarcerated in Babylon.[12] And not only the gods gained freedom: " I [also] gathered all their peoples and returned them [to] their habitations." [13] This was in truth an unexpected, almost unprecedented, development. It had reference to gods and people not only of central Babylonia but of Ashur in the far north, Susa in the south, Der and the old Guti lands in the east, and who knows what others besides? Even as propaganda it would build morale; but as promise gave way to reality, as rebuilt temples became tangible proof of a new order,

10. References in *Journal of the American Oriental Society, 52* (1932), 304. Add: Nabu-naid-Cyrus Chronicle, col. 3: 8 ff.

11. Cyrus Cylinder, ll. 9 f.

12. Nabunaid-Cyrus Chronicle, col. 3: 21; Cyrus Cylinder, l. 32; Verse Account, col. 6: 12–16. That this, too, is not mere propaganda is apparent from the biblical account (on which, see below), and from the prosaic letter published by A. T. Clay, *Neo-Babylonian Letters from Erech,* Yale Oriental Series (1919), Vol. 3, No. 86; cf. *JAOS, 52,* 304.

13. Cyrus Cylinder, l. 32; cf. Verse Account, col. 6: 25 ff. (on which see Benno Landsberger and Theo Bauer, *Zeitschrift für Assyriologie,* Neue Folge, *3* (1927), 94, and Oppenheim in Pritchard, p. 315).

what wonder that others, too, such as the captive Babylonian Jews, should see in Cyrus their own savior, should pen their expressions of hope in him, and that their words should still appear in Holy Writ? It is Cyrus who comes

> . . . from the east,
> Whom righteousness meets at every step,
> Setting nations before him,
> And subjecting kings.[14]

To the Jews, of course, it was not Marduk but Yahweh

> Who says of Cyrus, " My shepherd,
> Who shall fulfill all my pleasure ";
> Who says of Jerusalem, " She shall be built,"
> And of the temple, " Your foundations shall be laid."
> Thus says Yahweh to his anointed,
> To Cyrus, whose right hand I have grasped,
> To bring down nations before him,
> And to ungird the loins of kings.[15]
>
> . . . . .
>
> I have roused one in righteousness,
> And all his ways will I level;
> He shall build my city,
> And shall set my exiles free.[16]

The words so closely parallel the contemporary propaganda documents that one wonders if the authors might actually have read them.[17]

Thus ends the first insight we are given into the motivations of those who, in earliest Persian times, were compiling, for con-

14. Isa. 41:2. Biblical quotations generally follow (sometimes in a slightly revised form) *The Complete Bible: an American Translation* (Chicago, 1939).

15. Isa. 44:28–45:1.

16. Isa. 45:13.

17. Cf. A. T. Olmstead, *History of the Persian Empire* (New York, 1948), p. 55. In this perspective, the edict incorporated in Ezra 6:1 ff. bears many marks of authenticity.

temporaries as for successors, the propagandistic yet historical documents. The appeal was twofold. The first was to a respect for legitimacy, to the "eternal seed of kingship"; in this there was nothing not known from the postdiluvial monarchs of olden times, and the Persian merely showed that he was learning the mechanics of rulership in an old land.[18] The second, more basic appeal was to justice replacing injustice, to truth and righteousness versus inequity: "He [Cyrus] constantly sought after order and equity for the black-headed people whom [Marduk] made him conquer." [19] The end result could be only that "In the faith that he had made the dead live, that he had spared them all from extermination and disaster, they [the people] drew near him joyfully and sang his fame." [20]

That the new-found method was effective may be judged from the declaration of Herodotus that the Persians called Cyrus "Father" because "he was gentle and procured them all manner of goods." [21]

IV. "HUCKSTER" DARIUS AND HISTORY REMADE

The Persian Darius, who ascended to sovereignty seventeen years after Cyrus conquered Babylon, is justly given even greater fame. To begin with, we have a large number of his own historical records upon the rocky walls at Bisitun, the terraces of his splendid city Persepolis, his royal tomb at Naqsh-i-Rustam, and elsewhere. He was infinitely better known to that famed Greek storyteller, Herodotus, of whom his son and grandson were con-

18. It must be assumed that Cyrus would attempt to improve his knowledge of these mechanics in the following years, and one of the indicated tools was the simple production of written documents. Excavations at Cyrus's royal city, Pasargadae, have revealed that the practice of writing trilingual inscriptions can scarcely be denied him. See Ernst Herzfeld, *Altpersische Inschriften* (Berlin, 1938), pp. 2 ff., and Roland G. Kent, *Old Persian*, American Oriental Series *33* (New Haven, 1950), 12, nn. 4, 5.

19. Cyrus Cylinder, ll. 13 f.

20. *Ibid.*, l. 19.

21. Herodotus, *History* iii, 89.

temporaries. Finally, from his reign there has come down to us a vast quantity of written materials—economic transactions, court records, private correspondence, and the like.

It will be our task to determine whether these documents are mere bombastic, traditional utterances or whether there are expressed or implied concepts of the past which operated in their composition. If we find such concepts, we shall endeavor to discover whether they, in turn, were challenged, modified, or replaced.

Superficial examination of the major inscriptions of Darius would lead to the conclusion that because of their physical situation they must be explained as documents prepared for show and that they cannot be interpreted as compositions intended to be read and understood by the people. Although the Bisitun relief and inscriptions overlook the major highway leading from Iran to Babylon, they are carved at an altitude of 315 feet above that highway and were deliberately made inaccessible to men. Likewise the writings that appear on the tomb at Naqsh-i-Rustam can be reached and read only after the utmost physical exertion. This much must be granted, however, even if we were to adopt this view: without exception the monuments are impressive. More significantly, they obviously were *intended* to impress, which indicates that the author was concerned with the effect of his achievements on contemporary and succeeding generations.

Parenthetically, it may be said that Darius had well mastered the techniques handed down to him by the intellectual giants of the past. He had learned how to make monuments for show. He had learned how to write the traditional formulae and how to compose his documents within the old framework of 1) an introduction, containing a genealogy and invocation to the god or gods; 2) a factual statement of achievements or deeds; and 3) a conclusion, embodying blessings upon those successors who preserve, and curses upon those who damage, the monuments.

Other factors, too, reveal Darius' admiration for, and acceptance of, the wisdom of the ancients. At the newly founded capital, Persepolis, administrative records were kept in the Elamite language; this was so simply because of the fact that within the Persian Empire, which had advanced from penury to more than plenty in a few short years, there were insufficient numbers of native Persians equipped with the technical knowledge of Elamite accountants.[22] Furthermore, almost without exception royal monuments are inscribed in both Babylonian and Elamite, thus reflecting a desire not only to disseminate more widely the information contained in them but also to perpetuate traditions, for inscriptions had been prepared for millennia in both of these languages.[23]

Something new was added, however. In every instance attention is focused not upon the Babylonian or Elamite text but upon the Old Persian version, to the invention of which Darius himself lays specific claim. He wrote, he says, "in [the] Aryan [language, a method] which formerly was unknown." [24] The claim is quite in line with his often repeated assertion: "I am . . . a Persian, son of a Persian, an Aryan, having Aryan lineage." [25]

Now the claim may not be valid. Inscriptions have been found at Cyrus' capital, Pasargadae, and some of these are written in Old Persian. But this is quite beside the point. Too often that which is significant in the minds of men is not what really happened but what they believe or wish others to believe has

22. Cf. George G. Cameron, *Persepolis Treasury Tablets*, Oriental Institute Publications, *65* (Chicago, 1948), 17–22, 24 ff.

23. The Aramaic rescript of a portion of the Bisitun inscription, the possibility that an Aramaic version preceded the composition of the Babylonian text, and the evidence for Aramaic speakers at Persepolis all argue for the translation of official records into Aramaic also (for references, cf. Cameron, *Tablets*, pp. 19 ff., 28 ff.). The presence of Aramaic, of course, is an appeal not to the past but to the contemporary situation.

24. The Bisitun inscription of Darius (hereafter abbreviated as DB), sec. 70; for the revised reading of this section, see George G. Cameron and Roland G. Kent in *Journal of Cuneiform Studies*, *5* (1951), *52*, *55*, and Roland G. Kent, *Old Persian* (2d. ed., 1953), *ad loc.*

25. DN*a*: 13–15; DS*e*: 12–14; imitated by Xerxes in XPh: 12–13; cf. also, DBI: 48 f.; DP*e*: sec. 3; DN*a*: 43–7; DZ*c*: 7–8. For all these abbreviations see Kent, *Old Persian* (either edition), pp. 4–5.

occurred. The claim, therefore puts us in quandary: did it originate because the sovereign sought to *imitate* his predecessors or because he endeavored to *surpass* them? Even this enigma leads to only one conclusion: in either case, although the claim reflects a deep measure of admiration and respect for the past, *that past might be imitated and improved upon.* Simultaneously, we are forced to accept the further conclusion that Darius was deeply aware of, and took great pride in, his Aryan descent and language. The old order, then, was an outmoded one giving place to new. The old was permeated with confusion, injustice, and the Lie; the new brought equity and truth. This very thought is the motivation, the *raison d'être,* of the Bisitun inscription.

Darius' first appeal in that document, as he traces his own genealogy back to the eponymous ancestor Achaemenes, is to legitimacy, a recognition that in and of itself the past had merit: "Says Darius the King: For this reason we are called Achaemenids: From long ago we have been noble, from long ago our family have been kings . . . Eight of our family were formerly kings; I am the ninth: nine in succession[?] have been kings."[26]

This statement, however, is immediately followed by a declaration that the new regime (i. e., that of Darius) was god-given in order to re-establish justice and equity: "Says Darius the King: By the favor of Ahuramazda I am King; Ahuramazda bestowed the kingdom upon me . . . Within these countries the man who was excellent, him I rewarded well; who was evil, him I punished well."[27] The atmosphere is that of a courtroom where the divinely appointed plaintiff can plead his case and present a bill of particulars. The immediate past is pertinent. Our accuser says in effect: "There was a king before me named Cyrus; he was of our family and therefore a descendant of Achaemenes. Cyrus had two sons: Cambyses, who became king, and Bardiya. Cambyses secretly killed Bardiya and then went off to conquer Egypt. In his absence a man named Gaumata, claiming to be the murdered brother, raised a standard

26. DB, secs. 3, 4.
27. DB, secs. 5, 8.

of rebellion to which flocked many of the provinces. With Cambyses' death, this usurper—vicious, cruel, and a stifler of free speech—became sole monarch." When, therefore, with the aid of six other conspirators, Darius eliminated the usurper, the kingdom was logically and justly his. The logic is somewhat involved, since we learn subsequently that Darius' father and grandfather were still living at the time,[28] and one wonders why one of these should not have inherited the throne instead of the youthful Darius. Justice, too, was blind; with few exceptions the provinces, misled by lies, refused to accept the divinely ordained new order. The bulk of the Bisitun text and relief portrays the conquests of the separate rebels. Here it is apparent that no sooner was one revolt quelled in each province (even at the very heart of the kingdom—in Persia, Elam, and Babylonia) than another broke out anew in the same area. "Says Darius the King: These are the provinces which became rebellious. The Lie made them rebellious, so that these deceived the people." [29]

This was the official story. It may even have been substantially true. Cyrus *may* have been a descendant of Achaemenes, as Darius was, though by a collateral branch. The real Bardiya, son of Cyrus, *may* have been killed by Cambyses, and he whom Darius assassinated may indeed have been a usurper. However this may be, the official story, true or not, needed promulgation, and our document concludes with a twice-stated appeal to future sovereigns first, to protect themselves from the Lie and its consequences; [30] second, to believe and preserve the account of Darius' accomplishments, even though these might seem incredible; [31] and third, to promulgate and spread the word among all people, even as Darius himself had done.[32]

28. DB, sec. 36 and DS*f*, sec. 3.

29. DB, sec. 54.

30. DB, sec. 55, substantially repeated in secs. 62–4 where Darius regards himself as a model.

31. DB, secs. 56–9, rephrased in secs. 65–7.

32. DB, secs. 60–1, with Darius' example provided in sec. 70, on which see also Roland G. Kent, "The Oldest Old Persian Inscriptions," *JAOS, 56* (1946),

Traditional methods of promulgation are approved, but even these have been inadequate, and it is here that Darius proudly makes his claim, referred to above, of writing in a way hitherto unknown, i. e., in the Aryan language.

Thus the pattern introduced by Cyrus was clarified and refined. Always there is emphasis on the accrued wisdom of the old; but always, too, there is insistence upon the addition of new values to old, outmoded ones. The new values are based on an expressed desire for truth and justice; they are intended to eliminate confusion and the Lie, and they are to be broadcast for the enlightenment of all people. That the official story was effective when presented in this light may be adduced from the fact that it was told to, and related by, Herodotus, whose account differs only in details.[33]

Propaganda alone would never be adequate, of course, and promulgation of the official account was immediately followed by other, more persuasive acts. Even in his autobiography Darius had asserted: "By the favor of Ahuramazda these countries showed respect toward my law; as was said to them by me, thus was it done."[34] This was no idle boast. As early as his second regnal year, Darius' collection of existing laws was in use among the Babylonians where, for the usual guaranty by the seller, there is substituted the phrase: "According to the king's law they shall make good."[35] Obviously, the new book could not have been so quickly formulated had it not been based on one already in use. But even the term for "law" is new; instead of the long familiar "judgments," we now have the good Iranian *data* familiar from Ezra and the Book of Esther.[36]

206 ff., and W. Hinz, "Die Einführung der altpersischen Schrift," *Zeitschrift der Deutschen Morgenländischen Gesellschaft*, Neue Folge, 27 (1952), 28 ff.

33. Herodotus, iii, 30–1 and 61 ff. See also, Ctesias, *Pers.* xii, *Epit.* 41–4; Plato, *Epist.* vii, 332A, *Leg.* 695B; Justin, i, 9, 4 ff.; Polyaenus, vii, 11, 2.

34. DB, sec. 8.

35. J. N. Strassmaier, *Babylonische Texte, Inschriften von Darius* (Leipzig, 1897), No. 53. The phrase referred to is *data ša šarri*.

36. Cf. A. T. Olmstead, *History of the Persian Empire* (Chicago, 1948), pp. 119 ff.

Similarly, the monarch lost no time in preparing the groundwork for a recodification of laws in Egypt. To his reinstated satrap he wrote: "Let them bring to me the wise men among the warriors, priests, and scribes of Egypt who have assembled from the temples, and let them write down the former *laws* of Egypt . . . *The law of Pharaoh, temple, and people let them bring*." [37] The new lawbook, in other words, was not to be confined to royal decrees. Religious laws and the hitherto unwritten customary procedures were also to be standardized. This, too, was a new departure.

References to the Book of Ezra remind us that under Darius, as under Cyrus, there was a return of Jews to Jerusalem. The leaders were subjected to considerable pressure, not only from local zealots like Haggai and Zechariah but also from royal administrators who demanded to know by what authority the newcomers were reconstructing the temple. When the Jews claimed that the construction had been authorized by a decree of Cyrus, "Darius, the King, issued a decree, and search was made in the house of the archives where the treasures were stored there at Babylon. And at Ecbatana, in the castle that is in the province of Media, a roll was found." [38] The authorization thus having been verified, no further obstacles were presented by the Persian officials. The incident would be of little moment in this context were it not for the interesting sidelight that it throws upon Darius' acceptance of previously issued decrees.

This attempt to define the Persian concepts would be inadequate unless we endeavored to analyze, however briefly, the political ethos and structure of imperial policy, which in many ways was the direct antithesis of the preceding Assyrian policy. Assyria had not been content simply to rule the territories which she had so vigorously annexed; she had sought to assimilate them as well. Systematically the later Assyrians obliterated previous frontiers and substituted an arbitrarily mapped-out network of

37. W. Spiegelberg, *Die sogenannte Demotische Chronik* (1914), pp. 30 ff.; cf. Diodorus, i, 95, 4–5.

38. Ezra 6:1–2.

Assyrian provinces. The Persians, by contrast, originally sought to reconcile their subjects by keeping to a minimum the imperial government's interference with existing habits and customs and by permitting a maximum amount of local self-government. As long as their subjects kept the peace and paid their taxes, the Achaemenids were content to let them live as they pleased in other respects; they were slow to anger, even when they had to deal with inveterate rebels.

On the plane of administrative geography this policy preserved the *status quo* and therefore signified Persian willingness to accept the lessons of the past; it was rudely interrupted, however, by the wholesale revolt of province after province at the accession of Darius. The Great King found himself compelled to reduce to a narrow compass the once broad basis of voluntary support on which the former regimes had safely rested. Even certain areas of the homeland Persia were detached; Media was partitioned; Armenia was broken into fragments; and so were other important satrapies that might be politically dangerous.[39] This was a deliberate break with the past, which had a marked effect on Persian interpretations of past events. It added to the assertion already made by Cyrus that Persians were divinely appointed saviors whose mission was to bring justice, order, and tranquility to the peoples of the earth. In one of two inscriptions carved during his lifetime on the rocks where his tomb was being prepared, we read:

> Says Darius the King: Ahuramazda, when he saw this earth in commotion, thereafter bestowed it upon me, made me king. By the favor of Ahuramazda I put it down in its place. What I said to them, that they did, as was my desire. If now thou shalt think: "How many are the countries which King Darius held?" look at the sculptures of those who bear the throne. Then shalt thou know . . . the spear of a Persian

39. The evidence for the foregoing statements has been amassed and assessed by A. J. Toynbee in an Annex to his *A Study of History*, 7 (1954), 580 ff.

> man has gone forth far . . . a Persian man has delivered battle far from Persia. . . . O man, that which is the command of Ahuramazda, let it not seem repugnant to thee; do not leave the path which is right; do not rise in rebellion.

The second inscription is even more significant, for it is concerned exclusively with the contemporary situation. Darius is portrayed as the exemplar of ideals of conduct and as the earthly deputy of the supreme deity. He is the mighty ruler to whom resistance is treason, who puts to death those who would set themselves in his place or who follow seekers after the Lie. He praises the doers of right, the worshipers of Ahuramazda, and condemns the doers of wrong; he seeks justice with all his mental and physical powers.[40] Not once is reference made to the past; in effect, the whole inscription is a denial of the previously held concept that traditional values had merit.

V. RETURN TO OLD IDEAS

Perhaps we shall never know what led Darius to the expression of this extreme view, which could not and did not last in the ancient world. The Persian Empire was the sum of its component parts, in each of which there was, as there is today, a conviction that old and cherished ways of life and thought must be saved from destruction. Slowly but surely the successors of Darius revert to this latter point of view.

Xerxes represents a transition—but here we ourselves must break with a traditional view. Greek sources, which the Western world long blindly accepted, portray Xerxes as a weakling dominated by eunuchs and as the barbarian author of an insane attack on " civilized " Greece. Oriental sources picture a very different character. At his accession he was in the prime of life, trained for the throne by a dozen strenuous years of administration. His military venture in Greece was a failure, to be sure, although it

40. DN*b*; for translation and explanation cf. Roland G. Kent in *Journal of Near Eastern Studies, 4* (1945), 39 ff., 232, and *Old Persian*, pp. 138 ff.

was by no means as significant to his imperial subjects as the Greeks would have us believe. This one failure was more than offset by a whole series of victories, including the recovery of Egypt and the retention of control over most of the Greeks themselves. Although the architects of Darius had laid out the grand plan of the terrace structures at Persepolis, it was Xerxes who brought the main buildings to completion and who initiated construction of most of the others. In his inscriptions he is proud of the accomplishments of his father; he is prouder still that he himself has turned to good effect that which had been badly done aforetime.[41] Thus it may be said that in some respects Xerxes marks an even greater break with the past; perhaps the clearest demonstration of this came with his sack and terrible punishment of Babylon, that great old intellectual giant.

It was also Xerxes, however, who began to compensate for military defeat by employing a method of conquest as old as time itself: diplomacy backed by imperial gold, i. e., bribery. As a useful tool it need not, of course, have been learned from Greeks, Babylonians, or Egyptians; yet a man is known by the company he keeps and " For himself doth a man work evil, in working evils for another." [42] Darius had said:

> I am a friend to what is right,
> I am not a friend to what is wrong;
> It is not my desire that the weak man should
> have wrong done to him by the mighty.[43]

Xerxes' policy, by contrast, is a denial that Persian rule was different from its predecessors.

It was also Xerxes who first became involved in matters which had always plagued oriental monarchs: harem and court intrigues. Fostered by mothers, sisters, wives, and sweethearts, those intrigues revolved around questions of legitimate claims to the throne. By its very nature, the claim to legitimacy is an appeal

41. Cf. XP*f* and *g*, XV, and XS*a*, *b*, and *c* with XPh, sec. 4.
42. Hesiod, *Works and Days* 265.
43. DNb, sec. 8.

to past history; such an appeal, when crisis came, proved to be stronger than the claims of Cyrus and Darius that with the coming of the Achaemenids a new order had begun.

The years of crisis were 404 to 401 B. C. when, aided and abetted by the queen mother, brother was pitted against brother in contest for the throne. Xenophon relates how ten thousand Greeks, under the one brother Cyrus, penetrated almost to Babylon, where they won their battle but lost their leader, and then made their arduous way northward to the Black Sea and home to their coastal cities.

This incident, however, left a deep impression on the Persian victor, Artaxerxes II. He and his brother were sons of a Darius, but the very name of his brother, Cyrus, suggested with some poignancy that other Cyrus who had first led the Persians to conquest and whose line had been superseded by that of the Great Darius himself. There was need to substantiate the claim of Darius that by the assassination of the false Bardiya and the assumption of the crown he, Darius, had merely restored to its rightful place the line of the eponymous ancestor, Achaemenes. There was also need to discredit the royal line of the older Cyrus.

Two methods were at hand. One involved a falsified account of the origin of Cyrus the Great prepared by Artaxerxes' personal physician, Ctesias. According to this account, Cyrus was no Achaemenid by birth but a lad of base origin, the son of a lowly shepherd. The other method required the preparation of a series of inscribed monuments glorifying the grandfather and great grandfather of the Great Darius.[44] Thus came into being the inscriptions of Ariaramnes and Arsames. These were forgeries, to be sure, but ancient forgeries, prepared more than a century after their ostensible makers had been laid to rest.

Grandiose as was this plan, it was at the same time an acknowledgment that in the minds of Persian history writers the past had claimed its own. Gone now was the effort to visualize current

44. Now partly in Roland G. Kent, *Old Persian*, pp. 107, 116 (see also, pp. 158–9); cf. Kent, " The Oldest Persian Inscriptions," JAOS, *66* (1946), 206 ff.

situations as the antitheses of those which had preceded; gone the assertion of a new order, based on truth, justice, and equity, replacing the old dependence on the Lie, injustice, and confusion. Now men claimed sovereignty exclusively on the age-old basis of legitimacy. The cycle was complete.[45]

45. It was, then, no mere accident that the supremacy of Ahuramazda was henceforth challenged—also in the reign of Artaxerxes II—by the gods Anahita and Mithra; see A^2Sa and *d*, A^2Ha and *b*, and A^3Pa in Kent, *Old Persian*, pp. 154 ff.

ANCIENT ISRAEL

Millar Burrows

I. THE NATURE OF THE SOURCES

THE situation we face in trying to formulate the idea of history in ancient Israel is very different from that which we have met in dealing with Egypt, Mesopotamia, and Persia. It is different in two ways: in the nature of the sources at our disposal and in the relative prominence of the idea of history in those sources.

Our sources for the Hebrew idea of history are not firsthand, contemporary records like the innumerable cuneiform texts on clay tablets or the inscriptions and pictures on the walls of Egyptian and Assyrian temples and palaces or on the cliff at Bisitun. They are literary documents which have themselves gone through a long history of compiling, editing, and copying. What the Assyrian King Sennacherib thought, or wanted others to think, about his invasion of Judah, laying waste cities, and shutting up King Hezekiah " like a bird in a cage," is known to us from his prism inscription. We have no comparable document from Hezekiah to tell us what he thought about it.

We have no Hebrew royal inscriptions. The inscription of King Mesha of Moab shows that the Hebrews could have had royal inscriptions. The nearest thing to a Hebrew building inscription ever discovered is the one found in the Siloam tunnel, which does not even name the king under whom the work was done. Absalom is said to have set up a monument in the King's Valley to preserve the memory of his name (II Sam. 18:18). It has been suggested that the account of David's victories and the list of his officials in II Sam. 8 may have been taken from a royal victory stele.[1] The fact remains that no Hebrew royal inscription has been preserved. We have almost no Hebrew inscriptions of any kind.

1. E. Sellin and L. Rost, *Einleitung in das Alte Testament* (Heidelberg, 1950), p. 89.

Such sparse records as the ostraca of Samaria and Lachish give us some historical information but nothing about the idea of history. For that we are entirely dependent upon literary sources in late copies.

In this literature the idea of history plays an extraordinary part. It is a religious literature, of course, and history was of basic importance to the religion of Israel. The literature consists very largely of historical narratives, all presented under a dominant conception of the meaning of history. Yet it is not a single, uniform idea. Rather, we have in the Old Testament many ideas of history. Our first difficulty therefore in discussing the idea of history in ancient Israel is an embarrassment of riches. I may add that while my predecessors in this series have been breaking virgin soil, my own plot has already been cultivated almost to the point of exhaustion.

The literature of ancient Israel has been preserved because it is accepted as sacred literature by Judaism and Christianity. It has therefore become an integral part of our own cultural heritage. This fact makes it easier for us to interpret Hebrew ideas with the sympathetic understanding of those who stand within the tradition. For this very reason, however, we must be especially on guard against the danger of reading our modern Western ideas—or theological conceptions derived from Greek philosophy—into the ancient Hebrew writings. The sources must be allowed to speak for themselves, and what they say must be understood, as far as possible, in terms of their own cultural background.

Back of the rather sophisticated presentation of history in the Old Testament lie early popular traditions and legends. Some of these have been taken up into the later historical literature and preserved almost intact; others are preserved merely in fragments or faint echoes. Sometimes the old tradition and the later interpretation can be easily distinguished; sometimes it is difficult or impossible to disentangle them. In some cases an earlier motive can be dimly seen behind the particular purpose for which the story is used by the historian. The story of Cain and Abel, for example, reflects the conflict between pastoral and agricultural societies, but as the story is used in Genesis this motive is replaced by the later writer's interest in the history of sin and judgment. Again, the story of the tower of Babel was undoubtedly in the first place an etiological legend to account for the diversity of men's languages. A religious idea also is implied, the naïve, primitive idea of the jealousy of the gods toward man and their fear of human progress. As used by the Hebrew historian, however, the story becomes another incident in the history of sin and judgment.

Since the records, in their present form, are the result of prolonged reflection on the nation's history, our attention in this lecture will have to be given chiefly to this relatively advanced historiography. Before proceeding to the quasi-philosophical or theological ideas of history, however, we may pause to sketch briefly the nature of the traditions which the Hebrew historians used as source material and the popular conception of history more or less consciously implied by these traditions.

Folk tales of popular heroes, with the usual motives and interests found in such stories the world over, are embodied in the historical books of the Old Testament. The accounts of the exploits of the judges, especially Samson, are examples. The story of David and Goliath is a typical hero legend, illustrating also the common tendency in such legends to attribute the exploits of obscure individuals to more illustrious heroes, for in II Sam. 21:19 the same feat of valor is attributed to an otherwise unknown townsman of David named Elhanan. The stories of Elijah and Elisha belong to the same general category, though the heroes in these stories are not warriors but prophets. Such legends serve various popular interests, including sheer love of the extraordinary for its own sake, and sometimes, too, compensation for personal or national failures and frustrations.

Sometimes, of course, stories are told for the sake of moral or spiritual edification. In many of the Old Testament narratives this element is conspicuous by its absence, at least from our point of view, though the early Hebrews may have enjoyed sly craftiness or brutal cruelty with fewer inhibitions than we. Some stories are undoubtedly included because of their exemplary character, from the accounts of the patriarchs to the stories of Daniel and his companions.

Many of the accounts of the earliest periods reflect an etiological interest, the interest in explaining facts of present experience in terms of their origins. The explanation of place names by a simple and transparent kind of folk etymology is especially prominent. Here is an example: " And Deborah, Rebekah's nurse, died, and she was buried under an oak below Bethel: and the name of it was called Allon-bachuth," i. e., the oak of weeping (Gen. 35:8). The name of the city Beersheba is explained not once but twice (Gen. 21:31, 26:33), with a suggestion of a third explanation (Gen. 21:28–31a). The name of Bethel also is explained twice (Gen. 28:19, 35:15).

This etiological interest appears in the frequent use of the phrase " to this day," especially in Joshua; e. g., " Yahweh said to Joshua, ' This day I have rolled away [*galal*] the reproach of Egypt from you.' And so the name of that place is called Gilgal to this day " (Josh. 5:9).

There are vestigial fragments of culture legends in Genesis, such as the statement that Jabal was " the father of those who dwell in tents and have cattle," that Jubal was " the father of all those who play the lyre and pipe," that Tubal Cain was " the forger of all instruments of bronze and iron " (Gen. 4:20–2), and that Noah was the first to till the soil and plant a vineyard—with the unfortunate consequence that he was also the first drunkard (Gen. 9:20 f.). There are stories told to explain the origins of cult objects and practices, such as the account of Jacob's stone at Bethel (Gen. 28:18) and the double tradition of the twelve stones at Gilgal (Josh. 4:9, 20). Accounts of the origins of the festivals come under this head. The Book of Esther may be called a late etiological legend designed to legitimize the feast of Purim, which was of late origin and was not included in the sacred calendar of the law.

Conceivably many such stories were first told in a playful or semiplayful spirit and only later were prosaically taken at face value. The etiological interest, however, appears not only in folk tales incorporated by the historians in their narratives; the writers themselves were clearly still interested in explaining present facts by their origins or supposed origins.

II. MOTIVES AND INTERESTS IN EARLY NARRATIVES

The narratives of the patriarchs include incidents which reflect an interest in the growth of the nation and the justification of its supremacy over neighboring peoples. The story that when Jacob and Esau were born Jacob took hold of Esau's heel and was therefore called Jacob (connecting the name with a word meaning heel), the story of Esau's selling his birthright to Jacob, and the story of Jacob's cheating Esau out of his father's blessing give three different explanations of the superiority of Israel to Edom, for as stated expressly in Gen. 36 : 8, " Esau is Edom." Still another explanation appears in the divine oracle given to Rachel before the birth of Jacob and Esau:

> Two nations are in your womb,
>   and two peoples, born of you, shall be divided;
> the one shall be stronger than the other,
>   the elder shall serve the younger.
>
> (Gen. 25 : 23)

This last is an example of the " blessing poem," illustrating a favorite method of accounting for Israel's supremacy over other peoples and the relative positions and power of the different tribes. The conception which lies at the root of this characteristic Hebrew literary form is important for the more developed ideas of history in the Old Testament, and not least, for the prophetic interpretation of history. It is the very primitive conception of the spoken word as an active force, which has power to bring about what is said. For the ancient Hebrew, as for the Semites in general and other peoples also, a curse or a blessing is not merely the expression of a wish; it is a powerful instrument for good or evil. Consequently the prosperity of a tribe can be explained naturally by saying that its ancestor pronounced a blessing on it.

A poem in the form of such a blessing is then an effective literary vehicle for describing the group's history and present condition. The Canaanites are doomed because Noah cursed Canaan; the Hebrews and the peoples they believed to be related to them are destined to prosper because Noah blessed Shem, their common ancestor (Gen.9 : 24–7). When Isaac, under the impression that he is blessing Esau, blesses Jacob, he cannot revoke the blessing; he can only give poor, cheated Esau a second-rate blessing (Gen. 27). The most elaborate examples of this type of poem are the blessing of Jacob in Gen. 49 and the blessing of Moses in Deut. 33. The former celebrates the supremacy of Judah as the tribe of the royal family; the latter, evidently written in the northern kingdom after the division of the monarchy, pities Judah as separated from the main part of the nation and beseeches Yahweh to "bring him to his people."

The oracle received by Rachel, which I have quoted, shows a further development of the idea of the blessing. Here we have not merely the words of a man; Rachel "went to inquire of Yahweh, and Yahweh said to her" thus and so (Gen. 25 : 22). So the oracles spoken by Balaam in Num. 23–4 are not his own but divinely inspired and unchangeable: Balaam would be glad to oblige Balak and curse Israel if he could, but

> How can I curse whom God has not cursed?
> How can I denounce whom Yahweh has not denounced?
> (Num. 23 : 8)

The all-powerful word of Yahweh overwhelms and cancels out the word of the seer.

This same idea underlies the conception of the covenant-promise in the stories of the patriarchs. When God tells Abraham that he is to be the father of great nations and that one of these will possess the land of the Canaanites the promise is sure. So, too, the word of Yahweh which comes to the prophet is not merely a prediction of something foreseen; it is one of the means by which

God accomplished his will. The History of the Davidic Succession in II Sam. 6–I Kings 2 exhibits the working out of the promise to David spoken by the prophet Nathan in II Sam. 7. Centuries later, when the doom pronounced by the earlier prophets had already fallen, the prophet we call Second Isaiah said:

> For as the rain and the snow come down from heaven,
> and return not thither but water the earth,
> making it bring forth and sprout,
> giving seed to the sower and bread to the eater,
> so shall my word be that goes forth from my mouth;
> it shall not return to me empty,
> but it shall accomplish that which I purpose,
> and prosper in the thing for which I sent it.
> (Isa. 55 : 10–11)

The attempt to explain the present by the past involved sometimes a rather free attitude to the past, producing a picture more like historical fiction than sober history. It involved especially, and inevitably, a phenomenon so frequent that it may conveniently be designated by the quasi-technical term "retrojection," i. e., anachronistically attributing present ideas, attitudes, or practices to earlier times. (Modern writers often speak of projecting ideas back into the past, but projecting backward is a contradiction in terms.)

An interesting example of retrojection is the account of the institution of the Hebrew monarchy in I Sam. 8 and 12. Here all the later disillusionment as to the effect of the monarchy on the life of the people is expressed by Samuel in the form of a warning to the people, who were demanding a king. Of course it is quite possible that there were conservative Israelites who from the beginning had grave misgivings about the monarchic form of government. The parallel and earlier account, however, attributes the initiative in the inauguration of the monarchy to Samuel himself, acting at the direct behest of Yahweh (I Sam. 9–11, except 10 : 18b–19a). Especially interesting, even somewhat amusing, is the way in which Moses is represented in Deut. 17

as telling the Israelites before the conquest of Canaan what the king they will choose after the conquest must not do and putting this in terms that specifically and obviously describe the reign of Solomon: " he must not multiply horses for himself . . . And he shall not multiply wives for himself, lest his heart turn away; nor shall he greatly multiply for himself silver and gold " (Deut. 17 : 16 f.) —almost a literal quotation of what is said about Solomon in I Kings 10 : 26–11 : 1.

By a particularly characteristic kind of retrojection the laws of Israel are presented in a framework of historical narrative, by which the whole corpus is attributed to Moses. The priestly stratum of the Pentateuch in particular is so dominated by this conception that George Foot Moore aptly entitled it, " Origins of the Religious Institutions of Israel."[2] The institution of the Sabbath is carried back to the creation of the world; the prohibition of eating meat with blood to the covenant with Noah, circumcision to the covenant with Abraham, and so on through the time of Moses, to whom all the rest of the system is said to have been revealed. Sometimes an incident in the journey through the desert gives occasion for a new law, as in the case of the daughters of Zelophehad, who had no brothers and were allowed to inherit their father's property on condition that they married within their own tribe (Num. 36). More often, as in the law of the Nazirites (Num. 6), the retrojection goes no further than the stereotyped formula, " Yahweh said to Moses, ' Say to the people of Israel . . .' " The motive in all this is clearly to establish the divine origin and authority of the law.

An interest in justifying and so maintaining the *status quo* may be seen in the accounts of the distribution of the land among the tribes and the fixing of the tribal boundaries by Joshua (Josh. 13–19), where it has been shown that records from the time of the monarchy or earlier have been used.[3]

2. G. F. Moore, *The Literature of the Old Testament* (New York and London, 1913), pp. 43 f.

3. A. Alt, " Das System der Stammesgrenzen im Buche Josua," *Sellin-Festschrift* (Leipzig, 1927), pp. 13 ff.; M. Noth, *Das Buch Josua* (Handbuch

Various other special interests can be detected in the use of history in the Old Testament. Some motives often found in other ancient records are not so prominent in the Hebrew historical literature. Official documents, such as royal inscriptions, often are motivated by the desire for personal or dynastic aggrandizement. There is sufficient evidence in the Old Testament that the Hebrew kings, from David on, tried to build up a doctrine of the divine origin and sanction of the royal authority and its commitment to the descendants of David. The Royal Psalms, whatever one may think of the popular hypothesis of an annual enthronement ceremony, indicate at least that in the official ritual of the temple the claims of the monarchy were recognized and supported. The prophets and historians, however, rejected all such pretensions. To them the king was merely what Andrew Melville called James I, "God's silly vassal." In fact, as already noted, the writers of Deuteronomy and the Deuteronomic stratum in I Samuel regarded the very institution of the monarchy as a grave mistake, a rejection of the sole kinghsip of Yahweh.

The treatment of Saul and his family in I Samuel certainly evinces a partiality for David.[4] The history of the kingdoms of Judah and Israel given in I-II Kings is definitely partial to Judah and the Davidic dynasty as against Israel and the successive kings and short-lived dynasties of Israel. All the rulers of both kingdoms are represented as neither good or bad. Most of the kings of Judah are bad, and only a few relatively good; but *all* the kings of Israel are *wholly* bad.

What may be called class or party interests are sometimes evident in the Old Testament narratives. The priestly historians, for example, in attributing the origin of their prerogatives and institutions to the divinely inspired regulations of Moses, betray a desire to justify the vested interests of the priesthood. After the Babylonian exile, the people of what had been the territory

zum Alten Testament), Tübingen, 1938; but cf, S. Mowinckel, *Zur Frage nach dokumentarische Quellen in Josua 13–19*, Oslo, 1946.

4. A. Spiro, "The Vilification of King Saul in Biblical Literature" (abstract), *Journal of Biblical Literature, 71* (1952), ix.

of the kingdom of Israel were considered by the little Judaean community centered in Jerusalem as a mongrel horde, hardly better than pagans. The little groups which had returned from Babylon considered themselves the only real Israelites. An intense and bitter rivalry developed between Jerusalem and Samaria as the rightful centers of the worship of Yahweh, and this is a prominent motive in the work of the Chronicler (I-II Chronicles, Ezra, and Nehemiah). In fact, Torrey has shown good reason to believe that the major motive of the Chronicler's work was to vindicate the authority of the " mother church " of Jerusalem.[5] The whole history of the northern kingdom is simply omitted in II Chronicles, except as it impinges on the history of Judah.

What has been said thus far may produce the impression that there is no real history or historical interest in the Old Testament at all. That would be quite erroneous. The importance of the Old Testament as a source book for ancient history is becoming more and more evident. It is quite true that the events of the past are recounted almost exclusively for some particular purpose, polemic or apologetic or didactic. A disinterested curiosity as to what actually happened and a desire to preserve an accurate record of events for posterity may have been at work in some of the records consulted and quoted in the historical books, but for the most part these have been preserved only in fragments through their use for the purposes of the historians. There is one outstanding exception to this rule. The full, frank, objective account of David's reign in II Sam. 9–20, which gives the impression of having been written by an eyewitness, or at least a contemporary, has been widely recognized as one of the finest examples of historical narrative in any ancient literature. It shows no inclination to idealize David or the nation, though it has been incorporated in the History of the Davidic Succession, which clearly seeks to vindicate Solomon as the successor of David. The only motive apparent in II Sam. 9–20 is a sense of important events which should not be forgotten, the feeling that often impels a person living in stirring times to keep a diary.

5. C. C. Torrey, *Ezra Studies* (Chicago, 1910), p. 153.

III. THE FIRST HISTORIANS AND PROPHETS

Thus far we have been dealing with special motives apparent in the treatment of particular portions of the nation's history. The idea of history in the Old Testament, however, involves not only the treatment of separate events and persons; it includes a comprehensive view of the whole history of the nation and its orientation in world history. Although this is first clearly formulated in the extensive works of historiography which together make up the Pentateuch and the historical books, it is rooted in very ancient conceptions lying at the heart of the religion of Yahweh. Much attention has been given recently [6] to the brief historical confession of faith given in Deut. 26:5–9 as a formula to be repeated by the worshiper in presenting his offerings of first fruits:

> A wandering Aramean was my father; and he went down into Egypt and sojourned there, few in number; and there he became a nation, great, mighty, and populous. And the Egyptians treated us harshly, and afflicted us, and laid upon us hard bondage. Then we cried to Yahweh the God of our fathers, and Yahweh heard our voice, and saw our affliction, our toil, and our oppression; and Yahweh brought us out of Egypt with a mighty hand and an outstretched arm, with great terror, with signs and wonders; and he brought us into this place and gave us this land, a land flowing with milk and honey.

Here is the Hebrew idea of history in a nutshell. The stress on the deliverance from Egypt as the decisive divine act by which the nation was constituted is characteristic of the Old Testament as a whole. Recent research has dealt in detail with the formation of the traditions of the exodus and the conquest and the ways in which they came to be combined. We shall not deal with these

6. G. von Rad, *Das formgeschichtliche Problem des Hexateuchs*; G. E. Wright, *God Who Acts*.

matters here; the point for our present purpose is that the conception of Israel's history as grounded in a divine choice and a divine act of deliverance from bondage and as consisting in the fulfillment of promises made to the remote ancestors of the Israelites was already dominant in the religious tradition of the people before the works of history were written. In the annual festivals the great events of the past were recalled, re-enacted, and made real and present to the worshipers.

So far as our evidence indicates, however, the first to present this distinctive conception in a clear, systematic form was a profoundly original, constructive thinker, whose work survives as the basic literary stratum of the first books of the Old Testament. His account begins in the second chapter of Genesis and continues through the fourth chapter, after which materials from other sources have been woven into it by later editors. This first Hebrew historian is known to Old Testament scholarship by the letter *J* because from the beginning he uses the divine name *Yahweh* (spelled, of course, with a J in German). He probably lived and wrote in the days of Solomon or soon thereafter, i. e., in the 10th century B. C. Using traditions handed down from earlier times, he combined and presented them in such a way as to stress the goodness of God; the weakness, selfishness, and foolish pride of man; and the stern judgments executed by God in the Flood, the confusion of languages, and the overwhelming of Sodom and Gomorrah, always accompanied by the merciful preservation of a righteous remnant to be heirs of the promises given to their forefathers. After the captivity in Egypt, the tribes delivered under the leadership of Moses entered into a solemn covenant with Yahweh at Mount Sinai to the effect that he alone would be their God and they would be his people and obey his laws. Still they rebelled and were punished by forty years of wandering in the desert. At last the promised land was reached and conquered; many enemies were defeated; under David the nation was securely established; and under Solomon "Judah and Israel dwelt in safety, from Dan to Beersheba, every man under his vine and under his fig tree" (I Kings 4:25).

Here this first great history of Israel probably ended, with the promise to Abraham of innumerable descendants and the possession of the land apparently fulfilled. But although the J history stopped at this point, if indeed it went this far, history did not stop. The people and their kings still followed their own evil ways and even behaved worse than before by imitating the ways and worshiping the gods of the Canaanites, whom they had conquered. The kingdom was split into two: the northern kingdom, Israel, after a turbulent existence of about two hundred years, was destroyed by the Assyrians; and Judah, except for a few brief and halfhearted efforts at reformation, went from bad to worse.

In this critical period began that extraordinary succession of Israel's prophets, to whose profound insight and moral courage we owe a unique body of religious literature, as significant for the idea of history as for other phases of Israelite thought. For the prophets, as for the historians, the course of history was governed by the sovereign will of God. For them, too, as for the historians, the direction of history was understood under the category of promise and fulfillment. Just as Second Isaiah later presents Yahweh as challenging the gods of the nations to bring forward their witnesses and show that they have ever announced in advance what they were going to do, as he has done—" I am God, and there is none like me, declaring the end from the beginning, and from ancient times things not yet done " (Isa. 46 : 9f.) —so Amos, centuries earlier, had said, " Surely the Lord Yahweh does nothing without revealing his secret to his servants the prophets " (Amos 3 : 7) .

God's choice of Israel as his people, the covenant, the deliverance from Egypt, and the possession of the promised land are recalled again and again by the prophets. Amos reminds Israel that other nations too are guided and governed by Yahweh: " ' Are you not like the Ethiopians to me, O people of Israel? ' says Yahweh. ' Did I not bring up Israel from the land of Egypt, and the Philistines from Caphtor and the Syrians from Kir? ' " (Amos 9 : 7) . Yet Israel is still Yahweh's own chosen people:

" You only have I known of all the families of the earth " (Amos 3 : 2) . Hosea mentions not only the exodus but other events in Israel's history. Isaiah does not make so much use of the past history of the nation, yet he shows his acquaintance with it by allusions to the wickedness of Sodom and Gomorrah (Isa. 1 : 9 f.) , to " the slaughter of Midian at the rock of Oreb " and what the Egyptians did (Isa. 10 : 24) , and to the less distant " day that Ephraim departed from Judah " (Isa. 7 : 17) . No other prophet states so strongly as he does the sovereign power of God in the events of his own time. Even the world-shaking power of the Assyrian Empire is only a tool in the hand of Yahweh, to be discarded when he is through with it (Isa. 7 : 20, 10 : 5–19) .

But for these prophets of the Assyrian period and the ensuing Neo-Babylonian period it was impossible to feel the proud satisfaction in Israel's position in the world which had found expression in the old blessing poems and in the J history. Something had gone terribly wrong. The division of the kingdom, the recurrent revolutions in Israel, the humiliation and final destruction of the northern kingdom by its enemies, and the weakness and insecurity of Judah did not promote confidence that the promises made to the fathers were being fulfilled. For the prophets, however, there was no problem in this; the answer was at hand before the question arose. Many in Israel, perhaps the nation as a whole, might think of their position under the covenant as a guarantee of security and prosperity. But the prophets knew that the covenant meant warning as well as promise; its blessings depended upon the people's obedience. Israel had broken the covenant and thus brought upon itself the certainty of fearful punishment: " You only have I known of all the families of the earth; therefore I will punish you for all your iniquities " (Amos 3 : 2) . Only Habakkuk questioned the fairness of God in punishing Israel by the still more wicked Chaldeans, and he found the answer to that question in the assurance that justice would be established in due time.

Considering the conditions of their own day and looking back over the generations that had gone by, the prophets saw the whole history of their people as a history of stubborn, stupid rebellion against the God who had made them a nation and given them the land of the Canaanites. The same evil thoughts and intents of the heart that had been pointed out in the J history as characteristic of the first generations of men were still evident.

Not only were the old sins committed; with the acquisition of the promised land Israel had learned new sins from the Canaanites. Worship of the fertility deities of the country had brought with it debasing practices which corrupted the moral life of the people. Moreover, the transition from the seminomadic life of the desert, with its simple social organization, to the settled life of Canaan and the growth of commercial relations with other peoples from the time of Solomon on had brought about the emergence of a wealthy class, with oppression of the poor, corruption of courts and rulers, and all the evils of luxury, intemperance, and violence. " They build Zion with blood and Jerusalem with wrong. Its heads give judgment for a bribe, its priests teach for hire, its prophets divine for money; yet they lean upon Yahweh and say, 'Is not Yahweh in the midst of us? No evil shall come upon us' " (Mic. 3:10–12). So said Micah, and more than a century later Jeremiah recalled the destruction of Shiloh by the Philistines to show that the presence of the temple could not guarantee the safety of Jerusalem (Jer. 7:12–14, 26:1–9).

This understanding of Israel's history is poignantly expressed by Hosea in the form of a parable of Israel as the unfaithful wife of Yahweh, who left him to follow the gods of the land: " For she said, I will go after my lovers, that give me my bread and my water, my wool and my flax, my oil and my drink. . . . And she did not know that it was I who gave her the grain, the wine, and the oil, and who lavished upon her silver and gold, which they used for Baal " (Hos. 2:5, 8). Jeremiah later takes up the same parable with some elaboration, and still later Ezekiel with brutal realism elaborates it to the point of repulsiveness. Hosea uses also the figure of father and son for the relation between Yahweh and Israel: " When Israel was a child, I loved him, and out of

Egypt I called my son" (Hos. 11:1). Isaiah pictures the nation as Yahweh's vineyard, which he has cultivated with loving care, only to have it bring forth wild grapes instead of the good grapes he had every right to expect (Isa. 5:1–7). Jeremiah denounces the kings of Judah as unfaithful shepherds, who instead of caring for their sheep and feeding them have scattered the flock. Again Ezekiel characteristically elaborates the parable. Later, when the Babylonians have taken into exile King Jehoiachin of Judah and the nobles of Judah are trying to gain security by negotiation with Egypt, Ezekiel depicts the situation and its implications in a characteristically elaborate and rather confused parable of a vine and two eagles (Ezek. 17).

Although the denunciations of national evils by the prophets and their proclamations of impending doom were couched in new language of overwhelming power, the central idea was still the same as that of J's history of sin and judgment. The other aspect of J's interpretation of history is present also in the prophets' announcements of coming judgment: the destruction of the nation will be almost complete, but there will be, or at least may be, a few survivors, as in the days of Noah. Amos cries, "Hate evil, and love good, and establish justice in the gate; it may be that Yahweh, the god of hosts, will be gracious to the remnant of Joseph" (Amos 5:15). But at best the remnant will be small, "As the shepherd rescues from the mouth of the lion two legs, or a piece of an ear" (Amos 3:12). With somewhat more confidence Isaiah predicts that "the remnant of Israel and the survivors of the house of Jacob will no more lean upon him that smote them, but will lean upon Yahweh, the Holy One of Israel, in trust. A remnant will return, the remnant of Jacob, to the mighty God" (Isa. 10:20 f.).

The wicked kings have been rejected, but in place of the unfaithful shepherds, Jeremiah hears Yahweh say, "I will gather the remnant of my flock out of the countries where I have driven them . . . I will set shepherds over them who will care for them . . . Behold, the days are coming, says Yahweh, when I will raise up for David a righteous Branch, and he shall reign as king and deal wisely, and shall execute justice and righteousness in the land" (Jer. 23:3–5). And Isaiah says: "There shall come forth a shoot from the stump of Jesse, and a branch shall grow out of his roots" (Isa. 11:1). And an oracle added to the Book of Amos says: "In that day I will raise up the booth of David that is fallen and repair its breeches, and raise up its ruins, and rebuild it as in the days of old" (Amos 9:11).

IV. THE DEUTERONOMIC HISTORIANS

During this same period history was being written also. Interwoven with J's history in the Pentateuch are sections of narrative, often including duplicate accounts of the same incidents. Since the divine name Yahweh is avoided in these passages until the time of Moses, and the common word for God, *Elohim*, is used instead, the source from which they are supposed to have been taken is commonly called *E*. It is not entirely clear whether this was a complete history comparable to that of J and running parallel to it or whether the E sections were simply supplementary material added to produce a revised and enlarged edition of J. In any case, aside from the author's view that the name Yahweh was not used by Israel until the time of Moses and his tendency to retroject his own antipathy to idolatry into the patriarchal period, there seems to be no new or distinctive idea of history in this E material.

Later, however, during the Assyrian period, an effort was made to bring the nation to its senses by a new account of its origin and the spiritual foundations of its existence. This was the book we know as Deuteronomy, first so named in the Greek version because in it Moses, just before his death, delivers to the tribes encamped in the plains of Moab a second proclamation of the law, combined this time with fervent and eloquent exhortations. The same writer, or more probably others whose point of view and literary style were dominated by his, continued the story through the times of the conquest, the judges, and the kings, down to the destruction of the monarchy and the Babylonian exile. The result was another great history of Israel, comprising what we now have as the books of Deuteronomy, Joshua, I-II Samuel, and I-II Kings. Drawing again, as J did, upon early traditions, incorporating perhaps with little or no change narratives from J and E, and using more or less official records and other historical works which are occasionally referred to by name, these Deuteronomic historians organized the history of the nation from the time of Moses to the downfall of the kingdom of Judah in a clear pattern embodying a distinctive idea of history.

The fundamental thesis is still that of J and the prophets: Israel's success and prosperity, indeed its very existence, depend upon obedience to Yahweh. From the beginning, however, with occasional exceptions, the nation's history has been one long story of disobedience leading to disaster. To this common theme the Deuteronomists add several characteristic variations. In the first place, the major factor in Israel's failure to realize its destiny as the chosen people of Yahweh is the corruption due to contact with the Canaanites. It would have been far better had Israel destroyed them ruthlessly, and that was what Yahweh intended. Moses had strictly enjoined them: "When Yahweh your God brings you into the land which you are entering to take possession of it, and clears away many nations before you . . . then you must utterly destroy them; you shall make no covenant with them, and show no mercy to them" (Deut. 7:1 f.).

Joshua carried out his commission faithfully: "So Joshua defeated the whole land, the hill country and the Negeb and the lowland and the slopes, and all their kings; he left none remaining, but utterly destroyed all that breathed, as Yahweh God of Israel commanded" (Josh. 10:40). And again: "As Yahweh had commanded Moses his servant, so Moses commanded Joshua, and so Joshua did; he left nothing undone of all that Yahweh had commanded Moses. So Joshua took all that land . . . And he took all their kings, and smote them, and put them to death. . . . For it was Yahweh's doing to harden their hearts that they should come against Israel in battle, in order that they should be utterly destroyed, and should receive no mercy but be exterminated, as Yahweh commanded Moses" (Josh. 11:15–17, 20).

So says the book of Joshua; but apparently the editor of this book let his harsh idea of what should have been done lead him into rather reckless retrojection of his own wishful thinking, for the book of Judges begins; "After the death of Joshua the people of Israel inquired of Yahweh, "Who shall go up first for us against the Canaanites, to fight against them?" (Judg. 1:1). This is followed by a specific statement of parts of the country from which the tribes did not succeed in expelling, to say nothing of slaughtering, the previous inhabitants. The editor of this part of the history, frankly facing these facts, has an explanation: because the Israelites did not obey the command to annihilate the people of Canaan, Yahweh sent a messenger to them, saying, "I brought you up from Egypt, and brought you into the land which I swore to give to your fathers. I said, 'I will never break my covenant with you, and you shall make no covenant with the inhabitants of this land; you shall break down their altars.' But you have not obeyed my command. What is this you have done? So now I say, I will not drive them out before you; but they shall become adversaries to you, and their gods shall be a snare to you" (Judg. 2:1–3). This is somewhat qualified by the further statement that the remaining inhabitants are spared in order to serve as a means of testing Israel's fidelity to Yahweh (Judg. 2:20–3).

Israel did not meet the test but again and again succumbed to the insidious temptations of pagan influence. Even repeated experiences of disaster following apostasy and of deliverance following repentance and reformation did not teach the nation the clear lesson of its whole history. The editor of the Book of Judges, after a little prefatory section summarizing the meaning of the history, gives a series of stories taken from earlier sources, enclosing each in the framework of a stereotyped introduction and conclusion. With monotonous insistence the introduction says that the people of Israel forsook Yahweh, who therefore delivered them to the Moabites or the Midianites or whoever the particular enemy was in each instance. An account of their suffering at the hands of the foe follows; then it is said that they cried to Yahweh and he sent them a deliverer. Now comes the story of the deliverance, and the conclusion states that the land had rest for forty (or eighty) years.

Not only did Israel have plenty of opportunity to learn by experience; it was also given repeated and specific warnings. A characteristic technique of the Deuteronomic historians is the introduction of anonymous prophets or " men of God " at critical junctures in the story, reminding the people of their obligation to Yahweh and warning them of the consequences of disobedience, to make sure that the moral of the tale is not overlooked. The first such prophet is the " messenger " whose warning I have already quoted (Judg. 2 : 1–3). At the end of the period of the judges, when the sons of Eli at Shiloh exploit their priestly privileges and behave scandalously, a man of God comes to Eli and proclaims that the priesthood will be taken from his family and given to another (I Sam. 2 : 27–36). Here it is easy to see an etiological explanation and justification of the ascendancy of Zadok and his family in the priesthood at Jerusalem and the deposition of Abiathar, a survivor of the Shiloh priesthood, in the time of Solomon. In telling how Solomon, after his accession, removed Abiathar from the priesthood, the historian observes: " So Solomon expelled Abiathar from being priest to Yahweh, thus fulfilling the word of Yahweh which he had spoken concerning the house of Eli in Shiloh " (I Kings 2 : 27).

Looking back over the whole sad story after the fall of the northern kingdom and attributing the disaster to the persistent idolatry of the people, the Deuteronomic historian says: " Yet Yahweh warned Israel and Judah by every prophet and every seer, saying, ' Turn from your evil ways and keep my commandments and my statues, in accordance with all the law which I commanded your fathers, and which I sent to you by my servants the prophets ' " (II Kings 17 : 13). Here we have again an underlying presupposition of the J history and the whole prophetic interpretation of history, the close connection between history and the word of God. Just as the early historian saw the occupation of the promised land and the establishment of David's kingdom as the fulfillment of the promise, so now the Deuteronomic historians, together with the prophets, see the calamities of the nation as the fulfillment of the divine warning against disobedience. So Jeremiah reports the word of Yahweh: " For I solemnly warned your fathers when I brought them up out of the land of Egypt, warning them persistently, even to this day, saying, Obey my voice. Yet they did not obey or incline their ear, but every one walked in the stubbornness of his evil heart. Therefore I brought upon them all the words of this covenant, which I commanded them to do, but they did not " (Jer. 11 : 7 f.). He further states: " I have spoken persistently to you, but you have not listened. You have neither listened nor inclined your ears to hear, although Yahweh persistently sent to you all his servants the prophets " (Jer. 25 : 3 f.).

V. POSTEXILIC PROPHETS AND HISTORIANS

The blow fell; the end came; but no, the end was not yet. The memory of the deliverance from Egypt, which had been recalled over and over again by historians and prophets as a reproach to the ungrateful and disobedient nation, now served in the darkness of the exile and the postexilic period to awaken new hope and confidence. The warning had come true; the promise still remained. This is the jubilant proclamation of Second Isaiah, the anonymous prophet of the days just before and after the fall of Babylon and the beginning of the Persian period. His magnificent poems, beginning probably in Isa. 34 and 35 and continuing in Isa. 40 and subsequent chapters of the Book of Isaiah,[7] refer again and again, either explicitly or by plain implication, to the exodus, the crossing of the Red Sea, and the journey through the desert to the promised land as the pattern of the new deliverance about to be accomplished.

7. C. C. Torrey, *The Second Isaiah*, New York, 1928.

Go forth from Babylon, flee from Chaldea,
declare this with a shout of joy, proclaim it,
send it forth to the end of the earth;
say, " Yahweh has redeemed his servant Jacob! "
They thirsted not when he led them through the deserts;
he made water flow for them from the rock;
he cleft the rock and the water gushed out.
(Isa. 48 : 20 f.; cf. 35 : 1–10, 43 : 16–18)

Here we note a feature characteristic of much Hebrew thought about the past in connection with the future, the tendency to think of the future as a return of the conditions of the distant past. Not only the historic deliverance from Egypt but the traditions of the beginnings of human history and the creation of the world entered into the picture of the future. Second Isaiah connects the deliverance from Egypt with the myth of the primeval conflict between God and the dragon of chaos:

Was it not thou that didst cut Rahab in pieces,
that didst pierce the dragon?
Was it not thou that didst dry up the sea,
the waters of the great deep;
that didst make the depths of the sea a way
for the redeemed to pass over?
(Isa. 51 : 9 f.)

The garden of Eden served as a model for the final bliss of the redeemed. Abundance and ease, peace among men, and peace between men and animals appear fairly early in prophetic pictures of the future (e. g., Isa. 11 : 6–9). The divine consummation of history was thought of in terms of the primeval paradise, and by the same token, the beginnings of history were conceived in terms of the desires whose fulfillment was expected at the end of time. The result, of course, was that the conceptions of both beginning and end were profoundly affected.

The exodus is not the only episode in Israel's history alluded to by Second Isaiah. The Egyptian captivity is coupled with the Assyrian oppression (Isa. 52:4). Israel is exhorted: "Look to the rock from which you were hewn, and to the quarry from which you were digged. Look to Abraham your father and to Sarah who bore you" (Isa. 51:1 f.). The story of the flood is recalled:

For this is like the days of Noah to me:
as I swore that the waters of Noah
should no more go over the earth,
so I have sworn that I will not be angry with you
and will not rebuke you.
(Isa. 54:9)

The most original and distinctive contribution of Second Isaiah, however, is his interpretation of the recent history of his people under the figure of the Servant of Yahweh. Many and widely divergent are the interpretations put upon this figure by the commentators. I can here only state my conviction that in the Servant poems, including the one in Isa. 52–3, the prophet means by the Servant of Yahweh Israel itself, as in the many places where the context explicitly states this identification. Two main points are involved in the picture of Israel as the Servant of Yahweh. The first is that the sufferings of the nation in the destruction of the kingdom, the devastation of the land, and the exile and dispersion of the people are not merely punishment for the sins of past and present generations but part of a divine discipline and preparation for a special mission in the world. The other point, closely connected with this, is that Yahweh has chosen Israel not only to be the recipient of his blessing but to be used for the redemption of the nations. This is the idea already suggested by the early historian of Judah, that Israel was chosen from among all the peoples not only for its own sake but for the sake of becoming a blessing to all the families of the earth.[8]

During the Persian period which followed the Babylonian exile

8. The Hebrew expression in Gen. 12:3 probably did not mean just that originally, but it may have received that interpretation fairly early.

another important work of Hebrew historiography was brought to completion, again using much more ancient materials and expressing ideas and attitudes doubtless much older than this time, but impressing upon all the material the stamp of another distinctive theological view of history. This is the priestly history and law code, conventionally and conveniently called *P*, which is interwoven with J and E in the Pentateuch. Here the main stress is upon the divine ordering of nature and history as enduring and final, and so upon God's covenant with Israel as permanent and indestructible. Over against the prophetic conception of the covenant as irretrievably broken by Israel's sin, so that only by an entirely new and different covenant could the chosen people be restored to favor, the priestly historians held that sin interrupted Israel's communion with God, but in the rites and institutions of the cult a divinely ordained means of atonement and restoration had been provided. Yahweh would never break his covenant, and Israel could not.

Instead of making the covenant at Sinai central and normative, P says nothing of a covenant in the time of Moses, although the laws, including the whole ritual system with all its apparatus, are attributed to Moses. Instead of the Sinai convenant there is in P a series of concentric covenants: when the original order of creation, with its first commandment given for all mankind, was brought to an end by the Flood, God established a covenant with Noah. Within this a fuller covenant was granted to Abraham and his descendants, not only promising innumerable progeny and the possession of the land of Canaan but adding, " And I will be their God " (Gen. 17 : 6–8) . With the elimination of Ishmael, and then of Esau, the covenant is still further narrowed down to the descendants of Jacob, i. e., Israel, the people among whom God has chosen to make his dwelling. With the erection of the tabernacle the story reaches its climax, the fulfillment of the promise that God would dwell among his people and be their God.

This is not merely a romantic reconstruction of the past or an attempt to give divine sanction and permanent validity to the institutions of the cult and the prerogatives of the priesthood, though we have seen that these motives entered into it. What the priestly writers and editors were trying above all to do was to express in the form of history their ideal for Israel, their conception of the will of God for Israel. It has been pointed out that what P represents as realized in the history of the Mosaic period appears in the last part of the Book of Ezekiel as eschatology, and that this is its real nature. In other words, what P presents as history is really hope.[9]

In some of the Psalms, as in the prophetic writings, episodes from the history of the nation are used in homiletic and devotional fashion for warning or encouragement. During times of distress, God is reminded of his great acts on behalf of his people in the past and passionately besought to come again to their aid. The use of the nation's past for such purposes inevitably leads to some distortion of the picture, particularly in the direction of an idealization of earlier times. The period of the wilderness is sometimes especially idealized. By contrast with the vices of Canaanite civilization it tends to be regarded as a time of simple justice and virtue, its crude barbarity being overlooked. The use of David's reign as a pattern for the rule of the righteous king who is to come leads to similar idealization.

To the late Persian or early Greek period belongs the work of the Chronicler. This has been mentioned earlier, and the chief motive governing his version of Israel's history has been described. To his championship of Jerusalem and its temple as the legitimate center of worship may be added here an inordinate interest in ecclesiastical matters, especially the duties and privileges of the Levites. The Chronicler exalts and idealizes David, but the main stress is laid on his supposed service as the originator of cultic institutions, and the glorification of him as the ideal monarch is qualified by the fact that he was a man of blood and therefore disqualified for building the temple.

It is further characteristic of the Chronicler that he attempts

9. Zimmerli, "Verheissung und Erfüllung," *Evangelische Theologie, 12,* No. 1/2, p. 49.

to interpret the whole past in terms of individual retribution, even though this sometimes involves a radical reconstruction of what could be known from the more ancient sources, as in his story of the repentance and restoration of Manasseh, the wicked king to whose bloody deeds the Deuteronomic historians ascribe the fact that in spite of Josiah's subsequent reforms the doom of Judah could not be revoked (II Kings 23 : 26).

The Chronicler's idea of the past involves also a kind of unrealistic, wishful thinking, which probably reflects a disillusionment not unlike that prevailing is some quarters today. His conception of the work of God in history is that everything is accomplished by direct acts of God, while men need do nothing but pray and sing hymns; even battles are won by miracles without any fighting. This should not obscure the fact that the Chronicler has used and so preserved some important sources, substantially supplementing the data of I-II Kings at some points and giving us all the materials we have for the Persian period of Jewish history.

VI. THE APOCALYPTIC INTERPRETATION OF HISTORY

Throughout the generations and centuries following the end of the Babylonian exile the hope of redemption and restoration was so long and repeatedly disappointed that a general disillusionment with history as a possible sphere of divine redemption was produced. Under these circumstances the apocalyptic hope arose as an expression of invincible faith in spite of all catastrophe and discouragement. The old promises of judgment on the enemies of God and redemption for Israel and the world were now deferred to a new, supernatural world to be created on the ruins of the old. With this, however, went a new interpretation of past history, viewing it as a series of world empires decreed by God that would lead up to the final establishment of his own eternal empire. This scheme finds its first and classic expression in the Book of Daniel. In a series of symbolic visions, becoming more and more elaborate and detailed, the events of the Persian and Greek periods down to the persecution of the Jews by Antiochus Epiphanes in the 2d century B. C. are set forth with sufficient interpretation to make clear what is meant. One kingdom is to follow another until, finally, " the God of heaven will set up a kingdom which shall never be destroyed, nor shall its sovereignty be left to another people. It shall break in pieces all these kingdoms and bring them to an end, and it shall stand for ever " (Dan. 2 : 44).

This new idea of history rests on conceptions as old as the blessing poems of Genesis. Here again past history and present conditions are described in the guise of prophecy. As the conditions of David's time are attributed to Jacob's blessings and the oracles of Balaam, so now the predicament of the Jews under the Seleucid rulers is stated in the form of visions granted to Daniel in the time of Nebuchadnezzar and Belshazzar. The history of the Babylonian and Persian periods is somewhat confused: an empire of the Medes is inserted between the Neo-Babylonian and Persian empires, and the conquest of Babylon is attributed to a Darius the Mede, who cannot be identified successfully with any historic person. As the symbolic representations of history come down into the Greek period, however, they become so specific and accurate as to constitute an important source for that period of Jewish history.

Through all the ancient Israelite interpretations of history runs a consistent and characteristic understanding of time as proceeding in a straight line, with a beginning and an end. This is in sharp and obvious contrast with the ideas of history prevalent among many other peoples as consisting of an endless recurrence of cycles leading nowhere.[10] Only the writer of the Book of Ecclesiastes in the Old Testament thinks of human life in such terms. A recent study [11] describes the Hebrew conception of time as rhythmic rather than cyclic, but this does not seem to me correct. Time moves on steadily in a straight line; history is like

10. B. Kristensen, " De Godsdienstige Beteeknis der Gesloten Perioden." *Ex Oriente Lux*, *2*, No. 8 (1943), 15-26.

11. T. Boman, *Das hebräische Denken im Vergleich mit dem griechischen*, Göttingen, 1952.

a graph, with many ups and downs but a clearly perceptible trend and direction. The end to which history is leading, moreover, in all forms of the Hebrew conception of history, is not a Götterdämmerung with a conflagration consuming earth and heaven, man and gods alike; it is a new heaven and a new earth in which dwells righteousness. Even the 8th-century prophets, with their insistence on overwhelming doom, had some idea of a better future for the remnant of the people. In the apocalyptic literature, where a cosmic catastrophe is contemplated, it is only a removal of ruins by the divine builder to clear the ground for the new building of the future.

VII. SUMMARY

The basic, distinctive presupposition of all ancient Hebrew ideas about history is the conviction that in human history the one eternal, living God is working out his own sovereign purpose for the good of his creatures, first for his chosen people, and through them for the rest of mankind. History therefore cannot be a matter of recurring cycles without essential change or a matter of undeviating, automatic, and irresistible progress in civilization. It is the work of a personal divine will, contending with the foolish, stubborn wills of men, promising and warning, judging and punishing and destroying, yet sifting, saving, and abundantly blessing those found amenable to discipline and instruction.

Through all this long struggle, in many stages of selection, opportunity, failure, rejection, and new beginnings, the divine purpose of creating a holy people, a kingdom of priests, through whom all the families of earth may be blessed, is painfully and patiently wrought out. At the darkest hour, when human pride and self-will seem to have completely frustrated the divine program through the destruction of the chosen nation because of its refusal to follow the guidance given through lawgiver, prophet, and sage, the note of promise, the assurance of another new beginning after severe discipline, sounds more strongly than ever.

One generation after another may fail and be excluded from the promised reward of obedience, but the promise still stands, and through all the vicissitudes and changes of human history the purpose of God moves toward its ultimate consummation.

At the heart of the Hebrew idea of history is the assurance that Israel is God's chosen people, but this involves not merely privilege but obligation. We have noted Second Isaiah's idea of Israel as the Servant of Yahweh. There were lapses from this high level of thinking. The Book of Esther, the latest book of the Old Testament, manifests what may fairly be called a national inferiority complex under oppression by foreign powers. In the celebration of a marvelous deliverance from past enemies and a bloody vengeance upon them, the oppressed Israel of later days found comfort for the present and hope for the future. Even Second Isaiah sometimes pictures the Gentile nations as subjugated rather than redeemed. But the vision of a divine world mission for Israel is not lost. The book of Jonah, treating history very freely, satirizes the proud exclusiveness which did not want to be a light to the Gentiles and asserts God's loving concern even for the wicked Assyrians: " And should not I pity Nineveh, that great city, in which there are more than a hundred and twenty thousand persons who do not know their right hand from their left, and also much cattle? " (Jonah 4:11).

This must be said: the Old Testament doctrine of the chosen people is no dogma of racial superiority. Heredity is assumed as the normal basis of membership in the chosen people. The ethnic origins of Israel are no doubt oversimplified in being traced to one father, but even so, the grouping of Jacob's twelve sons as the sons of four mothers, corresponding to geographical divisions of the country, preserves some recollection of the diverse derivation of the tribes. After the exile Nehemiah and Ezra tried to counteract pagan corruption by abolishing intermarriage between Jews and other peoples, but it was then much too late. The Book of Ruth gently recalls the fact that King David himself had a Moabite great-grandmother—a pretty nice person, too! The introductory stories and genealogies of Genesis emphasize the common ancestry of Israel and other nations. Edom is Israel's brother; Ishmael is his uncle; all the peoples are his blood relatives. Israel is in the center of history not by racial origin but by divine election.

The purpose of God is a moral purpose. When disaster comes to the chosen, favored nation, it is recognized and accepted as deserved judgment, and the necessity of repentance before restoration is acknowledged. This involves a moral standard of national success and welfare. "Righteousness exalts a nation, but sin is a reproach to any people" (Prov. 14:34). National disasters are attributed to social injustice and political corruption. Even such natural calamities as earthquakes are regarded as divine punishment. Doubtless the connection is sometimes drawn too closely to fit the facts of history and life, but as time goes on, there is a growing recognition of the fact that the wicked often prosper and the righteous, both individuals and nations, often suffer. In the apocalyptic interpretation of history, with which our story of ancient Hebrew ideas of history ends, it is expressly indicated that the accomplishment of God's righteous will and the final establishment of his kingdom will not come about on the plane of human history in the present order of the universe.

BIBLIOGRAPHY

NOTE: Since a great deal has been written on the biblical idea of history, this bibliography is of necessity highly selective. The standard Old Testament introductions are not included, although they contain much relevant material. Quotations from the Old Testament, with minor exceptions, follow the Revised Standard Version.

Walther Eichrodt, "Offenbarung und Geschichte im Alten Testament," *Theologische Zeitschrift, 4/5* (Sept.-Oct., 1948), 321–31.

——— *Das Menschenverständnis des Alten Testaments*, Basel, 1944; English trans., *Man in the Old Testament*, Studies in Biblical Theology, No. 4, London and Chicago, 1951.

Otto Eissfeldt, *Geschichtsschreibung im Alten Testament. Ein kritischer Bericht über die neueste Literatur dazu*, Berlin, 1948.

Johannes Hempel, *Altes Testament und Geschichte*, Gütersloh, 1930.

C. R. North, *The Old Testament Interpretation of History*, London, 1946.

Martin Noth, "Die Vergegenwärtigung des Alten Testaments in der Verkündigung," *Evanglische Theologie, 12*, No. 1/2 (July-Aug. 1952), 6–17.

Gunnar Östborn, *Yahweh's Words and Deeds: a Preliminary Study of the Old Testament Presentation of History*, Uppsala and Wiesbaden, 1952.

Robert H. Pfeiffer, "Facts and Faith in Biblical History," *Journal of Biblical Literature, 70* (1951), 1–14.

Gerhard von Rad, *Das Geschichtsbild des chronistischen Werkes*, Beiträge zur Wissenschaft vom Alten und Neuen Testament, Vol. 4, No. 3, Stuttgart, 1930.

——— *Das formgeschichtliche Problem des Hexateuchs*, Giessen, 1938.

——— *Deuteronomiumstudien*, Göttingen, 1948; English trans. *Studies in Deuteronomy*, Studies in Biblical Theology, No. 9, London and Chicago, 1953.

——— "Theologische Geschichtsschreibung im Alten Testament," *Theologische Zeitschrift, 4* (Basel, 1948), 161 ff.

Artur Weiser, *Glaube und Geschichte im Alten Testament*, Beiträge zur Wissenschaft vom Alten und Neuen Testament, Vol. 4, No. 4, Stuttgart, 1931.

Ernest G. Wright, *God Who Acts*, Studies in Biblical Theology, No. 8, London and Chicago, 1952.

Walther Zimmerli, "Verheissung und Erfüllung," *Evangelische Theologie, 12*, No. 1/2 (July-Aug., 1952), 34–77.

THE HELLENISTIC ORIENT

C. Bradford Welles

THE Hellenistic Orient is a concept involving both space and time. Territorially I should expect it to include the territory of the Seleucids and the Ptolemies at its widest extent, i. e., Egypt as far south as the Wadi Halfa, with the Cyrenaica and Cyprus, western Asia Minor, the Levant, the Fertile Crescent, Iran, the Indus valley, Afghanistan, and Russian Turkestan as far north as the Syr Darya and as far east as the Pamirs. This is our proper area, and it is large enough; but since, with Rostovtzeff,[1] we must admit the essential unity of the Hellenistic mentality, we cannot ignore the shores of the Black Sea, Thrace, Macedonia, and the peninsula of Greece itself, or for that matter, the Roman or Punic West.

To define the chronological limits of our subject is more difficult. Obviously we may not be satisfied with the so-called Hellenistic Age, the three hundred years between Alexander's campaigns and Caesar's victory at Actium. The field of the student of Hellenism is the Greco-Roman period, which includes everything between the end of the Achaemenian Empire and the rise of Islam, the thousand years of Wilhelm Schubart's Egypt.[2] It is true that much of our area during much of this time was free of Greek domination, but it is equally true that the process of " Hellenizing " the Orient began long before Alexander. Thus Egypt in the fourth century B. C. had been run very largely by Greeks, adventurers or Point Four missionaries.[3] Even Persia under the second and third Artaxerxes made use of Greek talents in various technical fields, while Greek influence on Persian art goes back

1. Rostovtzeff, *Social and Economic History of the Hellenistic World,* especially pp. 1032–53.

2. *Ein Jahrtausend am Nil; Aegypten von Alexander dem Grossen bis auf Mohammed.*

3. The evidence is summed up in my paper in the *Journal of Juristic Papyrology, 3* (1949), 21–47.

to the great Cyrus.[4] As to Anatolia, the Germans at Miletus,[5] if not yet the British at Smyrna,[6] have found Mycenaean influence or at least Mycenaean imports, and some have imagined that the Danunim of Karatepe were vagrant Danaans from Homeric Greece.[7] Egypt was in cultural contact with the world of the Aegean as early as the Middle Bronze Age,[8] whether or not we have the right to call such Aegeans " Hellenic." [9]

I. THE EARLY PERIOD

It should be pointed out, also, that the process of Hellenization is only one aspect of a cultural exchange between the Aegean world and the Orient which began at a very early period. Greeks accepted as well as gave, although the historical Greeks had very little recollection of it. The archeologists, our admired but not

4. H. Frankfort, *American Journal of Archaeology, 50* (1946), 6–14; Gisela M. A. Richter, *ibid.*, pp. 15–30.

5. Carl Weichert in *Bericht über den VI. Internationalen Kongress für Archäologie, Berlin, 21–26 August, 1939*, Archäologisches Institut des Deutschen Reiches (Berlin, 1940), pp. 325–32.

6. The earliest level found by the excavators at Old Smyrna dates from about 1000 B.C.; see *Illustrated London News* (Feb. 28, 1953), pp. 328 f.

7. Julian J. Obermann, *Discoveries at Karatepe*, Publications of the American Oriental Society, Offprint Series, No. 26, 1948; R. T. O'Callaghan, *Orientalia*, N.S., *18* (1949), 193–7; Arne Furumark, *Opuscula archaeologica, 6* (Acta Instituti Romani Regni Sueciae, Vol. 15) (1950), 243 f.

8. A. J. B. Wace and C. W. Blegen, *Klio, 32* (1939), 131–47; Fritz Schachermeyr, *ibid.*, pp. 235–88; S. Smith, *American Journal of Archaeology, 49* (1945), 1–24; Helene J. Kantor, *ibid.*, *51* (1947), 1–103; M. P. Nilsson, *Archiv Orientální, 17* (Symbolae ad studia Orientis pertinentes Frederico Hrozný dedicatae, Vol. 2) (1949), 210–12; Furumark, *op. cit.*, pp. 203–49.

9. This is the thesis of Pierre Montet concerning the " Haou-Nebout," proposed *Revue archéologique*, Ser. 6, *28* (1947), 129–44, attacked by J. Vercoutter, *Bulletin de l'Institut Français d'Archéologie Orientale, 48* (1949), 107–209, and defended by Montet, *Revue archéologique*, Ser. 6, *34* (1949), 129–44. The interpretation of A. H. Gardiner, *Ancient Egyptian Onomastica, 1* (1947), No. 276, pp. 206–8, is rather different. In the present state of our knowledge, it is probably judicious to say that there is more against the theory than in favor of it, but it remains at least not impossible.

always unanimous guides in these fields, are apt to think that Greek-speaking peoples came into the Aegean world at about the beginning of the 2d millennium B.C., and from the north: from the Eurasian steppe, that is, not from the European forest belt.[10] Their views are supported by the linguists, our other learned friends who long have been busy with the affinities and geographical locations of the speakers of what is variously called the Indo-European or Indo-Germanic or Aryan family of languages.[11] But if the Greeks did come from the steppe, they brought little with them, in contrast with the Aryans of India and the Iranians of Persia.[12] The religion even of the Bronze Age Greeks, beyond Zeus, Hestia, and possibly Poseidon, shows no trace of such an environment.[13] Their cults are local and their divine names derive usually from an unknown language. As to their literature, as Professors Heidel, Kramer, and Obermann show us—and this is the vehicle of their first approach to history—this comes from the

10. For this and the related problem of Aegean chronology, cf. C. W. Blegen, *American Journal of Archaeology, 32* (1928), 146–54; Myres, *Who Were the Greeks?* (1930); Schachermeyr, *loc. cit.*; S. S. Weinberg, *American Journal of Archaeology, 51* (1947), 165–82; E. W. Hutchinson, *Antiquity, 22* (1948), 61–74; Gaul, *The Neolithic Period in Bulgaria*; Friedrich Matz, *Historia, 1* (1950), 173–94; V. Milojčić, *Jahrbuch des Deutschen Archäologischen Instituts, 65/66* (1950–51), 1–90. Respect for tradition should not blind us to the circumstance that although the archeological evidence indicates that immigrants came into Greece in the Bronze Age, it does not prove that these were Greek-speaking, and such remarkable scepticism as that expressed by Elias J. Bickerman, *Classical Philology, 47* (1952), 65–81, and *American Journal of Philology, 79* (1953), 98, is very useful.

11. C. D. Buck, *Classical Philology, 21* (1926), 1–26; A. Meillet, *Aperçu d'une histoire de la langue grecque*, 3d ed. Paris, 1930. For an interpretation of the Pylos tablets as Greek cf. M. Ventris and J. Chadwick, *Journal of Hellenic Studies, 73* (1953), 84–103.

12. So Franz Altheim has recently noted the lack of tradition brought with them by the Goths from northern Europe, in contrast with the "Reiternomaden" of the steppe, *Niedergang der alten Welt, 1*, 122.

13. Nilsson, *1*, 313–16; C. Picard, *Les Religions préhelléniques (Crète et Mycènes)*, Paris, 1948; Schachermeyr, *Poseidon und die Entstehung des griechischen Götterglaubens* (cf. Nilsson, *American Journal of Philology, 74* (1953), 161–8); R. Pettazzoni, *Mnemosyne*, Ser. 4, *4* (1951), 1–8.

Orient; comparison with the Sumerian, Babylonian, and Ugaritic epics shows a clear influence from East to West.[14] But for the purposes of these lectures, we have not to begin our survey with the Bronze Age.

And yet, in a larger sense, we cannot ignore the Greeks' consciousness of their own background either, however remote, because that was, in one way, their idea of history. Now the word " history " has a number of meanings. It includes historiography, the writing of an intelligible account of events of the more or less remote past by someone who may be styled an " historian," but it includes as well the systematic exploration of the past.[15] That is what Herodotus, who introduced the term *historia,* meant by it.[16] Neither of these, however, is " the idea of history." We look to a third concept, as when we say that " man has a history," meaning that he is the product of a long sequence of events in time. His background lies in space too, and an historian, ancient or modern, must take account of environment, but it is the element of time which distinguishes an " historical " account of something from its description on a purely static basis. In the case of man, this involves a consideration of what he has been and considers the changes—and the reasons for the changes—which have brought him to be what he is. By implication, if not expressly, it involves the consideration of what he will be, since there are no ends in history, and the present is a moving, not a stationary, spot in time, which like Conrad's ship

14. Heidel, *The Gilgamesh Epic and Old Testament Parallels; The Babylonian Genesis*; S. N. Kramer, *Journal of the American Oriental Society, 64* (1944), 7–23; *Crozer Quarterly, 22* (1945), 207–20; *Proceedings of the American Philosophical Society, 90* (1946), 120–30; *Bulletin of the University Museum, 17* (Philadelphia, 1952), 2; Obermann, *How Daniel Was Blessed with a Son.*

15. Cf., for example, Croce, *History: Its Theory and Practice*; Shotwell, *An Introduction to the History of History*; Toynbee, *Greek Historical Thought from Homer to the Age of Heraclius* (a very useful collection of passages from the Greek authors), and *A Study of History,* abridgement by D. C. Somervell, Oxford, 1947; Collingwood, *The Idea of History*; Walsh, *An Introduction to the Philosophy of History.*

16. *Histories,* Preface.

remains forever in the center of its great circular world of sea and sky.[17] The idea of history includes man's future as well as his past. We may say that it is man's idea of his place in history. For us, since the 17th century, this has been connected with the so-called idea of progress,[18] and men are concerned for their places in the onward surge of events.

I have been preceded by scholars who discussed this topic in the ancient Oriental kingdoms and in Judaea. I am to be followed by those who will discuss the same phenomenon in the worlds of Christianity and Islam. My function is that of a bridge, to explain through the mentality of the Hellenistic East the transition from the older notions to the newer ones. My task is to identify and to explain the gradual dissipation of the energy and optimism of the Greeks in their first contacts with the Orient and the growth of the resignation and humility with which the Hellenistic man later turned to the two great new religions of authority and salvation.

These first contacts were early. We should probably start with Homer and Hesiod, that is, with the 8th or 9th century B. C., or possibly the 10th, as does W. F. Albright.[19] Although the roots of the mythology in which the epic is grounded go deep, and it may be that, with Whatmough,[20] we should recognize that the epic tradition in Greece reaches back into the Middle Bronze Age or even further, the conscious world of Homer is that of Greek recovery following the so-called Dark Ages.[21] I refer rather

17. *Lord Jim*, chap 3.

18. Bury, *The Idea of Progress*; Teggart, *Theory of History*.

19. *American Journal of Archaeology*, *54* (1950), 162–76.

20. Joshua Whatmough, *American Journal of Archaeology, 52* (1948), 45–50.

21. Rhys Carpenter has been for long a strong advocate for a low dating. Cf., in addition to the many valuable studies of the problem by M. P. Nilsson, H. L. Lorimer, *Homer and the Monuments*, and H. T. Wade-Gery, *The Poet of the Iliad*, Cambridge, 1952. It may be suspected that, lacking further evidence, the possibilities of dating the poems have been pretty well canvassed, with the result a *non-liquet*. There is general agreement that the poems represent a very long epic tradition; cf. especially C. Picard, *Annuaire de l'Institut*

to the material environment of the *Odyssey* than to the intellectual climate of the *Iliad.* The latter, with its insistence on the moral ordering of the universe and man's duty to live up to what has been called the heroic ideal [22] is important for us in so far as it serves to establish a basically pessimistic but practically vigorous attitude toward the world in later Greeks. One may not lightly minimize its influence on Alexander.[23] Nevertheless it is rather the *Odyssey* which we can date, at least in its main outlines. This essentially " unmoral " epic belongs to the early days of Greek sea-roving by small bands of adventurers. These engaged in trade or piracy, depending on the situation, and established factories in the western Mediterranean which grew presently into cities.[24] In the East they were in not always friendly contact with those other traders, robbers, and colonists, the Phoenicians, and they

de Philologie et d'Histoire Orientales et Slaves, 9 (Mélanges Henri Grégoire (1949), 489–502. There is equal agreement that both poems show the impress of a single author, although not necessarily the same one. But since the development of the poems notoriously did not stop with that author, as G. M. Bolling has repeatedly shown, he may be placed at a number of dates from Mycenaean times to Pisistratus. Support for an earlier date may be expected, perhaps, with our continuously growing knowledge of the Mycenaean period and of the oriental contacts of the Mycenaean Greeks. Cf., for example, R. Dussaud, *Annuaire de l'Institut de Philologie et d'Histoire Orientales et Slaves, 9* (Mélanges Henri Grégoire) (1949), 227–31.

22. Werner Jaeger, *Paideia, 1* (Berlin and Leipzig, 1936), 23–37.

23. Estimates of the romantic elements in the life of Alexander vary enormously with the individual historian, reaching their maximum, perhaps, in the remarkable book of Georges Radet, *Alexandre le Grand,* Paris, 1931. On Alexander's attitude toward Achilles see Tarn, *Alexander, 2,* 52 f.

24. While it is usual to understand the accounts of the western Mediterranean in the Odyssey in the light of Greek seafaring of the 9th and early 8th centuries B.C., and while the model for Scheria in Bk. VI could be any one of a number of 8th-century colonies, the fabulous stories about the same regions in the *Odyssey* are hard to imagine being current when Greeks were becoming familiar with the actual situation. Since it is clear that Greeks knew the West very well in the Mycenaean period, this mixture of real knowledge and myth need not stand as proof of a late date. Cf. T. J. Dunbabin, *The Western Greeks,* Oxford, 1948; *Papers of the British School at Rome, 18,* (N.S., Vol 5) (1950), 104–116.

paid their first visits to Egypt, which seemed to the Greeks to contain the oldest civilization of all, puzzling, repelling, attracting, but always interesting its transmarine visitors. While the people of the Odyssey take for granted the traditional view of their past in the Age of Heroes, they give no indication of being motivated by a consideration either of the past or of the future. Like practical men, they were concerned with improving their immediate material situation in any way that offered, little possessed of that romantic love of adventure and curiosity credited to them by our nostalgic 19th century. Odysseus was quite content to stay at home, after the recovery of his possessions—in Homer, if not in Tennyson.

But Odysseus and his comrades learned from their travels, even without intending it. What they may have learned from the Phoenicians, beyond a system of writing, techniques in the applied arts, and how to make money in business, we do not know. Perhaps much, if we knew it. But from Egypt they learned history, along with more practical matters. Herodotus, later, is only one of a great series of Greeks who had been coming to Egypt from the times of the Saite dynasty down. When Herodotus spoke with the priests at Thebes, they recalled the earlier visit of Hecataeus the historian, who had boasted of his sixteen-generation ancestry headed by a god. In comparison they had showed Hecataeus the statues of their priests, who had held the office in succession, son following father. Their 345 generations impressed upon the Greek upstart the immensity of the Egyptian past.[25] Similarly, Solon had been told by the priests that the Greeks were all children; a Greek old man did not exist.[26] Herodotus dutifully learned what he could of Egyptian history, not entirely at variance with what modern scholars think. The Greeks met people to whom the present was important not in its own right but only as an extension of the past. It is true that conduct in Greece was generally conditioned by ancestral customs,

25. Herodotus, II, 143; cf. Kurt von Fritz, *Transactions of the American Philological Association*, 67 (1937), 315–40.

26. Plato, *Timaeus*, 22B.

τὰ πάτρια. Cowardice in battle was not the Spartan way—*οὐ γὰρ πάτριον τᾷ Σπάρτᾳ*—as Tyrtaeus had sung without scientific documentation, but in the wider world of the Orient the Greeks met people who could give dates and facts. And there were customs as well as traditions which challenged vital principles of Greek belief. It was the mad Persian King Cambyses—whimsey is a heady trait in kings—who, in Herodotus' words, set himself to deride religion and custom, that custom which Pindar had called king of all; [27] but it was his sober successor Darius who made the dramatic demonstration of its relative nature. Summoning the Greeks with him, he asked them what would persuade them to eat their fathers' dead bodies. Enjoying their shocked amazement, he brought in certain Indians and asked them what would make them willing to burn their fathers' bodies. Their astonishment and anger was answer enough, and the question being translated to the Greeks, they learned something of the complexity of human experience.[28]

From the earliest times the Greeks were inclined to regard this experience, in their own case, as a progressive deterioration.[29] Hesiod presents us with the conception of the succession of the four ages, from Gold to Iron, each worse than the preceding. He does not state whence this notion came; he had lived in Asia Minor, and it may have an Oriental origin. This was to color the thought of the Greeks and Romans throughout antiquity. Even Herodotus, who exhibits generally the bouncing confidence of the Age of Pericles, nevertheless characterized the 5th century as a time of wars and suffering, in contrast with the happier times which had preceded it.[30] At this distance we may wonder at this judgment, but it is notable that the historian of the

27. Herodotus, III, 38, 4

28. Herodotus, III, 38, 3–4.

29. Traces of the belief in a cyclic theory of history also exist, although with an oriental coloring, cf. Plato, *Timaeus* 21–23.

30. Herodotus, V, 97, 3, a comment which evoked the astonishment of W. W. Howe and J. Wells, *A Commentary of Herodotus*, Oxford, 1912, and others ancient and modern who have not understood his point of view (as Plutarch, *De malignitate Herodotei* 24).

glorious wars of liberation from Persia should have been so little pleased with them. He was proud of the victory, of course; so also Aeschylus earlier. But like Aeschylus, he seems to have felt that it would have been better had there been no wars and no victory.[31] Both feel, as did the author of the *Iliad*, an essential tragedy in human existence. In the *Agamemnon* (l. 177), Aeschylus expresses the same pessimism: " in experience is learning," *πάθει μάθος*, but the learning is an individual matter and usually comes too late. Man as a whole faces no automatic amelioration of his lot, and history is futility, not progress.

In a similar vein, seventy years later, Xenophon was to conclude his *Hellenic History* with the indecisive battle of Mantinea (VII, v, 26–7):

> When these things had taken place, the opposite of what all men believed would happen was brought to pass. For since well-nigh all the people of Greece had come together and formed themselves in opposing lines, there was no one who did not suppose that if a battle were fought, those who proved victorious would be the rulers and those who were defeated would be their subjects; but the deity so ordered it that both parties set up a trophy as though victorious and neither tried to hinder those who set them up, that both gave back the dead under a truce as though defeated, and that while each party claimed to be victorious, neither was found to be any better off, as regards either additional territory, or city, or sway, than before the battle took place; but there was even more confusion and disorder in Greece after the battle than before. Thus far be it written by me; the events after these will perhaps be the concern of another.[32]

31. So the theme of the *Persae* is rather lament at Persia's disaster than joy at the Greek triumph. A Greek, of course, would have regarded it as ill-omened to gloat over a fallen opponent. Cf. the quotations of T. B. L. Webster, *Political Interpretations in Greek Literature* (Manchester, 1948), pp. 31–34.

32. Trans. Carleton L. Brownson in the Loeb Classical Library.

II. GREEK HISTORIOGRAPHY

In later times, Greek criticism was in no doubt as to what constituted good historical writing. Historians themselves explained their own methods and disparaged those of their rivals in introduction and excursus, while such literary pundits as Dionysius of Halicarnassus and Lucian of Samosata discussed the virtues and vices of historians at length.[33] Both agreed that the criterion was truth.[34] Lucian's " say how it happened," ὡς ἐπράχθη, εἰπεῖν,[35] is an anticipation of Ranke's " wie es eigentlich gewesen." Nevertheless, Lucian speaks of the historian as a sculptor, a Phidias or a Praxiteles, whose materials—gold, ivory, and marble—are supplied him by someone else, but he must fashion them himself.[36] So the historian. The facts of his story are supplied him, but he must shape them in a mold. His narrative must have all the usual classical stylistic excellences: rhythmic clausulae and the avoidance of hiatus, properly selected words and figures of speech, emotion, pathos; and an equable distribution of praise and blame. But before all else his work must have form, i. e., a beginning, middle, and end.[37] The great pair of classical Athens, Herodotus and Thucydides, remained the models

33. Dionysius of Halicarnassus, *De Thucydide*; Lucian, *Quomodo historia conscribenda.*

34. Lucian, *op. cit.*, 9; Dionysius, *op. cit.*, 8; cf. Dionysius, *Antiquitates romanae* I, 1: τὴν ἀλήθειαν . . . ἀρχὴν φρονήσεώς τε καὶ σοφίας. Cf. also, Cicero, *De oratore* 2, 15: " Nam quis nescit primam esse historiae legem, ne quid falsi dicere audeat? Deinde ne quid veri non audeat? Ne quae suspicio gratiae sit in scribendo? Ne quae simultatis? "

35. *Op. cit.*, 52.

36. *Op. cit.*, 63.

37. Cf. the full discussion by Wilhelm Schmid and Otto Stählin in Wilhelm von Christ's *Geschichte der griechischen Litteratur* (Ivan von Müller, ed., Handbuch der Altertumswissenschaft, Vol. 7), *2*, Pt. 1 (Munich, 1920), 204–45. For a modern counterpart of this theory cf. E. Renan, *Essais de morale et de critique* (2d ed. Paris, 1860), pp. 104 f., as quoted by Emery H. Neff, *The Poetry of History* (New York, 1947), p. 162: " History is as much an art as a science; perfection of form is essential to it."

beyond approach though not beyond criticism, but it was regretted that the masters had selected their particular subjects. These were not rounded and closed. Both historians left their histories unfinished, actually trailing off. In contrast, Polybius and Dionysius and their many lesser co-workers wrote of Rome: [38] the successes which fell to Roman arms and to Roman virtues. Biography was good too. Alexander was a favorite topic during his own lifetime and for centuries afterward. That was another success story, with the additional advantage that it contained material for praise and blame and room for speculation on what would have happened had the hero lived longer. Other popular subjects of the later period were monographic: histories of cities or kings or single wars. Lucian describes amusingly the flood of histories written and recited at Corinth in honor of the eastern campaigns of Avidius Cassius in 165, including one tract which was so admirably compendious that the title was almost longer than the text.[39] Antiquarian or eulogistic, we cannot but lament the loss of these histories because of what they would have told us. Their mere fragments are impressive in Jacoby's monumental collection.[40] But paradoxically enough, though their value to the ancient world was primarily literary, we should find them—with certain notable exceptions—literarily valueless in contrast with the great classics which the ancient critics found imperfect. They were essentially compositions written in the pursuit of distinction of some sort. Herodotus, and still more Thucydides, wrote from the heart.

For the period from the 5th century on down through the 4th to the death of Alexander, and on for nearly another hundred years, was characterized by a conscious effort on the part of the Greeks to change their environment for the better. The discouragement of Herodotus and Xenophon was due to their feeling

38. This introduced the idea of progress. Cf. Dionysius, *Antiquitates romanae* I, 2, where Rome is the latest in a progressively larger sequence of empires.

39. *Quomodo historia conscribenda* 28–41.

40. Felix Jacoby, *Die Fragmente der griechischen Historiker*, Berlin and Leiden, 1923–50.

that nothing was being accomplished. Herodotus was a part of the Ionian enlightenment. From Thales on, men were eager to discover the laws of the universe, its nature and extent, its ways and customs, and its history. Men were exploring and questioning, telling of their results, and defending their theories, while discussion waxed hot, and interest soared. With the 5th century Athens became the center of all this activity, and to Pericles and the democrats of Athens it may well have seemed that democracy, with its release of men's energies for self-improvement within the frame of the Greek city, might lead the way to a better world. Athens felt no limits to her powers. As her rule over her formerly free allies approached the tyranny of an imperial power, it is probable that many Athenians felt that they were only spreading benefits by their domination, like modern colonialism. Probably it was beneficial, in many ways. We do not need to go to Plato to be shown that freedom as such is not an unmixed blessing or untouched by danger. Our criticism of the Athenian Empire comes from the comedians, bent on either flattering the Demos or defaming its leaders, or from political speeches in the historians, no more reliable than political speeches in other places. Some of the allies revolted as soon as they had the opportunity, but by no means all. Some of them stuck to Athens through thick and thin, notably Samos,whose loyalty the Athenians rewarded with a touching monument.[41] Aside from the specific grievances of individuals or communities under the Athenian Empire, there is good reason to suppose that the empire presented the Aegean area with a degree of prosperity and independence which it would never have attained otherwise.[42]

41. Illustrated in Johannes Kirchner, *Imagines Inscriptionum Atticarum* (2d ed. by Günther Klaffenbach, Berlin, 1948), No. 43, pl. 19.

42. Rostovtzeff, *The Social and Economic History of the Hellenistic World,* p. 94. The Anatolian coastal cities, nevertheless, prospered much less than Athens, because of the centralization of the empire and their lack of contact with the interior of Asia Minor. They flourished in the 4th century because of the change in both these conditions, and their competition may well be a factor in the decline of Greece at this time, which Rostovtzeff noted (pp. 90–125).

Thucydides was a part of this environment. As an Athenian general and statesman he shared in the city's objectives. He knew what Athens stood for and let Pericles sum it up in the Funeral Speech. He felt Athens' mission and enjoyed her intellectual opportunities, until a mistake in judgment in his command caused his exile. Then he learned what her rivals felt. His history shows his familiarity with the science of the time. In his introduction he sketches the early development of Greece in the form of a progress from barbarism to civilization, a rather exceptional point of view, although Plato reflects it in Book III of the *Laws,* and it became part of the school of Democritus of Abdera and appears later in Lucretius. Almost alone of ancient historians, he was interested in disease, psychology, economics, and historical determinism. His successors in these scientific directions were to be found in the schools of Plato and Aristotle rather than in that of the rhetorician Isocrates, who largely shaped the direction of Greek (and Latin) historical writing for the rest of antiquity. And yet the greatness of his history lies in its treatment of the essentially humanitarian problem, why did Athens fail? The tragedy of his history lies in the fact that the failure was not merely that of one more undistinguished imperial power, which overreached its resources and excited an overpowering group of enemies. The tragedy lies in the fact that Athens, with all her faults, should have won, or at least, the idea which Athens represented should have won. Greece might have been something short of happy if Athens had won; instead it endured a century of war because Athens lost.

III. THE SEARCH FOR PEACE

For the Greek world was troubled by the dilemma which continues to beset men in this world, the reconciliation of the objectives of political survival for the community and the good life for the individual. Poverty and Greece were neighbors from of old, but with the rise of the merchant city, the prosperity of which brought it consumers' goods and a plentiful supply of slaves, the well-being of the individual seemed assured. He had food, shelter, independence, and leisure, but all of these fine things came to him through his citizenship. Were his status to change or were his city to suffer disaster, the happy picture would alter. The more cities which crowded Grecian coasts and dotted the interior and the greater the growth of population in response to these favorable conditions the more precarious became security. Greece was only rarely threatened from outside, but the rival cities were a constant threat to each other. Precautions were necessary if Greece was not to fall into a war of all against all, or on the other hand, to be cut up into numerous little uncommunicative areas to the detriment of trade and culture.[43] This security was supplied to some extent in the 6th century by the amphictionies around the temples and the Peloponnesian League under the hegemony of Sparta. With the Persian Wars and the growth of Athens, Greece was split into two rival leagues, constituting a kind of balance of power. Their conflicting policies led to the Peloponnesian War and the dissolution of the Athenian Empire. To Thucydides, convinced that the Athenian policy had much to offer the Greeks, this presented a political problem of both complexity and tragic force. But a satisfactory answer was difficult.

The Greek 4th century inherited the original problem, still unsolved and with the old Athenian solution discredited.[44] For the Athenians had sought to substitute for the hegemony a kind of empire, which might have grown into a state, just as Athens had once united all of Attica into one city. Greece was thrown back on the hegemony once more, but the Greek states were growing too numerous and too powerful to be controlled, as of old, by one hegemon. Sparta succeeded for a few years. Thereafter the century saw constant wars and political regroupings based

43. This isolation was Plato's answer in the *Laws* to Greece's troubles. Cf. my paper in *The Journal of Economic History*, suppl. 8 (1948), pp. 101–14.

44. So André Aymard, *Annuaire de l'Institut de Philologie et d'Histoire Orientales et Slaves, 9* (Mélanges Henri Grégoire) (1949), 74, remarks that the Peloponnesian War was the end of the πόλις concept: νόμος gave way to σωτήρ.

on the rivalry of the great powers and the scramble of the little ones to be on the winning side without being absorbed. Being Greeks and having experienced the enlightenment, however, people did not accept the situation without protest or examination.

Early in the century the principle was enunciated that the natural condition of states was peace.[45] By nature, and therefore according to natural law, the Greek states must share a general peace.[46] This was the formula according to which were held, at times, almost yearly peace conferences to which all the states came, all accepting the principle, although never able to agree on precise terms of applying it. It became evident that some sanction was necessary. Many looked to Persia to supply this, as a kind of superhegemon.[47] Others presently began looking at Macedonia, which was growing rapidly under the brilliant leadership of her king, Philip II.[48] This ideal was presently to be consummated, through conquest, in the League of Corinth, of which Philip was president and the dominant power. It promised peace, although it did not include all of the peninsula. It might have been an answer to one of Greece's problems.

But there was no assurance that Philip's solution would satisfy the other demand, that for individual well-being. It certainly curbed individual freedom, which in some sense was included in the objective. On the purely economic plane it might cause some to be prosperous, but it lessened the likelihood that the rich would share with the poor. And inevitably this question was complicated by another: what was well-being? Well-being for whom?

45. Expressed by Andocides in the speech " On the Peace with Lacaedemon," cf. especially sec. 17: " See, Athenians, this too, that now you create a peace and freedom common to all the Greeks, and give all the power to share everything."

46. B. Keil, *Eirene*, Berichte der Sächsischen Gesellschaft, Vol. 68. No. 4, 1916; cf. especially, Victor Martin, *La Vie internationale dans la Grèce des cités*, Geneva, 1940.

47. This is the conception represented by the Peace of Antalcidas, although it finds little expression in our surviving authors.

48. The publicist and theoretician for this group was Isocrates; see his oration " To Philip," and *Letters 2* and 3.

Understandably the discussion shifted to the philosophers with the inevitable result: much talk and little agreement. Here, however, perhaps for the first time, the Greeks tried consciously to learn from history.

The Greek background itself offered few attractive suggestions.[49] If discipline is an important, even the essential, element in well-being, if well-being concerns the inner and not the outer man, then the disciplined states of Greece, which had at least a relatively successful foreign policy, might have something to offer. Plato's *Republic* owes much to Spartan institutions, which Xenophon also admired and publicized in two tracts.[50] But Sparta was based on a rigid system of classes, which a democratic state, with its broad base of education, financial independence, and political consciousness, would not accept voluntarily. Constraint might be impossible or might produce the reverse of the result desired; education might help but surely very slowly. If people would be equal or at least functionally equal, was there not another way in which this could be arranged? Whether the model be the philosopher, who claims the right to lead through wisdom, or the head of a family, a domestic benign despot, people's thoughts naturally strayed to monarchy, or rather, kingship—since a king was by definition an embodiment of all the virtues of a ruler: the shepherd, guiding and protecting his flock for its own good. One had examples to hand. Plato imagines that somewhere, some time, there has been or is or may be such a king—thinking perhaps wistfully of Dionysius II.[51] Others went further. Xenophon drew such a picture in Cyrus the Great of Persia and imagined another in Cyrus the Younger, whose unhappy fortunes he had shared himself.[52] Isocrates saw in Philip the realization of this ideal.[53]

49. But Plato, at the beginning of the *Critias*, finds in the early history of Athens an historical justification of his *Republic*.

50. *Res publica Lacedaemoniorum* and *Agesilaus*. Plato's debt to Sparta would be easier to determine if we knew more about the real Sparta, but he himself explains his view of this in the opening books of the *Laws*.

51. *Republic* VI, 499 C/D.

52. *Cyropedia* and *Anabasis*, especially *Cyropedia*, I, ii.

53. See above, n. 48.

It was left for Alexander, the young, gifted, romantic king who conquered the Persian Empire and marched as far as India, to make the dream come true. It is unimportant what Alexander himself may have thought, although he would not have been a Greek had he not felt himself in some sense, and progressively with his amazing successes, a reincarnation, not only of Achilles but of those wonder-working benefactor kings of mythology, Heracles and Dionysus.[54] Aristotle had already written that such a king would be a very god, who proved himself by his deeds.[55] It is little wonder that the Alexander biographies bear in many ways a resemblance to the Cyropedia, for Alexander had created what Xenophon had dreamed of, a world state which would end war and distribute to its people what each should have. They would have freedom also, since the benefits were so manifest that they would freely choose to accept their assigned positions. This is the other side of the theory of kingship, as in the Song of Deborah: " for that the people gave themselves willingly, praise ye the Lord." [56]

There is no doubt that the enthusiasm was genuine. Alexander's sudden death and the confusion which followed hardly put his huge realm to the test, but we can see the excitement which Ptolemy's kingdom of Egypt aroused. Theocritus, subsidized but not bought, wrote Ptolemy's panegyric:

> there's no country so fruitful as the low-country of Egypt when Nile comes gushing up to soak the soil and break it, nor no country, neither, possessed of so many cities of men learned in labor. The cities builded therein are three hundreds and three thousands and three tens of thousands, and threes twain and nines three, and in them the lord and master of all is proud Ptolemy. . . . For wealth, his would outweigh the

54. Cf. Tarn, *Alexander*, *2*, 45–52, who doubts much influence. Cf., however, Fritz Schachermeyr, *Alexander der Grosse*.

55. *Politics*, III, 1384a; Tarn, *Alexander*, *2*, 366–9. Cf. however the criticism of J. P. V. D. Balsdon, *Historia*, *1* (1950), 363–88; Fritz Taeger, *Historische Zeitschrift*, *172* (1951), 225–44.

56. Judg. 5.

> wealth of all the princes of the earth together—so much comes into his rich habitation both day by day and from every quarter. And as for his peoples, they occupy their business without let or hinderance, seeing that no foeman hath crossed afoot that river of monsters to set up a cry in alien townships.[57]

" Ptolemy," in Theocritus' words on another occasion, was " the best paymaster a freeman can have," and thousands of Greeks took the poet's advice to enter his service: " So an thou be'st minded to clasp the warrior's cloak about thee, and legs astride to abide the onset of the hardy foeman, to Egypt with thee." [58] In Egypt, according to the contemporary Herodas, the Greeks found " wealth, grounds of disport, power, climate fayr, fame, exhibiciouns, sages, gold, children, the demesne of the Brethren Gods, right noble the king, the Museum, wine, all boons man mote crove, women more than sky vaunteth of stars, and in contenance as what goddesses of yore come unto Páris for deeming of their beautie." [59] Certainly they came to improve their lot, and they were a mixed company, as we see them in the papyri, scientists and poets, politicians and soldiers, capitalists, but day laborers also, who cleared the Fayum desert of brushwood for a few cents a day.[60]

IV. THE EGYPTIAN SOLUTION

With all its Macedonian government and its great influx of Greek adventurers, Egypt continued largely in its traditional ways, and while King Ptolemy quietly made such changes in administra-

57. Theocritus, XVII, 79–86, 95–99, trans. J. M. Edmonds in the Loeb Classical Library.

58. Theocritus, XIV, 59, 65–68.

59. Herodas, I, 27–35, trans. A. D. Knox in the Loeb Classical Library. Cf. also, the royal encomium studied in the schools, O. Guéraud and P. Jouguet, *Un Livre d'écolier du IIIe siècle avant J.-C.*, Publications de la Société Royale Egyptienne de Papyrologie, Textes et Documents, Vol. 2 (Cairo, 1938), ll. 155–61.

60. Préaux, *Les Grecs en Egypte d'après les archives de Zénon.*

tion as seemed desirable,[61] he did not fail to capitalize on Egypt's age-old reputation for dong things well. Hecataeus of Abdera was hired to write a history of the country with the aim of establishing its reputation as the home of the Greek ideal of kingship.

> The life which the kings lived was not like that of other men who enjoy autocratic power and do in all matters exactly as they please. In the matter of their servants, for example, not one was a slave, but all were sons of the most distinguished priests, in order that the king, by virtue of his having the noblest men to care for his person and to attend him throughout both day and night, might follow no low practices.[62]

He was a model of docile regularity. "The hours of both the day and night were laid out according to a plan, and at the specified hours it was absolutely required of the king that he should do what the laws stipulated and not what he thought best."[63] "For there was a set time not only for his holding audiences or rendering judgments, but even for his taking a walk, bathing, and sleeping with his wife, and, in a word, for every act of his life. His whole diet was ordered with such continence that it had the appearance of having been drawn up, not by a lawgiver, but by the most skilled of their physicians."[64] Such kings, "by virtue of their having cultivated a manner of life which had been chosen before all others by the most prudent of all men, fell into the fewest mistakes. And since they followed so righteous a course in dealing with their subjects, the people manifested a good will towards their rulers which surpassed even the affection they had for their own kinsmen."[65]

Not only were the kings of Egypt the most exemplary of men.

61. Cf. my paper in the *Journal of Juristic Papyrology, 3* (1949). 21–47.
62. Diodorus Siculus, I, 70, 1–2, trans. C. H. Oldfather in the Loeb Classical Library.
63. *Ibid.*, 3.
64. *Ibid.*, 10–12.
65. *Ibid.*, I, 71, 3–4.

Their subjects were the happiest, because everything was ordered for their good. The population was divided into permanent functional groups, practically as in Plato's *Republic,* each gladly contributing its services to the beatitude of the whole. In return, they received tangible benefits from their rulers. For one third "of the country has been taken over by the kings for their revenues, out of which they pay the cost of their wars, support the splendor of their court, and reward with fitting gifts any who have distinguished themselves; and they do not swamp the private citizens by taxation, since their income from these revenues gives them a great plenty "[66] (as well it might!). It is little wonder that in this perfectly constituted land, deficiencies should seem due to backsliding. Toward the end of the 3d century B.C. a set of instructions to a financial official contains the item: "Take particular care that no peculation or any other wrong takes place. For every one resident in the country must clearly understand and believe that all acts of this kind have been stopped and that they are freed from the bad conditions of the past, no one having a right to do what he likes, but everything being managed in the best way."[67]

Thus was history made useful in Ptolemaic Egypt, even if not precisely in the sense which Thucydides had imagined. If it did not save men from committing mistakes already committed by others, it as least justified them in their chosen course and furnished them with a favorable psychological climate for fashioning the future as they wished.

V. THE NEW CITIES

It would be pleasant to parallel this description of the idea of history in Ptolemaic Egypt with its functioning in the other Hellenistic kingdoms, but our evidence is inadequate. We know shockingly little about the mentality of the Seleucids and the

66. *Ibid.,* I, 73, 6.

67. Arthur S. Hunt and J. Gilbart Smyly, *The Tebtunis, Papyri, 3,* No. 1 (London, 1933), No. 703 ll. 222–32 (translation of the editors).

Attalids, who ruled the most of Anatolia and Hither Asia,[68] and even less about the Bactrian kingdom on the Oxus. The rulers generally were capable and hard working, with a confidence in their mission to rule by improving things. It may be that the kings of Bactria were only a line of white rajahs, maintaining their positions by tact and ability, rather than, as some have thought, architects of a new policy of racial harmony between Greeks and Iranians, heralds of a new era wherein Greeks would forsake their ancient conviction of being better than other men. It seems actually that there were few Greeks who came to this relatively inacessible and outlandish country.[69] And as to the Attalid kings in their mountain stronghold at Pergamum, it is supposed that they enjoyed very little popularity with the Greeks in general, subjects or otherwise.[70] We may well be led astray by slight evidence, and the Attalids created the second greatest library of the age and turned their capital into a spectacle which yielded nothing to the magnificence of Alexandria,[71] but they do seem, in any case, irrelevant to our discussion. We have no evidence whatever that they attempted consciously to make the world a better place to live in or that they quoted history in their support. The Seleucids are, quite possibly, a different matter.

I refer to their activity in founding cities. Alone of the Hellenistic royal families, they created hundreds of new cities, finding for them locations, plans, constitutions, and settlers, together with the money to pay for all this. We know little enough about it. In some cases we do not know even the precise location of the settlements. In so large a project, we must assume that the cities followed a relatively small variety of patterns. Some have been

68. The royal letters show that the Seleucids, at least, were influenced by past history and refer to the dynastic tradition in support of a policy; cf. my *Royal Correspondence in the Hellenistic Period* (New Haven, 1934), Nos. 15, 25, 44.

69. Tarn, *Greeks in Bactria and India*; Franz Altheim, *Weltgeschichte Asiens im griechischen Zeitalter*; my review in *Gnomon*, *22* (1950), 53–61.

70. Witness the impudent comment and severe punishment of Daphidas, Tarn, *Hellenistic Civilization*, p. 164; Hansen, p. 39.

71. Hansen, chs. 7–9.

excavated, but these have been either too large and overgrown with Roman and Byzantine remains, like Antioch, or untypical, as is supposed to be the case with our own Dura-Europos, although it was listed as a city in the official Parthian records.[72]

But whatever these new cities may have been, they embodied a conception of progress. We know nothing of the feelings of the Greeks or Macedonians who migrated to the new islands of Hellenism in the sea of Asia. Probably few of the Greeks came from Metropolitan Greece, and some of them certainly did come from Seleucid-controlled Asia Minor; their removal may not have been voluntary.[73] On the other hand, the few incriptions which we find here and there, notably at Susa, indicate that they accepted their lot and went briskly about their business, whether they liked it or not.[74] Democratic forms were maintained, with an essentially oligarchical control. The Greek amenities were preserved, literature, learning, and gymnastic.[75] Many of the settlements flourished, notably Seleucia on the Tigris, which became one of the great cities of the Hellenistic times and a symbol of Hellenism in the East.[76] Certainly the Seleucids planned to hold their realm with a net of cities tied together by routes made safe for trade and administrative travel. Certainly they expected that the Hellenic population would make common cause with them against the Asiatics and supply them with reliable

72. Isidorus of Charax, *Parthian Stations* 1.

73. So Antioch in Persis (Bushire) was a colony of Magnesia on the Maeander; cf. Jones, pp. 23–25; Rostovtzeff, *Hellenistic World*, p. 480 (for the emigration in general, see pp. 1054–7); Tarn, *Hellenistic Civilization*, p. 156; and in general, Bikerman, *Institutions des Séleucides*, pp. 159 f.

74. For Susa, cf. *Supplementum epigraphicum graecum*, Vol. 7 (1934), Nos. 1–34, especially hymns 11–14.

75. Rostovtzeff, *Hellenistic World*, pp. 1057–98; Tarn, *Hellenistic Civilization*, chs. 3, 8, 9.

76. The Greek population was not large, probably, and the degree of Hellenism which the city possessed is variously estimated. It throve on the transit trade until the later times of the Parthian Empire. Cf. Strech in Pauly-Wissowa, *Real-Encyclopädie*, Ser. 2, Vol. *3* (1921), cols. 1148–84. For the excavations carried on by the University of Michigan, cf. the references in Rostovtzeff, *Hellenistic World*, p. 1424, n. 227, and p. 1645.

troops. It is not impossible that they envisioned the emergence in the rather distant future of a national state, with a homogeneous population of largely Greek culture, although one would hesitate to assert it.[77]

It is possible that their thought ranged further. The founder of a city, the creator of a new body politic, was in Greek eyes something more than human. In addition to their other claims to divinity, the Seleucids could claim heroic worship as *κτίσται* in their foundations—as we actually see in our relief Seleucus Nicator worshiped as the founder of Dura.[78] And in a world which was filled with ideas about the function of the ideal king in an ideal society, we cannot categorically deny that the Seleucids may have fancied that they were setting up model communities for future generations to enjoy. It is morally certain, at any rate, that their advisers and court poets told them that they were doing so. It was an age that saw the writing of Utopias become very popular. Euhemerus, a courtier of King Cassander of Macedon, described a fabulous island in the Indian Ocean, populated by emigrant Cretans. Its name was Panchaea, and it was phenomenally rich; but all its inhabitants contributed to the common store and private property was restricted to a house and garden. Its priests and soldiers were supported by the farmers, but no one was unhappy and no one had to work very hard.[79] A similar island, peopled by Sun-Citizens, Heliopolitans, was discovered by by Iambulus. These had double tongues and could carry on two different conversations at the same time. They possessed women

77. The problem centers on Antiochus IV and his Jewish policy, as well as his supposed desire to spread the cult of Zeus Olympius; cf. Walter Otto, *Zur Geschichte der Zeit des 6. Ptolemäers*, Abhandlungen der Bayerischen Akademie der Wissenschaften, Philosophisch-historische Abteilung, Neue Folge, Heft 11, Munich, 1934; Rostovtzeff, *Hellenistic World*, pp. 1492 f.; H. L. Jansen, *Die Politik Antiochos' des IV*, Oslo, 1943; Altheim, *Weltgeschichte Asiens*, *2*, 35–50.

78. Rostovtzeff, *Dura-Europos and Its Art*, frontispiece; F. E. Brown in *The Excavations at Dura-Europos, Preliminary Report of the Seventh and Eighth Seasons of Work* (New Haven, 1939), pp. 258–60.

79. Diodorus Siculus, VI, 1.

and children in common and did practically no work at all. The land produced crops by itself, and the sweet, turbulent, tidal waters surrounding the island kept off enemies, so that they needed no armed forces. But they did have a king, who was put to death at the ample age of 150 years, a tactful figure which no Seleucid king came close to reaching.[80]

All of this was supported by the Stoics, some of whom later were to try Plato's experiment of being crown councilors. It is unfortunate that we have lost the *Republic* of Zeno of Citium, the founder of the order. It seems to have had most of the standard features and to have insisted: "As in the life of a man, so in that of the whole city does happiness come from virtue, and from concord within it, so that they may continue always free, independent and temperate."[81]

VI. ENERGY AND DECLINE

With this energy and enthusiasm, accordingly, and a certain optimism, together with at least a selective and functional use of history to support them, did the Greeks enter upon what properly is called the Hellenistic Age. All of these favoring qualities were soon put to a severe test.

Franz Altheim is only the most recent to urge that the stage of ancient history extends from the Atlantic Ocean to Mongolia, if not to the Pacific.[82] Greco-Macedonian kings and historical philosophers were destined to find their world of peaceful experimentation threatened from West and East, and it is to these essentially extraneous considerations that we must credit what is called the failure of the Hellenistic states. It is true that these states showed the same inability to get along peaceably with one another as had the little city-states in Greece one hundred years

80. *Ibid.*, II, 55–59. For these texts cf. Rostovtzeff, *Hellenistic World*, p. 1523, n. 81; Tarn, *Hellenistic Civilization*, p. 129.

81. Joannes ab Arnim, *Stoicorum veterum fragmenta 1* (Leipzig, 1905), No. 263, p. 61.

82. Notably in his *Niedergang der alten Welt.*

earlier. The historical writing of this period, notably the accounts of the *Diodochoi* and *Epigonoi* down to 266 by the seemingly very able Hieronymus of Cardia, deal mainly with wars. He was a strong advocate of the unity of Alexander's empire, a partisan of his countryman and Alexander's secretary Eumenes, and later, of Antigonus I. Doubtless it was the struggle to maintain this unity which gave him his central theme, although he was a practical man of affairs also, had governed Nabataea, knew the Arabs, and lived to a vast age, doubtless saddened by the victory of the separatists. We lack his own expression of his political philosophy. Doubtless he wished peace as well as unity. Perhaps the quarrelsomeness of the Greeks was deplorable. They were little ready to let go any advantage to another, although this may have been only a consequence and an extension of the qualities which made them unique as a people—their restless and aggressive curiosity, their impatience of authority, and their reluctance to acknowledge a superior. The wars of the Hellenistic states may have weakened them for the coming life struggle with Rome, although these wars were conducted to a great extent in a humane and gentlemanly fashion [83] and may have served only to keep their armies in trim and acquainted with the newest developments in military science. At all events, it is pure humbug when Roman historians smugly justify Rome's occupation of the Hellenistic East on the ground that these states had "failed." [84] Their primary failure consisted in their inability to defeat the Roman legions.

83. Tarn, *Hellenistic Civilization*, pp. 80–4. Rostovtzeff, *Hellenistic World*, pp. 140–54, 191–203, points out that Greece was an exception. Although the armies of the kings in Asia did relatively little damage to themselves or to others, the independently minded cities in the Greek peninsula suffered very much from rival claimants of their allegiance. Xenophon in the *Cyropedia* (V, 4, 24–8), had noted the sensible plan of Orientals for the armies to fight each other and leave the peasants to go about their work in peace.

84. This point of view is widespread and natural. Roman historians become partisans of Rome, loyally enough, and justify her policies from a humanitarian point of view, while disparaging her rivals. The comment of F. E. Adcock, *Cambridge Ancient History, 9* (Cambridge, 1932), 713, is typical: "The

They had started out bravely enough, and the 3d century B. C. seemed destined to anticipate the modern age of science. The great scholars of the Alexandrian Museum and Library, utilizing ideas and methods worked out in Athens' Academy and Lycaeum, made enormous and very rapid advances both in the natural and the theoretical sciences. This group was by no means isolated. All of the Greek world was astir with excitement, and great things seemed in prospect. Archimedes of Syracuse, the discoverer of the calculus and many of the principles of mathematical physics, showed the way to new sources of power in hydrostatics, pulleys, windlasses, and screws. With these and his experiments with the concave lens he contrived much that the military put to practical use. Later on, Hero of Alexander invented the steam engine, but through the favor of providence Hellenistic man escaped a machine age. One has remarked that the ancients wisely knew these things for toys and refused to stultify their souls by taking them seriously.[85] It would be pleasant to credit our Greeks with such perspicacity, but science is a primrose path which no amount of better judgment will keep men from pursuing so long as their intellectual energy is unimpaired. Rather is it likely that with the end of the 3d century, the Hellenistic man was beginning to falter in his idea of history. He was becoming less confident of his ability to create a world of his own designing and began to look instead to the problem of getting along in the world about

Ptolemaic dynasty had outlived its usefulness, and the machine of government could be readily adapted to serve a new master." In a similar way classical historians have little but contempt for what they call Oriental. Helmut Berve, *Gestaltende Kräfte der Antike* (Munich, 1949), repeats the old and deservedly outworn notion that Rome took over the mission of the Hellenistic monarchies to protect the Greeks from the Orient. Dura provides the refutation, as I have tried to show in my paper " The Population of Roman Dura " in P. R. Coleman-Norton, ed., *Studies in Roman Economic and Social History in Honor of Allan Chester Johnson* (Princeton, 1952), pp. 251–74. Tarn has been commendably free from this attitude and has made the telling observation that literary Greeks in the East tended to migrate to the Mediterranean during the Hellenistic period, but remained at home after the Roman conquest (see *Greeks in Bactria and India*, p. 39).

85. Tarn, *Hellenistic Civilization*, ch. 9.

him. This may or may not have affected his ability to repulse the armed might of Rome and Parthia. It reconciled him, in any case, to living in a world which he no longer dominated.[86]

What caused this change is hard to say. It did not happen everywhere at once. The esurient Greekling who could and would do anything for a price must have appeared in the West early, eager to advance his fortunes by serving the new master. On the other hand, Greeks fought the hated Roman barbarian with fanatical fury as late as August of 30 B. C., when Hellenism's last champion went down to defeat before Alexandria. On the other hand, Octavian's victory was won only with the help of such stout sea captains as Seleucus, the son of Theodotus, of Rhosos in Syria; [87] and culturally, the East possessed vitality enough to teach and instruct its Western conquerors. It is not possible to say that the energies of Hellenism were expended by 200 B. C., although it is suggestive that the brilliance of the 3d century dims progressively with the growth of Roman influence. Can scientific optimism exist without political optimism? Perhaps. It may be that this problem will be put to the test in the years which lie ahead of us. Certainly it is true that the modern scientific and industrial revolution has coincided with a period of intense political excitement, and it would be hard to insist that there is no connection.

VII. THE ROMAN BLIGHT

A little positive evidence comes to us from Dura. This little Macedonian colony of Dura-Europos, lying on the Euphrates just north of the present boundary between Iraq and Syria, was excavated over a period of ten years by a Yale expedition and yielded many inscriptions which throw light on its history.[88] It

86. Rostovtzeff, *The Mentality of the Hellenistic World and the After-Life*, Cambridge, 1939.

87. Louis Jalabert and René Mouterde, *Inscriptions grecques et latines de la Syrie, 3*, 1 (Institut Français d'Archéologie de Beyrouth, *Bibliothèque archéologique et historique, 46*) (Paris, 1950), No. 718, pp. 395–411, with revised text and full commentary and bibliography.

88. See *The Excavations at Dura-Europos, Preliminary Reports*, New Haven, 1929–1952.

was founded about 300 B.C. under the first Seleucus. The original citizens of the town were Macedonian, which meant that Dura was a city without many of the usual Greek features; there was no theater and no palaestra, and the constitution and officials of the city were different from the usual Greek pattern. Nevertheless the language was Greek, men and women bore Macedonian names and intermarried very little with the surrounding Bedouin. Although they largely worshiped native gods in native temples, lived in native houses, and wore native dress, they remained as a proud and self-conscious group, not assimilating in any essentials,[89] until the Roman conquest under Marcus Aurelius in the 2d century. Then they disappeared almost completely, and the city was occupied by soldiers and their people of the mixed Greek, Roman, and Oriental type which had been found in Syria since the Roman conquest.[90] As first argued by J. Beloch [91] and more recently maintained by Rostovtzeff,[92] it was probably the eastern imperialism of Rome which changed the Greeks of the Hellenistic Orient.

That, at all events, or something like that, is the story of the idea of history in the Hellenistic East. With the loss of confidence came a loss of feeling for the future as a part of man's historical experience. Harold Mattingly has recently written of the man in the street under the empire: "The Roman . . . had a very feeble sense of the remaining dimension of time." [93] History

89. They adopted Oriental architecture, dress, and other externals, but remained Greek in culture and in law. For the latter, cf. most recently Fritz Pringsheim, *Ausbreitung und Einfluss des griechischen Rechtes*, Sitzungsberichte der Heidelberger Akademie der Wissenschaften, Phil.-hist. Klasse (1952), No. 1. Testimony to the former is the late graffito from the house of Nebuchelus mentioning Demosthenes and the Boule of the Athenians, *The Excavations at Dura-Europos, Preliminary Report of the Fourth Season of Work* (New Haven, 1933), No. 184, pp. 81 f., as well as the finds of Greek literary papyri in the city reported in *Transactions of the American Philological Association, 70* (1939), 203–12.

90. Cf. my paper cited above, n. 84.

91. *Historische Zeitschrift, 84* (1900), 1–38.

92. *A History of the Ancient World, 2,* 169.

93. Mattingly, *The Man in the Roman Street*, p. 102.

became something which was respectable, even admirable, and possibly also useful, but dead, a purely intellectual pursuit. Great men collected historians to preserve the memory of their achievements and spoke and acted in conscious imitation of the worthies of the past. Lesser men summarized their careers on their tombstones to impress passers-by. Cicero praised history, echoing some Greek predecessor: "Not to know what happened before you were born is to be forever a child. For what is the span of life of a man unless it is tied to that of his ancestors by the memory of earlier events?"[94] Well, what? Education is education, and you cannot be educated unless you know history. So everyone wrote and recited and read and listened to history, histories of every conceivable sort—local histories, special histories, cultural histories, long histories, short histories. Abridgements and condensations were especially popular, for as in modern times people were impatient, and surely anything that was said in fifty books could be said better in one.[95] Many were seriously concerned to find out what had happened. Dionysius of Halicarnassus spent twenty-two years of study in Rome, learned Latin, questioned everyone and read everything he could find, to write the definitive history of early Rome.[96] Much of this flood of historical writing was trivial, but some of it, preserved or not, was excellent. No one has excelled Tacitus in dramatic force and mordant prejudice. Flavius Josephus has given us detailed and trustworthy accounts of the events of his own time and the historical background of his own people. The *Jewish War* is a dramatic and penetrating, albeit hardly an impartial, piece of historical writing by an eyewitness and a scholar. We should have learned much from Nicholaus of Damascus.[97] How much poorer should

94. *Orator* 120; cf. also, *De oratore* 2, 36.

95. It is currently reported that one of our great foundations is supporting the preparation of a definitive history of the world in fifty volumes by a group of leading scholars. The work will then be abridged to ten and two volumes, and finally, to one volume.

96. *Antiquitates Romanae* I, 7.

97. Richard Laqueur, *Real-Encyclopädie*, Ser. 2, Vol. 33 (1936), cols. 361–424.

we be without the history of Dio Cassius, himself a statesman and a man of affairs in the times of the Severi. History there was in plenty, in the later Hellenistic East, so that the memorable deeds of men might not be forgotten, so that people in trouble might console themselves with the disasters of their forefathers, and so that students might not lack for political or moral guidance.[98] But the idea of history had changed. It was no longer a part of man's progress to a better future.

VIII. THE NEW MENTALITY

Instead, for getting along and improving his lot, man turned to other things, religion and magic. It is symptomatic that astrology rises as science sinks.[99] Fate controls man's fortunes, but fate can be controlled in turn in a variety of ways, if one knows how or can come upon a practitioner who does. Our papyrus collections are full of spells and incantations, and our museums are full of amulets and charms. Serious men, anxious to help humanity on its otherwise hopeless path, wrote learned treatises that have survived to our day.[100] Material existence grew pleasanter and more comfortable with the advent of the empire, although taxation and controls grew also. It was hard to attain security and independence on one's own. Instead of a competence, one looked for a pension. Instead of acquiring property, it was safer to become a member of the bureaucracy or to attach oneself to someone who was, and to spend one's time in anticipation or contemplation of the rarer but more exciting pleasures: the public festivals, with free distribution of food and wine, and the great pageants, especially the games, with their gladiatorial contests and hunting of wild animals. If one were more refined, one

98. Cf. especially Polybius, I, 1/2.

99. In one of the most remarkable observations on human nature remaining from classical antiquity, Polybius (VI, 56, 6–15) comments on the effective use of political religiosity by the Romans that it would have been unnecessary had the state been composed only of wise men.

100. Cf. the materials used by Franz Cumont, *L'Egypte des astrologues*, Brussels, 1937.

would become a philosopher or a poet, and make a living composing epitaphs for people pathetically fearful of being forgotten after their death. Frightened, selfish, unhappy, and above all, helpless, it was inevitable that people should turn their minds to the possibility of a better life in another world. Socrates in Plato's *Apology* expresses pleasure at the prospect of talking with Homer and Musaeus in the Elysian Fields, but this is irony. It is not ironical when the tombstones of thousands of undistinguished persons in the Hellenistic East reflect a belief in immortality,[101] while the faiths promising salvation in some form—Orphism, Mithraism, the worship of Sarapis and of Isis—spread rapidly and numbered their adherents by the tens of thousands. Man needed comfort, and man needed company.[102]

His idea of history was no longer a source of strength and joy to him, and he would only escape from it. Messianism was in the air. The imperial propaganda was built upon it.[103] In spite of the optimistic slogans on the coins, however, and the heartening epithets applied to the emperors, man no longer believed that the Age of Gold would be restored on earth. His *reparator temporis felicis* [104] was not of this world.

101. See Cumont, *Lux perpetua.*

102. This is a point usefully stressed by A. D. Nock, *Conversion.*

103. Especially in the form of legends on the coins, a material drawn upon heavily by such students of the Roman mentality as A. Alföldi, M. P. Charlesworth, H. Mattingly, Michael Grant, and C. H. V. Southerland.

104. Cf. the slogan " felicis temporis reparatio " used by Constantius II; Henry Cohen, *Description historique des monnaies frappés sous l'Empire Romain,* 7 (Leipzig, 1930), 448.

BIBLIOGRAPHY

F. Altheim, *Niedergang der alten Welt*, 2 vols. Frankfurt a. M., 1952.

——— *Weltgeschichte Asiens im griechischen Zeitalter*, 2 vols. Halle, 1947–48.

E. Bikerman, *Institutions des Séleucides*, Paris, 1938.

J. B. Bury, *The Idea of Progress*, London, 1921.

R. G. Collingwood, *The Idea of History*, Oxford, 1946.

Benedetto Croce, *History: Its Theory and Practice*, New York, 1921.

F. Cumont, *Lux perpetua*, Paris, 1949.

James H. Gaul, *The Neolithic Period in Bulgaria*, American School of Prehistoric Research, Bull. 16, 1948.

Esther V. Hansen, *The Attalids of Pergamum*, Ithaca, 1947.

Alexander Heidel, *The Babylonian Genesis*, Chicago, 1951.

——— *The Gilgamesh Epic and the Old Testament Parallels*, Chicago, 1949.

A. H. M. Jones, *The Greek City from Alexander to Justinian*, Oxford, 1940.

Helene J. Kantor, *The Aegean and the Orient in the Second Millennium* B. C., Cambridge, 1947.

H. L. Lorimer, *Homer and the Monuments*, London, 1950.

H. Mattingly, *The Man in the Roman Street*, New York, 1947.

J. L. Myres, *Who Were the Greek?*, Sather Classical Lectures, Vol. 4, Berkeley, 1930.

M. P. Nilsson, *Geschichte der griechischen Religion*, Vol. 1: W. Otto, ed., *Handbuch der Altertumswissenschaft* (Munich, 1941), Vol. 5, Pt. 2.

A. D. Nock, *Conversion*, Oxford, 1933.

Julian Obermann, *How Daniel Was Blessed with a Son*, Publications of the American Oriental Society, Offprint Series, Vol. 20, 1946.

Claire Préaux, *Les Grecs en Egypte d'après les archives de Zénon*, Brussels, 1947.

M. Rostovtzeff, *A History of the Ancient World*, 2 vols. Oxford, 1926–27.

——— *Dura-Europos and Its Art*, Oxford, 1938.

——— *The Social and Economic History of the Hellenistic World*, 3 vols. Oxford, 1941.

F. Schachermeyr, *Alexander der Grosse*, Graz, 1949.

——— *Poseidon und die Entstehung des griechischen Götterglaubens*, Salzburg, 1950.

W. Schubart, *Aegypten von Alexander dem Grossen bis auf Mohammed*, Berlin, 1922.

——— *Ein Jahrtausend am Nil*, Berlin, 1912.

J. T. Shotwell, *An Introduction to the History of History*, New York, 1922.

W. W. Tarn, *Alexander the Great*, 2 vols. Cambridge, 1948.

——— *The Greeks in Bactria and India*, 2d ed. Cambridge, 1951.

——— *Hellenistic Civilization*, 3d ed. Cambridge, 1952.

F. J. Teggart, *Theory of History*, New Haven, 1925.

A. J. Toynbee, *Greek Historical Thought from Homer to the Age of Heraclius*, London, 1924.

W. H. Walsh, *An Introduction to the Philosophy of History*, New York, 1951.

EARLIEST CHRISTIANITY

Erich Dinkler

I. DEFINITION OF THE TASK AND METHOD OF PROCEDURE

Our question is directed toward the idea of history in earliest Christianity in the apostolic and postapostolic age. The sources for our inquiry are almost without exception to be found in the New Testament, which is to say that we are dealing with the writings transmitted to us in Greek in which early Christianity confessed its faith in Jesus of Nazareth as the Christ, that is, the Messiah, as the Son of God, and as Lord.[1] These writings are distributed over a full century beginning with the First Letter to the Thessalonians written about 50 A. D. and ending with the Second Letter of Peter written about 150 A. D., though to be sure earlier oral traditions are incorporated in the various books. In other words, we have before us in the canon of the New Testament writings which represent both original Christianity and early Catholicism, and correspondingly we have a mirror of the history of theology throughout a decisive century.

The first point to be noted is that the word " history " does not occur in our sources.[2] This poses the fundamental question of whether in that case the idea of history is also lacking; but before we come to this crucial problem we must grapple with the difficulty implicit or explicit in all of the previous lectures, namely that our modern word " history " has itself been fashioned by history

1. As primary sources we use the writings of the New Testament, as secondary sources we shall mention the Apostolic Fathers.

2. The verb ἱστορεῖν occurs only once in the New Testament, in Gal. 1:18. The term is used here in its Hellenistic meaning: to visit in order to get acquainted with. Cf. H. Schlier, *Der Brief an die Galater* (1949), p. 30, and Liddell-Scott, *Greek-English Lexicon* (9th ed. 1940), *1*, 842; also W. Bauer, *Griechisch-deutsches Wörterbuch zu den Schriften des Neuen Testaments und der übrigen urchristl. Literatur* (1952), *s. v.*

and is freighted with philosophy. The concept of history has been given to us by Greek science and to this very day is employed by us in a Greek sense. From Thucydides to Toynbee the common and connecting assumption has been that history is a rational, intelligible continuity, an integrated nexus or concatenation, operating in a unified world, capable of investigation and illumination by historical method. History is not conceived as a riddle or a threat established on Olympus or arbitrarily fashioned by Moira or Fate, but rather as the eternally valid, the constant, and the law-abiding. From the time of Thucydides, history has been known as a rational comprehensible unity, the object of scientific thought, a part of the Greek insight about the world, since the cosmos is understood as a work of art. Every part is a portion of the unity, history included.[3] This view of history as a nexus where everything that has happened from the very beginning, from the ἀρχή, is intelligible, where the causal relationship is assumed and investigated, has stamped itself upon the West. It is simply taken for granted when we talk about history, even when we speak with scientific exactitude and whenever we do research work in the field of history.

For our present purpose this means that in the first place we shall have to discard the term "history" because our modern view cannot be neutralized and divested of its Greek imprint. We shall have to ask rather about the judgment on past and present, about *the concept of time* in the New Testament, if we are to avoid a philosophical restriction of the conclusion through inadequate phrasing of the question. Only at the end of each section and at the end of the paper can I return to the question whether in this concept of time there is contained any definite idea of history.

This question with regard to the concept of time is directed to a literature which spans a century and lies before us in our New Testament. Although this period is brief compared with

3. Cf. H. Holborn in *The Interpretation of History*, ed. J. R. Strayer, Princeton, 1943; R. Bultmann, *Das Urchristentum im Rahmen der antiken Religion* (1949), pp. 113 ff.

those treated in the previous papers, the method for arriving at an answer is by no means simple. We have to recognize at the outset that our New Testament is not a theological unity but includes *varied* theological conceptions. We have to differentiate and proceed chronologically before venturing general and comprehensive judgment. In treating a subject like ours, a frequent mistake is to take the New Testament writings all on one level with no regard to the nuances presented by early Christian chronology and with no differentiation between the quite varied writings. Such harmonization postulates unity in advance and yields a biblical dogmatic, but historical investigation must take account of the nuances both in theology and in the theme of history.[4]

Earliest Christianity embraces the first and second generations who believed in Jesus Christ as crucified and risen from the dead, since there was no Christianity until after the cross and the resurrection. This presupposes, of course, that for earliest Christianity the historical Jesus and His message are the basis for the understanding of the world of time and of itself. For that reason we begin with the message of Jesus as the determinative presupposition of the thought of apostolic Christianity.

II. JESUS' PROCLAMATION OF THE NEARNESS OF THE REIGN OF GOD

The sources from which we derive the message of the historical Jesus, namely the Synoptic Gospels, are naturally historical witnesses, but they are neither historiographical annals nor biographi-

4. Oscar Cullmann, *Christ and Time*, 1950, is harmonizing the New Testament evidence and thus building up a Christian theology of history. In spite of the fact that Cullmann's book is important as well as stimulating, I must object to his main thesis, namely that the real scope of the New Testament is given by " Christ as the center of History." My paper is somehow a constant dialogue with Cullmann's book, and I cannot deny that one can learn from it even when not agreeing with its theological conclusions and presuppositions. See also R. Bultmann in *Theologische Literaturzeitung* (1948), pp. 659–66, a critical review of Cullmann's book.

cal accounts. The primary intent of the Evangelists, whether the Synoptics or John, was missionary in character and is tellingly expressed at the end of John's Gospel (20:31): "These [signs of Jesus] are written that you may believe that Jesus is the Christ, the Son of God, and that believing, you may have life in His name." We see that the Evangelists are not concerned with knowledge but with faith. They are giving not an account of facts but a confession of faith. They are not writing objective history but are rather pointing to an occurrence which has fashioned their very existence. The motive for writing is thus determinative for the content. The interest determines the choice and the form of the material. To be sure, the Evangelists regard their confessions as historically accurate accounts, yet we as critical historians cannot for that reason assume historical and chronological accuracy. On the other hand, we must not forget that behind the confessions and interpretations of faith lie historical occurrences, objective facts of history, yet these facts are scarcely to be disentangled from the theological interpretations with which they are interwoven.[5]

When we come to the concept of time in the message of Jesus, we cannot lift it directly out of the Synoptic Gospels because even the very words of Jesus have received a theological interpretation; but since in accord with modern critical methods we are able to bring together and compare three Gospels, Matthew, Mark, and Luke, we can reconstruct the message of Jesus with a high degree of probability, though obviously not with absolute assurance. Some points are generally accepted and some are controversial.

The most pregnant summary of the preaching of Jesus is preserved in the earliest Gospel, in Mark 1:15, which reads: "The time is fulfilled and the Reign of God is at hand, repent."[6] Here

5. See also C. H. Dodd, *History and the Gospel* (London, 1938), pp. 11 ff.

6. The following words: καὶ πιστεύετε ἐν τῷ εὐαγγελίῳ, i.e., and believe in the Gospel, are additions of the Evangelist. Mark 1:14 f. sounds like an earlier opening of "the Gospel of Christ Jesus." Mark 1:15 is formulated by the Evangelist himself. He connects the message of the coming of the Reign of

we have the concept so central for the message of Jesus, the Reign of God: *ἡ βασιλεία τοῦ θεοῦ*. The near approach of God's Reign or Lordship is announced, and a demand is laid upon the hearers—repent (*μετανοεῖτε*) —a summons plainly based upon the imminence of the coming event. The concept of the Reign of God is nowhere defined, but from all the contexts we see perfectly that the reference is to something marvelous, an event which will take place without the hand of man, solely through the act of God.

The decisive question is: How is the Reign of God related as to time and content to the present and to the world? Along with this is the further question of whether the proclamation of God's Lordship and the nearness of its coming contain an implicit judgment on the past and a particular concept of time.

There is no doubt that in all three Synoptic Gospels the Lordship or Reign of God as preached by Jesus himself is characterized as something yet to come. The not yet and the soon are equally plain (cf. Mark 9:1). All the words of Jesus about the nearness of God's Reign demand that men decide and divide. Nobody can be indifferent, nobody can be neutral. Equally significant

God with the demand for repentance (cf. Matt. 10:7 = Luke 10:9 ff.) and the demand for faith in the Gospel (on the basis of the Gospel!).

εὐαγγέλιον is not the message of Jesus concerning the nearness of the kingdom but the message about Christ Jesus (as in Mark 1:1) which gives promise for repentance. *Genitivus auctoris* of *εὐαγγέλιον* is *τοῦ θεοῦ* (see Mark 1:14. The reading: *τῆς βασιλείας τοῦ θεοῦ* is secondary and influenced by Matt. 4:23, 9:35). The christological-soteriological meaning of *εὐαγγέλιον* is easily to be understood on the basis of Paul. Nothing can support the assumption that the christological usage of Paul is a development of an earlier non-christological usage of the term. It is characteristic for the naïve identification of the Gospel of the faith in Christ with the message of the historical Jesus in the Gospel according to Mark that with Mark Jesus speaks five times about the *εὐαγγέλιον* in an absolute sense: 1:15, 8:35, 10:29 f., 13:10, and 14:9 (in secondary readings 3:14 and 16:15 can be added). On the other hand we must acknowledge that Matthew and Luke were more critical with regard to Mark. In their parallels they correct or circumscribe the tradition: Matthew repeats the word only four times (4:23, 9:35, 24:14, 26:13), and Luke nowhere. The assumption that in an earlier layer of Mark the demand to believe in the Gospel was not given has against it the evidence of the Synoptic tradition.

is the insistence that because the coming is certain but the hour uncertain there can be no delay of the decision. In all the different layers of the Synoptic tradition, the Reign of God is described as coming, therefore, as still future; but at the same time it is rapidly approaching. Yet it is not coming in the future like a war or a revolution but rather as the turning point of all time, as the end of history in the current and modern sense of the word. It is still future but will come as an event which will terminate future history. It is the *αἰὼν ἐρχόμενος*.[7] With reference to this coming Reign of God Jesus prayed, " Thy kingdom come " (Matt. 6:10). And because this Reign cannot come as a development, as a process or a product of this world, therefore its coming is synonymous with the end of the world. Here once more we see the temporal horizon of futurity.[8]

7. Whether the phrase *αἰὼν ἐρχόμενος* goes back to the preaching of Jesus is not decided. There are more arguments against such an assertion than for it. Cf. W. G. Kümmel, *Verheissung und Erfüllung* (2d ed. 1953), p. 42, n. 98.

8. The main objection to this conception is given in Luke 17:20 f., which is translated in the King James Version as follows: " And when he was demanded of the Pharisees, when the kingdom of God should come, he answered them and said: The kingdom of God cometh not with observation. Neither shall they say: Lo here! or: lo there! For behold, the Kingdom of God is *within you.*" According to this translation, which is similar to Luther's German text, the Reign of God would be " in the nature of spiritual force, a power which sinks into a man within, and can be understood only from within," as formulated by A. v. Harnack, *What Is Christianity,* p. 66, and E. v. Dobschütz, " Zeit und Raum im Denken des Urchristentums," *JBL,* 41 (1922), 217 f. However this translation is based on a theological misunderstanding. The word, which is—as much as one is able to decide—an authentic saying of Jesus, means: " The Reign of God is not coming with signs to be observed " (*μετὰ παρατηρήσεως—cum observatione*). This requires a contrast like " it comes suddenly, without signs, without development to be observed. And therefore one *will* not say [notice the future] Lo here or there the Reign of God is coming." The Greek word *ἐντός* means in Latin *intra,* in English " in the midst." There is no parallel in Greek to the idea that *ἐντός* points toward the inwardness of the soul. The meaning of our passage is therefore: while you are looking around for the coming Reign of God, whether it can be observed here or there, it arrives, as soon as it comes, suddenly in the midst of you. See K. Clark, *JBL,* 59 (1940), 367 ff., and recently, Kümmel, *op. cit.,* pp. 17 f., 26 f., and 100, where the complete literature on this problem

If now the entire message of Jesus is shot through with the proclamation of the nearness of God's Reign which is to come, and indeed, already arriving, the emphasis is thereby placed upon the future which stands before us alike with threat and promise. This eschatology enshrines a judgment upon the present and upon the past and, indeed, upon history and mankind. That which is believed to take place in the future is the criterion for passing judgment upon the present and upon the past. And that which is believed to take place in the future is announced with authority as knowledge. It is conceived as something which has actually taken place. It is not a question of the future in general but of the very concrete future, namely, the *breaking in* of God's Lordship and *the breaking off* of the world of men. This is the point from which to understand the judgment on the present: now is the time of decision with reference to the future, and that means for all those who hear the message. Man is called upon to repent, that is, he must turn about and seriously fulfill God's will by renouncing himself and his love of self. This demand contains also a judgment which affects primarily the past. Man is evil (Matt. 7:11). He belongs to an adulterous and sinful generation (Mark 8:38; cf. Matt. 12:39, 41 f., 45). This means that in the past, prior to the summons and the decision of the present moment, man lived for his own advantage and for the love of self, not for the love of God and neighbor. Man lived for his own will and not for the will of God.

All judgment depends upon the proclamation of Jesus with regard to that which is to come, that which is already breaking in but is not yet fully developed. That which is to come is announced with authority and proclaimed as utterly imminent. Thus the present and the past are judged from the standpoint of the future. Note should be taken of the mythological form

is cited. Luther's translation and the King James Version were recently defended by E. Hirsch, *Frühgeschichte des Evangeliums* (1941), *2*, 157, obviously taking up arguments of A. Merx, *Luke*, p. 347. The theological viewpoint of Hirsch, Harnack, etc., goes back to Tertullian, Hippolytos, Cyril, Ephraim and perhaps also to *P. Oxyrh.* 654:3.

of this judgment inasmuch as Jesus conceives of the world as under the lordship of Satan and the demons and thinks of his own work as a conflict with them. But alongside this mythological element stands another which is not mythological: man is evil, the world is fallen. That these two lie side by side gives to the myth its meaning, namely that what is said about man and his future is presented in pictures supplied by the tradition. The myth has no independent significance. It is simply the symbolic language of the period.

Nevertheless, the question arises whether Jesus entertained a dualistic view of the world and of history, so that the world and its history are no longer thought of as an absolute creation but rather as the basis for conflict between God and Satan. Are we to find here an anticipation of Christian Gnosticism with its cleavage between the God of creation and the God of redemption? In the form of myth are we to discover here a metaphysical speculation? The answer must be no. The doctrine of creation in the preaching of Jesus follows the tradition of the Old Testament and of Judaism. God is Creator and Lord over the world and its time. God is at work in all that happens: " Whatsoever the Lord pleased, that did He in heaven and in earth " (Psalms 135: 6) . The same concept of God's omnipotence comes to expression in the words of Jesus: " [a sparrow] shall not fall to the ground without your Father's will " (Matt. 10: 29) . No one " can add to his stature one cubit " (Luke 12: 25) . " The very hairs of your head are all numbered " (Matt. 10: 30; cf. *ibid.*, 6: 25–35) . And then there is the saying which was making trouble for early Christianity: " But of that day and that hour knoweth no man, no, not even the angels which are in heaven, neither the Son, but the Father " (Mark 13: 32) . All of these sayings declare the same thing: that God is Lord over the world and everything that happens in it and also the Lord over time.

How then are we to understand the claim that the world is ruled by demons and is evil? The apparent discrepancy is resolved if this concept of the world is understood anthropologically. The world, which is pictured as fallen and under judgment, is not any cosmic entity but rather man himself; man who has made God into an object and who has elevated himself to the level of a subject, man who withdrew himself from the order of creation, that is, from obedience to God. This picture is drawn not only in late Jewish apocalypticism, for instance, in the Assumption of Moses (10:1) where we read: "Then will the Reign of God appear above all His creatures and the devil will come to an end." Also Jesus said: "I saw Satan falling like lightning from heaven" (Luke 10:18). This is not meant in cosmological terms. The point is rather that to men is announced the advent of the new world era. We might say more precisely, an era of salvation. The coming is so near that it already colors the present. In the person of Jesus is set the sign of this era and if there is to be a brief respite before the actual advent of God's Lordship—a respite which both provides for and requires repentance—nevertheless, a glimmer of the dawning new day is already apparent to the inner eye of faith.

The eschatology of Jesus thus has twin accents: 1) that the Reign of God is just around the corner, and though it is still future, its powers are here and now to be discerned; 2) the man who is challenged by this proclamation must decide for or against the coming event.

We are warranted then in reading from this eschatology a judgment upon history, to be sure, a judgment on the history of man, his past and his future, and on the emergent present. This present is qualified: "The time is fulfilled." It is a present lifted out as *καιρός* with reference to the imminence of the coming. An either-or is set before man. The summons of Jesus is directed toward the will of the individual, toward man's understanding of himself. The import of the situation is laid bare, in that once and for all the possibility of an existential reversal is presented to man in the cry of the herald: "the turning point of the ages is at hand." At the same time the demand resounds: "you yourself must decide now and at once."

In contrast to the Old Testament concept of the kingly rule of Yahweh, Jesus' picture of the Reign of God is not an event to be expected in the history of a people; rather it is thought of in strictly eschatological terms. And in contrast to late Jewish apocalyptic the new element is that the future is not portrayed in the language of heavenly delights; likewise all speculative elements are lacking. Instead the Reign of God is a supernatural event (Mark 12:25) which transcends the ethnic limits of the people (Mark 8:11 f.). This is not a case of the realization of the reign of peace or salvation within the framework of history,[9] nor is it something which gradually develops in the course of history. Rather it is a new epoch of salvation, supernatural in character, which breaks in with the termination of history. This Lordship of God comes to pass without effort on the part of man.

The intent of this proclamation is undoubtedly directed toward men. To man who is branded, bound, and burdened through his past is offered future forgiveness and release from the burden of the past. To sharpen the conclusion we may say that the preaching of Jesus offers no theology of history but a soteriology of the eschatological man. The idea of history consists paradoxically in this: that the end of history proclaims the redemption of man from history.

9. Against our interpretation of the "Reign of God" in the teaching of Jesus are often cited the parables of growth: Mark 4:26–9, 4:30–2, Matt. 13:24 ff., 33; and parallels. They are used as examples for the assertion that the kingdom is already here and growing in the form of an immanent process or development. However, the idea of development and process must be introduced; it is not inherent in these parables. For a detailed discussion of the parables of growth, see N. A. Dahl in *Studia theologica, 5* (1952), 132 ff.; and for literature concerning the problem cf. Kümmel, *op. cit.*, pp. 117 ff. C. H. Dodd, *The Parables of the Kingdom*, pp. 175 ff., takes them as a support of his "realized eschatology": "the eschaton, the divinely ordained climax of history, is here" (p. 193). Cf. A. N. Wilder, *Eschatology and Ethics in the Teaching of Jesus*, pp. 43 f., where he deals with Dodd. Recently Dodd has obviously changed his conception of "realized eschatology"; see his *Interpretation of the Fourth Gospel* (1953), p. 447, n. 1.

III. THE ATTAINMENT OF SALVATION IN CHRIST AND THE UNDERSTANDING OF TIME

We have already said that one can speak of Christianity and the Christian Church only since there was a faith in Jesus Christ as Lord, that is, faith in a redemption through Christ. Christianity dates from the cross and the resurrection. Now we are first able to turn to our theme in the proper sense. The scene shifts. Out of *Jesus, the messenger,* there has come to be *the message about Jesus Christ* as preached by the Apostles. The carrier of the message has become the object and the content of the message. At the same time, the accent of the preaching of Jesus is shifted because the concept of the eschatological Reign of God is from now on so understood and interpreted that the Christian community itself becomes the breaking in and the start of the new aeon, the realization of the Reign of God. The decisive break in the continuity of time for Christianity has already happened. What for Jesus was future is for the early Christian congregation already present. Where, then, does one recognize the turning point in the world epochs?

In the cross and resurrection. Does that mean, then, in an historical occurrence? We might better say in an occurrence within history understood by faith as a decisive act of God for the world, a faith which is indeed related to historical data, an act which in its final truth can be supported only by that which faith supplies and not through any objective historical investigation.

1. PAUL

" But when the fullness of time had come, God sent forth His Son " (Gal. 4:4). So wrote the Apostle Paul, the first great theologian of earliest Christianity, whose letters were written in the decade 50–60 A. D.[10] In II Cor. 6:2 he cites the Deutero-Isaiah

10. We use here as authentic Pauline letters Romans, I and II Corinthians, Galatians, Philippians, I Thessalonians, and Philemon.

49:8: "For He [God] says: I have heard thee in the acceptable time and in the day of salvation have I succored thee." And Paul adds triumphantly: "Behold *now* is the accepted time; behold *now* is the day of salvation."

This is not the fixing of a date on a calendar but rather and primarily a message which affects man. "Therefore if any one is in Christ, he is a new creature: the old has passed away; behold the new has come" (II Cor. 5:17). This means that he who believes in Christ *is* a new being, that for him the Christian era of salvation *has* come, the past *is* ended, and forgiveness has graciously been bestowed. The breaking in, the turning point, the caesura in the continuity is given in the act of God once and for all (ἐφάπαξ). This has taken place *within* the framework of history but is nevertheless understood as an eschatological event. Thus, Rom. 10:4 says: "For Christ is the end of the law for righteousness to everyone who believes." He who is familiar with Pauline terminology will understand that the word *nomos* (law) comprises what we call history. We may, therefore, formulate the thought of Paul in the statement: *Christ is the end of history.*[11]

11. With Paul the term νόμος has different meanings, which cannot be discussed here. For a complete picture, cf. G. Kittel, ed., *Theologisches Wörterbuch zum Neuen Testament, 4,* 1061 ff., and R. Bultmann, *Theology of the New Testament, 1,* 259 ff. For the understanding of our passage the following is decisive: the contrast of δικαιοσύνη τοῦ θεοῦ, which is marked by a *genitivus auctoris,* and ἰδία δικαιοσύνη (Rom. 10:3), which man tries to establish and thus neglects the peculiarity of God's righteousness. There is no doubt that the "righteousness of God" does not mean a special quality of God, but an action of God, by means of which righteousness is bestowed upon man. This is demonstrated by the phrase δικαιοσύνη ἐκ θεοῦ and by the quotation of Ps. 51:4 in Rom. 3:4. There is no moral connotation involved, but God's acting with man is pointed out. The attempt of man to establish his own righteousness is obvious in the works of the law, in man's building up of his future, of his own history, in all kinds of religio-social activism in order to gain God's blessing. Here it becomes evident that man intends "to boast before God," that he tries to take his future into his own hands and thus brings "history" to pass. Against this stands the event of the cross. From here the νόμος receives its new evaluation and disqualification. Therefore Paul can say in Gal. 2:21: εἰ γὰρ διὰ νόμου δικαιοσύνη, ἄρα Χριστὸς δωρεὰν ἀπέθανεν. Cf. also, Rom. 7:1 ff. and 8:1 ff.

This is indeed a paradoxical and intriguing assertion. Had Paul, then, no feeling for the givenness of the historical period in which he himself stood, lived, and worked? Was he entirely lacking in historical consciousness? Was not the hard reality of history the great and constant impediment to his missionary journeys? Does this not mean, however paradoxical it may sound, that for Paul the end of history was itself an event within historical continuity and not simply the abrogation of history in a cosmic drama?

The problem is only accentuated if one asks: Are the expressions " Christ is the end of history," " the Christian is a new creature," " the time is fulfilled " applicable to all men in the world? Plainly this cannot be Paul's meaning because the nonbeliever has no part in the new creature. He remains in the old aeon. To be sure the event of Jesus Christ has indeed a certain meaning even for nonbelievers, namely that they share in the judgment by which the old aeon is condemned once and for all but are excluded from the turning of the epochs, from the new creation, because they are still captive to the old aeon. Hence, it follows that two aeons—the old aeon of subjection to the demons and the new aeon of salvation and of the new creation—lie side by side, and both fill out the dimension of time and reality. This conjunction of aeons which exclude each other shows that this concept is not a cosmology or a periodization of world history. This is rather a case of portrayals and concepts which refer to man and his relation to God and Christ, because the aeon to which the Christian is dead (and thereby a new creature) is understood as the aeon of sin. From this aeon, he who believes in Christ is free (cf. Rom. 6). This means that the turning of the aeons is to be understood not mythologically but existentially, since, as a Christian, I am delivered from the bondage and the burden of the old aeon; thereby there is given to me freedom from the past for the future, i. e., from *my* past for *my* future.

At the same time the theology of Paul in its eschatological aspect is not as unified and consistent as we might wish, since alongside of the concept that the present for a believing Christian is the hour of salvation stands a second concept: man awaits a definitive event in the near future, and conceives of this event as a cosmic catastrophe through which death, sin, and the devil will be finally and universally eliminated. It is the concept of the return of Christ to judge the world. It is the picture of the parousia. Here Paul is able to paint also the coming event in apocalyptic and mythological pictures. Here the accent appears to be shifted again and transferred to the future, as it was with Jesus, and the present appears to be an existence in between the times, a period of waiting, a life of suffering for and with Christ. To be sure there is a heightened quality of existence, but there is also a not yet. Here Christ is the *prelude* to the end of the world and its history.

Within this second concept of time, which may be characterized as the expectation of the parousia, one sometimes finds in Paul an attempt to delineate a plan of God for mankind, a sort of history of salvation. Perhaps we would do better to avoid using the concept of history in conjunction with salvation and to speak rather of a sketch of an economy (*οἰκονομία*), a plan of salvation.[12] The attempt is made to interpret the past, the present, and the future up to the time of the parousia as a period planned by God Himself and predestined from eternity. Irenaeus would call it a " divine pedagogy " of mankind.[13]

In Rom. 9–11 Paul poses the question: Is Israel rejected as the people of the promise? Behind the very question lies the problem of the unified and unshakable action of God in the past, the present, and the future. Would God fail to keep a promise which he had made to Israel? Impossible! The grounds which Paul assigns to his further argumentation are not altogether free from difficulty because the concept Israel for him sometimes means

12. Our meaning of *οἰκονομία*, namely, plan of salvation, is not to be found with Paul. However, it is found in the Deutero-Pauline letter to the Ephesians (1:10 and 3:9), later in Ignatius (Eph. 18:2, 20:1), Justin (*Dialog.* 30:3, 45:4), Irenaeus, and Clement of Alexandria. The term means what Cullmann, *op. cit.*, 35, calls " the continuous redemptive line." See also, Kittel, *Th. W*, *5*, 154 f., and Bauer, *Wörterbuch, s. v.*

13. See the paper by R. H. Bainton which follows this.

the *empirical* people of Israel, and then again it means the *eschatological* people of Israel, namely, the members of the eschatological congregation of Christ. The whole discussion shows clearly a wrestling with the problem of the οἰκονομία of God. In his conclusion Paul reverts to the historical people of Israel (Rom. 11:1–32) and in the crucial portion (Rom. 11:25–32) refers to this as a *mysterium*. What Paul here calls μυστήριον is perhaps to be interpreted as hope. Yes, it might even be called a prophecy of faith. The diction of Paul shows clearly that he is himself aware of his temerity in referring to this mystery.[14] What has he basically said?

The whole of Israel will come to salvation and this will be as Israel actually *is* in the last phase. The present partial blindness of Israel with reference to salvation in Christ is only for a restricted time, " until the full number of the gentiles come in " (Rom. 11:25). The Israelites " are enemies of God for your sake " (Rom. 11:28). That is to say, Israel, the historical people of the old covenant, is involved in a dialectic of history where the opposition to the event of Christ serves the mission among the heathen, but in the end " God has mercy upon all " (Rom. 11:32).

The result of the discussion about the elect and the rejected now and those of the historical Israel who are called to ultimate redemption is not in accord with the customary thinking of Paul in christological, theological terms. We have here rather a prophetic interpretation of the future, a speculation about the coming events, which, strictly speaking, is theologically illegitimate. Paul, indeed, seems to be aware of this when in the concluding verses of the whole section (Rom. 11:33–6) he in fact relativizes his prophetic mystery in that he confesses the unfathomable wisdom of God and lauds His plan whereby the ignorance of man is confessed. One concludes, then, that man is not in a position to

14. A more detailed exegesis of Israel in Rom. 9–11 by this author will be published soon. For μυστήριον, cf. G. Bornkamm in Kittel, *Th. W, 4*, 829. For the eschatological conception of Israel, see W. D. Davies in *Harvard Theological Review* (1953), p. 11.

sketch out a philosophy or a theology of historical dialectic for God. On the other hand, one cannot overlook the fact that here an attempt is being made to interpret God's working in the past, in the old aeon, and God's activity in the present, through Jesus Christ, and in the coming aeon. In other words, he views the periods as an entity and in that way accommodates the future prior to the parousia as a brief preliminary yet to be completed in the plan of salvation. A tendency toward universalism is unmistakable, even toward optimism.

At first glance the two conceptions of Paul seem to be in tension: here the view that before the coming of Christ to judgment, salvation must be completed in time; there the message that Christ is the end of history. But the tension is a seeming one. When isolating the two views and pointing out their implications and logical consequences, they may contain contradictions. But with Paul himself the concept of a plan of salvation and the message "now is the time of salvation" are well balanced and support each other. The *οἰκονομία* idea is the underlying faith for all his apostolic activity;[15] this is the frame and basis of his missionary task: that the fullness of time has come because the final event of Christ's parousia is around the corner because Christ Jesus has risen and the final drama of God's plan as the definite goal is at hand. The inner balance of both conceptions is marked by the fact that the sequence of periods, past, present, and future, is brought together in its entirety in order to make manifest God's will with men and men's responsibility for a response now. The two conceptions, which we first separated, are in fact an inherent unity, because also the future time may be *καιρός*, namely, according to God's plan (cf. I Cor. 15:20–8).

In the attempt to bring into relation the occurrences of past, present, and future, and to understand the various occurrences in their interrelation, correlation, or even antithesis, Paul uses an appropriate *method* of interpreting the Scripture, that is our Old Testament, in order to make it fruitful for faith in Christ:

15. Cf. A. Fridrichsen, *The Apostle and His Message* (Uppsala, 1947), p. 3 ff.

the *typological interpretation.* This method is of prime importance for the understanding of patristic and medieval culture, as Erich Auerbach has basically demonstrated.[16]

In Rom. 5: 14 Paul speaks of Adam as " a type of the one who was to come," that is to say, as a type of Christ. In I Cor. 10: 6 the Israelites in the wilderness are referred to as " types " of Christians, and just above (I Cor. 10: 1–4), the passage of Israel through the Red Sea and the journey under the cloud were taken as a prefiguration of Christian baptism. Likewise the manna and the miraculous water from the rock were taken as a prefiguration of the Christians' Lord's Supper. And even though the key word " type " may be lacking, one cannot miss the typological interpretation when Paul speaks of the new creature (II Cor. 5: 17) or of the " first man " and the " last Adam," the " second Adam," and so on (I Cor. 15: 45–9).

These examples of typology,[17] which might readily be multiplied, presuppose a particular concept of time and history, and we must recognize that in the combination of type and antitype *historical* persons or events are brought into relation, so that one is tempted to talk about a " historiosophy " inherent in typology.[18] For our purposes the primary point is that the conception is shot

16. Erich Auerbach, " Figura," *Archivum romanicum*, Vol. *22* (1938); see also his *Neue Dantestudien*, Bern and New York, 1944; " Typological Symbolism in Medieval Literature," Yale French Studies, 1952; *Mimesis*, Princeton, 1953. L. Goppelt, *Typos*, 1939, and J. Daniélou, *Sacramentum futuri*, 1951, which, unfortunately, were written without knowledge of Auerbach's contributions, are lacking a clear definition and distinction between typology and allegory. See also R. Bultmann, " Ursprung und Sinn der Typologie als hermeneutischer Methode," *Pro regno pro sanctuario, Festschrift für G. v. d. Leeuw*, 1950, who takes up Auerbach's definitions, which do indeed clarify our exegetical terminology. In this paper we are primarily interested in the theological implications of this typological method.

17. See Bultmann, contribution just mentioned.

18. The difference between typology and allegory may be defined as follows: In *typology* historical events of the Old Testament (or events believed to be historical) are related to historical events of the new age and are interpreted as prefiguration, as τύπος, as *figura*. The literal meaning and the historical uniqueness of these events are thereby preserved. The best example

through with the idea of a repetition of similar or antithetical occurrences. A cyclical movement of time seems to be hinted at by a return of the similar, although possibly of the dissimilar, so that we have a varied representation, as in the concept in the Book of Acts of the restoration of all things: *ἀποκατάστασις πάντων* (3:21). To be sure, this cyclical idea is not carried through consistently because there is no thought of another repetition of the cycle, but rather through the scheme of eschatology the cycle is completed and cut off because fulfilled.

The past as delineated in the Bible of Israel is interpreted by this typological method in terms of the present. On the basis of fulfillment one recognizes the prefiguration as prophecy! There is no doubt that this method is not to be called historical, critical. There is here no historical concept in the modern sense, nor is there any doubt that by this method the truth of the Christ-event cannot be demonstrated; but if this method is not historical, nevertheless it has an historical significance because here again the attempt is evident to interpret individual historical events on the plane of providential design as prefiguration or fulfillment, as type or antitype, as a correspondence between the primitive and the final periods.[19] Whereas in our modern idea of history individual historical occurrences are related on the horizontal plane as cause and effect, in the typological interpretation the vertical relationship of God's plan of salvation is the cause of the unity of the aeons.[20] In contrast to our understanding of

may be seen in the sacrifice of Isaac as a prefiguration of the sacrifice of Christ. In *allegory* the correlation of historical events is missing. We find here that different features of a story (one feature can even be historical) are interpreted with regard to their deeper or real meaning and thus replaced by different qualities or truths or expected occurrences. The tendency of abstraction is prevailing. See especially, the method of Philo or the earliest Christian interpretation of the parables of Jesus (e.g., Matt. 13:36–43).

19. The classical formula is given by Barnabas 6:13: *ἰδού, ποιῶ τὰ ἔσχατα ὡς τὰ πρῶτα.*

20. Dobschütz, *loc. cit.*, pp. 212 ff., tries to prove (p. 222 f.), that typology as a temporal way of thinking is Jewish, while allegory is Greek or Hellenistic. This distinction is not tenable. Both methods work with the category of time, but both work also with space, as soon as they turn to cosmological perspec-

history, namely through posing questions to the sources and opening ourselves to be questioned by them, in this method a hermeneutic is employed which brings with it knowledge about the present and projects, or better retrojects, it into the past. Thus the past serves as a confirmation of the knowledge which faith gives with regard to the present, but this does not strike us as a question directed to us and affecting us.

Now alongside of and co-ordinated with this interpretation, which later was so profoundly influential,[21] stands the other conception which is interested only in the present, the *kairos*, in men between the aeons, in the new being, in the new creature in Christ. Here Christ is the end of a development and actually in His person and work He is the end of history. Here the eschaton is already present. Death is overcome already, sin is set aside already, the Christian is basically no longer in the flesh but in the Spirit. The Christian as a new creation is thus emancipated from the world, in spite of his being in this world, and therefore beyond history.[22]

But Paul has *both* of these conceptions: the apocalyptic, which concerns itself with a plan of redemption, and the existentialist,

tives. In other words, *both* methods, the allegorical and the typological, have their roots in Hellenistic thought and represent alterations or changes of the Old Testament scheme of prophecy and fulfillment. They are demonstrating the Hellenistic attempt to solve the hermeneutical problem, namely, to understand the events of the past for the present. That there is a concern for spatial thinking with the Greeks and a priority for time with the Jews is beyond discussion. See also the excellent monograph by T. Boman, *Das hebräische Denken im Vergleich mit dem griechischen* (1952), pp. 104 ff.

21. The early Church and medieval theology, with the exception of Augustine, have taken up and developed only the one side of Paul, the *οἰκονομία* conception, the idea of a plan of God. In the apologetic interest of the early Church the delay of the parousia and its everlasting truth had to be explained; this was done in outlining inferences of the *οἰκονομία* idea, which is in itself a Jewish apocalyptic one. Cullmann, *op. cit.*, unfortunately delineates only this idea and asserts that it is *the* biblical one. However, he eliminates the *καιρός* conception, which is even more characteristic for the eschatological faith of earliest Christianity.

22. Cf., for instance, Phil. 3:19 f., which describes in other words the statement of I Cor. 7:29 ff.

which emphasizes the fulfillment in the now and in the kairos. Yet if we ask what is common to the two concepts, we are brought to *the picture of man* whereby our problem is again thrown into a new perspective.

Greek and Roman antiquity looked on man as a part and organic member of the cosmos, and each individual had the capacity to develop himself into a work of art. But for Paul man is never able to arrive by his own power and is never thought of as a part of the cosmos. Man for Paul is first of all a *persona* (in the Augustinian sense) when he surrenders himself to Christ, when he surrenders himself in service to his neighbor and lives through power from beyond himself. In antiquity, history is seen in relation to nature and is integrated with it. But in Paul, as well as in Jesus and the Old Testament, history fulfills itself independently of nature. For Paul history means the perpetually new decision of the individual.

Thus as critical and discriminating historians and theologians we cannot get away from the conclusion that in Paul two conceptions of eschatology are in tension *and* in balance, two ways of knowing time and temporal occurrences. We have *on the one hand* a conception related to Jewish apocalyptic in its variations of a divine plan of salvation, of an οἰκονομία. Here the emphasis is upon the nearness of the final drama of the parousia of Christ, of the last judgment, of the general resurrection of the dead. Here we have eschatological perspective on time. *On the other hand* we have an existentialist conception of eschatology and time in which the past and the future are drawn together in the present, in the kairos, in which there is a radical conversion into the present of that which eschatologically has taken place. It is primarily in this second conception that the problem of history as the problem of *man's temporal being* comes to the fore. In other words, the anthropological theme finally emerges.[23]

23. With Paul the two conceptions of "history" correspond finally to the *indicative* (*now* is the time of salvation, we as Christians *have* overcome sin and death, Rom. 6) and to the *imperative* (the time of fulfillment is at hand, therefore . . . .). Just as these two elements of Paul's theology are correlated,

Paul, however, is not the only author in the New Testament, even though he is the earliest. As we go further, we shall pursue these two already delineated concepts. We look first at those writings in which most markedly we observe an interest in the plan of salvation entailing a temporal perspective and historical future.

2. THE SYNOPTIC WRITERS

We commence with the Synoptic Gospels. A word of explanation, however, is necessary at the outset. Our Evangelists were not biographers of the historical Jesus of Nazareth, rather they were redactors who collected and set into a literary framework oral traditions of the words of Jesus and the stories about Jesus, particularly with reference to his passion, already largely cast in fixed molds. But in assembling this material the Evangelists also worked into it their own theological point of view. As members of the Christian community they interpreted the tradition which lay before them, and in their interpretation, they presupposed faith in Jesus Christ, the crucified and the risen Messiah. An established result, at any rate for those who are dedicated to critical scholarship, is that no longer can we assume that the Christian congregation, in the course of its history, started out with Mark and then proceeded to elaborate the Gospel in Matthew and Luke. Rather we must realize that Mark's Gospel also is a fruit of the selective and formative work of the congregation in an earlier stage, just as the Gospel of Matthew in a later. For that reason we cannot methodologically assume that in Mark we have a life of Jesus which can be taken simply as history and in which one can regard the dogmatics of Mark as the dogmatics of Jesus.[24] If we so approach the question, what can we say

so also the *οἰκονομία* and the *καιρός* conception. Not by chance are the two balanced *and* in tension, since this balance and tension are reflecting one's being " in between."

24. Albert Schweitzer, " The Struggle Against Eschatology," *The Quest of the Historical Jesus* (1911), pp. 241 ff., somehow was *nolens-volens* a follower of this assertion.

with regard to the theology of the Synoptic Evangelists as over against the theology of Paul or the message of the historical Jesus?

In Mark 13:1–27 we have a passage which is commonly designated as the Synoptic apocalypse.[25] Plainly this passage is not to be ascribed to Jesus. Rather it is a unit in which, indeed, single words of Jesus may be incorporated, but in its totality it is a later composition in which an original Jewish apocalypse has been attributed to Jesus.[26] Whether the Evangelist Mark composed this passage or merely took it over from some other source is difficult to say, and for our present purpose, inconsequential. In any case an historical situation is reflected here which is characterized by the postponement of the parousia of Christ and by a growing reflection concerning the future. That is to say, the delay in the final act of history, the parousia, has become a problem and apologetic reflection has begun, one which

25. Mark 13:3–36 = Luke 21:7–36 = Matt. 24:3–36. The "little Apocalypse" has its real beginning in Mark 13:3, not 13:1. Mark 13:1 f. is a separated logion, which belongs to the preceding dialogue in the temple. The two verses have, of course, an apocalyptic character, expecting perhaps the destruction of the temple, together with the arrival of God's Reign. In secondary texts Mark 13:2 is harmonized with 14:58 (15:29) = Matt. 26:61 (27:40); cf. Acts 6:14. In Mark 13:3 ff. the temple is not destroyed! Mark 13:3 ff. is highly complicated in its different layers. Basic is the observation that the question of v. 4 is twofold and that the answer for the first question is given in vv. 30 ff. Matt. 24 combines Mark 13 and Luke 17:22–7; the latter is a tradition of Q (see n. 28), but does not present an authentic entity. For recent research dealing with our passage, see F. C. Grant, *The Earliest Gospel* (1943), p. 63; C. J. Cadoux, *The Historic Mission of Jesus* (1941), pp. 11 f., 273 f.; V. Taylor, *The Gospel According to Mark* (1952), pp. 636 ff. Fantastic is M. Barth, *Der Augenzeuge* (1946), pp. 127 ff.; most informative about the discussion is Kümmel, *op. cit.*, pp. 88 ff.

26. C. C. Torrey, *Documents of the Primitive Church* (1941), pp. 12 ff., thinks that Mark 13 (with the exception of 13:14a) is a unit in itself and probably goes back to the historical Jesus. That the passage as a whole cannot be traced back to the preaching of Jesus has its evidence in the contrast to Luke 17:20. I consider as Jewish apocalyptical fragments: Mark 13:7 f., 12, 14–20, 24–7, partially following R. Bultmann, *Geschichte der Synoptischen Tradition* (2d ed. 1931), p. 129.

seeks to explain the postponement. Whereas Jesus said: " The time is fulfilled and the Reign of God is at hand, Repent " (Mark 1:15) and " The Reign of God comes not with signs to be observed " (Luke 17:20), now, after the manner of the apocalypses, anticipatory signs of the coming of God's Reign are given, and its appearance is subjected to observation (contrary to Luke 17:20), although the beginning of these anticipatory signs remains uncertain. In Mark 13 the coming of God's Lordship in the form of the advent of the Son of Man is bound up with the coming of the end of the world and the end of history and is described in terms of the Jewish apocalyptic scheme of the two aeons. Signs of the end are the appearance of false prophets and Messiahs (Mark 13:5 f., 21–3), wars and natural catastrophes (Mark 13:7 f.), as well as severe persecution of the disciples of Jesus (Mark 13:9–13). Nevertheless, before the end the Gospel will be proclaimed to all peoples (Mark 13:10). Further, the distress of the last days in Judea is particularly described. The abomination of desolation will appear, standing where it ought not, namely, in the temple of the holy city, and speedy flight from the houses is commanded (Mark 13:14–23). Then will follow darkening of the sun and the moon and the falling of the stars (Mark 13:24). Under these mighty signs, the Son of Man will appear and through His angels will gather the elect from all of the four winds (Mark 13:26 f.). This entire section reflects clearly the experiences of the congregation and their speculations about the postponement of the end.[27] It has nothing to do with the preaching of Jesus where the Reign of God is announced as coming suddenly and immediately and where any observation of signs is expressly forbidden. Here we find ourselves in a situation in which the attempt is being made to use the experiences of history, which did not correspond to the message of Jesus, as themselves a prediction;

27. The experiences of the earliest Church are even more clearly stated in the additions of Matt. 24:12 to Mark 13:13 *ψυγήσεται ἡ ἀγάπη τῶν πολλῶν*. The term *οἱ ἐκλεκτοί* in Mark 13:20, 22, 27, never occurs elsewhere in the Synoptic tradition; besides, the passage as such is already suspicious because it is the only composition of a speech of Jesus within Mark.

but the entire reflection concerning that which must yet take place before the end of the world and the judgment shows at the same time a mood of resignation, and the sense of standing in the midst of the kairos plainly is disappearing. Doubt is growing, and speculation with regard to the future sets in, that is, with reference to the coming history which must unroll before the parousia. At the same time, the coming event is conceived in cosmic and mythological terms as the final judgment, as the world drama, and the ultimate catastrophe. The certainty of being at the end of the times is waning, indeed already in the final stage. Time and history have become a speculative problem.

This is even plainer in the Gospel of Matthew, which has as its source the Gospel of Mark together with a collection of the sayings of Jesus.[28] All these have been worked over. Here, too, the postponement of the parousia is a problem, and that is why it emphasizes " The day will come as a thief in the night " (Matt. 24:43; Luke 12:39; Matt. 25:1–13). The idea that this day is the end of this world is a peculiarity of the Gospel of Matthew, and because of the preferential place occupied by this Gospel in the later history, it was peculiarly influential on the Church's subsequent understanding of the message of Jesus.[29] Only in Matthew do we find the expression *συντέλεια τοῦ αἰῶνος*, that is, the close of the age (Matt. 13:39, 49; 24:3; 28:20).[30] This end

28. We here presuppose the theory—indeed a hypothesis for sixty years, but not yet replaced by any better solution—that besides Mark there was an independent source containing mainly sayings of Jesus. This hypothetical source is called Q (from the German *Quelle*, meaning " source "). Where Matthew and Luke have material in common which is not taken from Mark, Q is the probable source.

29. See also the influence of Matt. 25:31 ff. upon early Christian art.

30. The apocalyptic scheme of two aeons is found as well in Matt. 12:32 (against Mark 3:28 f. and Luke 12:10) as in Mark 10:30 ff. (= Luke 18:30 against Matt. 19:29) and in Luke 20:34 f. (against Mark 12:25 = Matt. 22:30). In all these passages we see an increasing predilection for the conception of the two *αἰῶνες*. On the whole it is remarkable that the specific apocalyptic terminology is rarely represented in the Synoptic tradition. The expression *συντέλεια τοῦ αἰῶνος* in Matt. 13:49 may go back to the teaching of Jesus, in spite of the fact that the interpretation of this term in the context

of the world coincides with the coming of the Son of Man; with regard to his coming thère is an extensive section at the end of chapter 24 and in chapter 25. An interest here is unmistakable, not simply in time as such but also in history as an integrated context of events. This interest is directed to the future *before* the coming of the parousia and also to the past. It is not without significance that in this Gospel the figure of Jesus is transformed into the divine, and on this account we have the relations of the antecedent history of Jesus, his genealogy, and his miraculous birth, in order to provide an historical basis for the divine Sonship of Jesus. This is all of a piece with the appeal to the fulfillment of prophecy. We have here a piece of apologetic, a kind of historical proof. To this end Matthew often uses in varied form the expression, " All this took place to fulfill that which had been spoken by the prophet " (Matt. 1:22, 2:17, 8:17, 13:35, 21:4, 27:9). In this way the drama of redemption in Jesus Christ is brought into unity with Old Testament prophecy, and through the scheme of prophecy and fulfillment, the present time is itself interpreted as fulfillment. This proof, from a prophecy which confirms the truth of that which happens in the present and correspondingly strengthens the meaning of the present, is derived from a genuine Old Testament view of a teleological course of history and has as its presupposition the concept of a linear course of time. To be sure, this picture is not to be regarded as that which the Evangelist Matthew had consciously made his own, for at the same time he makes use of the typological method, which rests upon a cyclical concept of time. This means that the Evangelist had not reflected on the presuppositions of his method and was ready to use the cyclical or the linear. He had not seen the problem. His perspective on time, which he developed mythologically into a final drama, was rather naïve, that is to say, nonreflective.

The literary man among the Synoptists was Luke. Was he a historian in our sense? Certainly of all the authors in the New

seems to be secondary. See also J. Jeremias, *Die Gleichnisse Jesu*, pp. 66 f.; Cadoux, *op. cit.*, p. 200; and Bultmann, *Theology*, *1*, 5.

Testament he comes the closest to it in that he sees connections and endeavors to explore their meanings and explains sequences through a motive and a power, which is for him the working of the Holy Spirit. He is indeed more concerned than the other Synoptists with history as a luminous continuity of events, so that, with a grain of salt, we may refer to him as the historian of the apostolic age. The prefaces to the Gospel and the Acts of the Apostles reveal a writer who wishes to be an historian and who will relate that which has occurred accurately (ἀκριβῶς) and orderly (καθεξῆς). His purpose is to record a portion of Christian history. The very fact that Luke writes in literary fashion points to a period which could not conceive of an event without anticipations—literature always reckons with a temporal future—and the manner of his writing marks an epoch in early Christian composition.[31] This is less true of the Gospel, where the earlier materials were merely more closely integrated and arranged in literary style, than for the Acts of the Apostles, where the author in part had no precursors and displays his tendency to universalism, even expresses his concept of the restoration of all things (ἀποκατάστασις πάντων). The transition from the mission of Peter to the mission of Paul, the road from Palestine over Asia Minor and Greece to Rome, was, in fact, an historical datum which demanded form and meaning. This has to do not with stories but with history. And now the motive of the mission comes into the foreground as an historical and a theological factor. The point which appeared in Mark in the Synoptic apocalypse (13:10) and then at the end of Mark (16:15), and which in Matthew (28:18–20) was emphasized as the commission of the risen Lord, becomes in Luke (Luke 24:47 and Acts 1:8) the hidden motive of his two works, namely that the announcement of the message must go into all the world *before* the parousia.

The inferences of this conception are twofold: 1) For Luke the

31. Cf. M. Dibelius, *Aufsätze zur Apostelgeschichte* (1951), p. 165; I am dependent in this section upon Dibelius' book and upon Jackson, Lake, and Cadbury, *The Beginnings of Christianity*. Cf. also O. Bauernfeind, *Die Apostelgeschichte*, Leipzig, 1939.

early Christian " in-between " becomes a time for the unfolding of an economy of world history. The event of Christ Jesus at the beginning of the Christian Church and the expected parousia at the end are the frame, the borderlines of history. In the midst of this frame world history as an economy-plan progresses. 2) Luke explains historical events on the line of cause and effect. He recognizes immanent contingencies and thus inaugurates a " history of salvation." *The secularization of history in Christian theology begins with Luke.* And secularization means also universalism. The event of Christ Jesus is fixed into a chronology, connected with secular occurrences (Luke 1:5, 2:1–3, 3:14, etc.).

With Luke we stand in the last quarter of the 1st century, probably in Antioch, and we have before us a strongly Hellenized Evangelist. His mind takes the immediacy of the present as a point of departure, and he interprets and sees the past, the present, and future in a nexus of events. The transition from a time of the eschatological expectation of the imminent event has passed over into a time when the end of history and of the world is projected indefinitely into the future, and all this has taken place in Luke without any observable disillusionment.

3. THE LETTER TO THE HEBREWS

From Syria we go to Egypt where presumably the so-called Letter to the Hebrews was composed, presumably, also in the last quarter of the 1st century. Perhaps in this letter, more markedly than in any other book of the New Testament, we have a concept and an interpretation of past, present, and future in the sense that may be called the divine plan of salvation. The author desires to present to the now acutely imperiled congregation their situation before God and in the world, which stretches before their eyes in the realm of time. He must, therefore, set forth the historical situation and the historical past of the Christian congregation. The point of departure is this: now at the end of these days God has spoken to us through Christ (Heb. 1:2), now at the end of the ages Christ is revealed (Heb. 9:26; cf. The Shepherd of Hermas, sim. IX, 12, 3). This means that our author knows nothing less than an historical Now and that the present is to be understood as a definite transition from an old to a new aeon. Again this awareness of the situation, this knowledge of an eschatological Now is found to be a problem. The enthusiastic tone of Paul has disappeared. Paul could write to the Romans: " salvation is nearer to us now than when we first believed. The night is far spent, the day is at hand " (Rom. 13:11 f.). The author of the Letter to the Hebrews—who he was we do not know, that he was not Paul we may be sure—has to encourage the congregation with exhortations which plainly show that the confidence of standing at the end of the epochs directly before the great break in history and the incoming of the time of salvation has grown feeble. The tenor now is: " Cast not away, therefore, your confidence which has great recompense of reward, for you have need of patience that after you have done the will of God, you might receive the promise. For yet a little while and He that shall come, will come and will not tarry " (Heb. 10:35 f.). Plainly with reference to the last events and in view of the delay, the time in between is regarded as a problem, and therefore he makes the attempt to confirm the certainty of the coming by arguments taken from the past and prophecy.[32] This leads, on the one hand, to a depicting of the future as an epoch of salvation, a period of rest (*κατάπαυσμα*), a Sabbath (*σαββατισμός*). The present life is looked upon as a pilgrimage. On the other hand, the past is compared with the present. The accent is laid also upon the future, but without the expectation that the future is imminent.

The idea of history appears in the Epistle to the Hebrews in that a chain of faithful witnesses separated from the world through a sure hope in ultimate salvation reaches from the old covenant in the past through the present to the future (Heb. 11:1–12:6). The emphasis is laid upon a future which is still

32. W. Manson, *The Letter to the Hebrews*, 1951, is correct in stressing the eschatological tenor of our letter. Unfortunately, the author has not made use of E. Käsemann, *Das wandernde Gottesvolk*, 1938, where the motive of " pilgrimage " is demonstrated on the basis of pre-Christian Gnostic sources. The motive as such was recently also taken up by C. Spicq, *L'Epitre aux Hébreux* (Paris 1952), Vol. *1*, Introduction.

closed but unquestionably sure, which lies on the other side of world history in heaven, beyond the continuity of time. This eschatology makes the present for the Christian a suffering and militant pilgrimage in which Christ is the precursor and Christians are to follow in His steps. This conception tends to dissociate the presence of Christians from the world and to make them strangers upon the earth (Heb. 11: 13), but this lifting of human existence out of the world also means a dissociation from historical reality. It means that history is taken out of the existence of Christians. This is all with reference to the coming break in history. By reason of hope which is identical with faith, the future, the " city which is to come " (Heb. 13: 14), is already drawn into the present. And out of this hope arises the power to understand the present life of conflict, persecution, and suffering in a positive sense, namely that the love of God and the grace of Christ can be understood as operative in the midst of this suffering.

4. THE DELAY IN THE PAROUSIA AND THE PROBLEM OF HISTORY

We have seen thus far in the writings of the New Testament, both in the preaching of Jesus and in Paul, that the fundamental notion was the knowledge of the nearness of God's Lordship. We have seen, furthermore, that in the Synoptic Gospels, and particularly in Mark and Matthew, the postponement of the parousia was explained and gave occasion for reflection with regard to the period of history which must elapse before the parousia. Parables were placed in the mouth of Jesus which undoubtedly had their origin in this period of the deferred parousia and which exhort to watchfulness in the lengthening time (particularly Matt. 25: 1–13).[33] The disillusionment is mitigated in that Jesus Himself gives instructions for the deferred parousia. In the Acts of the Apostles the expectation of the imminent end no longer plays a role. The parousia of Christ has lost its theological import. The

33. See G. Bornkamm in *In Memoriam Ernst Lohmeyer* (1951), pp. 116 ff.

Gospel is on the march throughout the world in an apparently unthreatened continuity of time. The Letter to the Hebrews points in the same period to a crisis, namely that the suffering through persecution has produced weariness and weakening of faith. No longer is the Christian able to make the original confession of hope (Heb. 10:23, ὁμολογία τῆς ἐλπίδος). The eschatology has become a *theologoumenon*, a theoretical utterance, a chapter in dogmatic theology, which no longer has any existential significance. The author of the epistle makes every effort to stress the reality of that which is about to come and to prove it. The picture given in the Deutero-Pauline letters to the Colossians and Ephesians shows that the question of the immediate expectation of the parousia plays no decisive role. Likewise the Pastoral Letters no longer find the delay of parousia to be a problem. The incorporation of eschatological Christianity into the world as an enduring force has already begun. The eschatological community, the Church as the *Qahal Yahweh*, has become an historical Church. And the historical Church demands acceptance of churchly doctrine. This development is brought to a conclusion in II Peter. The doubt thrown upon Christian eschatology by the continuance of world history is cited: " Where is the promise of His coming, for ever since the fathers fell asleep, all things have continued as they were from the beginning of creation " (II Pet. 3:4), and the answer is this that God has other reckonings than do men. " With the Lord one day is as a thousand years, and a thousand year as a day " (II Pet. 3:8), but this only reveals the embarrassment which had arisen from the unfulfilled expectation. One must return time and history to God and abandon human reckoning. The relativity of time is stressed, and actually the parousia is no longer conceived as that which must first come to pass. Disillusionment with regard to the delay leads over into a theology of history, a theology of the history of salvation which operates with the concept of a world mission, of a " pedagogy of mankind," or with the idea of a thousand year interval. That under these circumstances the Second Letter to the Thessalonians should take over the Jewish idea of an adversary, a son of perdition, and a rebellion prior to the final victory is readily understandable. The theology of history thus becomes a teleology of history.

We may say then that the history of the world and of mankind became a conscious problem only after the expectation of the imminent end of the parousia had gone through a crisis. The continuance of history with reference to the expectation of the end of history led thus to a recognition of history as a problem. It is decisive that history itself discloses its problematic nature in the refutation of the early Christian expectation of the near approach of the end.

We must add, of course, a somewhat more precise delineation, for the transition took place only gradually. If we survey the whole, the development appears to have gone forward without a break and without difficulty, as can be seen in the Pastoral Letters, the Letter to the Hebrews, or I and II Clement and the Shepherd of Hermas. But on the other side, the development is not uniform.[34] The Book of Revelation, which received its present form at the end of the 1st century, shows a renewal of the eschatological expectation in very vivid forms. It brings in the new trait that the eschatology applies not only to God and man but also to God and world history whereby generalizations are carried over from man to the history of mankind.[35]

The disunity of the eschatology of the New Testament and in the apostolic and postapostolic age cannot be brought into order through an historical development. We can observe a tendency that runs through the development, but we cannot deduce from it a law of development. We recognize, to be sure, that the deferment of the parousia now and again makes the problem crucial as to the meaning of the further course of history from the point of view of the history of salvation. The outcome is that

34. Cf. R. Bultmann in *Man in God's Design* (1952), p. 42, where the one-sided picture of M. Werner, *Die Entstehung des christlichen Dogmas* (1941), is corrected.

35. Cf. L. Goppelt, " Heilsoffenbarung und Geschichte nach der Offenbarung des Johannes," *Theologische Literaturzeitung*, 77 (1952), 513 ff.

eschatology ceases to be the very basis of the early Christian faith and instead becomes one chapter among others in early Catholic dogmatic theology. From this two things result: first, the ethic becomes an independent discipline dissociated from the eschatology, and second, the *καιρός* idea, which was well balanced with the *οἰκονομία* conception in Paul, is replaced by the doctrine of the Holy Spirit and then by an early Catholic sacramentalism.

5. HISTORY ACCORDING TO JOHN

The problems which have thus emerged are implicitly solved in the Johannine writings, the Gospel and the letters. Here we have a conception reminiscent of the kairos view of Paul, that is an eschatology made present through the way of conceiving time. And since the Johannine writings come at the end of the 1st century in a later stage of theological interpretation and stylistic form, and since historiography was foreign to the thought of the author, we must see in these writings the last great protest of the early Christian attitude against incipient early Catholicism. Who the author of these writings was we do not know; that the Gospel and the letters go back to the same author is probable. Neither are we in a position to determine the precise locale of these writings, but that the Orient is speaking here, that Aramaic tradition has been incorporated, that Semitic thought and pre-Christian Gnostic mythology are here combined, all of this can be said with highest probability.[36]

This historical significance of that which happened in Christ and its implications for man in faith, apart from any naïve chronological reckoning, is the theme of John. Past and future are brought together in Christ, and likewise, become a unity in the believing man. The accent again is on the present, upon the Now. That which is to come is made absolutely present. The future will bring nothing which is decisively new.

"Truly, truly I say to you, the hour is coming and now is

36. Cf. Bultmann, *Theology*, Vol. 2 (1955), and C. H. Dodd, *The Interpretation of the Fourth Gospel.*

when the dead will hear the voice of the Son of God and those who hear will live " (John 5:25). " Truly, truly I say to you he who hears my word and believes Him who sent me has eternal life. He does not come into judgment, but has passed from death to life " (John 5:24). Jesus said to her (Martha): " I am the resurrection and the life. He who believes in me though he die yet shall he live, and whoever lives and believes in me shall never die " (John 11:25 f.). " Now is the judgment of this world. Now shall the ruler of this world be cast out " (John 12:31). " He who believes in Him [Christ] is not condemned. He who does not believe is condemned already because he has not believed in the name of the only Son of God. And this is the judgment, that the light has come into the world and men love darkness rather than light because their deeds were evil " (John 3:18 f.).

These quotations make it plain that for John the eschatological crisis is accomplished in the present and precisely there where man hears or rejects the Word of God. Here and now is the eschatological hour. In faith, life has been given in the absolute sense; in unbelief, however, condemnation is already present. For John the parousia, the resurrection from the dead, and the judgment are already accomplished in Jesus Christ. The coming of Jesus as the Son and the Word of God into the world and His return out of the world to the Father constitute the eschatological event (cf. John 3:1–21, 31–6; 7:15–36), and wherever man knows himself to be confronted by this event, judgment is pronounced upon him both as κρίσις and κρίμα. That is to say, in the confrontation with Jesus or the Word which He proclaims, judgment operates as division whereby belief or unbelief are made manifest in man. Life or death, light or darkness appear. Thus the eschatological judgment has become entirely present, kairos in the pregnant sense of the decisive moment in the eschatological occurrence (cf. the usage in John 7:6, 7). If now the eschatology of John applies to the present for the Christian, then consequently the apocalyptic idea of a cosmic drama at the end of history falls out of the picture. That is why we read (John 9:39) that Jesus *came* (ἦλθεν) for judgment upon the world, and the present is not a time between the times, but it is the definitive consummation which does not have to wait for any end of the drama yet to come.

This is not an eschatological perspective on time. It is not the idea of the οἰκονομία. There is no waiting for any *telos*, for any development in time; nor is there any reflection about time. And for the first time there is no trace of the dualism of the aeons derived from Jewish apocalyptic and running through the other New Testament writings. Also, the combination of the concept of salvation with cosmology is lacking. Instead there is the dualism taken from Gnosticism between light and darkness, truth and falsehood, believers and world, that which is above and that which is below.[37]

If, then, in John there is no conception of an eschatological future in the sense of the temporal, if there is no interest in the history of the past but only a contemporizing of eschatology, then history has assumed an entirely existential category, and what has taken place in the world is to be judged with reference to the *krisis* in Jesus Christ. It is, of course, something that has happened among men and is never to be dissociated from man. In other words, history here becomes an anthropological entity. Thereby the historicity of man comes to expression, namely, that man through faith in Christ moves from decision to decision, and the end of history is sought in the vertical while the horizontal relationship in time is regarded as an indifferent ground for life.

37. In giving this outline of the Johannine eschatology we presuppose that R. Bultmann, *Das Evangelium des Johannes* (2d ed. 1950), is right in his basic assumption, that our present Fourth Gospel is the result of a later churchly revision, which however, still preserves essential parts of the first conception. It is only in this first conception that we find the unbroken καιρός eschatology; the churchly revision adds passages with a temporal eschatology, thus including the οἰκονομία line. The fact of this addition is of course remarkable, since the καιρός idea is not eliminated but complemented, so that finally both ideas are presented. The difference between Paul and the churchly revision of John is this: with Paul the two conceptions are balanced and correlated; in John they are obviously in tension and somehow contradicting. Bultmann's hypothesis is not accepted by Dodd, *The Interpretation of the Fourth Gospel*, or E. C. Colwell and E. L. Titus, *The Gospel of the Spirit*, 1953.

Here again, then, is the faith that in Christ the end of history has come. We are never able to go beyond it because here past and present are conjoined. The causes of human life lie on the other side of the world and history, even though they may be within its domain. The key for this eschatological existence of man is to be found in *agape*, in love.[38]

IV. SUMMARY AND A RESUMPTION OF THE QUESTION CONCERNING THE IDEA OF HISTORY

1) The course thus far followed through the New Testament and the varied stages of the earliest Church reveals with all of the nuances essentially two distinguishable concepts of time and eschatology. In the one, the parousia is expected as coming either immediately or remotely in the future and, correspondingly, the present time is conceived as a progress toward the cosmic conclusion of the drama, i. e., the final act of the history of the world and salvation. Here there is reflection about the economy, about God's design; and the more time goes on, the more acute is the problem from the standpoint of faith. The problem of the intervening time is felt more acutely where either the ethical conflict with the world calls for a Christian solution or where the deferring of the parousia constitutes an offense.

In the other concept, the contemporizing of eschatology in the *kairos*, in the *krisis*, in the *pneuma hagion*, in the *zoē*, yes, in the *kainē ktisis* is completed and is not referred to any decisive, final act of God in the future. In fact, especially in the Johannine concept, the decisive break in the history of the world has already taken place in the past, in the incarnation and the exaltation of the Son of God. The future does not appear to bring anything essentially new. The history of redemption is fulfilled, and in the present faith already there is the transition from death to life, " The old has passed away. Behold, the new *has come* " (II Cor.

38. John 13:32–5; cf. R. Bultmann, *Das Evangelium des Johannes*, pp. 403 ff., 417 f.

5: 17). However, even here the new is not without its problems, but in his historical existence the Christian is always confronted by situations demanding new decisions.

2) Before we take up the question whether these two concepts of eschatology are mutually exclusive, because they are logically incompatible, we must inquire after historical sources for both conceptions whether they are genuine anticipations or only analogies. Finally, the historian who stands in the succession of the Greek conception of history must seek in every direction for connections and anticipations.

The *first* of the above-mentioned conceptions, which assumes a final act and connects the return of Christ with the end of the world, is plainly derived from the tradition of Jewish apocalyptic. Here we have the apocalyptic teaching of the aeons, which in turn goes back to Iranian sources and was transmitted to Judaism during and after the period of the Babylonian captivity.[39] The only specifically Christian element in this eschatology is that *Jesus Christ constitutes the turning point of the aeons.* With Jesus Christ either the concluding aeon or the intermediate aeon of the Messianic time begins, but the chronological structure expressed in the teaching of aeons is apocalyptic, not genuinely Christian. Our modern chronological scheme with its division of the two aeons, before and after Christ, is a secularized survival of this Jewish apocalyptic reckoning according to aeons and is Christianized only because it is brought into relationship with the birth of Christ. But it would be false to see in this the New Testament theology of history.[40]

Fourth Ezra says: " The Highest has created not one aeon, but two " (IV Ezra 7: 50, 8: 1).[41] What we have here is simply a

39. Cf. W. Bousset, *Die Religion des Judentums* (3d ed. 1927), pp. 242 ff., 478 ff.

40. Cullmann, *op. cit.*, pp. 17 ff., is following this line of thought, as is T. Preiss, " The Vision of History in the New Testament," *The Journal of Religion*, *30* (1950), 157 ff.

41. See also IV Ezra 7: 112 f.: *praesens saeculum non est finis* . . . ; 8: 1: *saeculum futurum*; 7: 47: *saeculum venturum*. Cf. Syriac Apocalypse of Baruch: 83: 8: *utrumque saeculum*.

further development of that which was already to be found in the Slavic Enoch, namely, the differentiation of one aeon as the period of the world and another as the period yet to come of timelessness and eternity. Plainly there is here an influence of Parsiism.[42] And all of the additional elements derivative from this scheme, such as the intermediate interval, the appearance of an antichrist, and the final judgment, are to be understood only in terms of apocalypticism. We saw at the beginning of this lecture that the preaching of Jesus assumes the structure of the apocalyptic view of the world but does not share the apocalyptical speculative interest. From this incorporation of the apocalyptic structure there emerges what has been called the history of salvation, in which the association of the word history with salvation carries, however, quite a different sense from that which is associated with history when applied to the world. And in the concept of the history of salvation, there are traits derived from Gnostic cosmology and therefore not from the apocalyptic. This is particularly plain in the letters to the Ephesians and the Colossians, where such ideas as the pre-existence of Christ serve to elevate Christ to the position of an associate in the creation and a reconciler of the entire cosmos, so that in this combination of the history of salvation with cosmology, the distinction between that which has occurred in history and that which has occurred in nature is entirely eliminated. Thus, we see that the concept of the *oikonomia* is made up of syncretistic components and is Christianized only because applied to Jesus Christ, the Redeemer in whom the Christian believes as the inaugurator of the new aeon.

It is not so easy to trace the sources and the analogies in the history of religion for the *second line* of approach, which contemporizes eschatology. It appears to me, however, that the decisive impulse is derived from pre-Christian Gnosticism.[43] At

42. Cf. W. Bousset, *op. cit.*, pp. 242–86; P. Volz, *Die Eschatologie der jüdischen Gemeinde* (2d ed. 1934), p. 63 ff., and H. Sasse in Kittel, *Th. W, 1*, 202 ff. See also T. Klauser, *Reallexikon für Antike und Christentum, 1*, 193 ff.

43. I am well aware that the presupposed phenomenon of a " pre-Christian Gnosis " is still a controversial point. In line with F. C. Burkitt, *Church and*

the outset we see clearly in the New Testament that the kairos conception is particularly current in the Hellenistic congregations where the christology was conceived in terms of the Gnostic myth of redemption. When the Gnostic myth of the " redeemed Redeemer " was applied to Jesus Christ and thereby made historical, then the pre-existent Son, who came down from heaven, assumed human form, humbled Himself even to the cross, and again returned to His Father in the heavenly home. The movement from above to below and from below to above is continued no further, for the cosmic victory of Christ is already accomplished with the resurrection and the ascension.[44] In all of this one observes the absolute stressing of the present as the time of salvation. And repeatedly the pre-Christian Gnostic vocabulary is employed to express the being and the having of the Christian. Yet one must also emphasize the differences, because the being and the having of the Christian in this charismatic present is no quality or guarantee as in Gnosticism, but is always something eschatologically conditioned. That is to say, it is given only in hope and in faith. One can find analogies in Philo, who himself was affected by Gnosticism; but in Philo as in Stoicism the kairos hope is converted into a human disposition, yes, even into human

Gnosis, 1932; R. P. Casey in *Journal of Theological Studies*, *36* (1935), 45 ff.; C. H. Dodd, *The Interpretation of the Fourth Gospel*; and W. D. Davies, *loc. cit.*, pp. 113 ff., the term Gnosis should be preserved for 2d century Christian Gnosis. On the other hand, we cannot deny the researches of W. Bousset, *Hauptprobleme der Gnosis*, 1907; R. Reitzenstein, *Das iranische Erlösungsmysterium*, 1921; H. Schlier, *Religionsgeschichtliche Untersuchungen zu den Ignatiusbriefen*, 1929; E. Käsemann, *Leib und Leib Christi*, 1933; W. Bauer, *Rechtgläubigkeit und Ketzerei im ältesten Christentum*, 1934; H. Jonas, *Gnosis und Spätantiker Geist*, 1934; R. Bultmann, *Das Evangelium des Johannes*, and *Theology*, *1*, 164 ff.; R. Bultmann in Kittel, *Th. W*, *1*, 688 ff. and the important article by W. Baumgartner in *Theologische Zeitschrift*, 1950. F. C. Grant in *JBL*, *71* (1952), 52 f., points out the scholarly divergencies, but agrees upon the existence of a pre-Christian Gnosis. The discussion is perhaps more one about its definition than one about its existence. Recently, Kurt Schubert in *Theologische Literaturzeitung*, *77* (1953), 495–506, has contributed a significant article to the problem.

44. Cf. Phil 2:5-11; Col. 1:19 f., 2:15; I Tim. 3:16; I Pet. 3:22.

wisdom (Sophia) and thereby is deprived of its historical basis. Nature and history are so blended in the Gnostic conception that it cannot serve to illuminate the paradoxical existence of man. In spite of the impulses derived from these sources one must recognize in *the contemporizing of eschatology a genuine Christian conception.* That which has happened in Christ is believed to be the final chapter in God's drama of salvation. The new aeon is already there and the resurrection of the dead has already commenced.

But perhaps one ought not to stress too heavily the Jewish apocalyptic and the pre-Christian Gnosticism as sources, because the basis for both conceptions may already be present in the preaching of Jesus. In His message that which is to come, the nearness of God's Reign, and at the same time, the charismatic present as a time of decision and repentance are equally emphasized. The disciples of John the Baptist came with a question: " Art thou He who is to come, or look we for another? " and the answer was, " Go tell John what you hear and see, the blind receive their sight and the lame walk, lepers are cleansed, and the deaf hear, and the dead are raised up, and the poor have good news preached to them. And blessed is he who takes no offense at me " (Matt. 11:3–6). At the same time Jesus taught His disciples to pray: " Thy kingdom come " (Matt. 6:10; Luke 11:2). With the emphasis on the future and the present in the preaching of Jesus we readily understand that after His crucifixion the early congregation developed these two points in terms both of Jewish apocalyptic and Hellenistic mythology.

3) The primary question of our theme remains yet to be answered, namely, *which idea of history is contained in the early Christian treatment of time and eschatology?* We have already seen that world history is not treated as a rational, intelligible unity. There is nothing whatever about history in the modern sense as conditioned by the ancient Greek usage. The idea is discoverable only implicitly when reference is made to the cosmos or to the nomos, when the reference is to the immanent world of men, i. e., the world and history which men themselves construct

or a world autonomy out of which man is redeemed by Jesus Christ. This is the meaning of the assertion that in Christ history comes to an end. Time still goes forward, of course, but history only seemingly continues. Any genuine development has ceased. In the presence of God it has terminated.[45]

To be sure, this concept is not carried through consistently and is not held in all of the writings of apostolic Christianity. There is, in fact, a development away from the eschatological perspective of time which we have designated as the kairos concept. The expectation of a concluding event in the program of salvation through the return of Christ plus the disillusionment with regard to the deferment of this event bring the problem of history into focus. Now on the basis of the past, a necessary period preceding the advent of the parousia is postulated, and a disposal of future events by God is prophesied in such fashion that a concept of the history of salvation is mapped out. Yet even this is not properly to be called the history of salvation, rather it is a view of those occurrences in the process of salvation which still remain to be completed, which God, one by one, will bring to pass. This " history " of salvation is of such a character that it does not rest on any laws of history within the structure of the world. One cannot talk about *res gestae* of the future in continuity with the past but only about *gesta Dei,* which have their meaning only in the still hidden will of God, though announced in Christ.

All of this adds up to the conclusion that one cannot derive a philosophy of history from the New Testament. One cannot extract a Christian methodology of history or any indication for a Christian periodization of history. The writings of apostolic Christianity provide no key to unlock the secret of world history and to determine its meaning. None of these attempts has support in the sources of our period. And for the Christians of the early Church, *the history of our human world remains a riddle.*[46]

What, then, are *the positive conclusions* of Christian eschatology

45. Against Cullmann, *op. cit.*, p. 92, who is without reason in attacking K. Barth, *Kirchliche Dogmatik, 2,* Pt. 1 (1940), 705 ff.

46. See K. Löwith, *The Meaning of History,* Chicago, 1947.

for our question about the idea of history? If, as we have insisted, eschatology contains a judgment on the present and the past, then we have here a judgment on that which *has* happened, even if we do not call it history. But that which has happened is bound to the category of time in the past, and as an object under judgment, provides an example for our question. History begins always with an interest in the past and is recognized as soon as coherences are seen. How, then, on the basis of Christian eschatology, is the past actually judged? The peculiarity that the judgment is rendered on the *men* of the past and specifically on their relationship to God and the understanding of the self to be derived therefrom at once comes to light. Derived from this point of view an entire people can come upon the scene, yet not as a political or a sociological entity but only as a community of men *before God*. The point of view, then, is *anthropological*. And in the New Testament *the past* is recognized as a modus of existence in which man has not yet begun to live by faith in Christ. The past is to be recognized as existing where the new aeon of salvation by faith in Christ has not begun. And the judgment on the past consists in this: that time is characterized by disobedience to the will of God, by an attempt on the part of man to construct a future for himself. This epoch is the age of the law, a time of transgression and failure, therefore an aeon of death. In mythological terms it is the time under condemnation by reason of Adam's fall. In nonmythological terms it is the time when man perverts religion into the deification of himself, and in so doing, displays actual disobedience against the God of creation. Obviously in this sense, the past is not conceived in historical but rather in anthropological terms, or more exactly we might say in *soteriological* terms, as the aeon *before the soteria* which has been disclosed in Christ.

The present begins at that point where man surrenders himself and relies upon Christ, when man experiences and recognizes himself as delivered through Christ, i. e., from the outside, from the beyond. At this point the new aeon in which the new powers are at work and in which man again attains to deeper freedom is disclosed and realized.

But this soteriological view of past and present, conditioned by the No or the Yes with reference to Christ, shows that finally the two aeons do not basically resolve each other, but that the resolution comes only through the decision in faith of the individual man. The past continues into the present at the very point where man denies Jesus as Christ. And here we see very plainly that past and present are *not seen as historical epochs* of universal validity.

Moreover where the New Testament talks about man as he stands under faith in Christ, that is, where the reference is made to the present in the sense above defined, this very present is itself to be understood as a condition of man in an *interval*, because for the present of the Christian the *no longer* of the *past* and the *not yet* of the *future* are decisive. And also the *continued working* of the *past* and the operation *already* of the *future* are determinative. In other words, here we have the paradoxical existence of faith which still lives in the world and history, yet is already emancipated from the world and history. Thus the problem of history is finally comprised in *the historicity of man.*[47]

The historicity of man consists in the fact that human beings are conditioned by their past, which they can neither transcend nor do away with, and by their future, namely, the threat of

47. We use the term historicity according to R. G. Collingwood, *The Idea of History* (1946), pp. 210 ff., and E. Frank, *Philosophical Understanding and Religious Truth* (Oxford, 1945), p. 133, n. 1. Frank says: " in a literal sense the word ' historicity ' can be applied only to men. Cf. R. G. Collingwood . . . It is the distinctive character of man not only to be, but to know that he is, and to actualize this knowledge. In being, thinking, and acting, he is always confronted, therefore, with what he himself and others before him have been, done, and thought. This is what I call his historicity. In this sense the term is used also by Collingwood and by contemporary German philosophers such as Jaspers and Heidegger." For Heidegger's definition, see especially, *Sein und Zeit, 1,* 19 f., 372 ff. An excellent treatment of history and historicity with regard to present theological issues was recently published by F. Gogarten, *Kirche und Entmythologisierung*, 1953. For a critical review of contemporary philosophies of history, see H. Ott, " Neuere Publikationen und Probleme von Geschichte und Geschichtlichkeit," *Theologische Rundschau, 21* (1953), 63–96.

the possible and the hope for bliss. In Christian thought this phenomenological situation is even more concrete: the believer in Christ is conditioned by a decisive event of the past, namely, Jesus Christ, and at the same time by an event expected in the future. The interval, which is characterized by the no longer and the not yet, stamps itself upon the Christian existence. The classic passage for this is given in Phil. 3:12–14: "Not that I have already obtained this or am already perfect; but I press on to make it my own, because Christ Jesus has made me His own. Brethren, I do not consider that I have made it my own; but one thing I do, forgetting what lies behind and straining forward to what lies ahead, I press on toward the goal for the prize of the upward call of God in Christ Jesus." Of course, the term historicity does not occur, but the phenomenon of man's historicity is clearly stated: man as *conditioned by his past*, which is always with him and which he tries to hold down on the basis of his knowledge in faith that Christ has made him His own. Faith in Christ means therefore that the Christ event is understood as a part of my own past because it occurred for me. And at the same time: man as *conditioned by his future*, which is conceived as the "goal for the prize of the upward call," as "what lies ahead." This future is not a mere fancy but a certainty marking my present, as certain as my own past which is with me.[48]

The historicity of man is perhaps best expressed in the Christian conception of freedom (ἐλευθερία) and of hope (ἐλπίς), which are special features of Christian faith (πίστις), according to the New Testament, especially Paul. Freedom means that the Christian is set free with regard to his own past, that he is able to transcend history as a nexus, that he can therefore decide within history for history and actualize his historicity. Hope means that the future is no more a threat of still hidden powers but is unlocked and disclosed and safe in God's hand. And this knowledge again sets in actions my own decision for history in its best possible way, because my intentions can be free from the danger that I might be caught again by my own self and my past.

48. Cf. R. Bultmann, *Theology*, *1*, 322.

This is finally and actually the positive contribution of the New Testament to the history of the idea of history: that history is not thought of in cosmological or metaphysical terms but in terms of the historicity of man. It is indeed an irony of history that this was forgotten after Augustine, not seen again before Søren Kierkegaard, and not taken up *explicitly* until our 20th century. It may be that the reason for this fact should be seen in our eschatological " neighborhood " to earliest Christianity.

Emphasizing thus the historicity of man as the decisive contribution of earliest Christianity to the idea of history, we must recognize also that the further development in the 2d, 3d and 4th centuries was much more concerned with the metaphysical problem of history than with a further definition of man's historicity.[49] In other words, the οἰκονομία conception, the idea of God's design with and within history and world history, became the predominant churchly interest. The dialectic statement of Paul and also the Johannine conception of the historical Now were forgotten.[50]

Looking upon the development as a whole we may say that the *Greeks* were the first to recognize time as a problem. The *Christians* of the New Testament first discovered the historicity of man. It remained for *Augustine* to raise alongside of these two problems the still more fundamental problem of history as such.

49. See also, Jean Daniélou, *Essai sur le mystère de l'histoire*, Paris, 1953, and K. Löwith, *The Meaning of History*. For Augustine cf. my article: " Augustins Geschichtsauffassung," *Schweizer Monatshefte, 34* (1954), 514–26.

50. The following article and monographs of importance for our theme were published after this paper was finished: R. Bultmann, " History and Eschatology in the New Testament," in *New Testament Studies, 1* (1954), 5–16; Conzelmann, *Die Mitte der Zeit*, Studien zur Theologie des Lukas, Tübingen, 1954; P. Minear, *The Christian Hope and the Second Coming*, Philadelphia, 1954; J. Munck, *Paulus und die Heilsgeschichte*, Aarhus, 1954.

PATRISTIC CHRISTIANITY

Roland H. Bainton

In this series we have been employing the concept of history as embracing the entire span of man's life in time upon this earth with the obvious sequence of birth, begetting, and death. The idea of history seeks to disclose other more elusive sequences, and possibly laws, to comprehend the meaning of the whole. This may be done by deductions from observation, but the Christian can never rest content to interpret events by events, nor will he essay to understand man's terrestrial course without invoking the celestial. The idea of history must encompass the origin and destiny of man.

Our concern is with early Christian thinking in the first five centuries after the New Testament and primarily in the East. This geographical delimitation is for this period, however, largely fictitious, for truly the twain did meet. To which, for example, would one assign Jerome writing in Latin at Bethlehem or Irenaeus writing in Greek at Lyons?

I. CHRIST THE END OF HISTORY

The point of departure for any such study must, of course, be the New Testament because Christian thinking was simply an elaboration, interpretation, and application amid the course of ongoing events of New Testament concepts. With regard to the significance of the New Testament for the idea of history two assertions have been made, apparently contradictory. The first is that Christ marked the end of history. The second is that Christianity for the first time supplied a meaningful philosophy of history. The first of these statements can be understood in more than one sense. If it means that Christ ended the sequence of births, begettings, and deaths, then obviously it is not true. What we can say is only this: that the early Church expected Christ to be the end of history. The assumption was that he would come again to inaugurate a new order in which there should be no marrying or giving in marriage, but this expectation was never realized, and in the words of II Peter 3:4, "All things continued as they were from the beginning of the world."

In another sense Christ may be said to have been the end of history in that he elevated men into a new dimension of living in which the immediacy of the vertical relationship to God superseded and almost obliterated the horizontal relationship of man to man. Paul affirmed that he no longer lived, but Christ lived in him.[1] And John asserted that they alone truly live who eat and drink of the Son of Man.[2] This view was amplified in the early Church into the doctrine of the deification of man, who in Christ becomes so truly a new creature as to put off corruptibility and mortality and to share in the very nature and being of God. According to Irenaeus, God became man in order that man might become God. The change was assumed to be effected particularly through the sacrament of the Lord's Supper, for just as the bread and wine after consecration are no longer common elements, so also is the believer altered, divesting himself of the distinctively human and putting on the divine nature.[3] He who thus becomes God with God is indifferent to and above space and time. Such thinking was congenial especially to the theologians of the East from Irenaeus to Athanasius and John of Damascus and explains why to this day the Eastern liturgy concludes the mass not with the cross but with the resurrection and the assurance of newness of life.[4]

Yet, not here is one to find the essence of the Christian concept of history. To begin with, this view is not specifically Christian. Did not the mystery cults also aspire to make man divine and immortal? Did not Plotinus pray for that experience of ecstasy in which the spatial and the temporal become unreal? Cannot one in fact say that mysticism spells the end of history? At the

1. Gal. 2:20.
2. John 6:53.
3. Irenaeus, *Against Heresies*, III, 18, 7; IV, 18, 5.
4. Cf. the works of Bauer, Bornhäuser, Butterworth, and Lot-Boradine.

same time mysticism does not end history. He who experiences ecstasy experiences it in the body. He who becomes oblivious to time will be snapped back by the crying of a babe or the burning of the toast, and even if the raptures of the mystic were continuous, which is never the case, he would be living two lives, in the spirit and in the flesh. The reader becomes vividly aware of this in perusing Bunyan's *Pilgrim's Progress*, for in the beginning, when Christian is distraught as to his destiny, his family seek to cure his distemper by "harsh and surly carriage," and he is compelled in consequence to set out upon his pilgrimage alone, but after the trumpets have sounded for him on the other side, we discover that his family have been with him in the flesh all the time, and he with them. The Christian, then, though not of this world, is not out of this world. He may be at times beyond time, but he lives in time. We may perhaps say that though he transcends history, he is enmeshed in history.

II. DELAY OF THE PAROUSIA

The early Christian fathers became increasingly aware of their involvement as time passed without the coming of the Lord. They began to consider when He would appear and why He delayed. Speculations with regard to His coming entailed a theory of history which was constructed by a combination of two Old Testament ideas. The first was that of the Sabbath rest, after the work of the week was done, on the seventh day. The other was the statement of Ps. 90 : 4: "For a thousand years in Thy sight are but as yesterday when it is past." The assumption, then, was that the course of world history would run for six thousand years. To calculate the end one must first have determined the beginning. This might be done by constructing a chronology for the Old Testament and thus arriving at the date of creation. This computation many of the early Christians attempted, but others preferred a much more fundamental mode of reckoning in terms of the amount of time required between the first and the second comings of Christ. Some time was plainly needed, because the Lord had distinctly said that before the end "The Gospel must be preached to all nations,"[5] and the Apostle Paul had envisaged the gathering in of the Jews.[6] Many of the fathers held that the denouement was being deliberately held back by God to provide time for the world mission of the Church. Some even interpreted the expression in II Thess. 2 : 7, "The power which restrains," as referring to the great missionary commission.[7]

How long would this take? Hippolytus answered that the work would require one half of a day of a thousand years. The incarnation of Christ was thus assumed to have fallen exactly in the middle of the sixth period and the end would be around A. D. 500. Since Hippolytus flourished at the beginning of the 3d century, this would leave close to three hundred years. Lactantius, in the days of Constantine, employed the same scheme, but since he was a century later than Hippolytus, the time before the coming of the Lord was reduced to approximately two hundred years. Such speculations continued in the West until St. Augustine broke with all millenarianism and projected the coming indefinitely into the future. In the East the development was not essentially different from that in the West. In the 2d century in Asia Minor Papias indulged in the lush imagery of Jewish apocalyptic and described the new imminent age in crassly materialistic terms; but these chiliastic expectations speedily declined. The Alexandrians spiritualized eschatology, and Gregory of Nyssa performed the same function as Augustine when he rejected the scheme of the Sabbath in the 7th millennium. Instead, for him, the seven thousand years embraced the whole of time without a break, and the Sabbath was the eighth period of eternity.[8]

Thereafter, alike in the East and the West, the established churches centered attention more on the day of judgment than on the return of the Lord. Recurrently, however, the masses

5. Mark 13 : 10.
6. Rom. 11.
7. Cullmann (1) and (2).
8. Daniélou (1) and Frick.

stimulated by some natural calamity, some unusual conjunction of the planets—for astrology was admitted to the courts of the Lord—would flare up in apocalyptic reveries. The year 1000 in the West in certain circles inspired such speculations, and in the East, curiously, the year 1492 was assumed to be the seven thousandth year from the creation of the world. In the West in the late 12th century Joachim of Fiore revived primitive eschatology by manipulations of the figure 1,260, the number of days spent by the woman in the Apocalypse in the wilderness, and these days converted into years. Even in Bolshevist Russia the authorities have been disturbed by popular agitations inspired through proclamations of impending cataclysms.[9] But the great established churches, perhaps precisely because they were established, have been less disposed to look for the end of the world, and even the church of the martyrs early grew dubious as to whether the end was soon to be desired, since the coming must be preceded by an accumulation of woes. Should the Christian then pray " Come quickly, Lord Jesus " [10] or for a delay of the end, *pro mora finis?* [11]

III. NOT CYCLES BUT SUCCESSIVE CREATIONS

The distinctive contribution of Christianity to the idea of history, then, was not the view that Christ had ended history. In a literal sense it was not true; and in a spiritual sense the life in the spirit was lived and was expected to be lived in the ongoing framework of events in time. The distinctive element lay rather in the flat rejection of the cyclical theory of the Greeks. A Christian could never have behaved like Scipio Africanus who, when he committed Carthage to the flames, wept not out of pity for the fifty thousand survivors whom he was about to enslave but only from the reflection that the revolving wheel of time

9. Vasiliev.

10. *Didache* X.

11. Tertullian, *Apology* XXXII and XXXIX. Cf. Bainton (2), n. 72.

would at long last bring the same fate to Rome.[12] The Christian could never say of Christ what Aristotle said of Plato: that in another age there might be another Plato. The Christian could not think of himself as living prior to the incarnation of God in Christ as Aristotle said that he was living prior to the fall of Troy quite as much as afterward, since in the recurrent cycle Troy would fall again.[13] "Once and for all Christ died unto sin."[14] "Once and for all He entered into the holy place."[15] "Once and for all we are sanctified by the offering of His body."[16] Only one early Christian author was ever so much as suspected of a cyclical view of history, and he did not entertain it. This was Origen, who said that life on earth is a purgation and for this purpose one life may not suffice. In other words, he suggested the idea of purgatory. Moreover when the purgation is complete, said he, inasmuch as man is free, there is the possibility of retrogression, and the whole process may have to start over again. Yet this is not to say that in each life there will be another Redeemer, because there is no foundation other than that which has been laid for us once and for all in Christ Jesus.[17]

The affirmation that Christ was at once new and definitive was an assertion about the course and the nature of history. The possibility of something new is involved, and this concept is rooted in the picture of God the Creator, the Lord of Life, bound by no ineluctable sequence, able by a supreme act of His omnipotent will to summon being out of nonbeing.[18] This He did at the creation, and the statement of the Creed, "I believe in God, the Father Almighty, the Creator," was an assertion not only about God but also about history. God created, in the Christian view, not in the sense of shaping up previously existing materials as in Plato's *Timaeus* but by saying, "Let there be," and there

12. Polybius, *Hist.* VI.
13. Cf. Puech.
14. Rom. 6:10.
15. Heb. 9:12.
16. Heb. 10:12.
17. Koch, p. 92.
18. Frank, p. 57.

was. "Let there be light," and the universe was suffused with radiance before ever the suns were sent hurtling upon their courses.[19]

The Creator God is forever creating, for "He who commanded the light to shine out of darkness hath shined in our hearts to give the light of the knowledge of the glory of God in the face of Jesus Christ."[20] The incarnation is a new creation, and the Christian is a new creature. Gregory of Nyssa declared that history "goes from beginnings to beginnings by means of beginnings which have no end."[21] That which is new can therefore be definitive, in no need of repetition. Christ is thus the beginning and the end, truly the alpha and the omega, the pivot of all history, as our chronology has eventually recognized by dating not forward from the creation of the world to Christ, but backward from Christ to the creation.[22]

Yet this does not mean that history is simply a series of disjointed episodes. There are sequences, first the blade, then the ear, and then the ripened corn. God has a plan for the ages. For the early Church the first practical question was to know the significance in the divine plan of the interval between the first and the second comings. The Church was all the more driven to give some meaningful content to this period because of the judgment of the Gnostics that time itself is a calamity. The Gnostic exclaimed: "In this world of darkness I have lived for a million myriad of years and no one knew that I was there. The years succeeded to the years, the generations to the generations. I was there, and they did not know that I was there, in their world." A Gnostic prayer declared: "Now our gracious Father, innumerable myriads of years have passed by since we have been separated from Thee." The Gnostic was bound to regard time on earth as a calamity because life in time is spent in the flesh, which

19. Daniélou (3).

20. II Cor. 4:6.

21. *Hom. Cant.* VIII, *Patrologia graeca* (Migne), Vol. 44, col. 1043b. Cited in Daniélou (3), p. 68. Does not check.

22. Cullmann (3).

is an impediment and an imprisonment. Marcion spoke brutally of the ignomy of existence, engendered in obscenity and brought forth in impurity. The body is a sack of excrements which death will turn into a stinking cadaver.[23]

No Christian ever talked that way. The Apostle Paul might desire to depart and be with Christ. Ignatius might hope that his martyrdom would not be impeded; but even Origen, who was closest to the Gnostics, did not stigmatize life in the body as an imprisonment. God gave us bodies for a good purpose: that in them we might receive our instruction, perfect our training, and complete our probation.[24] The interval, then, between the first and second comings had a twofold purpose: to gather in the Gentiles and to effect the purgation of the Christians. The Shepherd of Hermas remarked, for example, that for the heathen there is always repentance, and for the Christian who has lapsed there is one more chance.[25]

IV. HISTORICAL SEQUENCE: THE CHURCH AND THE PRE-CHRISTIAN DISPENSATION

The above expressions all apply to individual Christians, but these individuals were not isolated, and history was regarded as something more than the progress of particular persons in the way of salvation. They are members of the Church and the Church has her role in the divine economy. She is called the bride of Christ,[26] and thus she is affirmed to be in intimate communion with her unique source. She is the new Israel of God.[27] In early Christian literature she was called the new Eden, the restorer of paradise.[28] Thus to relate the Church to Israel was to connect her with the course of Jewish history prior to the

23. Quispel, p. 93.
24. Koch, p. 37.
25. Hermas, *Vis.* II, ii, 5.
26. Eph. 5 :32.
27. Gal. 6 :16.
28. Irenaeus, *Against Heresies* V, 20. Cf. Bainton (2), n. 99.

coming of Christ. Here a most difficult problem confronted the early Christians, both to assert the continuity of Christianity with Judaism against the Gnostics and to assert the superiority of Christianity to Judaism against the Jews. The Gnostics, because they condemned the creation, condemned also the Creator and His chosen people together with their sacred book. Since the world is evil, said they, He who made it must be evil. He is not, then, the God and Father of our Lord Jesus Christ but a malevolent demiurge, and all those in the Old Testament who regarded him as evil and all those who defied him are to be considered good, such as Cain, Seth, Dathan, Kore, and Abiron. The whole scale of values was reversed, and the coming of Christ in consequence was considered to have been absolutely new, a complete break in history. Until that time the supreme God was hidden in obscurity. Truly he was an unknown God. Then with shattering suddenness he stepped into the course of time in the fifteenth year of Tiberius.

The Christian Church on the contrary affirmed the goodness of creation and the identity of the Creator God with the Redeemer God. The Old Testament was then retained, but only with qualifications. How, then, could this previous development be related to the revelation of God in Christ? Several devices were employed to integrate the new covenant with the old. One was the device of dispensations, that is to say, God dealt with his chosen people by stages. From the side of man's behavior the course was marked not so much by progress as by deterioration. First Adam fell, then the human race was so perverse as to incur the Flood. The covenant with Abraham was only with a saving remnant, and Moses because of the hardness of men's hearts had to give a bill of divorce. The fathers stoned the prophets and when the Son came, He was slain upon a tree.

From God's side, however, there was a progressive self-disclosure culminating in the cross and the resurrection. The dispensations were linked together by certain anticipations cast according to a similarity of pattern. The Old Testament was interpreted in terms of typology. " As Moses lifted up the serpent in the wilderness, so should the Son of Man be lifted up." The sacrifice of Isaac prefigured the sacrifice of Christ; the four-winged creatures in the vision of Ezekiel, namely the man, the eagle, the lion, and the ox, foreshadowed the four evangelists; and so on. This is not a cyclical theory of history because the new covenant did not repeat precisely the old. The sacrifice of Christ was not a repetition of the sacrifice of Isaac. As a matter of fact Isaac was not sacrificed, and no one would pretend that the four gospels repeated the four creatures of the prophet's vision. The point was rather that a certain identity of meaning, a similarity of structure linked each dispensation with that which was to come. The more so was this the case because of the assumption that the pre-existent Christ in the form of Wisdom or Logos was on occasion partially disclosed even in the Old Testament. He it was who appeared to Abraham at the oak of Mamre. He it was who stood before Moses in the burning bush. The uniqueness of the incarnation was at times almost imperiled by this projection backward of the work of Christ.[29]

This was obviated by assuming a progressive revelation culminating in the Incarnation. In the realm of ethics, God led his people through successive stages to a more advanced level. In former times acts were condoned or enjoined by God which are no longer allowed. Polygamy was conceded to the patriarchs, says Tertullian, because of the need at that time to replenish the earth more rapidly, though even then it was contrary to God's preferred intent, since he used only one rib to make a helpmate for Adam.[30] Other discrepancies from the Christian code, such as the despoiling of the Egyptians, the suicide of Samson, or the extermination of the Canaanites, were explained sometimes as due to a special revelation no longer valid, or allegorized and thus denuded of any literal meaning.[31]

The Old Testament era, in general, however, was assigned to

29. Daniélou (2).

30. Tertullian, "Exhortation to Chastity," *Ante-Nicene Fathers, 4,* 53. Cf. "To His Wife," *ibid.*, p. 39.

31. Bainton (1).

the period of the fall, and the Christian Era marked a new dispensation, a restoration of the state of the garden of Eden prior to the transgression of Adam. The Church was described as the new Eden of God whose mission it was to restore the lost splendor. In her fellowship the lion and the lamb should lie down together. This idea, incidentally, readily lent itself to combination with a similar concept prevalent particularly among the Stoics of a golden age in the past without war, without property, without slavery, progressively lost in deterioration through the ages of Silver, Bronze, and Iron. The Christians did not appropriate the whole of this program. War alone should be repudiated. Slavery, however, was simply to be Christianized. The attitude toward property is the most interesting as an illustration of discriminating borrowing and adaptation. The Church did not espouse a communal ownership of all goods, but at the same time often echoed Cynic-Stoic praises of poverty. A drink, said the Cynic, is no more refreshing because from a silver or a golden cup, and sleep is no sweeter on an ivory bed.[32] The Christian would make the same observation and then inquire whether Christ came from heaven with a silver footbath to wash the disciples' feet.[33] Note that Christ came from heaven and not from the lost Atlantis. The motivation for poverty was also different. The Cynic sought to insure inward tranquility by divesting himself in advance of everything of which by Fortune he might be despoiled. When Diogenes saw a boy drinking out of his hands, the sage smashed his cup, saying, " Fool that I am to have been so long encumbered with superfluous baggage." [34] The Christian Tertullian inquired rather whether a neck adorned with a necklace would bow before the ax of the executioner.[35] For the Christian poverty was a part of the discipline necessary to maintain morale for martyrdom. The point was not reinforced by assuming such simplicity to have

32. Lovejoy (1), pp. 142–3.

33. Clement of Alexandria, *Ante-Nicene Fathers, 2*, 247, Tertullian, *ibid., 4*, 16–17; Cyprian, *ibid., 5*, 279–80.

34. Seneca, *Ep.* XC.

35. Tertullian, " On the Apparel of Women," II, 13, *Ante-Nicene Fathers, 4*, 25.

been the original condition of mankind. Only Lactantius referred to the Church as the restorer of the age of Saturn.[36] Ambrose made much of poverty but little of the theme of the lost paradise, though he did borrow from the philosophers the view that the accumulation of private wealth is against nature.[37]

All such appropriations from classical theories are noted mainly to emphasize the way in which the Church transformed in borrowing. The main point in the whole concept of the Church as the New Eden was not that the external conditions of the garden were recovered but rather the condition of man. The Christians were new creatures who exemplified in their behavior the love, joy, peace which are the fruits of the spirit.

V. SECULAR HISTORY

Thus far in our discussion the Christian theory of history has been delineated solely from the point of view of God's plan for man's redemption. Have, then, the Christians no conception of a secular history? Basically, no, but still as the Christian Church found itself operating within the framework of the empire, attention was devoted to the relations of the Church to the state and to society, and reflections emerged as to the course of empires. The Church was in the anomalous position of being persecuted by an emperor who claimed to be god and of being assisted by an empire which rendered accessible to the Gospel the remotest corners of the known world.

Diverse attitudes developed. They are all adumbrated in the New Testament. The most favorable attitude to the empire is to be found in the Lukan writings, which note the coincidence of what one might call sacred and secular chronology. Christ was born under Augustus and baptized under Tiberius. In the Book of Acts the Roman magistrates are represented on the whole as curbing the fanaticism of the Jews. The most hostile attitude is that of the Book of Revelation, which portrays Rome as Babylon

36. Lactantius, " Divine Institutes," *Ante-Nicene Fathers*, 7, 140–2, cf. 219.
37. Lovejoy (2).

drunk with the blood of the saints. The intermediate position is that of Paul and the Pastorals. For Paul in II Thessalonians the man of sin who sets himself forth as God appears to be the deified Roman emperor, but the power which restrains the chaos of the apocalyptic woes may be the Roman Empire. At any rate, in the succeeding period, whereas some interpreted " the power that restrains " as the missionary activity of the Church, others saw in it a reference to the empire.

In the period between the New Testament and the age of Constantine these three general positions recur. The most favorable was that which saw in the empire a providential provision for the dissemination of the Gospel (so Origen) and rejoiced that the roads were open and the seas were clear (so Tertullian). The most hospitable to Rome was Melito of Sardis, who looked upon Christianity and the empire as two conjoint works of God for the benefit of mankind. At the other extreme was Commodianus, who would welcome an invasion by the Goths to overturn the empire.

The main line followed the thought of Paul. The deified emperor should be resisted until death, but the empire was viewed as a force restraining disorder. The judgment on the empire was qualified. The encomia of the Roman panegyrists were blended with the execrations of the conquered. The exigencies of polemic drove Christian apologists to deprecatory views of Rome. When the pagans charged that Christianity was responsible for whatever calamities befell, the reply was first of all that the calamities antedated Christianity and must therefore have some other source. Roman literature itself supplied the refutation in the view that a virus of corruption had infected the blood stream of Rome from the very outset of her history. When the founding fathers, the twins, were suckled by a wolf, and when Romulus slew Remus, then Rome was established by fratricide. This theme is to be found in Horace and was avidly appropriated by Tertullian and Minucius Felix. Another similar theme went back to a speech made by Scipio Nasica in the Roman Senate at the time when the fate of Carthage was under debate. He opposed destruction on the ground that a great state needs a rival to keep her from internal dissension. When, then, Carthage was actually demolished and Rome subsequently succumbed to civil wars, Sallust reverted to this prediction as the explanation of Roman degeneration. This note recurs in the apologetic of Lactantius.[38] The Christians also were not unwilling to burrow in the anti-imperial literature of the East, even though some of it may have become traditional and comparatively devoid of animus. Older even than Daniel was the theory of the four monarchies which should pass away to be superseded by a fifth. The application to an empire of either the number four or the number five was thus both a judgment and a prediction. If the empire was called the fourth, then its collapse was imminent; if it was the fifth, it was about to overthrow and succeed its predecessors. A note of hostility, then, is observable in that chronology which declares that Assyria was followed by Rome in the position of the fourth monarchy. This sequence runs through not a few of the fathers, though perhaps they merely perpetuated a tradition without being altogether aware of its implications.[39]

With the accession of Constantine Christian theologians in the first flush of enthusiasm for their victorious champion reverted to the view of Melito of Sardis, arguing that coincidentally Rome had pacified the world and Christianity had overcome the demons and tamed belligerent peoples. The Roman peace and the Christian peace together had turned swords into plowshares. Christ was therefore made into a Roman citizen, and Augustus almost into a Christian. The close affiliation of Christianity and the empire received a theological undergirding. The argument was advanced mainly by the Antiochian theologians with their strong emphasis upon the divine unity. They contended, notably Eusebius of Caesarea, that polytheism had been appropriate to a congeries of city-states inspired by demons to incessant turmoil, but now monotheism and monarchy called for each other: one

38. Bainton (2), pp. 203–5.
39. Swain.

God, one Lord, one faith, one baptism, and one Constantine.[40] Hear the words of Eusebius:

> The wars of antiquity were due to polytheism. Then the demonic gods were overcome by Christ, then divergent governments and wars ceased as one God was proclaimed to all mankind. At the same time one universal power, the Roman empire, arose and flourished, while the enduring and implacable hatred of nation against nation was now removed: and as the knowledge of one God, and one way of religion and salvation, even the doctrine of Christ, was made known to all mankind; so at the self-same period, the entire dominion of the Roman empire being vested in a single sovereign, profound peace reigned throughout the world. And thus, by the express appointment of the same God, two roots of blessing sprang up together for the benefit of men; the Roman empire and the teaching of the Christian religion.[41]

This attitude toward the empire was to run through a long line of Eastern theologians.

But the West was confronted with a new situation. Rome was sacked by the troops of Alaric in the year A.D. 410. The shock was profound. *Roma aeterna* was no longer impregnable. The pagans revived the ancient reproaches and ascribed calamity to the neglect of the old gods. Augustine retorted by a recital of all the crimes and all the calamities from the fall of Adam to the fall of Rome. "Great cities without justice are but robbery on a large scale." Well did the anti-Roman historian Pompeius Trogus trace the succession of robber states from Assyria to Rome. Was she not founded on fratricide and extended by the rape of the Sabines and the demolition of Carthage? What then of the benefits conferred by Rome; what of the one language and the bond of peace? Yes, but by how many wars, how much bloodshed, were they achieved? Had it not been better that such

40. Peterson.

41. "Oration on Constantine," XVI, *Post-Nicene Fathers*, *1*, 606.

benefits be conferred with the consent of the peoples? Talk not of glorious victories. Look at naked deeds, at the lust of dominion with which Sallust reproached mankind. The glory of the empire rests on lust and blood. Thus all the imprecations of the vanquished reverberate through the pages of Augustine, and when he comes to Augustus and the founding of the empire, he is no more favorable. There is no talk here of Christ as a Roman citizen. Roman history first reaches a point of turning with the conversion of Constantine, and if there be Christian emperors like Constantine and Theodosius, then may their sway increase.[42]

By this conclusion Augustine appears to have wrecked his argument. He seemed to be contending that Rome had fallen because of her sin. Why, then, should she collapse precisely at the time when some measure of improvement had been introduced by the Christianizing of her ruler? The real answer is that Rome no more fell because of her sins than rose because of her virtues. She was quite as bad,and indeed much worse, in the days of her ascent. The point is rather that empires rise and fall according to the economy of God. He can use even the Assyrian as the rod of his anger and is dependent on none for the achievement of his ends. Ultimately, the only history is the history of God's great plan.

Modern writers somewhat divide when they come to deal with the outworking of this philosophy of history in which we do observe a difference between the East and the West. How do the lines run from Eusebius and Augustine to the Caesaro-papism of the East and the papal theocracy of the West? A recent writer [43] contends that the East provided the political and historical thinking for the West, that not Augustus but Eusebius is the father of the *Sacrum Imperium* of the Middle Ages. Augustine is held in no sense to have endorsed the empire. The mere conversion of an emperor did not mean for him the Christianizing of the empire. Now to be sure, Augustine was not naïve, but certainly he did not, like Tychonius, place all kings on the side of the devil.

42. *The City of God*, Bks. I-V, XVIII-XXII.
43. Kamlah.

The empire enshrined for him values not lightly to be relinquished, and when Boniface, the general of Rome, proposed on the death of his wife to become a monk, Augustine remonstrated, " For God's sake, not now! " [44] The empire must be defended. Moreover, under the guidance of the Church, the empire might achieve some semblance of justice. In the indeterminate period of man's life to come on earth, Church and state in collaboration might accomplish, if not a restoration of paradise, at least something better than demonic chaos.

Moreover, the thinking of the Easterners came in time more nearly to approximate that of Augustine. The age of exuberance was succeeded by disillusionment with regard to the sons of Constantine when they embraced heretical Arianism and persecuted the orthodox. Then Hilary, Hosius, and Athanasius reminded the ruler that " The purple makes emperors not priests." [45] In the East almost more than in the West the idea took root of Rome transplanted to the East and destined to be eternal by reason of consecration at the hands of the Holy Orthodox Church.

Neither in the East nor in the West did Christians ever contemplate an ideal consummation on earth. Never did they forget that life is but a pilgrimage and man's eternal blessedness and supernal rest lie beyond this veil of tears.

Such a conclusion validates the apparently contradictory judgments that Christ is the end of history and that Christianity offers the first meaningful philosophy of history. If history be defined as a chain of events, each linked to the other in causal sequence, then Christ makes plain to us that in this sense there never was any history because God is Lord of all events. He can break all sequences with that which is altogether new. Yet there is in events a sequence arising solely from the purpose of God to culminate the drama of redemption. This, rather than either the wickedness or the goodness of man, explains the rise and fall of empires, and this enables man to survive the rise and the fall of empires because hope is fixed upon Him who sitteth above the circle of the earth.

44. *Ep.* 189.

45. Setton.

BIBLIOGRAPHY

Roland H. Bainton, (1), " The Immoralities of the Patriarchs," *Harvard Theological Review, 23,* No. 1 (Jan., 1930), 39–49.

——— (2), " The Early Church and War," *Harvard Theological Review, 39,* No. 3 (July, 1946), 189–212.

Ludwig Bauer, " Untersuchungen über die Vergöttlichungslehre in der Theologie der griechischen Väter," *Theologische Quartalschrift, 98* (1916), 467–91; *101* (1920), 28–64, 155–86.

Hand Bietenfeld, " The Millenial Hope in the Early Church," *Journal of Scottish Theology, 6,* No. 1 (Mar., 1953), 12–30.

K. Bornhäuser, " Die Vergöttungslehre des Athanasius und Johannes Damascenus," *Beiträge zur Förderung christlicher Theologie, 7,* No. 2 (1903), 7–198.

Emile Brehier, " Quelques traits de la philosophie de l'histoire dans l'antiquité classique," *Revue d'histoire et de philosophie religieuses, 14* (1934), 38–40.

G. W. Butterworth, " The Deification of Man in Clement of Alexandria," *Journal of Theological Studies, 17* (1915–16), 157–69.

Hans Campenhausen, " Weltgeschichte und Gottesgericht," *Lebendige Wissenschaft,* Vol 1, 1947.

Oscar Cullman (1), " Le Caractère eschatologique du devoir messianique et de la conscience apostolique de S. Paul," *Revue d'histoire et de philosophie religieuses, 16* (1936), 210–45.

——— (2), " Quand viendra le Royaume de Dieu? " *Revue d'histoire et de Philosophie religieuses, 18* (1938), 174–86.

——— (3) *Christus und die Zeit,* Zollikon-Zurich, 1946.

Jean Daniélou (1), " La Typologie millenoriste de la semaine dans le Christianisme primitif," *Vigiliae Christianae, 2* (1948), 1–16.

——— (2), " *Sacramentum futuri,* Études sur les origines de la typologie biblique," *Etudes de théologie historique,* Paris, 1950.

——— (3), " The Conception of History in the Christian Tradition," *Papers of the Ecumenical Institute, 5* (1950), 67–79. This paper appears also in *The Journal of Religion, 30* (1950), 171–9.

Franz Dölger, " Rom in der Gedankenwelt der Byzantiner," *Zeitschrift für Kirchengeschichte, 56* (1937), 1–42.

Ecumenical Institute, Papers of, Vol. 5 (1950), " The Meaning of History."

Hans Eger, "Kaiser und Kirche in der Geschichtstheologie Eusebs von Caesarea," *Zeitschrift für die Neutestamentliche Wissenschaft, 37/38* (1938–39), 97–115.

Erich Frank, *Philosophical Understanding and Religious Truth,* New York, 1945.

Robert Frick, "Die Geschichte des Reich-Gottes-Gedankens in der alten Kirche bis zu Origenes und Augustin," *Beihefte zur Zeitschrift für die Neutestamentliche Wissenschaft,* Vol. *6* (1928).

Harald Fuchs (1), *Der geistige Widerstand gegen Rom in der antiken Welt,* Berlin, 1938.

——— (2), "Augustin und der antike Friedensgedanke," *Neue philologischen Untersuchungen,* Vol. 3, Berlin, 1926.

M. Goguel, "Eschatologie et apocalyptique dans le Christianisme primitif," *Revue de l'histoire des religions, 106* (1932), 381–434, 489–524.

Jean Guiton, *Le Temps et l'eternité chez Plotin et St. Augustin,* Paris, 1933.

Wilhelm Kamlah, *Christentum und Geschichtlichkeit,* Stuttgart, 1951[2].

Franz Kampers, "Roma aeterna und sancta Dei ecclesia rei publicae Romanorum," *Historisches Jahrbuch, 44* (1924), 240–9.

Hal Koch, "Pronoia und Paideusis, Studien über Origines," *Arbeiten zur Kirchengeschichte,* Vol 22, 1932.

Ernst Lewalter, "Eschatologie und Weltgeschichte in der Gedankenwelt Augustins," *Zeitschrift für Kirchengeschichte, 53* (1934), 1–51.

M. Lot-Boradine, "La Doctrine de la 'déification' dans l'Eglise grecque jusqu'au XI siècle," *Revue de l'histoire des religions, 150* (1932); 5–43, 525–74.

Arthur O. Lovejoy (1), *Primitivism and Related Ideas in Antiquity,* 1935.

——— (2), "The Communism of Saint Ambrose," *Journal of the History of Ideas, 3,* No. 4 (Oct., 1942), 458–68.

Karl Löwith, *Meaning in History,* Chicago, 1949.

Theodore Mommsen, "St. Augustine and the Christian Idea of Progress," *Journal of the History of Ideas, 12,* No. 3 (June, 1951), 346–74.

Wilhelm Nestle, "Griechische Geschichtsphilosophie," *Archiv für Geschichte der Philosophie, 41* (1932), 80–114.

Hans-Georg Opitz, "Euseb von Caesarea als Theologe," *Zeitschrift für die Neutestamentliche Wissenschaft, 34* (1935), 1–19.

Erik Peterson, *Der Monotheismus als politisches Problem: Ein Beitrag zur Geschichte der politischen Theologie im Imperium Romanum,* Leipzig, 1935.

Henri Puech, "La Gnose et le temps," *Eranos Jahrbuch, 20* (1951), 57–113.

G. Quispel, "Zeit und Geschichte im antiken Christentum," *Eranos Jahrbuch, 20* (1951), 115–18.

Kenneth M. Setton, *Christian Attitudes toward the Emperor in the Fourth Century,* New York, 1941.

Joseph Ward Swain, "The Theory of the Four Monarchies: Opposition History under the Roman Empire," *Classical Philology, 35* (Jan.-Oct., 1940), 1–21.

A. A. Vasiliev, "Medieval Ideas of the End of the World: West-East," *Byzantion, 16* (1942–43), 462–502.

Helmut Werner, "Der Untergang Roms," *Forschungen zur Kirchen und Geistesgeschichte*, Vol. 17, 1939.

EARLY ISLAM

Julian Obermann

I. RESISTANCE TO REFORM

AMONG the several religious and cultural areas considered within the frame of the present series, Islam alone is characterized by the fact that it has a precise chronological beginning—precise as to the year and even as to the month and day. One need only look into a pertinent history book to find that the islamic era began on the day following Mohammed's flight from Mecca to Medina, that is, on Thursday, July 15, of A. D. 622.[1]

This is only a graphic way of saying that, unlike any major religion or cultural epoch of the ancient Near East, Islam makes its appearance in history as a sudden, punctual, i. e., revolutionary, break with the past. Within less than two decades virtually the entire Arab nation embarked upon a new way of life—a mass conversion of unheard-of proportions accomplished with unprecedented speed. How is this to be accounted for? Was it solely because here a lowly, inferior form of national existence was readily given up for much higher stakes?

Seen superficially, that is, from our modern viewpoint, the past with which Mohammed and the new community of believers had broken might indeed have been easily forgotten and speedily eradicated. It had acquired none of the possessions that normally resist being swept away by a reformer; it had developed none of the institutions that are apt to generate a struggle for survival, for historic continuity, and against oblivion. Prior to the emergence of Mohammed, the people of North Arabia had evolved no religion of any spiritual vestige, no kingship, no constitutional government whatsoever, no authority either central or regional, no code of laws—excepting only the self-imposed duty to avenge the slaying of one's kin and to protect one's guest, client, and

1. On this date, see M. Plessner, art. " Ta'rīkh," *EI*, suppl., p. 231a.

ally—no material civilization, no sedentary communities except in the two or three cities at the western fringe of the peninsula, Ṭā'if, Mecca, and Medina, and above all, no written monuments, indeed, no writing at all to speak of.

Actually, however, the old way of life was by no means swept away by the mass conversion to Islam. On the contrary, the past did linger on with so much vibration and repercussion, so stubborn and enduring a tenacity, that no aspect of Early Islam can be critically understood without close consideration of its prehistory, that is, of the period of Arab history prior to the rise of the new religion. So far from being swept away by the reformer, the old way of life left profound imprints on the shape and direction in which his reform was to be consolidated.

It is important to realize at the outset that conversion to Islam was first conceived of as a voluntary " covenant " between Mohammed and any Arab individual willing to accept " guidance " and " admonition." On this basis, however, only a small number of the people of Mecca, Mohammed's native home and the starting point of his mission, proved susceptible to his appeal. The vast majority refused to have any part of it, so that the city of Mecca had to be brought into the fold of Islam by force of arms, and this long after the start of his prophetic activity, in fact some seven or eight years after his flight to Medina. Nor was his mission at first more successful outside of Mecca, among the clans and tribes of the desert. Even such Bedouin groups as in due course had been converted by Mohammed renounced the " covenant of Allah " subsequently and returned to their old pagan ways and had to be reconverted by the " sword of Islam." Already, then, during the lifetime of Mohammed, conversion to Islam had changed from conversion of individuals by choice and moral persuasion to conversion of groups by force and physical compulsion.

Mohammed himself, we shall see, is fully aware of the core of the opposition to his message: a deep-seated notion on the part of the Arabs that the new faith would destroy the mode of life they inherited from their " fathers," the very roots of their ethnic heritage; that, in other words, for them to become Moslems would mean to cease being Arabs. It would be inaccurate, however, to account for this notion solely on the grounds that to the people of Arabia Mohammed's teaching was an unheard-of imposition, a blank and stark innovation. Rather, we have to do here with a conflict between two rudimentary ideologies: an antinomy between Arabism and Islamism that was to remain a crucial factor in the life of the Moslem community through all major eras of its history—indeed, a crucial factor in the mission and personality of Mohammed himself. The nature of this conflict has been variously treated in the largely pioneering researches of von Kremer, Sprenger, Caussin de Perceval, Robertson Smith, and particularly, in the works of Wellhausen, Nöldeke, and Ignaz Goldziher, all of whom have furthered the critical study of this field in a variety of ways.

For the present inquiry a clear understanding of this antinomy is of the very first importance. For the fact is that in the pagan heritage of the Arabs, no less than in the basic documentation of Islam, the Koran, we find much stress laid upon the meaning and consideration of the past. In the case of the Koran, such a stress may be observed at the very surface, as we shall see. In the case of pre-islamic Arabia, this is less apparent but no less demonstrable. It is true, of course, that owing to their natural environment, the Arabian Desert, to their Bedouin mode of life as tent dwellers and breeders of sheep and camels, and above all, to their nomadic wanderings, the pagan Arabs of the North left us no archeological or epigraphic monuments of any kind. In this, as in some other respects, they form a parallel to the pre-Mosaic Hebrews. Of neither do we own contemporary written documents comparable to those of Egypt, Babylonia, Ugarit, Phoenicia, or South Arabia. Nevertheless, the pre-islamic Arabs of the North, much more than the pre-Mosaic Hebrews, did leave a vast literary heritage accumulated during the era preceding their conversion to Islam—a vast store of narratives, legends, poems, and proverbs which had been handed down from generation to generation by oral transmission, and which had remained alive, effective, and articulate down to the time of Mohammed and indeed long after his time. Only thus is it understandable how an enormous bulk of that literary heritage could be collected and recorded in the *classical* era of Islam, to which we shall have reference later on.

In examining the witnesses to this pagan heritage of the northern Arabs, the preserved traditions of their ancient storytellers and the survived songs and odes of the pagan poets—Imrulqais,[2] 'Abīd b. al-Abraṣ, 'Amr b. Kulṯūm, al-Ḥāriṯ b. Ḥilliza, Zuhair, 'Āntara, Labīd, 'Āmir b. aṭ-Ṭufail, an-Nābiġah, al-A'sha, and many others—we come upon a preoccupation with the past which in its persistence and intensity is very surprising indeed; but it is an approach to history wholly incompatible with that conveyed by Mohammed in the Koran, and this, of course, is not surprising at all. I submit, indeed, that we shall have come to grips with the main problem of our inquiry once we fully understand these two conflicting conceptions of the past, that of the Arabs' ancient heritage and that of Mohammed's new orientation, in their tenacious effectiveness, their reciprocal impact, and in the attempts made in Early Islam toward their neutralization, that is, in the attempts made to render the pragmatic implications of each of these two conceptions compatible with those of the other.

II. ARABISM

1. PREOCCUPATION WITH THE PAST. TRIBAL AND INTERTRIBAL GENEALOGY

The interest in the past manifested by Arabs of the preislamic era is as intense and sensitive in expression as it is slim and tenuous in outlook. It is bound by a hypertrophied clan consciousness, an emotional overbearance of genealogy and blood kinship, and a complete lack of rational curiosity. In prose their preoccupation with the past is attested by numerous narratives concerning the so-called " Days of the Arabs " (*aiyām al-'arab*). Here their storytellers speak of a past in which terror and violence

2. Properly: Imru'u 'l-Qais.

had reigned supreme, and they speak of this aspect of their past to the exclusion of everything else. They tell of incessant blood feuds and tribal wars, of perpetual deadly struggles between brother tribes, kindred clans, and close neighbors, without ever reflecting upon guilt and merit, right and wrong. In verse, too, the past is spoken of exclusively in its sanguinary, warlike, fratricidal aspect. Here, however, the events of the past are recorded for the benefit and the glory of the poet's own clan and tribe: the superiority of *its* status over that of some other group or indeed of any group. Here, then, there emerges something like a code of values. The pagan poet magnifies the past record of his kin by dwelling on the nobility and prestige of its ancestors, nobility and prestige not only such as inherited by descent but particularly such as acquired by heroic prowess on the field of battle. Such a record of the past is the priceless possession of his kin and clan, for it in turn ennobles and enriches his clan's blood, hardens its courage and daring, renders it invincible.

Once again we come here upon a feature common to the pagan Arabs and the ancient Hebrews. In both instances, the champion of the people speaks in verse; in both, his spoken message recited in the swaying rhythms of Semitic prosody is infectious: as a shield and blessing to his kin or as a blast and a curse to its adversaries; and in both, the poet's impassioned exaltation or vilification often gives way to calm reflection and self-searching questioning. But unlike the Hebrew poet, the ancient Arab bard does not ever protest against the established order or denounce the validity of accepted premises and traditions. He often finds that nobility and prestige did not always protect either his ancestors or the latter's offspring against defeat and suffering, that their very courage and daring proved fatal and disastrous to them. Qualms and reflections of this kind are evidenced in the verses of nearly every Arab poet whose compositions have reached us in sufficient quantity; but they seem immune to intellectual re-evaluation: they never lead to a re-examination of the principles of Arab society or to a revision of its code of values. Instead, the ancient bard—often with profound poetic feeling, and always with a measure of touching despair—invariably relegates all such reflections to the realm of irrevocable destiny (*dahr*), to uncontrollable visitations (*ḥawādiṯ, manāyā*), in short, to a wholly irresponsible and inscrutable government of blind Fate.

One might feel inclined to account for the peculiar isolationism in the historical outlook of the northern Arabs by their lack of contact with the outside world. The fact, however, is that the Arabs of the Ḥijāz and the Najd did maintain contact of long standing with their Christian and pagan cousins in Syria, Iraq, and South Arabia, and with the Jewish-Arab tribes and clans in Khaibar, in Taima, and especially, in and around Medina. They thus had every opportunity to learn something about Byzantium, Persia, and Abyssinia, the Jewish Synagogue, and the Christian Church. The wide range of Judeo-Christian lore reflected in the sermon of Mohammed and the occurrence of Aramaic and Persian words in pre-islamic poetry attest to this.[3] Yet in their narratives, legends, and songs of the past, the northern Arabs are so wholly absorbed in their own affairs, their own intertribal feuds and wars, their own lineage and pedigrees, as to make it clear that as regards their notion of history the rest of the world simply did not exist.

Within the generation of Mohammed, and as far back as we can see, the people of North Arabia find themselves divided into a great number of large and small groups, all of which believe themselves to be related to one another, while each group holds itself supremely independent of any other. Their poets and storytellers do tell in effect how sporadic efforts were made toward political hegemony and centralization, by the Lakhmid petty kings in Iraq, the Gassanian phylarchs in Syria, or the Kinda princes in Arabia itself; but they also tell how each effort failed,

3. See, e. g., *arjuwān*, "purple"; *sājid*, "performing prostration"; ʿAmr, *Maʿall*, ed. L. Abel, ll. 44, 104; *malik muqsiṭ*, "a just king"; *barīya*, "creature"; *mahāriq*, "documents"; Ḥāriṯ, *Muʿall.*, ll. 28, 39, 67, (cf. Muf., ed. Lyall, No. 25:1, *mahāriq al-furs*); *bazārīq*, "troops"; Muf. No. 41:16 (cf. the scholion, *ad loc.*); *yamm*, "sea"; Aġ., XX, 24:1; see Nöldeke, *Fünf Moʿallaqāt*, in *Sitzungsberichte*, *140* (1899), 49, 73.

how it was resisted, or even severely repulsed. The remarkable thing is that the division and independence of the groups, on the one hand, and their notion of mutual affinity, on the other, are both based on the idea of kinship. Without a known exception,[4] each group holds itself, and is held by all others, to represent a unity of blood in the sense that all members of a given group, whether large or small, are assumed to have descended from a common ancestor. Also without a known exception, all groups of the Northern Arabs believe themselves to have ultimately descended, each by a direct successive line of ancestors, from the same eponym as their common forebear—who in tradition came to be known by the name of ʿAdnān—so that all these groups in turn were bound together as a single racial stock by the medium of blood kinship. The same principle of racial affinity is held to apply to the southern or Yemenite Arabs—whose ultimate eponym is said to have borne the name of Qaḥṭān—even though many of their tribes had long since migrated to the North, while some of them had for centuries occupied territories in the midst of those of the northern tribes.

Accordingly, a given group of pre-islamic Arabs may be found to speak of itself as the sons of its immediate common ancestor

4. Cf. the custom among ancient Arabs of ratifying a treaty by symbolic mixing of the blood of the contracting parties (see Herodotus, III, 8); this seems to have been indispensable in the case of a permanent *ḥilf*, that is, a permanent federation of two or more groups for the purpose of mutual aid and protection (in contrast to a *temporary* alliance, e. g., that between Asad and Ġaṭafān on the Day of Shiʿb Jabala or that between Mohammed and the people of Medina; see below p. 270 f.). This custom would well account for the consciousness of blood kinship—which, eventually, would come to be conceived of as descent from a common ancestor—even in the case of a group (e. g., the Tanūkh) that is remembered as having taken its origin in a ḥilf. On the other hand, the above custom may be best understood as having developed in a society in which no duty or obligation of any kind was conceived of as binding except among blood relatives, i. e., descendants from a common forebear. See J. Pedersen, *Der Eid bei den Semiten* (Strasbourg, 1914), pp. 21 ff., and the literature adduced there; see also G. L. Della Vida on the etymology of Khaṯʿam, *EI*, *2*, 924b; for materials on ḥilf, cf. Goldziher, *Muhammedanische Studien*, *1*, 63 ff.

or as the sons of any of its more remote ancestors, whereby each term of reference involves not only a different genealogical level but, as a rule, a different political affiliation. With each more remote ancestor the bond of blood that welds the group together becomes increasingly thinner, but the size of the group involved correspondingly larger. In other words, when an Arab clan, by which term we will understand the smallest independent group, identifies itself by its direct forebear, the term employed applies exclusively to that clan and to no other group, but when it speaks of its members as the sons of a more remote ancestor, the name used may be borne by many other groups, namely, all those descended from that remote ancestor.

As could hardly be otherwise, the a priori assumption that not only each clan and tribe, however large, but all Arab tribes of the North, and similarly all tribes of the South, constituted a racial nexus of blood, affected by descent from a common eponym, has been severely questioned by modern scholars.[5] In the present connection, however, it is sufficient to realize that to the Arabs themselves, and certainly to those of the generation of Mohammed, nothing is more axiomatic than that assumption. While ʿAdnān himself figures only rarely in ancient Arab tradition, at least as far as the available records indicate, his immediate offspring, the patriachs of the northern Arabs, are well accounted for in pre-islamic poetry: his son Maʿadd, his grandson Nizār, the latter's two sons, Muḍar and Rabīʿā, Muḍar's son Qais ʿAilān, and so forth. Again, at the time of Mohammed and long before his time, reference to the great Arab tribes of both the North and the South—Bakr, Taġlib, Tamīm, Hawāzin, Ġaṭafān, Asad, Kināna, Ṭaiyiʾ, Ḥimyār, Madẖij, and many others—is exceedingly common, although at that time those tribes no longer actually exist as units. Instead each of them had long since been separated into numerous subtribes, each subtribe into many branches, each branch into a variety of clans, with all these divisions bearing names of their own. Yet in their songs and traditions, the Arabs

5. Smith, *Kinship and Marriage in Early Arabia*, pp. 7 ff. and *passim*; Goldziher, *1*, 40 ff. and *passim*.

of the 6th and 7th centuries cling to their tribal genealogical nomenclature, and names such as Banū Bakr, Banū Tamīm, Banū Asad, always in reference to the same combination of respective groups, prevail throughout the peninsula. What is more, the same unanimity prevails, in song and tradition, with regard to *intertribal* kinships: Bakr and Taġlib are always spoken of as sons of Wā'il, Asad and Kināna as sons of Khuzaima, Hawāzin and Ġaṭafān as the offspring of Qais 'Ailān, Aus and Khazraj as the sons of al-Ḥāriṯa, and so forth. A few examples may here suffice to illustrate the terms of reference as regards tribal and intertribal genealogy that prevail during the century preceding the rise of Islam.

Tradition relates how at a contest of Arab chieftains held at the court of the renowned king of Ḥīra, al-Munḏir b. Ma'a 's-Samā' (A. D. 505–54), the latter opened the debate by bringing forth two pieces of precious cloth, saying that he would give them to the chieftain who could prove that his clan was of more noble status than that of anyone present. The contest is said to have been won by a Tamīmite of the branch of Bahdala named 'Āmir b. Uḥaimir. To prove the greater nobility of his group, it is said, he offered the following succession of ancestors down to his own generation: Ma'add, Nizār, Muḍar, Khindif, Tamīm, Sa'd, Ka'b, 'Auf, Bahdala. By the silence that followed this recital, the king realized that indeed none of the Arab chieftains present could boast of equal nobility of tribal lineage and, the assumption is, of equally glorious achievements of his ancestors on the field of battle.[6]

Imrulqais, universally celebrated as the foremost poet of pre-islamic Arabia, tells how he was unable to avenge fully the murder of his father by the tribesmen of Asad because of the protection they were given "by the sons of their forebear" (*bi-banī 'abīhim*),[7] that is, because the Asadites took refuge

6. Ḥam., p. 729; it is hard to see why 'Āmir's answer is to be considered as having been worked over "im Sinne der späteren genealogischen Details" (Goldziher, *1*, 55).

7. *Dīwān*, ed. W. Ahlwardt, No. 7:2; cf. the scholion, p. 221.

in the territory of Kināna, both tribes having their " forebear " in Khuzaima, as we have seen. It is well to remember that Khuzaima is only two generations removed from Muḍar, grandson of Ma'add, son of 'Adnān, and that here a poet who knows himself to be of Yemenite stock [8] expresses his awareness of the genealogical kinship of two northern tribes, that is, his awareness of a kinship reaching back a great many generations before his time. That an Asadite poet of the time of Imrulqais speaks of his tribe as sons of Khuzaima is therefore all the more natural.[9]

An example of particular interest in this connection is furnished us by the poet al-Ḥāriṯ b. Ḥilliza, a younger contemporary of Imrulqais. He belonged to the Banū Yashkur, a subtribe of Bakr b. Wā'il, and is said to have enjoyed the favor of 'Amr b. Hind, the renowned Lakhmid king of Ḥīra during the third quarter of the 6th century (562–74). The mother of this king, Hind, was the daughter of the famous king of Kinda, al-Ḥāriṯ (grandfather of Imrulqais), whose grandmother, named Umm Unās, belonged to the Banū Shaibān, another subtribe of Bakr b. Wā'il. Accordingly, her son, the father and predecessor of this Kindite king, was known by the name of 'Amr b. Umm Unās. Now in the best-known ode of our poet he tells of the many benefits which his tribe has bestowed upon King 'Amr b. Hind in times past. One of these benefits was that the poet's tribe, Bakr, through the medium of the Banū Shaibān, had provided the bride that was destined to become not only the mother of a ruler of Kinda but the maternal great-great-grandmother of the king of Ḥīra. This the poet expresses in the verse

And we did beget 'Amr, Son of Umm Unās,
as an immediate offspring, after a dowry was duly paid us.

Here, then, the poet's historical consciousness extends to an event, a minor event in itself, that occurred some six generations before, and to a genealogical item so minute that it would normally reach

8. Cf. *Dīwān*, No. 61:2–3.

9. 'Abīd b. al-Abraṣ, *Dīwān*, ed. Lyall, No. 12:21.

the attention of none but a professional genealogist. We shall see, however, that the ancient Arab odes, especially when dealing with events of the past, were intended to be didactic in nature and calculated to reach a very wide audience. Our poet, therefore, must have assumed that the cryptic verse just cited would be properly understood by anyone whom his composition would reach; if so, any Arab of his time and environment would have been as genealogically minded as the poet himself.[10]

The poet Labīd and his cousin, the poet ʿAmir b. aṭ-Ṭufail, contemporaries of Mohammed, speak of the sons of Jaʿfar as their next of kin, Jaʿfar being the immediate ancestor of their clan. But they also refer to their clan as the sons of Kilāb, or of ʿĀmir (b. Ṣaʿṣaʿa), or of Hawāzin, or of Qais ʿAilān.[11] In doing so, they give expression to a general awareness that the Banū Jaʿfar belong to the branch of the great tribe of Qais ʿAilān called Hawāzin, more specifically to the division of Hawāzin called ʿĀmir and still more specifically to the section of ʿĀmīr called Kilāb. Thus, only by the name of the Banū Jaʿfar do they identify their clan as a separate independent group of Arabs, distinct and apart from any other group. Upon occasion, moreover, Labīd also lends expression to the over-all division of the northern Arabs into the two genealogical twins of Muḍar and Rabīʿa, and to their being the "two offspring of Nizār." On another occasion he refers to the belief that no other descendants were left of the northern Arabs except those of ʿAdnān and Maʿadd;[12] while his cousin ʿĀmir b. aṭ-Ṭufail even refers to Qaḥṭān as the hero eponymous of the southern Arabs.[13]

10. Ḥārit, *Muʿall.*, l. 63; see Tibrīzī (ed. Lyall: *Ten Ancient Arabic Poems*, Calcutta, 1894), p. 142, ll. 9 ff.; Nöldeke, *Fünf Moʿallaqāt*, pp. 83 f.

11. See the Index to the *Dīwān* of ʿĀmir, ed. Lyall, pp. 172 ff.

12. Labīd, *Dīwān*, ed. A. Huber and C. Brockelmann (Leiden, 1891), No. 21:1, 3; No. 41:7. The meaning of No. 21:1 was questioned (unjustly, I believe) by Goldziher, *1*, 179, n. 2. In No. 41:7, the prep. *min dūna* can hardly mean anything but " besides " or " other than," thus having the sense of *ġaira* (see Lane, *Arabic-English Lexicon*, p. 930, col. a); Brockelmann (p. 39), " *seit* Adnān und Maʿadd," makes the context extremely difficult.

13. Suppl. to the *Dīwān*, ed. Lyall, No. 21:4 (from Aġ., X, 146, repeated

General awareness of a common ancestry in Ma'add-Nizār-Muḍar/Rabī'a, whether real or assumed, might have tended to generate among the northern Arabs a sense of national solidarity over against the social and political isolationism of the individual clan and tribe. In addition, several factors combined to make the substance of pre-islamic poetry, in so far as it dealt with events of the past, well-nigh national in scope, notwithstanding the extremely factional orientation of the individual bards. The same factors, moreover, did combine to render the compositions of outstanding poets accessible to nation-wide dissemination. Only one or two of these factors need be mentioned here.

Although the multitude of Arab tribes from Yemen to Palmyra and from the shores of the Red Sea to those of the Persian Gulf cannot possibly have used one and the same Arabic dialect in their speech, the compositions of their poets exhibit, as far back as our records go, a single idiom, the well-known idiom of Classical Arabic, so that a 6th-century poem produced in the heart of the desert could be understood equally well at the sanctuaries and fairs of Mecca, at the court of Ḥīra in Iraq, and at that of the Gassanian rulers in Syria—an astonishing fact that is still to be critically accounted for.[14]

Because of this uniformity in the language of their compositions, poets from every part of the peninsula could and did recite their odes and songs and thus exalt the past records of their respective clans and tribes before the truly nation-wide forum that was provided by the famous Fair of 'Ukāẓ in the vicinity of Mecca during the annual period of pilgrimage, which was also a period

Aġ., XVIII, 16): *al-qabā'il min banī Qaḥṭān*. For further examples of the general awareness of tribal and intertribal genealogy at the time of Mohammed, as well as the immediately preceding period, see Nöldeke's definitive review of W. R. Smith's pioneering work (above, n. 5) in *ZDMG*, *40* (1886), 174 ff. Especially noteworthy is his reference (p. 179, n. 2) to a pre-islamic poem incorporated in Muf. (but missing in several Mss., including that underlying Lyall's edition) which manifests the poet's awareness of the genealogy Kinda-Qaḥṭān; also the reference to Hassān's juxtaposition of Ma'add and Qaḥṭān (see now *Dīwān*, ed. H. Hirschfeld, No. 88:5). See also below, n. 110.

14. See G. Rabin, *Ancient West-Arabian* (London, 1951), pp. 1–24.

of sacred truce.[15] A tradition has indeed been preserved to the effect that it was here at 'Ukāẓ that the widely celebrated poems known as the Seven Mu'allaqāt, composed by seven bards from as many different tribes, were selected as the most excellent odes of the Arabs, whereupon they were inscribed in letters of gold upon choice Egyptian linen and hung at the Ka'ba in Mecca.[16]

Among the pagan Arabs propagation of historical records through the medium of poetry often assumed strategic importance, serving as first line of offense in times of war. Through the mouths of its poets and rhapsodists, each of two parties at war strove to intimidate and demoralize the rank of the enemy by reciting poems exalting its own status (*mufākhara*) and vilifying that of the opposite camp (*hijā'*)—a kind of cold war conducted by a peculiar kind of propaganda: the impact of history upon the imagination of poets.[17]

We have seen already that the pagan poet commemorates not only his clan's own achievements but also the nobility, prestige, and warlike prowess which the clan has inherited from its forebears and ancestors. Accordingly, his compositions often comprise a historic record of his entire tribe. Here, then, his political clan consciousness is greatly enhanced by his genealogical tribe consciousness. In addition, in recounting the Days of his clan or of his tribe, the poet is bound to refer to the group or groups that had waged aggressive or defensive warfare against his kin in each of those Days, so that his listeners are made well aware of past events concerning the *enemies* of their forefathers as well. For example, in recounting his own vicissitudes and those of his kin, the Kinda dynasty, Imrulqais is led

15. For a full description of the functions of the fair, see Wellhausen, *Reste*, pp. 80–9; see also, Ibn al-Aṯīr, *Kāmil*, ed. C. J. Tornberg, *1*, 413; Ağ., XI, 6; XIV, 41; and *passim*.

16. The sole interest of the story is that it illustrates the manner and the terms in which later Moslem writers conveyed to their readers the importance of 'Ukāẓ in pre-islamic times; that the details of the story have no basis in fact was brilliantly demonstrated by Nöldeke, *Beiträge*, pp. xvii ff.

17. Cf. Goldziher, *1*, 59–63 and *passim*.

to dwell on past events of several hostile groups that had been involved in those vicissitudes, especially clans of the tribes of Asad and Tamīm.[18] A particularly instructive case is that of 'Āmir b. aṭ-Ṭufail. Although this poet, too, is primarily concerned with his immediate clan, the Banū Ja'far, his divan could easily serve as a manual of the history of the great tribe of 'Āmir b. Ṣa'ṣa'a, of which the Banū Ja'far are but one of numerous subdivisions. Here we learn that in the course of the 6th century that tribe found itself alternately at war with nearly every major group of the peninsula, and the poet has something to say about each of these groups and even about some of their bards, chieftains, and warriors.[19]

What might have been the approximate age of the ultimate eponym of the northern Arabs? To put it differently: what might have been the maximum historical horizon of those to whom Mohammed's mission was primarily directed, the clans and tribes of the Ḥijāz and Najd in the first half of the 7th century?

Since prior to the rise of Islam the art of writing was virtually unknown in North Arabia, and altogether unknown among the Bedouins of the desert, and since the pagan Arabs had developed no systematic treatment of their genealogical traditions, it was only some time after the rise of Islam [20] that complete genealogical tables were first compiled and committed to writing, which listed pedigrees—not only of clans and tribes but of individual generations as well—back to 'Adnān and Qaḥṭān, respectively. At the time of Mu'āwiya (d. *ca.* 679) a number of genealogists had achieved sufficient renown to be invited to his court at Damascus

18. *Dīwān*, Nos. 51:3–8; 57; see especially the four poems cited in Hishām b. al-Kalbī's account of the Day of Kulāb that was incorporated in al-Anbārī's commentary on Muf.; to wit: Muf., pp. 435–8; the poems contain thirty-three verses not included in the *Dīwān* (Muf., p. 435, n. O). Anbārī's text was first published by Lyall in the "Nöldeke Festschrift," Vol. 1 of *Orientalische Studien* (Giessen, 1906), pp. 127 ff.

19. *Dīwān*, *passim*; cf. especially Nos. 2, 3, 7, 11, 12, 19, 27.

20. See below, pp. 287 f., 289 f., 301 ff.

to instruct the caliph in the art of their science. Henceforth, works on genealogy constitute an all-important branch of Arabic literature, and the pertinent data form standard equipment of Moslem historians. According to these data, twenty-two generations separate Mohammed from 'Adnān, while thirty-odd generations stand between his Yemenite contemporaries and Qaḥṭān. On the basis of these numbers modern scholars, such as Reiske and Wüstenfeld, arrived at a chronology whereby 'Adnān would have lived in the 3d, and Qaḥṭān in the 7th, pre-Christian century, so that the northern Arabs of Mohammed's generation would have been conscious, at the very utmost, of a span of about 1,000 years of their genealogical antecedence.[21] Their perspective as to pragmatic history, even in the limited sense exhibited by their storytellers and poets, must be seen to have been very much shorter than even that span.

2. BLOOD REVENGE. RECORDS OF THE DAYS. 'AṢABĪYA

The weakness and strength of the idea of kinship as a practical force may be seen by two characteristic features of pagan Arab society, both equally costly and fatal to its welfare. On the one hand, the idea of kinship did not prove strong enough to prevent kindred groups from waging war against one another. Indeed, the best-known Days of the Arabs, such as the wars of Basūs, of Dāḥis, of Bu'āṯ, involved warfare between brother tribes, Bakr and Taġlib, Aus and Khazraj, or even between two branches of the same tribe, 'Abs and Dubyān, both of Ġaṭafān. On the other hand, the idea of kinship did crystallize into an all but juridic force on the lowest genealogical level, namely, that of the clan, and this, into a force of the most forbidding kind. Within the fold of the clan—that is, as we have seen, within an independent group of families bound together by descent from a common ancestor whom they share with no other group—blood kinship is tantamount to blood solidarity in a virtually legal sense of the

21. See Wüstenfeld, *Register zu den genealogischen Tabellen*, pp. vii f.

word. Hence retaliation for the slaying of any member of the clan by an outsider is incumbent upon all its members. Conversely, when a member of the clan slays an outsider, the lives of all its members are held answerable by the clan of the slain until the bloodshed is duly avenged. In fact, blood feuds between clans of the same tribe or even of the same subtribe are a most common occurrence in pre-islamic Arabia. Here, then, clan consciousness takes precedence over tribe consciousness, both in the group of the slain and in that of the slayer. Within the clan, but not within the tribe or subtribe, the blood of the individual counts as an integral of the collective blood of the group in fact as well as in principle. It is as if the clan generates in its members a sense of uniqueness because only on this level do they descend from a common ancestor whom they share with no other group, so that his blood runs in their veins only.[22]

What makes this rule of blood revenge particularly devastating is that a single act of manslaughter may require many lives of both clans concerned before that act is considered properly avenged. Thus when the slayer himself is out of reach, the avengers may take the life of his next of kin or of any other member of his clan, and when subsequently the slayer is found, they may take his life as well. This may in turn lead the slayer's clan to retaliate for the additional members it has lost for only a single act of manslaughter. Nor does the matter end here. Where the identity of the slayer is unknown except to the extent that he evidently belonged to one of two, or to one of several, clans, the avengers may take a life of each of the groups concerned. Again the avenging clan often considers its blood more precious than that of the slayer's clan or considers the person of the slain superior in rank and prestige to that of the murderer; accordingly the avengers will proceed on the presumption that taking the life of the slayer is only part of the retribution due them, and here again, the added revenge is bound to result in a corresponding increase of counterrevenge.

The events best remembered in pre-islamic tradition—it is

22. Cf. Smith, *op. cit.*, pp. 22 ff.

safe to say the only events remembered—are those of conflict and collision between two groups that involved a more or less appreciable amount of bloodshed. Such an event is termed *yaum*, literally, " a day "; in the sense implied by the ancient storytellers and poets, the use of *yaum* here must be seen to denote a memorable occurrence in the history of the group or groups concerned, a notable chapter in their past record. Usually the term is qualified by the locale in which the collision came to a head, as the " Day of Kulāb," the " Day of Shi'b Jabala," the " Day of 'Ukāẓ "; sometimes it is qualified by the name of a person or object that figured prominently at the outset of the event, as the " Day of Basūs," the " Day of Ḥalīma," or the " Day of Dāḥis "; occasionally it is identified by an appellative characterizing the nature of the event, such as the " Day of Sacrilege," the " Day of Shaving of the Locks," or the " Day of Barred Gates." The recollections and traditions of such Days are preserved in narratives told in prose, the oldest and purest specimens of classical Arab prose to have come down to us. Nearly every tradition of a Day is interwoven with fragments of verse bearing on this or that detail or incident that marked its course—fragments from poems composed by spokesmen of one or the other of the two warring groups, often by spokesmen of both groups. Again, of nearly every major Day it is said—whether by the original storyteller or by its Moslem transmitter, it is often impossible to ascertain—that a great mass of poetry had been composed on its occasion. And in many cases much of this poetry has actually been preserved and has come down to us independent of the storyteller's account, often including the fragments cited *ad hoc* in his account.[23]

Starting as a collision between two single clans, of however close kinship, or merely as a dispute between two persons belonging to different clans, the event may develop into a blood feud between ever larger groups and gradually involve whole tribes or even federations of tribes. In cases of this kind tradition often remembers the whole cycle of events as the greater Day, con-

23. See W. Caskel, " *Aijām al-'Arab*," pp. 59 ff.

sisting of a series of minor Days. For example, the Day of Shaving of the Locks is remembered as the last of a cycle of clashes referred to as the great Day of Basūs, said to have lasted forty years, or the Day of Raḥraḥān as a prelude to that of Shi'b Jabala. The initial event may start with such insignificant an incident as the killing of a trespassing camel, as in the Day of Basūs, with a quarrel over a horse race, as the Day of Dāḥis, or with a dispute over watering rights, grazing privileges, and the like. Once, however, a life has been taken in the course of such an incident or quarrel, a blood feud of fatal consequences to both the group of the slayer and that of the slain is certain to ensue.

Most frequently, indeed, conflicts between Bedouin clans are precipitated merely by the dire economic conditions of North Arabia, a region for the most part sterile and arid, inhospitable to irrigation and cultivation. Especially in a period of drought with its inevitable result of scarcity of nourishment for man and beast, the raiding of a neighboring or distant settlement for sheep and camels is often the only means by which a clan can provide sustenance for its families.[24] Here, again, if in the course of a raid, one of the raiders or one of those raided is killed, this is apt to draw both parties into an unending strife of blood vengeance and may eventually engulf them and their allies and clients in a permanent state of war.[25] Essentially, then, the " Days of the Arabs " are cycles of blood feuds, of blood revenge and counterrevenge, that remained indelibly fixed in the historic recollections of the pagan Arabs together with, and as it were, in defiance of, their genealogical recollections.

The prose narratives of the Days are often told in great detail and nearly always with complete impartiality and anonymity. The ancient storyteller does not indicate with which of the two

24. An example of particular interest are the raids led by the poet 'Urwa b. al-Ward, which he himself describes at length; see his *Dīwān* (ed. T. Nöldeke, *Die Gedichte des 'Urwa ibn Alward*, Göttingen, 1863), Nos. 5 ff., and pp. 5 f.

25. Cf. above, n. 4.

opposing camps his sympathies are or whether he himself was an eyewitness to any part of the Day which he recounts. By contrast, the recounting of the Days in poetry is exceedingly terse and violently partisan. The pagan poet is not only a spokesman but as a rule also a chieftain and warrior of his clan and even of his tribe, so that he often describes raids he himself has instigated, Days in which he has taken a leading part. And as can be seen in the case of nearly each poet whose compositions have reached us collected in a divan, he returns to the theme of his clan's or tribe's Days again and again, except that he may vary in the number of Days he strings together and in the particular details of their course from one composition to another. When his compositions are seen as a whole, it appears that the poet has blended recent and less recent events into a single record of the past: he magnifies the warlike triumphs of his kin, boasting of the many lives that have been taken, the rich booty in camels and captives that has been made, in conjunction with similar triumphs achieved by the clan's forebears in bygone times. Only thus does he establish the heroic nobility and prestige of his kin and clan; for such prestige and nobility cannot be acquired; they must, like descent itself, be inherited by the medium of ancestral blood. Hence it is a matter of vital interest to the clan, often indeed a matter of self-preservation, to keep alive the memory of its ancestors' deeds and exploits on the field of battle and to convey this memory into an established record of the past through the mouth of its spokesmen and chieftains, its poets, rhapsodists, and storytellers. To the extent to which they deal with events of the past, which is very considerable indeed, nothing is more characteristic of the pagan Arab poets than their constant reiteration of assertions like " we have inherited nobility " (*wariṯnā 'l-majd*), " we have inherited prestige " (*wariṯnā 'l-ḥasab*), " we have inherited glorious lineage " (*wariṯnā 'n-nasab*).

It is impossible to appraise the character of any Arab personage known to us from pre-islamic antiquity without finding it necessary to dwell primarily on the extreme intensity of his clan consciousness as his dominant trait. It is a trait—sometimes termed *'aṣabīya*—that bespeaks total submergence of the individual in the collectivism of his ancestral heritage, and it is the source of both his perilous physical strength and his complete intellectual helplessness. As an individual, that is, outside the fold of his group, the pagan Arab is subject to no law, whether civil, moral, or criminal; in turn, his possessions, his family, and his very life are forever exposed to peril, except within that fold. As the guardian of his clan's heritage he clings to a record of the past which is essentially defined by the historic record of his clan alone; his genealogical consciousness may indeed reach back to the patriarchs of the northern Arabs, 'Adnān, Ma'add, Muḍar, Rabī'a, but it never goes beyond these patriarchs. As the bearer of the blood and the warlike prowess of his ancestors, he accepts as axiomatic the nobility and prestige of their past record, and hence he is unable to account for any flaw or mishap in that record except by postulating that it was governed by *dahr*, by a fate as blind and irresponsible as it is irresistible. In marrying the daughter of another clan, he may cause his offspring to pay dearly for the stain he has placed on their blood. In defending his clan, or in avenging bloodshed it has suffered, he is capable of inhuman cruelty, savage barbarism and treachery, and at the same time, of boundless gentility and devotion, fervent self-denial, serene self-sacrifice. In avenging the blood of his kin and clan, the pagan Arab is avenging his own blood; his thirst for revenge burns his insides like a consuming fever, a fever for which he seeks cure by bloodshed and which renders him insensible to any other reactions of sorrow or agony, his own no less than those of his victims.

Again a few examples out of a very great many must here suffice to illustrate the points at issue.

The war of Basūs comes to a head when Kulaib, the grand Shaikh of Taġlib, is killed by his brother-in-law Jassās, a prominent chieftain of the Banū Shaibān, a division of Bakr. Muhalhil, Kulaib's brother, sets out to avenge the slaying. After several sanguinary encounters between the two camps, a chieftain of the

Banū Ḥanīfa, a division of Bakr that had hitherto taken no part in the conflict, sends his young son Bujair with a message to Muhalhil, beseeching him to make peace and pointing out that enough blood has now been shed to avenge the murder of Kulaib. Upon receiving the message, and learning the identity of the messenger, Muhalhil kills the lad, exclaiming, "Die thou for Kulaib's shoe lachet." Upon occasion, however, this insatiable avenger is assailed by a sense of pity and remorse; but he finds it to be of no avail:

> Against the grief of our hearts, o people of Bakr,
> we attack you with spears well sharpened:
>
> We weep over you when we think of your fate,
> yet slay you as if we did not care.[26]

When the great Imrulqais learns about the slaying of his father by a man of Asad, the news affects him, in his own words, "like an earthquake that makes the mountain peaks tremble." He spends the rest of his days seeking to take more and more lives of the Banū Asad; for him, until the last day of his own life, the mountain peaks never ceased trembling. He dedicates his life to avenging the blood of his noble father on the entire tribe of Asad, spurred on by an all-engulfing sense of clan pride; but at the end of the road, he finds himself tormented by doubts. As he looks back to the whole of his clan's past, the poet is assailed by the realization that all might not be well with the axiom of ʿaṣabīya, which he had upheld so ardently and at so dire a cost. Clan heroism, clan nobility, clan virtues do not appear to have offered immunity to failure and disaster. Humiliation, treachery, and violent death had plagued the generations of Kinda's kings and princes: witness the infamous end of his royal grandfather al-Ḥāriṯ, of his royal father Ḥujr, of his princely uncle Shuraḥbīl on the Day of Kulāb. In this mood of reflection, he even doubts

26. Cited by Ibn Nubāṭa in J. L. Rasmussen, *Additamenta . . .* (Hauniae, 1821), p. 13; cf. Ḥam., pp. 93 f. and Rückert, *Hamâsa, 1*, 46; for the killing of Bujair, see Ibn al-Aṯīr, I, p. 394; Ḥam., p. 251, etc.

the wisdom of his own struggles for blood revenge, and significantly enough, he seems to question the worth of his and his kin's way of life: insatiable self-glory and self-indulgence coupled with avarice and cruelty. But he does not, as little as does any other pagan poet, suggest a solution of the riddles conjured up by his agonizing reflections. His qualms and queries simply come to a halt before the dark majesty of *dahr*, the impenetrable government of blind Fate:

I see ourselves hasten toward a goal unknown,
bewitched by the pleasures of food and drink:
[Like] sparrows, flies and insects,
yet more daring than ravenous wolves.

At the most noble of virtues did aim
my heart: by them only did I seek to profit.
My sinews did entangle the sinews of my kin—
yet death is to rob me of my youth:
Soon it will snatch my soul together with my body
and swiftly will it dispatch me to dust.

Did I not spur my camel through all manner of wilderness,
through long tracks of desert, in the glare of midday-mirages?
Yet how often did I journey about to the extremities of the land,
only to be satisfied with safe retreat in lieu of gain.

Could I, after what had befallen al-Ḥāriṯ the king,
after what had come over Ḥujr the noble, master of tents,
could I hope for leniency from the caprices of Fate
that leave not unruffled even the hardest mountain rocks?

Thus do I know that in but a short while
I shall be caught in the grip of tooth and claw,
even as my father Ḥujr suffered, and my grandfather,
and I have not forgotten the slain at Kulāb.[27]

A son of Zuhair b. Jaḏīma, the mighty chief of Qais 'Ailān, is

27. *Dīwān*, Nos. 43:2; 20:24; 5:1–2, 8, 4–5, 6–7, 9–13. De Slane, *Le Diwan*, p. 33:1–3, 5–9, 10–13; Rückert, *Amrilkais*, p. 80.

robbed of his possessions and killed while passing through the territory of Ganī, on his way home from visiting the court of Ḥīra. Having ascertained through an informer that the slayer was a man of the Ġanī tribe, Zuhair attacks them in force and takes a great many of their lives. When during the sacred months he attends the Fair of 'Ukāẓ and is challenged by Khālid b. Ja'far, then chief of the Banū Ja'far, maternal cousins of the Ganī, Zuhair meets the challenge by saying: "As long as strength is left to me, I shall pursue by it [my] blood revenge and there can be no cessation to it." [28]

The war of Dāḥis, between the two Gaṭafān tribes, 'Abs and Ḏubyān, breaks out in full fury after the chief of 'Abs, Qais, another son of Zuhair, has slain three brothers of a leading family of Ḏubyān—Auf, Ḥuḏaifa, and Ḥamal, sons of Badr—in avenging the slaying of his own brother Mālik. Eventually, Qais kills so many of the enemy camp that by his own confession he can never look at a Ġaṭafān woman without realizing that he must have taken the life of her father, her brother, or her lover. In reminiscing about his actions of 'aṣabīya, he moans:

> I did cure my soul on Ḥamal son of Badr,
> and the sword that slew Ḥuḏaifa did heal me.
>
> Yet though I cooled on them the fever of my heart,
> it's but my own fingers that I thus cut off.[29]

The renowned poet Mutalammis, uncle of the even more renowned Ṭarafa, was made to live a life of misery and desolation because he was the offspring of a mixed marriage, his father having been of the Banū Ḍubai'a, while his mother belonged to the Banū Yashkur, and neither group recognized him as fully their own. He himself cherishes equal loyalty to both, and in his own words, he would be "like a man who cuts off one of his

28. Ibn al-Aṯīr, I, 413 (*mā dāmat lī qūwatun 'udriku bihā ṯa'ran falā 'nṣirāma lahu*).

29. Ḥam., p. 96; on Qais' dictum concerning Ġaṭafān women, see Ibn al-Aṯīr, I, 434, l. 4, bottom.

hands with the other," if he were to renounce either side of his family. But this is precisely why he is despised by both, and why his treacherous patron, King 'Amr b. Hind, speaks of him with unconcealed sarcasm as of a person who falls between two stools.[30]

The poet 'Urwa b. al-Ward, although admired by his tribesmen for his boundless chivalry as well as his great poetic cunning, had to endure much suffering because he, too, was the offspring of an exogamous marriage, the two groups concerned being those of 'Abs and Nahd. He seems to have been forever reproached by his fellow 'Absites that his mother was a stranger (*ġarība*), a foreigner (*nazī'a*). He complains bitterly that although he himself is without taint, the fact that his maternal folk descended from Nahd deprived him of the ancestral glory (*majd*) for which he had striven. And in despair he exclaims that he wished he had been a slave, the son of a slave. Once he entreats the men of 'Abs not to blame his father for contaminating his son's lineage (*nasb*), seeing that among all the descendants of the Qais ('Ailān) he had been a man of undisputed prestige and nobility (*ḥasab*) until his association with the blood of Nahd.[31]

The poet Duraid, son of Ṣimma, an older contemporary of Mohammed, chief and captain of his clan—Ġazīya of the Hawāzin—is said to have fought in a hundred wars and raids. While returning from a successful raid against the Ġaṭafān, the raiders are ordered to halt by Duraid's brother 'Abdallāh, who led the expedition, in order to divide the spoils, although Duraid himself sternly warns against halting. They are overtaken by the pursuing Ġaṭafān, and in the battle that ensues 'Abdallāh is killed and Duraid severely wounded. Upon recovering from his wounds, Duraid avenges the slaying of his brother by visiting in succession each division of the Ġaṭafān and killing some of its members, thus taking the lives of men of 'Abs, Fazāra, and Ta'laba b. Sa'd

30. *Dīwān* (ed. K. Vollers, *Beiträge zur Assyriologie 5*, 1906, 166 ff.), No. 1:1 (*yu'aiyirūnī 'ummī*), 10–11; see the scholion, p. 166, ll. 9 ff.; see below, n. 31.

31. *Dīwān* (see above, n. 24), Nos. 9:9 (*hum 'aiyarūnī 'anna 'ummī ġarība*); 16; 19:1–3; 20:1 (*a'aiyartumūnī 'anna 'ummī nazī'a*); cf. above, n. 30.

for the single life of his brother. Referring to the incident Duraid says:

> Even when they disobeyed me, I still was one of them;
> I did see their folly, yet I followed not my own counsel:
>
> Am I not but one of Ġazīya? If they then err,
> I must err; and if they go right, I go right.[32]

Three other brothers of Duraid were killed in blood feuds. When asked why he does not weep over their deaths, he replies in effect that it was the trait of his nature to receive the visitations of fate with calm resignation (*bunītu 'ala ṣ-ṣabr*). He then proceeds to meditate upon his and his brothers' way of life, and in doing so, he offers one of the most revealing self-portrayals of 'aṣabīya to be found in pre-islamic poetry:

> Slaughter has desired none but the sons of Ṣimma,
> and they have desired naught but slaying: thus destiny meets destiny.
>
> Is it not that our bloodstream is forever haunted by
> relentless avengers—[haunted] to the end of time?
>
> Now it is *our* flesh with which the sword is fed,
> now, again, we are those that feed it with the flesh of others.
>
> Now it is *our* blood that is sought to give healing
> when it's shed; now it's we that slay, seeking cure.
>
> Thus we divide the blows of Fate between us,
> and it never comes to rest until we [both] receive our share.[33]

A different aspect of 'aṣabīya is described, in no less blunt and self-revealing terms, by the poetess Umaima, daughter of 'Abd Manāf, of the Quraish. It forms part of a dirge she is said to

32. Ḥam., 378, ll. 2, 4; for a different rendering, see Lyall, *Ancient Arabian Poetry*, p. 38; cf. Aġ., X, 3:13; 6:11 ff.; 11:13 ff.

33. Ḥam., 381 f. (cf. 380:5b); for a different translation, see Lyall, *Ancient Arabian Poetry*, p. 41.

have composed over those of her kin who fell in the Sacrilegious War—so-called because it came to a head at 'Ukāẓ during the period of sacred truce:

> If I bewail them, it's because they are my might:
> they are my pillar and they are my flank.
>
> They are my root and they my branches,
> theirs is the pedigree when mine I recite.
>
> They are my nobility and they my pride,
> they are my fortress when fear assails me.
>
> They are my spear and they my shield,
> they are my sword in all vexations.[34]

III. THE GREAT TURNING POINT

1. MONOTHEISM AND WORLD HISTORY

It is against this background and outlook of the pre-islamic Arabs that the revelation of Mohammed must be viewed to become historically coherent and ideologically tangible. That his theory of revelation and the substance of his message are deeply anchored in the teachings of the Jewish Synagogue and the Christian Church must be kept constantly in mind, to be sure; but in the present connection, this is merely of methodological interest. Of greater importance is the fact that his prophetic genius, his profoundly personal religious experience, spurred him on to make the essence of those teachings wholly and permanently his own and to strive to bring it to bear on the hearts and minds, the conduct and practice, of his fellow Arabs. The vital and decisive thing, however, is that when his mission of twenty-odd years is scrutinized in its entirety, we are forced to realize that he merely succeeded in superimposing the message of Judeo-Christian monotheism upon the legacy of his native environment, but that he failed to eradicate that legacy in himself and in his followers. Put to the test

34. Aġ., XIX, 82; cf. Caussin de Perceval, *Essai*, *1*, 318.

of sociopolitical leadership, he continues to speak in the tongue of monotheism, but his actions and deliberations reflect the ideas and mores in which he had been reared and among which he had spent the two thirds of his life that preceded his call.

Critical study of his career and his message has led scholars to propose that the phenomenon of Mohammed in Mecca is one thing, but that of Mohammed in Medina is quite another. Actually, even his teachings in the Mecca period occasionally foreshadow his conduct in Medina, while his sermon in the latter continues to re-echo that of the former period.[35] The plain truth is that the interplay between the religious ideals of Islamism and the ethnic forces of Arabism—an interplay which was destined to weigh so heavily on the community of the faithful throughout its history—becomes obvious in the development of Mohammed's mission itself.

Throughout his prophetic career, whether in Mecca or in Medina, the lessons of history dominate his pronouncements as recorded in the Koran. There is hardly a sura of any length in which those lessons do not occupy the center of his argumentation. There is even a certain resemblance between *his* preoccupation with events of the past and that of the pagan poets: both are characterized by emotional intensity, rhetorical pathos, incessant reiteration. But here the resemblance ends. In point of span, outlook, and moral applicability, Mohammed's concept of history differs immeasurably from that of the ancient Arabs and his own contemporaries. His knowledge of the great epochs and upheavals in bygone times, of their inner meaning for the past and their lessons for the present and the future, has been sent down to him by divine revelation. Of necessity, then, it is as new to his fellow Arabs as it is to himself.[36] His own salvation has come

35. For the Mecca period, cf. the reference to the deities al-Lāt, al-'Uzza, and Manāf; also to sacrifice (Sura 53:19 f.; cf. Nöldeke and Schwally, p. 110, n. 4; and Sura 108:2); for the Medina period, see below pp. 274 ff.

36. For example, of the Noah story, Allah says to Mohammed: "Thou didst not know it, neither thou nor thy people before this" (Sura 11:51); similarly, of the Joseph story (Sura 12:3). By contrast, he is told with regard

by an overwhelming experience of the existence of the one God of the world whose will and command had been proclaimed by all prophets of former generations: in the main, non-Arab messengers of God sent to non-Arab peoples. And as he begins to make his fellow Meccans share in his salvation, he employs as sole means of persuasion the argument from the manifestations of this God in the works of the universe and the history of the human race. Nor is this postulated correlation between monotheism and world history of Mohammed's own making. God himself vouches for the veracity of this correlation. Most of the great events and epochs of the past had indeed long since been made known by prophets of former times, or as Mohammed puts it, " had been sent down before." But to him the events are revealed anew; more than that, to him the events are revealed with special emphasis on their peculiar religious and moral significance, that is, we might say, with special emphasis on their historiological interpretation.

Mohammed's recounting of the events of the past goes back to the beginning of time: the creation of heaven and earth, of the first man and woman, by an act of God. The purpose and design of this act, while apparent from the beginning, became especially manifest in generations of great calamity and visitation. Mohammed hints at his awareness of a very great number of such generations,[37] but he dwells most frequently upon the biblical accounts of the Flood, the people of Sodom and Gomorrah, the fate of the Egyptians at the exodus, and the purely Arabic legends of the destruction of ʿĀd and Ṯamūd. In each of these and similar instances, a human messenger—Noah, Lot, Moses, Hūd, Ṣāliḥ—arose to warn that the impending disaster was a day of God's judgment, a retribution for the disregard of God's will and command. Now another visitation was impending, a cataclysm of

to incidents of Arab history: " Hast thou not seen how thy Lord did with ʿĀd? " (Sura 89:5); or " Hast thou not seen how thy Lord did with the fellows of the elephant? " which is generally seen to refer to the expedition of Abraha against Mecca (Sura 105:1).

37. Cf. Sura 14:9–10.

cosmic dimensions, this time to befall his own people, and he, Mohammed, was sent to warn them that the Day of Judgment was at hand.

He does not always present a given cycle of events of the remote past in chronological order, but he often indicates his awareness of their proper succession by such phrases as " and then," " and after that," " and before that." Of Abraham he says that this patriarch, the " friend of God," was not a Jew or a Christian, seeing that the Torah and the Evangel were not sent down except *after* his time.[38] In a passage that may well have been intended as a sarcastic reference to the Arabs' tribal-genealogical notions of history, he says in effect that " a thousand years of your counting " is but a single day in the history of God's doings, that is, in the true history of man and the world.[39]

At the beginning of his mission in Mecca, Mohammed speaks as an individual to individuals. He is only a warner like " the warners of old," an admonisher, not an overseer; and his is not the speech of a poet (*šāʿir*) or a soothsayer (*kāhin*). As a warner he is not answerable for the effect of his message, acceptance or rejection of which is put on an entirely voluntary basis. It is merely a reminder to men, a warning to mankind, " to whosoever of you wishes to be forward or to lag behind," " to whosoever chooses a way to his Lord "; it is an admonition to anyone " who has a heart and is willing to understand." [40]

In essence, his message proclaims that man is in great peril of the trial he is to face on the Day of Judgment, which in the eschatology of Mohammed coalesced with the Day of Resurrection. Depending on whether or not he lets himself be guided by God's warning and admonition, man will enter into the bliss of paradise or be condemned to the scourge of hellfire. In either

38. Sura 3:58; cf. 14:9 f.; 51:90; 53:55, and specifications such as *min qablu, min baʿdu*, throughout the Koran.

39. Sura 22:46; 32:4; 70:4 (here 50,000!); underlying is, of course, the biblical verse: *For a thousand years in Thy sight are but as yesterday when it is past* (Ps. 90:4); cf. A. Geiger, *Was hat Mohammed*, etc., p. 76.

40. Sura 50:36; 53:57; 69:41–2; 88:21–2, etc.

case his blessed or tortured life in the hereafter is to be everlasting. Here the past history of the race projects into the future, an infinite future, and God's plan and purpose at the time of creation is tested on, and experienced by, each individual. " I have not created jinn and man except that they worship Me. I desire from them no provision of any kind, nor do I desire that they should feed Me." Man should be aware that every whisper of his soul is known to God; indeed, God is " nearer to man than his jugular vein " (*ḥabal al-warīd*) .[41]

Nowhere in the first Meccan period does Mohammed stress cult and ritual, such as sacrifice, pilgrimage, or organized public service of any kind. Nor would this have been compatible with a message centered on man's individual responsibility to the one God of the world. He does speak of prayer, but rarely does he now use the word *ṣalāt*, which later was to become the term for the institution of regulated prayer meetings. Instead, he now speaks of prayer in the sense of private meditation and personal communion, begging for forgiveness, praise and thanksgiving; and apparently he believes that prayer of this kind is best performed at night when man is alone with his conscience.[42]

What, then, does God desire of man? Mohammed answers this question in the numerous pronouncements of the Meccan period in which he describes the Day of Judgment, the basic theme of his message in that period. On that day every ounce of man's own deeds on earth, good or evil, shall be weighed, and no account will be taken of man's blood kinship and earthly affiliations. On that day " man shall flee from his brother, from his mother and his father, and from his wife and his sons—each one of them that Day will have a concern to occupy himself [alone]." [43] Similarly, on that day " no man shall account for another in any way, for the affair will then be [wholly] unto God." [44] Thus clan consciousness and tribal nobility are here

41. Sura 50:15; 51:56–7.

42. Sura 50:38 f.; 51:17 f.; 52:48 f.; 53:62; 93:11; 96:19; etc.; cf. especially, Sura 73:6.

43. Sura 80:34–7.

44. Sura 70:8–14; 82:19; etc.

declared null and void. Only matters of the mind and the heart shall be of consequence in the ultimate computation of man's worth: whether or not he did believe in God and the Day of Judgment, whether or not he did engage in prayer and meditation, whether or not he did practice charity by setting free of slaves, feeding the poor, the orphan, and the prisoner, out of love for God, out of desire for God's presence.[45]

All this, however, would hardly have sufficed as basis for a new world religion—as little as the teachings of Amos and Hosea would have sufficed as foundation for the Jewish Synagogue, or the Sermon on the Mount would have been sufficient to precipitate the rise of the Christian Church. It was Mohammed's flight to Medina that brought about the great turning point not only in his own career and the history of the Arabs but indeed in the course of human civilization. For it was only during his ministry in Medina—his home for the last ten years of his life—that his Meccan " warning " and " admonition " crystallized into an ecclesiastic reality of durable force and of incalulable political consequence.

2. ARABISM AND ISLAMISM. FUSION OF IDEOLOGIES

In Medina, Mohammed is no longer an admonisher of individuals. Although he continues to know himself to be the Messenger of Allah, his status has undergone a change in two different directions. He is now the high priest of a sizable community of followers, and at the same time, the chieftain of a purely political confederacy comprising all the people of Medina, pagan and Jews no less than his converted followers. This alone should suffice to account for the far-reaching metamorphosis to which he now subjects his teachings. As his message becomes the established credo of a community it becomes more and more institutionalized, aug-

45. Sura 69:33 (expressed in negative terms); 70:22–6 (in positive terms); 74:44–7 (in negative terms); 76:8 f. (in positive terms); cf. especially, 90:13–16; 92:18–20; see Obermann, " Islamic Origins," pp. 107 ff.

mented by legal provisions, cult, and observances; and as he finds himself the political chief of an Arab *umma,* his deliberations tend more and more in the centrifugal direction of Arabism. Such was the inevitable, if paradoxical, price he paid for undertaking to convert the Arab masses within a single generation to the belief in one God of the world.

Upon his migration to Medina, Mohammed's followers consisted of three small groups, each belonging to a different tribe: those who migrated with him from Mecca, the so-called *Muhājira,* who were all of the Quraish, and his Medinan converts, called *Anṣār,* "Helpers," who belonged to respective branches of the two leading tribes of Medina, Aus and Khazraj. In keeping with the thesis of his early message that on the Day of Judgment no account will be taken of man's earthly affiliations, Mohammed unites the Muhājira and the Anṣār into a brotherhood of faith and institutes a number of observances that outwardly mark off this new, ecclesiastic, brotherhood. Still in keeping with his early conviction that he is one like the "warners of old," he adjusts those observances to the practice of the Jewish Synagogue and the Christian Church: he establishes in his quarters a *masjid,* a place of community service; he adds to the meditations of morning and evening, which he had postulated in his Mecca teachings, a daily midday prayer; he designates Friday as a day of divine public service; he instructs his followers to perform ablution before praying, to face in the direction of Jerusalem while praying, and to fast on the tenth day of Muḥarram, the first month of the Arab year, corresponding to the fast of Atonement on the tenth day of Tishri, the first month of the Jewish year.[46]

In contrast, however, to his provision that they enter a brotherhood of faith, Mohammed makes no attempt whatsoever to have

46. Ibn Hishām, pp. 336–8, 344 f.; Ibn Sa'd, ed. E. Sachau, I, Pt. II, 9 ff.; Ibn Qutaiba, *Kitāb al-Ma'ārif* (ed. F. Wüstenfeld), p. 85; Ibn al-Atīr, II, 88 (*ra'ā l-yahūd taṣūm 'āšūrā' fa-ṣāmahu wa-'amara biṣiyāmihi*); cf. Nöldeke and Schwally, p. 179, n. 1. See also Sura 2:136 (the former *qibla*); 2:39; 5:8; 62:9; cf. C. H. Becker in *Der Islam, 3* (1912), 379.

his followers sever the tribal and clan allegiances imposed upon them by their affiliations in pagan times. In setting forth the rules that were to govern the alliance he entered into with the people of Medina, he makes it abundantly clear that the three tribal divisions of his followers—the Quraish, the Aus, and the Khazraj—should continue to heed their former ties of blood kinship, and that, consistently, each of the numerous groups and subgroups that hitherto constituted the population of that city should retain its peculiar social and political constitution intact, whether the group be Moslem, Jewish, or pagan, or a combination of any of the three. Instead, the alliance was essentially military in nature: it pledged the contracting parties to a permanent truce and to mutual aid and assistance in case of war against any outside enemy.[47] It thus did not differ from similar political alliances between Arab groups in pagan times, except that the treaty of Medina was guaranteed and vouchsafed by Allah and by "Mohammed, the Messenger of Allah." Throughout the treaty he implies that the prospect of warfare is imminent, that clashes with outside enemies are certain to be forthcoming. He makes it plain that, by the instrument of the treaty, he seeks primarily to secure military aid in behalf of his followers; and hence he refers to the prospective warfare as *qitāl fi 's-sabīl Allāh*, "warfare in the cause of Allah." [48]

In point of fact, throughout his entire period at Medina Mohammed's main occupation is that of warfare: organizing raids and attacks, fighting off counterattacks. Moslem tradition itself refers to this activity of Mohammed during his mission at Medina as *maġāzī*, a term normally employed in reference to the raids and attacks during the pagan Days of the Arabs. It is indeed as if having become the leader of an Arab umma, Mohammed

47. Ibn Hishām, pp. 341–4; Wellhausen, *Gemeindeordnung*, pp. 67 ff.; Al-Wāqidī, *Kitāb al-Maġāzī*, p. 185:3 (*wa-kāna 'r-rajulu yakūnu musliman wa-'abūhu mušrikan*).

48. See above, n. 4. Cf. Ibn Hishām, p. 342:9 (*la yusālam mu'min dūna mu'min fī qitāl fi 'ṣ-sabīl allāh*); p. 343:11 (*wa-'anna 'l-yahūd yunfīqūn ma'a 'l-mu'minūn mā dāmū muḥāribīn*); see also the concluding passage, p. 344:2 ff.

gradually reverted to the warlike, marauding type of chieftain—the only type that hitherto had been known in Arab society.

During this period, Medina is at once the religious center of Islam and its military headquarters, with the Prophet as its warlord and the community of the faithful as its armed forces. Tradition has counted no fewer than seventy-four raids and wars in which Mohammed and his Moslem converts fought against many Arab tribes, and most particularly, against the Quraish of Mecca.[49] In most of these military engagements Mohammed is the aggressor; in all of them he is the commander-in-chief; in many of them he commands the Moslem forces on the battlefield as well. After the raid at Nakhla he even abolishes the age-old and universally honored observance of an annual sacred truce.[50] Hereafter, Arabs could fight against one another the year round without undue interruption. The battle of Badr, celebrated in Moslem history as one of Mohammed's greatest triumphs, involved no religious or missionary element of any kind, once we eliminate the angels said to have fought on Mohammed's side. In this battle, the first major encounter between Moslem Arabs and pagan Arabs, each of the three Moslem groups fights under its own tribal banner—Quraish, Aus, and Khazraj—as this would have been done in pagan times.[51] His warfare differs in no way from the intertribal warfare of the pagan past, with all its outward horrors and cruelties and all the irrational fanaticism of ʿaṣbīya. Their common objective is pillage, revenge, bloodshed, the difference being in name only. Mohammed firmly believes that *his* warfare is *jihād*, wars waged in "pious effort," *qiṭāl fi 's-sabīl*

49. See the list in Wellhausen, *Muhammed in Medina*, pp. 29–31; the number of expeditions led by Mohammed himself is given as twenty-seven both by Ibn Hishām (p. 972:4, bottom) and Wāqidī (Wellhausen, *ibid.*, p. 29, n. 1); but cf. Wāqidī, p. 6:13, where the number is given as 19. Cf. Ibn al-Aṯīr, II, 231:4 ff.

50. Wāqidī, pp. 8–10; Wellhausen, *Muhammed in Medina*, pp. 34–7; Ibn Hishām, pp. 424 f.; cf. Sura 2:214.

51. Wāqidī, p. 53:4 (bottom) ff.; on the Day of Sacrilege, the forces of the Quraish are formed according to their clans or genealogical grouping; cf. Ibn al-Aṯīr, I, 443:11 (*ʿalā kull baṭn minhā raʾīs*).

Allāh, " fighting in the cause of Allah." Yet, even on his deathbed, he orders Usāma b. Zaid to lead an expeditionary force against a settlement of Arabs at Mu'ta for the sole purpose of blood revenge, plain and simple. They were not to be offered the opportunity to accept Islam and thus be spared the attack. The order Usāma received from the Prophet was to burn and destroy, to kill, and to take captives.[52]

It seems impossible to dissociate Mohammed's remarkable victory at Badr from the persistent process of Arabization to which he now subjects his ministry and which he pursues to its ultimate conclusions. Some time after Badr, he orders that in future raids and wars in the cause of Allah he is to receive a fifth of the spoils, in keeping with a corresponding prerogative exercised by war chiefs in pagan times.[53] Having established a house of public worship shortly after his settlement in Medina, as we have seen, whereby he no doubt followed the practice of Jews and Christians, he now designates a special sanctuary outside the city to serve as substitute for the Ka'ba, the pagan shrine at Mecca. It is in this sanctuary, termed *muṣallā*, that he offers two animal sacrifices, one for himself and one for his umma, on the tenth day of Ḏu 'l-Ḥijja following his victory at Badr, and each year thereafter, in agreement with the age-old sacrifice ritual observed on that day during the annual pilgrimage feast at Mecca.[54] Although during his mission at Mecca he emphatically dissociated himself from poets, he now permits a number of bards —Ka'b b. Mālik, 'Abdallah b. Rawāḥa, and especially his laureate and champion, Ḥassān b. Ṯābit—to sing his praise and to contest with visiting Bedouin poets much in the manner that had long been practiced at the courts of Arab rulers and princes in pagan times.

52. Wellhausen, *ibid.,* (from Codex Prestonianus; cf. p. 6), p. 435; cf. the first battle of Mu'ta, pp. 309 ff.; Arabic text, pp. 401 ff.

53. Sura 8:42; cf., e.g., the share 'Abdallāh b. Ṣimma receives as leader of the successful raid against the Ġaṭafān (above, p. 262), Aġ., X, 6:3.

54. Tabarī, *Annales,* ed. M. J. De Goeje, I, 1362; Ibn Sa'd, I, Pt. II, 9:2 (*yuḍaḥḥī fī kulli 'ām*); 9:11 ff.; cf. Bukhārī, ed. M. L. Krehl, *K. al-Aḍāḥī,* No. 6.

As if he wished to rid himself of every vestige of the Jewish-Christian legacy he had at first so whole-heartedly embraced, he now modifies or cancels altogether even those observances he had introduced since his migration to Medina. Invariably, the modification or cancellation moves in the direction of Arabization. Blood kinship, he *now* declares in effect, takes precedence over the brotherhood in faith between the Muhājira and the Anṣār which he himself had provisioned and sanctioned.[55] The direction toward Jerusalem during prayer is now replaced by the *qibla* toward Mecca.[56] The weekly day of community worship, he now says, is a day of pious gathering and not a day of rest as well.[57] His revelation, he now constantly emphasizes, is an Arabic Koran, and not a foreign one.[58] The fast of the tenth day of Muḥarram is now cancelled and apparently replaced by the fast of Ramaḍān.[59] The truce of Medina, which his treaty had solemnly guaranteed to Moslems and Jews alike, is now rescinded with tragic results. It is hard to see how merely the refusal of the Jewish tribes of Medina to recognize him as a prophet should have led him to perpetrate their complete extermination, first by the expulsion of the Banū Qainuqā' and the Banū Naḍīr, and finally, by the massacre of the Banū Quraiza. Rather, we are all but forced to assume that in this, too, the Arabization process served at least as a strong contributing factor. The umma was now to be not only wholly Moslem but wholly Arab as well.

It is entirely inadmissible, however, to see in Mohammed's teachings and arbitrations during his mission at Medina a " betrayal " of the ministry he had initiated at Mecca. The cumulative testimony of his pronouncements offers, I believe, unequivocal evidence for the fact that the factors and circumstances

55. Sura 8:76; 33:6.

56. Sura 2:138–9; 2:144–5; cf. Ibn Sa'd, I, Pt. II, 3:20 ff.; cf. above, n. 46.

57. Sura 62:10; contrast 62:9 (*wa-ḏarū 'l-bai'a*).

58. Sura 12:2; 13:37; 16:105; 26:195; 39:29 (*qur'ānan 'arabīyan ġaira ḏī 'iwaj*); 41:2; 42:5; 43:2; 46:11.

59. Sura 2:179–81; cf. Nöldeke and Schwally, *1*, 179, n. 1; Ibn al-Aṯīr, II, 88:2, bottom (*falammā furiḍa ramaḍān lam ya'murhum bi ṣaumi 'āšūrā'*).

that came into play after his flight had merely forced him to vacillate between Arabism and Islamism—between the morale of Arab society, of which he was now an exponent, and his monotheistic piety as an individual—and made him aspire to a fusion of ideologies which he obviously thought could be reconciled. Therein lies the true significance of his mission, and also, the great enigma of his personality. In Medina, no less than in Mecca, his ministry is inspired by the power of prophecy, and nearly all his pronouncements bear the stamp of revelation. His arguments from world history and creation have now undergone a far-reaching change in style and direction, but not in force or persistence. Now as before he continues to draw on events of former millenia and to know himself as one with the " warners of old " —now especially with Moses, Abraham, and Jesus—apparently in complete unawareness that his terms of reference to those events and personages are at vast variance with the terms of his original mission, or that his daily conduct now makes even his present inspirations sound like a sham and a mockery.

Often, indeed, he feels prompted to mitigate his present acts of Arabization by invoking a word of God or re-echoing the spirit of piety he had preached at Mecca or citing the authority of the " warners of old." Thus Moses is to him now not the messenger sent to warn Pharaoh of the Day of Judgment but primarily the prophet who brought down the Book of Salvation to his umma only to find them rebellious, even as he himself found the Jewish tribes of Medina rebellious and had to eliminate them from his own umma. A similarly significant change marks his references to Abraham. In the midst of his unsparing raids and wars against the Arabs, of relentless spoiling and slaying in the cause of Allah, he recounts an ancient revelation to the effect that he who takes the life of another without due cause counts as if he had destroyed the whole human race.[60] He now pleads that total jihād is only a means of preventing the greater evil of *fitna*,

60. Sura 5:35 (*katabnā 'alā banī Isrā'il*); expressed in positive and negative terms (in agreement with Mishnah Sanh., 4:5; see Geiger, *op. cit.*, p. 102); cf. also, Sura 6:152; 17:35.

that is, of faction and dissension in matters of conversion to Islam: fitna, he now frequently exclaims, is worse than slaying! [61] Again, about the time he orders the change of the qibla from the temple of Jerusalem to the Ka'ba, he warns his followers: "To God belongs the East and the West: whichever way you turn, God's presence is there." [62] In a mood of pious indignation, he now finds words of rebuke against poets even sharper than those he used in Mecca,[63] although he has now admitted some poets to his entourage. Although, as we have seen, he now puts blood kinship above brotherhood in faith, he warns time and again that the Arabs' ethnic heritage, their cleaving to the ways of their "fathers," is the greatest hindrance to their acceptance of his "guidance." [64] In an utterance held by tradition to have been made by the Prophet on the occasion of his "conquest" of Mecca—the very climax of the process of Arabization he had pursued during his mission at Medina—he argues, from the creation of the first man and woman, that the Arabs have been divided into "tribes and subtribes" by God's own design, "in order that ye vie with one another [in piety]; lo, the noblest of you, in the eyes of Allah, is the most pious." [65] And repeatedly he chides the converted Bedouins that faith has not entered their

61. Sura 2:137, 214 f.; 8:39–42; etc.

62. Sura 2:109, 172 ("it is not piety that ye should turn your faces towards the East or the West, but [true] piety is . . .").

63. Sura 26:221–6.

64. Sura 2:165 ("Nay, we will follow what we found our ancestors doing"); 5:103; 7:27; 10:79 ("Hast thou come to us in order to turn us away from what we found our fathers practicing?"); 31:20; 43:21 f., etc. As pointed out by Goldziher (*1*, 10), Mohammed puts the same argument in the mouths of the former generations that had rejected the "warning" of *their* prophets; cf. Sura 21:54; 43:21, etc.

65. Sura 49:13; for the rendering "that you vie with one another," required by the context, see Lane, *s.v.* *'rf 6*; cf. Zamakhsharī, *Kashshāf* (Cairo, 1925), *2*, 399; for the various addenda by which this verse was expanded in tradition, see Goldziher, *1*, 70 ff.; it is remarkable that Goldziher prefers to follow a less attested tradition whereby the verse (49:13) formed part of a valedictory (*Abschiedsrede*) of the Prophet during the so-called Farewell Pilgrimage (*ḥajjat al-wadā'*); see below, p. 298, and n. 123.

hearts; therefore they must not say, "We believe" (*'āmannā*), but only, "We have submitted to Islam" (*'aslamnā*).[66]

Occasionally he betrays something like a troubled conscience, but this is soon overcome by the comfort of a reassuring revelation. Of particular interest, within the present inquiry, is the case of the pilgrimage ritual. Tradition relates that at no time during his ministry at Mecca did the Prophet partake in the great annual pilgrimage feast of the pagan Arabs.[67] This we would have been obliged to infer from the nature of his teaching prior to the flight. We have seen, however, that following his victory at Badr, he initiated an annual day of animal offerings at the muṣallā near Medina, corresponding to the "day of sacrifice" at the pilgrimage feast at Mecca, from which he and his followers had been banished. Eventually, he goes even further and declares that the pilgrimage itself, with its elaborate rites and sacrifices of purely pagan origin, is commendable, and that these rites and sacrifices are like the "observances" (*manāsik*) and "symbols" (*ša'ā'ir*) which, in all past history, God had "proscribed for each umma.[68] But even now he apparently feels uneasy at admitting into Islam so gross a monument of Arab paganism, and hence, in speaking of the pilgrimage rites, he merely says that there is "no sin" if a Moslem makes the circuit of Ṣafā and Marwa; and he seems to speak in a similar vein about the rites of 'Arafāt and Muzdalifa. He is, moreover, well aware

66. Sura 49:14. The verse was quite naturally destined to figure prominently in philosophical and theological discussions of later times on the distinction between faith (*'īmān*) and Islam; cf. e. g., Ġazālī, *Iḥyā* (Cairo, 1346), *1*, 103 ff.

67. Cf. Ibn Sa'd, II, Pt. I, 134:25 (on the authority of Anas); this, I take it, can only mean "a single pilgrimage" since the beginning of his prophetic career; hence the alternative tradition (on the authority of Mujāhid): twice before and once after the flight (Ibn Sa'd, II, Pt. I, 135:26); cf. Ibn al-Aṯīr, II, 232:5 (once before and once after the flight). In later times, it was apparently hard to imagine that the Prophet should have failed to perform the pilgrimage over a period of some twenty years; hence, no doubt, the fluctuation in tradition. See below, n. 72.

68. Sura 22:35, 37, 66; cf. 2:153, 196; etc.

that the flesh and blood of animal sacrifices cannot reach Allah, and that what alone does reach God is man's inner piety.[69]

But all his misgivings are finally removed by a revelation to the effect that the foundations of the Ka'ba had been laid by none other than Abraham himself, the true founder of monotheism; that the sanctity of Mecca and its cult have come about by a covenant of God with Abraham and his son Ishmael. Now Mohammed is able to speak without hesitation of the pilgrimage to Mecca as a fundamental tenet of Islam, as each Moslem's obligation toward Allah. For now Mecca has been put in a context of world history and religious universalism: " Behold the first sanctuary ever founded for man was that of Mecca—a blessed one and a guidance to all the world." No longer need he apologize, as it were, for its observances and rites; now they are " signs " of revelation, " evidences " of the truth, now that the Ka'ba has been transformed into the topos of Abraham (*maqām 'Ibrāhīm*).[70] The fusion thus has been curiously polarized. The Arabization of Islam had led Mohammed so far as to include the age-old national center of Arab worship in his institutionalized monotheism; now this stark residue of pre-Islamic paganism is in turn Islamicized by being anchored in God's primeval design for the salvation of man.

Having conquered Mecca, in the eighth year after the flight, by diplomatic maneuver and a show of force, Mohammed was able to decree in the following year, in a proclamation known as the *barā'a*, that hereafter no Arab would be allowed to participate in the pilgrimage except upon conversion to Islam.[71] Accordingly, when in the tenth year, he himself performs the pilgrimage—for the first time in twenty years[72]—the mass of pilgrims consists

69. Sura 2:153 (*lā junāḥ 'alaihi 'an yaṭauwafa bihimā*); 2:194 (*laisa 'alaikum junāḥ . . .*); 22:38 (Neither their flesh nor their blood does reach Allah; but your own piety will reach Him).

70. Sura 2:119–23; 3:90 (*Bakka* for " Mecca "); 3:91 (*'āyāt, baiyināt*; see, on these terms, Obermann, " Islamic Origins," p. 81).

71. Sura 9:1 ff.; cf. Wellhausen, *Das arabische Reich*, p. 14.

72. On the " little pilgrimage " alleged to have been made by Mohammed

entirely of Arabs converted to the belief in Allah and Mohammed as His messenger. The manifold rites and ceremonies executed by Mohammed on this memorable occasion, the "Farewell Pilgrimage," were the same as those that since time immemorial had been carried out annually by pagan Arabs in honor of their several gods and idols worshiped in and around Mecca: the circuit around the Ka'ba, kissing the Black Stone, running between Ṣafā and Marwa, halting at 'Arafāt and Muzdalifa, casting stones at al-'Aqaba, offering sacrificial animals at Minā, and so forth.[73] But now these ancient rites and ceremonies were carried out by the Messenger of Allah and a congregation of Moslems; now for the first time they were performed in the name and to the glory of the one God of all the world.

In a declaration he made during his mission at Mecca, Mohammed gives solemn expression to his complete severance from the pagan past of the Arabs:

> O ye unbelievers,
> I worship not what ye worship
> And ye are not worshipers of what I worship.
> I am not a worshiper of what ye have worshiped;
> Nor are ye worshipers of what I have worshiped.
> Ye have your religion—I have mine.[74]

Would he have been justified to stress a claim of this kind at the *end* of his career? The question would have to be answered decidedly in the negative if it were considered in the light of the

in the year 8 A. H., see F. Buhl, art. "Muḥammad," *EI*, *3*, 656a: "The prophet, although he was now lord of Mecca, did not yet take part in the pilgrimage in the year 8, which was so inexplicable to later generations that they invented an *'umra* unknown to many of his followers." See also, the literature cited by Buhl, *ibid.*; it is indeed remarkable that none of the transmitters adduced above (n. 67) refers to the alleged pilgrimage of 8 A. H.; see especially Ibn al-Aṯīr, II, 232 (giving Jābir as the authority), where the one pilgrimage made by the Prophet after the flight, i. e., the one of 10 A. H., is qualified by the words *ma'ahā 'umra*.

73. See the description of the *ḥajjat al-wadā'* in Ibn Sa'd, II, Pt. I, 124 ff.

74. Sura 109.

legal, social, and political provisions which dominate his teaching and conduct during his period at Medina—provisions of stark compromise, of cruel intolerance, of pitiless, aggressive warfare. But there can be no doubt that in one respect his breach with the pagan past remains complete and inexorable throughout his entire career, namely, his belief in one God of the world and its correlation with the idea of world history. In this Mohammed is uncompromising from beginning to end, even as idolatry is the one cardinal sin that Allah does not forgive.[75] After Mohammed's time various theologians were to evolve a variety of conflicting theories about his concept of God, all based on his own revelation. He himself never theorizes; his is the belief of an inspired, emotional visionary. His tone and mood of expression vary; his vision of Allah's rule and design remains constant. The monotheistic history of the world is ruled not by Fate but by Providence. The destiny of man and the works of the universe are governed not by the *dahr* of the pagan poets but by the *qadar* of Allah, by the all-transcendent power of God in consonance with His reign of mercy, forgiveness, and salvation. Even in Medina Mohammed has devised a word of his own coinage to underscore the great gulf that separated him from the pagan past of his people: *jāhilīya*—a term of contempt and condemnation that was to be employed by future generations of Moslem Arabs in reference to their own prehistory and in contrast to the world history of one eternal God.[76]

75. Sura 4:116 ("though He forgives anything short of that").

76. Sura 3:148; 5:55; 33:33, etc.; verbs and adjectives of the root *jhl* are used by pagan poets; but the abstract noun occurs, as far as one can see, for the first time in the Koran, and here it simply serves as an over-all designation of the spirit and mores that prevailed among the Arabs before their conversion to Islam; for the various specific connotations of forms of *jhl*, see Goldhizer, *op. cit.*, pp. 219 ff.

IV. THE TEMPER OF THE ERA

1. REMEMBRANCE OF THE ANCESTORS. TOTAL JIHĀD

It is only now that we may turn to the subject proper of the present inquiry: the idea of history in the era of Early Islam. The legacy of pre-islamic Arabia, on the one hand, and the teaching and conduct of Mohammed, on the other, provide a key necessary and, on the whole, sufficient for the understanding of the basic trends and currents that prevail in that era: a period of some 130 years, namely, from the flight of the Prophet in 622, through the ministry of the four "orthodox" caliphs—Abū Bakr, 'Omar, 'Othmān, and 'Alī—between 632 and 660, down to the disruption of the Umaiyad Caliphate about 750. In this eventful era the idea of history discernible among the adherents of Islam considered as a whole may be defined as a complex of notions derived from wholly heterogeneous spheres: the monotheistic and universalistic conception of the past as developed in the cultural evolution of Judaism and Christianity; the particularistic, genealogical, essentially factional conception inherent in the pagan-nomadic society of the northern Arabs; and the peculiar amalgamation of these two conceptions as exhibited in the teachings of Mohammed. As if he had intended to epitomize this composite idea of history that was to plague his followers in the future, Mohammed says in connection with the pilgrimage observance:

> And when ye have completed your rites,
> then remember Allah even as ye remember your ancestors,
> or even better than that.[77]

Actually, both kinds of remembrance—that of Allah and that of the ancestors—remain alive and active in all major eras of islamic history, except that in the period of Early Islam greater preponderance is held by the ancestors, i. e., the forces of Arabism,

77. Sura 2:196.

than in any future period. Indeed, the era of Early Islam is one in which remembrance of Allah is outweighed by that of the ancestors in an ever intensified degree. This is marked, externally, by the fact that the center of Islam is now moved from Medina, and even from Arabia, first to Kūfa in Iraq and then to Damascus in Syria; and internally, by the metamorphosis of the structure of Islam from an Arab community of believers, under Mohammed and Abū Bakr, to a Moslem empire, under 'Omar, and to an Arab monarchy under the Umaiyads. The sociopolitical temper of the era is that of subjugation, conquest, intertribal warfare, insurrection, and violent, intransigent partisanship. Its motto is jihād, in ever accelerated motion and ever wider application. It is applied by Mohammed and Abū Bakr to war of Moslem Arabs against all pagan Arabs; it is expanded under 'Omar to war of Moslem Arabs against all infidel non-Arabs, and after 'Omar, to war of Moslem Arabs against one another; eventually it is even applied to war of Moslem non-Arabs, the so-called *mawālī*, against Moslem Arabs.

In reality, jihād now is, even more plainly than it was during Mohammed's ministry in Medina, only a continuation of the militant factionalism inherited from pagan Arab times. It is this heritage that can be seen to account, directly or indirectly, for the incessant manifestations of cleavage, friction, and civil strife which so completely rend the Moslem community through the entire era—from its inception, through all its vicissitudes, down to its termination. Manifestations of this kind spring up even in Mohammed's immediate environment and among his closest kin: in the political tension among his oldest followers, namely, between the Muhājira of the Quraish and the Anṣār of Aus-Khazraj; in the conflict between his clan of the Banū Hāshim and its brother clan, the Banū Umaiya; and eventually, in the split of the Hāshimites themselves into the branch of 'Alī and that of 'Abbās. The manifestations continue with new violence and fanaticism after the death of the Prophet: in the apostasy (*ridda*) of the Bedouin tribes and their subsequent ferocious subjugation; in the assassination of 'Othmān, the murder of 'Alī, and the tragic slaying of Ḥusain, son of ʿAlī and grandson of the Prophet; and in the irreconcilable uprisings of the Khawārij and the Shīʿa. They stand out at the very height of the Umaiyad power: in the bloody ravaging of Medina, under Yazīd; in the battle of Marj Rāhiṭ between Qais and Kalb; in the crushing of the revolt of al-Mukhtār; in the siege of Mecca under ʿAbdalmalik and the pitiable end of the rival caliph, ʿAbdallāh b. Zuhair; and in the disastrous wars between the leading tribes of the era. And finally they reach their climax, or better perhaps their anticlimax, in the revolt of non-Arab Moslems, helped by ʿAbbāsid rebels and Shīʿite dissidents, against the assumed supremacy of Arab Moslems, which comes to a head at the battle of the Zāb and marks the downfall of the Umaiyad Dynasty.[78]

Apart from the caliphs themselves, the men of the era, the men of action and renown that make its political history, are ruthless generals and governors like Khālid b. al-Walīd (the " Sword of Allah "), Ziyād b. Abīhi, ʿUbaidallāh b. Ziyād, al-Muhallab, al-Ḥajjāj; warlike tribal chieftains like Ibn Baḥdal, Zufar b. al-Ḥāriṯ, ʿUmair b. al-Ḥubāb; and equally " warlike " tribal poets like Ḥassān b. Ṯābit, al-Akhṭal, Jarīr, al-Farazdaq, al-Quṭāmi. The stronghold of the tribes is no longer in Arabia. The flower of their manhood had been recruited under ʿOmar to fight in the cause of Allah, and the Arab tribes are now garrisoned in the provinces conquered from Byzantium and Persia; they serve as armies of occupation in Egypt, Palestine, Syria, Mesopotamia, Iraq, and Iran. Their physical composition, political affiliations, and economic conditions have undergone a vast change since their conversion to Islam under Mohammed and Abū Bakr. Accordingly, reference to the larger genealogical groups, such as Muḍar versus Rabiʿa or Maʿadd (ʿAdnān) versus Yemen

78. Wellhausen, *Das arabische Reich*, has remained the best treatment of the social and political movements of the Umaiyad period to date; essentially supplemented by his *Die religiös-politischen Oppositionsparteien im alten Islam* (*Abhandlungen der Königlichen Gesellschaft der Wissenschaften zu Göttingen, Phil.-hist. Klasse*), Vol. 5, No. 2 (1901); for a more recent critical survey of the dynasty, see Della Vida, art. " Umaiyads," *EI*, *4*, 998 ff.

(Qaḥṭān), is more frequent in the works of their poets than in those of the pagan bards; but their hypertrophied clan consciousness and genealogical factionalism have remained unaltered. Their fraticidal warfare, their incessant campaigns of blood revenge and counterrevenge now add fresh chapters to the Days of the Arabs, new glory to the nobility of their blood kinship.

The irony of this first era of islamic history is that having set out to divide the world into a " domain of Islam " (*dār al-'Islām*) and a " domain of war " (*dār al-ḥarb*) by the unspent life power of the Arab tribes, it made Islam almost a synonym of jihād. Whenever the converted tribes are not engaged in the great wars of conquest in the cause of Allah, in the subjugation of Romans, Persians, Berbers, in the unchecked slaughter and fabulous looting of " infidels," they wage wars of blood revenge against one another, often as if resuming the warfare which their forebears had waged before conversion: war between Bakr and Tamīm, between Tamīm and Azd, between Taġlib and 'Amir b. Ṣa'ṣa'a, between Kalb and Fazāra, or between the great confederacy of Qais 'Ailān and that of Kalb-Quḍā'a. Nor has the ethics of intertribal war undergone a change since the alleged banishment of jāhilīya: The head of a fallen chieftain is cut off by his rival and sent to the caliph, who rewards the messenger.[79] Pregnant women of a defeated tribe are ripped open by the victors—a barbarism that had been practiced by the pagan Arabs and long before them, by the Ammonites at the time of Amos.[80] Now and then Islam

79. Ḥusain's head was sent to Yazīd (*Al-Fakhrī*, ed. W. Ahlwardt [Gotha, 1860], p. 140, bottom); 'Abdallāh b. Zuhair's head was sent to Damascus by Ḥajjāj (Aġ., XIII, 43:3, bottom); the same treatment is given Qaṭarī, the famous leader of the Azāriqa Khawārij (see Della Vida in *EI*, *2*, 818a), and 'Umair b. al-Ḥubāb, one of the chiefs of Qais (Akhṭal, *Dīwān*, ed. A. Ṣālḥānī [Beyrouth, 1891], 106:1, and elsewhere); in the latter instances, the recipient of the dead man's head is 'Abdalmalik. A well-remembered instance of this custom in pagan times is the decapitation of Shuraḥbīl (see above, p. 259) by Abū Ḥanash on the Day of Kulāb; cf. Muf., p. 430:20 f. For the 'Abbāsid period, cf. *Al-Fakhrī*, pp. 175, 197, 227, 258, 262, 311, and especially, p. 323.

80. Aġ., XI, 60; Jarīr, *Dīwān* (Cairo, 1313 A.H.), I, 116:18 f. (*wa-kull mukhaḍḍarati 'l-qurbain tabtaqir*), and *passim*; for pre-islamic times, cf. 'Āmir b. aṭ-Tufail, *Dīwān*, Nos. 12:7 and 27:4; cf. below n. 81.

does stir up something like remorse. A chieftain of Sulaim, al-Jaḥḥāf b. Ḥukaim, about to launch a treacherous assault against Taġlib, finds it necessary to warn his tribesmen that if they follow him they will be condemned in the hereafter to hell-fire, but if they do not they will disgrace their tribe. The tribesmen thereupon choose hell and make the attack.[81]

2. REMEMBRANCE OF ALLAH

The *religious* temper of the era is indeed subdued by its turbulent political temper, but it is by no means dormant. The supreme tenet of Islam, the belief in a single God of the world, which had kept Mohammed's prophetic inspiration alive throughout his career, also saves the entire era of Early Islam from complete moral anarchy and religious disintegration. The word of this one God is now spoken in a still, small voice to be sure; but it is not drowned out even amid the tumultuous battle cries of intransigent partisanship and unrestrained ʿaṣabīya. In certain circles, moreover, specifically those of the Khawārij and the Shīʿa, the word of God is occasionally spoken in a voice both loud and harsh.

It is in this era that the Koran, the "Word of God" (*qaul Allāh*) par excellence, is canonized as unalterably binding for all time to come and augmented and interpreted by the Sunna, that is, the life and example of the Prophet. This work of canonization and, especially, of augmentation and interpretation proved to be of immeasurable, formative importance for the future of Islam. It became, in fact, an indispensable correlate to the divine revelation itself. It is carried out by faithful "companions" and their "followers" who, in keeping with the early sermon of Mohammed, have freed themselves from the shackles of clan and tribe, from the passions of partisanship, and are intent upon serving the one God of the world as individuals. In various moods of religiosity, which later were to develop into corresponding schools of Islamic theology, this type of individual piety recurs in each major center of Early Islam.

81. Aġ., *ibid.* (*innamā hiya 'l-nār 'au al-ʿār . . . fa-qālū naḥnu maʿaka*—to the extent of the barbarism just referred to).

In Medina, men like Abū D̠arr, 'Abdallāh b. 'Omar, Sa'īd b. al-Musaiyib, Muḥammad b. Sīrīn dedicate their pious efforts to the preservation of the Sunna of the Prophet, thus laying ground for the " unwritten " law (*ḥadīt̠*) of Islam.[82] In Basra, where political theology insisted that the qadar of Allah, just as the dahr of paganism, renders man morally helpless, void of all religious initiative, sages like Ḥasan al-Baṣrī and Wāṣil b. 'Aṭā have the courage to postulate freedom of will and individual responsibility as a fundamental thesis of Islam,[83] thus precipitating the remarkable emergence of islamic philosophical theory in the classical period. The type of piety centered wholly upon God and a secluded life of pious meditation and asceticism—a type of piety that was to blossom out into the important school of Ṣūfism—finds exponents in Kūfa and Basra as well as in Medina.[84] The movement of the Khawārij, which was to become hopelessly embroiled in jihād, starts out from a postulate to the effect that no decision concerning the community of believers has any validity unless it has been made by God.[85] Both the Khawārij and the Shī'a uphold the principle that all Moslems are equal before Allah. Although a pure Arab himself, al-Mukhtār, the " Moses of the Shī'a," is the first to rally the mawālī of Kūfa to armed uprising against one of the most perilous residues of paganism: the foregone conclusion whereby only an Arab could be considered a full-fledged Moslem and therefore entitled to special privileges over a Moslem of non-Arab descent.[86]

82. See E. Sachau, *Einleitung* to Ibn Sa'd, III, x ff.; on Abū D̠arr, cf. Ibn Sa'd, IV, Pt. I, 161 ff., and especially, Balād̠urī, *Ansāb*, ed. S. D̄. F. Goitein (Jerusalem, 1936), V, 52 ff.

83. On Ḥasan's position concerning the *qadar* question, see his *Risāla* (addressed to the caliph 'Abdalmalik), published by H. Ritter in *Der Islam, 21*, 67 ff.; see also Obermann, " Political Theology in Early Islam," pp. 138–62. On Wāṣil, see Shahrastānī in Haarbrücker, pp. 25 ff.

84. See Nicholson, *A Literary History of the Arabs*, pp. 224 ff., and *The Idea of Personality in Ṣufism*, pp. 7 f.; A. J. Arberry, *Ṣufism* (London, 1950), pp. 31 ff.

85. The postulate is summed up in the terse formula *lā ḥukma 'illā lillāh*; see, e. g., Ibn al-At̠īr, III, 279:1, bottom; *Al-Fakhrī*, p. 114:3, bottom.

86. Nicholson, *A Literary History*, pp. 218 f.

Even for the monumental islamic historiography that was to emerge as the crowning achievement of the classical period under the 'Abbāsids, the ground is prepared now, in the era of Early Islam. Notwithstanding the continued popular preoccupation with the Days of the Arabs, both past and present, individual ardent Moslems—learned men like Abū Mikhnaf (d. 157), Ibn Isḥāq (d. 151), 'Awāna b. al-Ḥakam (d. 147), Muḥammad al-Kalbī (d. 146), and many others [87]—devote their life work to collecting for themselves and transmitting to others an ever growing mass of detailed memorabilia bearing on the new millenium, its founder and early caliphs, its growth and spirit, its outer conquests and inner discords.

Blackened by their 'Abbāsid archenemies and the historians and theologians within the 'Abbāsid orbit, the Umaiyad caliphs have been characterized as " bad Moslems " even by modern scholars. They themselves consider their rule as God-given and their office as the heritage of God's Messenger. Not only the caliphs but their stalwart governors and generals act as *imāms* of their respective flocks and conduct the Friday service centered on the testimony of faith: " There is no god but Allah—Mohammed is the Messenger of Allah." It is customary, but not necessarily warranted in each given case, to assume that the conduct of the Umaiyad caliphs is invariably dictated by political opportunism, moral license, or religious laxity.[88] In the battle of Ṣiffīn the hostilities cease when Mu'āwiya's soldiers raise up copies of the Koran on the points of their lances.[89] He invites to his court the two leading genealogists of the period, Daġfal b.

87. See H. A. R. Gibb, " Ta'rīkh," *EI*, suppl. pp. 234b ff.

88. Cf., e. g., the characterization of their efforts in behalf of the *minbar* (Goldziher, *2*, 40 ff.: " aristokratischer Uebermuth . . . aristokratischer Dünkel "); see below n. 89, and cf. n. 92.

89. The incident is almost invariably spoken of as a maneuver by which the Koran was used merely as a subterfuge to confuse 'Alī's forces; cf. e. g., Wellhausen, *Das arabische Reich*, p. 36 (" einen elenden Kunstgriff "); Nicholson, *ibid.*, p. 192 (" Mu'āwiya bethought him of a stratagem. . . . The miserable trick succeeded ").

Ḥanẓala and ʿAbīd b. Sharya, in order to benefit from their learning, and he consecrates a third part of every night to the study of Arab history and ancient history in general.[90] During the assembly at al-Jābiya, where he was to be elected to the caliphate, Marwān b. al-Ḥakam is found sitting in a tent engrossed in the study of the Koran.[91] His son and successor ʿAbdalmalik writes to Ḥasan al-Baṣrī, in care of al-Ḥajjāj, requesting this saintly sage and ascetic to enlighten him as to the true sense of God's omnipotence (qadar) in relation to the moral and religious endeavor of man.[92] The same caliph, in replacing the Byzantine and Persian currency with one of Arab making, orders that the new coins be engraved with sayings from the Koran, one of them being the solemn utterance, "Say: He is God—One."[93] The caliph Hishām, son of ʿAbdalmalik, puts the education of his princes into the hands of al-Zuhrī, one of the foremost authorities of his time in matters of the sacred tradition of Islam.[94] The religious devotion of his successor, the caliph ʿOmar b. ʿAbdalʿazīz, has remained an object of veneration even among the ʿAbbāsids. Like ʿAbdalmalik, he seeks advice from Ḥasan al-Basrī on matters of the heart, specifically, it would appear, about the spiritual worth of meditation and asceticism.[95] During his reign, study of the

90. Masʿūdī, ed. C. Barbier de Meynard, *5*, 77–8 (*en un mot tout ce qui forme l'histoire du passé*); the subjects of Muʿāwiya's nocturnal study as specified by Masʿūdī agree closely with those said to have constituted the researches of Ibn Sharya that were ordered by the caliph to be recorded in a dīwān; see below, n. 130.

91. Balāḏurī, *op. cit.*, p. 129:4; cf. p. 125:17 ff. (*al-Madā'inī: kāna min 'aqra'i 'l-nās lil-qur'ān wa-kāna yaqūl*, etc.).

92. Ḥasan's *Risāla* to ʿAbdalmalik was in reply to a request from the caliph (in care of Ḥajjāj); see the articles cited above, n. 83; cf. Ibn ʿAbd Rabbihi, *ʿIqd* (Cairo, 1940), 2, 479:1 f., where ʿAbdalmalik is quoted as saying in effect that it was because he worried so much about his weekly sermon that his hair became prematurely gray.

93. Balāḏurī, quoted by Wellhausen, *Das arabische Reich*, p. 135; the Koranic saying is Sura 112:1.

94. Cf. the article on al-Zuhrī in Ibn Saʿd, II, Pt. II, 135 f., especially the last item, 136:4 ff.

95. Ḥasan's message to ʿOmar b. ʿAbdalʿazīz as preserved in the *Ḥilyat*

Koran forms the most frequent subject of conversation among the people of Damascus.[96] He shares with the Khawārij and the Shī'a, the militant enemies of his dynasty, in the thesis of the equality of all Moslems, whether Arab or "foreign," in the eyes of God; and his endeavors to realize this thesis in behalf and for the benefit of the mawālī assure him a lasting place of honor in the annals of the religious history of Islam.[97]

But when all is said and done, genealogy and poetry must be seen to enjoy far greater popularity in the early islamic era than Koran and Ḥadīṯ. Indeed, genealogy is now on the way to becoming part of the remembrance of Allah, a paradoxical, yet inevitable, concession made to Arabism in the best interests of Islam. From its very inception the community of believers had been a community of groups rather than individuals. The alms tax (*zakāt*), imposed by Mohammed upon the converted Arabs as one of the basic principles of Islam, was collected not from individual Moslems but from their respective units of blood kinship. The raids and wars he had waged in the cause of Allah aimed at conversion of entire genealogic divisions: tribes, subtribes, clans. The same is true as regards the reconversion campaigns under Abū Bakr by the "Sword of Allah." Similarly, all instances of peaceful submission were negotiated by "deputations" (*wufūd*) representing groups of well-defined genealogical character.[98] It was therefore only natural that when, under 'Omar, "registers" (*dawāwīn*) were drawn up for administrative purposes—such as allotment of stipends to Mohammed's family and

al-anbiyā' of Abū Nu'aim (died 430 A. H.) may well contain interpolations by later hands, but there is no reason to question its authenticity on the whole; see the translation of the message given by Arberry, *op. cit.*, pp. 33–5; see also, J. Pedersen, "The Criticism of the Islamic Preacher," *The World of Islam*, N.S., *2* (1953), 218 f.

96. Cf. *Al-Fakhrī*, 151 bottom.

97. Ibn Sa'd, V, 240-302; Wellhausen, "Umar II und die Mavāli," *Das arabische Reich*, pp. 167–94; Nicholson, *op. cit.*, pp. 204 ff.; K. V. Zetterstein, art. and bibliography, in *EI*, *3*, 977a–9a.

98. Ibn Hishām, pp. 933–63 (*sanat al-wufūd*); Ibn Sa'd, I, Pt. II, 38–86 (wifādāt al-'arab); Wellhausen, *Skizzen und Vorarbeiten*, IV, pp. 135 ff.

companions, division of the spoils from the wars of conquest among the Moslem warriors (*muqātila*), and the like—the listing was based on genealogical principles.[99] Apparently it never occurred to 'Omar that the stipends and shares might be paid out to Moslem individuals, without regard to tribe and clan, just as it had not occurred to the Prophet to have his Anṣār dissociate themselves from the clans and subtribes of Aus and Khazraj. Naturally, unless the pre-islamic divisions of the Arabs, both northern and southern, had remained generally intact and a matter of wide public information, the corresponding registration would have been plainly unfeasible, since, under 'Omar, the recipient warriors were recruited from the entire population of Arabia. Even so, the drawing up of the registers must have required systematic study of Arab genealogy, and their official use by the caliph was bound to lend that study a measure of religious sanction.

3. A NEW KIND OF GENEALOGY

Preoccupation with genealogy received a sort of nimbus, which eventually was to prove of great importance, from yet another direction. Wholly in the spirit of Arabism, but ultimately to the advantage of Islam, the triumphs of Mohammed made him the hero eponymous of a new kind of " nobility " and gave his blood the luster of a new kind of " glory." Accordingly, conversion to Islam added a fresh incentive to the genealogical consciousness of any group affiliated with the Prophet or at least with his tribe, the Quraish and, theoretically, all groups of the North, all descendants of Ma'add, could claim such affiliation. How even 'Omar, the most truly islamic figure in all the history of the caliphate, was unable to free himself from thinking in terms of Arab racialism may be seen from a pronouncement of his transmitted on ancient authority: " He [Mohammed] is our title to nobility, his tribe

99. Ṭabarī, I, 2749: 14 f. (*wa-huwa 'auwal man dauwana lin-nās fi 'l-islām ad-dawāwīn wa-kataba 'n-nās 'alā qabā'ilihim wa-faraḍa lahum al-'aṭā'*); *Al-Fakhrī*, pp. 101 f.

are the noblest of the Arabs, and after them those are nobler that are nearer to him in blood. Truly the Arabs are ennobled by God's Apostle."[100] It is an idea such as this that crystallized into the basic principle of the early Shīʿa: that no one is entitled to the office of the caliphate except the offspring of ʿAlī by Fāṭima, the nephew and daughter of the Prophet, there being none nearer to him in blood kinship.

Even among the Quraish, efforts were made to establish as close a genealogical nexus with Mohammed as possible. Thus the Banū Zuhra raised the claim, "We are the maternal uncles of the Prophet," because his mother ʾĀmina was an offspring of Zuhra, daughter of Kilāb b. Murra, Mohammed's paternal ancestor six generations removed![101] The situation is properly appraised by the ʿAbbāsid caliph, al-Maʾmūm, when he says that of the two main branches of Maʿadd, the Rabīʿa were angry with God ever since he had raised his Prophet from among the Muḍar rather than from among *their* stock.[102] Even the non-Maʿaddic Anṣār now seek to establish a genealogical tie with the blood of Mohammed. Because his paternal grandfather, ʿAbd al-Muṭṭalib b. Hāshim, was, or was held to have been, the son of a woman of the Banū Najjār, a subtribe of the Khazraj, the poet Ḥassān b. Ṯābit, the spokesman of the Anṣār, states triumphantly:

> It's we that begot from among the Quraish their Great one:
> we begot the good Prophet from among the clan of Hāshim![103]

100. Ṭabarī, *ibid.*, 2751:11 f.; translated by Nicholson, *op. cit.*, p. 188 f.; long after ʿOmar (d. 644), the historian Ibn Qutaiba (d. 889) is astonished when he comes upon tribesmen of the Quraish who do not know the exact genealogical degree that connects them with the Prophet! (*Maʿārif*, ed. F. Wüstenfeld, p. 3:13 f.).

101. Ibn Qutaiba, *Maʿārif*, p. 63:10 (*naḥnu ʾakhwāl an-nabī*).

102. Ṭabarī, III, 1142:12 (*wa-ʾamma ʾl-rabīʿa fa-sāxiṭa ʿala ʾllāh munḏ baʿaṯa nabīyahu min muḍar*).

103. *Dīwān* (see above, n. 13), No. 25:7 (Ibn Hishām, p. 938). For the genealogical basis of the claim, see Ibn Hishām, p. 88:1 ff.; Ibn Qutaiba, *ibid.*, p. 57:14; cf. p. 74:9, and the scholion on the cited verse (*Dīwān*, p. 45: *yaʿnī ʿAbd al-Muṭṭalib waladathu Banū ʾn-Najjār*).

We recall how, deep in the time of jāhilīya, a very similar claim was raised by al-Ḥāriṯ b. Ḥilliza in relation to King ʿAmr b. Hind of Ḥīra.

Merely by its logical implications, the new genealogy might have served—and in the realm of individual piety, we shall see, it did serve—to counteract the forces of factionalism inherited from pagan times. Yet in the realm of jihād, the political temper of Early Islam, it was bound to all but inflate those forces. Ḥassān, the court poet of Mohammed and himself a Khazrajite, perceives the new " nobility " of the Anṣār as a new element added to the former " glorious " record of Aus and Khazraj, new proof of their racial superiority over the Quraish, the Muḍar, and indeed, over all of Maʿadd. Thus the purely islamic designation anṣār, marking off those who helped the prophet consolidate his mission as the messenger of the one God of the world, is now transformed to function as a genealogical term, pure and simple. To a considerable extent this transformation was effected in keeping with the Arabicizing provisions of Mohammed in Medina; at any rate, it was done before his very eyes. In the words of Ḥassān, speaking in behalf of the Anṣār:

> We had been Princes of men before Mohammed,
> and when Islam came, superiority remained with us, too . . .
>
> Such is my tribe—the best of tribes altogether;
> whatever excellence be recounted—my tribe is worthy of it.[104]

And again:

> Sovereignty was ours in Heathendom, and precedence is ours in Guidance:
> in help to the Prophet, and the founding of nobility.[105]

In satirizing the Quraishite Ḥakīm b. Ḥizām, who had fought at Badr on the side of the pagans but was now a good Moslem,

104. *Dīwān*, No. 161:1, 4 (Ibn Hishām, p. 930).
105. *Dīwān*, No. 25:8 (wanting in Ibn Hishām).

Ḥassān ridicules him for having thrown away his weapons and fled from the field of battle:

> When he perceived Badr, its banks overflowing
> with the troops now from Aus, now from Khazraj.[106]

In the manner of the leading poets of the era Ḥassān exalts the fresh warlike glory of his tribe, the jihād under the banner of Islam, together with the glorious record that had been achieved on the field of battle by his tribe's ancestors in the period of jāhilīya:

> Is nobility aught but ancient lordship and bounty,
> and fame of Princes, and bearing of hardness? [107]

And consistently he refers to those against whom the Anṣār had fought in the wars of conversion by their genealogical designation, as if those wars had been intertribal feuds rather than wars of Moslems against pagans. Addressing himself to the Prophet, he says:

> And we were thine army on the Day of the Slopes of Uḥud,
> when, insolently, *Muḍar* mustered her troops to battle.[108]

Similarly, the present tensions between the Anṣār and the Muhājira, of purely sociopolitical nature, are combined by Ḥassān with the former great conflict "in the cause of Allah," in which these two groups of Mohammed's followers had fought against the genealogical cousins of the Muhājira, namely, the Ma'addic Quraish:

> We helped and housed Mohammed the Prophet
> whether this pleased the Ma'add or displeased them.[109]

And in the same spirit:

106. *Dīwān*, Nos. 80:4 (var. Ibn Hishām, p. 525:16); cf. No. 76:4.
107. *Dīwān*, No. 25:1 (Ibn Hishām, p. 938).
108. *Dīwān*, No. 131:11 (var. Ibn Hishām, p. 885).
109. *Dīwān*, No. 25:2 (Ibn Hishām, p. 938).

All the time, we have had from the Maʿadd
nothing but feuding or fighting or abuse.[110]

It is especially noteworthy that in the well-known satirical poem composed by Akhṭal at the behest of the Umaiyad prince Yazīd b. Muʿāwiya, the term Anṣār is used in a genealogical sense—precisely as in the verses of Ḥassān—even though the Anṣār's claim to islamic nobility is denied and ridiculed by the Umaiyad court poet:

The Quraish have now borne away all the honor and glory,
and baseness alone is beneath the turbans of the Anṣār,

So leave nobility alone—ye are not of its stock,
and stick to your shovels, o sons of Najjār.[111]

An early Islamic dictum—" Poetry is the register of the Arabs " —has been widely quoted and commented upon, by Moslem sages as well as modern scholars, as epitomizing the peculiarly close connection between Arab poetry and genealogy.[112] The dictum may be seen to apply no less to the era of Early Islam than to that of Arab paganism. We have seen already that the outstanding poets of the era perceived of the jihād of their time as if it were a continuation of the intertribal warfare of the

110. *Dīwān*, No. 1:17 (var. Ibn Hishām, p. 829); by the evidence of the above and similar utterances throughout the *Dīwān*, there can be no doubt that Ḥassān considers his tribe as of non-Maʿadic, i. e., Yemenite, stock; Nöldeke has indeed called attention to a verse of Ḥassān quoted by Yaʿqūbī, ed. M. T. Houtsma (Leiden, 1883), I, 321:4, bottom, in which the poet states explicitly that his tribal genealogy goes back to *Ġauṯ-Nabt-Mālik-Zaid-Kahlān*; cf. Wüstenfeld, *Tabellen*, Nos. 1 and 4; see above, n. 13.

111. *Dīwān*, p. 314:4 f.; first line translated by Nicholson, *op. cit.*, p. 241; cf. Aġ., XIII, 148; XIV, 122; whether " shovels " was actually intended by *masāḥī* is not certain; at any rate, the poet had in mind a tool used by carpenters, since he clearly plays upon the designation Banū 'n-Najjār (the leading division of Khazraj), literally: " Sons of the Carpenter."

112. The dictum seems to have consisted originally of the succinct epigram *aš-šiʿr dīwān al-ʿArab*, and in this form it may well have been coined by Ibn ʿAbbās; for its several expansions or expositions, see Goldziher, *1*, 45, n. 1; Lyall, Muf., Introduction, pp. xxvi f. and n.

time of jāhilīya. As was similarly the practice of their pagan predecessors, they see in the Days of the present new witnesses to the genealogical superiority and tribal glory of their clan whenever they deem it to have been victorious in a given conflict or armed encounter. Hence the constant reference to pre-islamic Days and conditions in the compositions of Ḥassān, Akhṭal, and Quṭāmī, and in the divans of, and especially the contests (*naqā'iḍ*) between, al-Farazdaq and Jarīr.[113] The new, intensified interest in genealogy to which we have referred could not but add to the popularity of poetry, both past and present. Only thus was it possible to save the enormous mass of poetic composition from oblivion by the work of compilers and philologists that was to be performed in the 'Abbāsid period. The tribesmen of Taġlib, we are told, seized upon each occasion to recite the famous ode of their great pagan poet, 'Amr b. Kulṯūm.[114] The poets of the era enjoy the hospitality and bounty of the court at Damascus, not so much because of the caliphs' particular devotion to the art of verse-making as because poetry continues to be a political weapon of first magnitude. Even at Mohammed's quarters in Medina poetic contests between the Prophet's court poets and the tribal bards of the deputations appear to have

113. Cf., e. g., references to the Day of Khazāz (dated by Caussin de Perceval, *op. cit.*, *2*, 272, as of A. D. 492!), Farazdaq, *Naq.*, p. 884: 11; the killing of Kulaib (precipitating the War of Basūs), Jarīr, *Naq.*, p. 897: 12; the (First) Day of Kulāb, Akhṭal, *Dīwān*, pp. 45: 1; 227: 1 f.; 228: 2; Quṭāmī, *Dīwān*, No. 13: 33 (cf. the scholion); Farazdaq, *Naq.*, pp. 289: 9; 292: 2; 451: 13, and *passim*; the assassination of 'Amr b. Hind by 'Amr b. Kulṯūm, Akhṭal, *ibid.*, p. 44: 1; Quṭāmī, *ibid.*, No. 13: 32 (cf. the scholion); Farazdaq, *Naq.*, p. 884: 10; cf. p. 880: 11; Ibn Qutaiba, *Shi'r*, ed. M. J. De Goeje (Leiden, 1904), p. 119: 10; Aġ., XI, 54: 17 f.; etc. A *systematic* study of all references to events and persons of pre-islamic history found in the *Naqā'iḍ* (below, n. 129) would, I believe, greatly enhance new critical research which this field is much in need of; a vital aid to such a study is already provided for, of course, by the voluminous scholia of Abū 'Ubaida and Bevan's excellent Indices.

114. Aġ., XI, 54: 14 f.; the verses (deriding the present-day Taġlib for their poetic impotence) are credited to " a certain poet of Bakr b. Wā'il "; cf. Nöldeke, *Fünf Mo'allaqāt*, p. 19.

been common. That the drawing up of genealogical registers under 'Omar was helped by data supplied in poetry may be taken for granted in view of the above dictum.

To reward him for an ode he composed in praise of the Umaiyads, the caliph 'Abdalmalik orders that Akhṭal be escorted through the streets of Damascus and that the escort cry out: " This is the poet of the Commander of the Faithful! This is the best poet of the Arabs! "[115] A poem recited by Akhṭal, in the presence of 'Abdalmalik, satirizing the Sulaim and 'Āmir for their defeat on the Day of Ḥashshāk, precipitates the treacherous assault of the Taġlib by al-Jaḥḥāf b. Ḥukaim, to which we have referred above.[116] The compositions of al-Quṭāmī enjoy so great a popularity in Iraq that because of the anti-Yemenite bias of his verses, his life is threatened by the Azd.[117] Something like nation-wide popularity is enjoyed by the poetic controversy between Farazdaq and Jarīr—a controversy of personal abuse and genealogical vituperation carried on in verses of all but unmatched poetic skill. While 'Abdalmalik's general, Muhallab, leads a campaign against the Azraqī Khawārij, his soldiers engage in passionate arguments as to which of the two poets outranks the other. Requested to arbitrate the issue, Muhallab recommends that the matter be placed before their Azraqī enemies, whose leader, 'Abīda b. Hilāl, makes the decision in favor of Jarīr.[118] Even

115. Aġ., VIII, 288:5.

116. Akhṭal, *Dīwān*, p. 286:8 ff:; al-Mubarrad (below n. 125), p. 286:18 ff.; Aġ., XI, 59 f.; see above, n. 81.

117. *Dīwān*, ed. J. Barth (Leiden, 1902), No. 7:1 f.; see Barth's quotation (from the *Lisān al-'Arab*), *ibid.*, p. 16, top, also p. xv.

118. Aġ., VIII, 42:14 ff.; Muhallab states here in effect that he does not wish to make the decision himself and thus be exposed to " these two dogs who would tear my hide apart "; the Azāriqa, on the other hand, he implies, have nothing to fear, for they are " an Arab tribe well-versed in poetry and capable of appraising it correctly." When the petition is then submitted to 'Abīda, he proves indeed competent to settle the dispute, but he is shocked at the petitioner: " May Allah punish thee! Thou dost neglect the study of Koran and Sacred Law, choosing to interrogate me in matters of poetry! " (*ibid.*, p. 43:6 f.); his shock must have been even greater to find the same condition within his own ranks; cf. below n. 119.

more significant is the following incident relating to ʿAbīda. This puritan warrior in the cause of Allah on the side of the Khawārij, we are told, was in the habit of inviting his men to call at his tent during lulls in fighting. Once, when two of his soldiers called on him, the following dialogue took place. ʿAbīda: "What do ye prefer: that I recite to you from the Koran or that I declaim poetry for you?" The soldiers: "The Koran we know as well as thou dost; so do recite for us poetry." ʿAbīda: "Ye sinners! By Allah, I knew well that ye loved poetry better than the Koran." Thereupon, it is related, he went on declaiming verse to them and making them recite poems to him until they became weary of it and took their leave.[119]

Sporadically, however, the intrinsic significance of the new genealogy and nobility, as believed to have been brought into being by the appearance of Mohammed, does make itself felt: the realization that the one God of the world to whom he had converted the Arabs is the God of man, and therefore, of all men. Although the struggle in behalf of the mawālī was motivated largely by political ambitions, especially the movement, under the ʿAbbāsid agent Abū Muslim, leading to the downfall of the Umaiyad Dynasty, it had been made possible and effective by the pious conviction that all believers are equal in the eyes of Allah. Learned Moslems, indeed, have sometimes undertaken to demonstrate that the new genealogy was prescribed by God in such utterances of His revelation to Mohammed as "Only the believers are brothers," and concerning Noah's wicked son, "He is not of thy kin; surely, he has wrought what is not right"; so that here "the authority [*wilāya*] of Islam establishes kinship between strangers . . . and revokes by it (the tie) between blood relatives." This is a bold interpretation of the Koranic passages, but it reflects the spirit of our era.[120] ʿOmar, we have seen, stresses the importance of blood kinship with the Prophet, but he makes it

119. Aġ., VI, 151:1 ff. (l. 4: *yā fasaqatu*).

120. See, e. g., Maqrīzī, *Kitāb an-nazāʿ*, ed. G. Vos (Leiden, 1888), p. 28:8 ff.; the Koranic passages are Sura 49:10 and 9:48; for a much older source of this "demonstration," see below, n. 127.

clear that such kinship alone is by no means decisive. In conclusion of his pronouncement, which we have quoted above, he says: "Nevertheless, by Allah, if non-Arabs accomplish good works and we accomplish none, they will be closer to Mohammed than we on the Day of Resurrection. Let therefore no one rely on blood kinship, but let him work for what is of worth in the eyes of Allah. For one who is held back by his works will not advance by his pedigree."[121] Wholly in keeping with this sentiment, tradition relates how 'Omar prohibited the recitation of ancient poetry in the controversies between the Anṣār and the Quraish, saying that this was "vilification of those living by recalling the conduct of the dead, thereby reviving the old hatreds. Yet God has uprooted the customs of paganism [jāhilīya] by the foundation of Islam."[122]

It is conceivable, of course, that traditions of this kind are apocryphal; but there can be no doubt that the sentiments they convey reflect the spirit of Early Islam as it was cultivated in circles of individual piety in contrast to that prevailing among the Arab masses and their warlike leaders. An early Medinan tradition, which may safely be assigned to our era, makes Mohammed deliver an address on the occasion of his conquest of Mecca, in the year 8 A. H., in the course of which he is made to say: "O people of Quraish! Behold, Allah has now removed from you the haughtiness of paganism [jāhilīya] and the boasting with ancestors. [All] men stem from Adam, and Adam was formed from dust." Following this, the Prophet is said to have recited the Koranic verse about the Arabs having been divided into "tribes and sub-tribes" by God's own design, to which we have referred above.[123] But perhaps the clearest expression lent to the new kind

121. Ṭabarī, I, 2751:14–17; for the first part of the pronouncement, see above, n. 100; "a trad." quoted by Lane (p. 215, col. 3:9, bottom, from *TA*), seems to be based on the concluding words of 'Omar's dictum, except for the variant *man baṭṭa'a bihi 'amaluhu* in lieu of *man qaṣara bihi 'amaluhu* in Ṭabarī, l. 16.

122. Aġ., IV, 140:6–9.

123. Ibn Hishām, p. 821:10 ff.; Wāqidī-Wellhausen, p. 358; Ṭabarī, I, 1642; cf. Zamakhsharī, *Kashshāf*, *2*, 399:10, bottom, and see above, p. 276, and n. 65.

of genealogy may be found in the poems of 'Imrān b. Ḥiṭṭān, a transmitter of Ḥadīṯ from 'A'isha and Abū Mūsā al-Ash'ari, and hence a contemporary, at least a younger contemporary, of 'Omar. A blue-blooded Arab, of the Shaibān of Bakr, he is praised in tradition for his sacred learning, asceticism, and devotion to prayer, and he is held to have been one of the outstanding poets of the Khawārij.[124] He was persecuted and haunted by al-Ḥajjāj, the famous governor of 'Abdalmalik, for his activity in behalf of the Khawārij, and he sought asylum with one tribe after another, concealing his identity for fear of being overtaken by Ḥajjāj's agents and posing as

> A Yemenite one day, when meeting a man of Yemen,
> and as of 'Adnān [another day], when meeting a man of Ma'add.[125]

Invariably, his hosts eagerly inquire as to his pedigree to determine whether he is worthy of their hospitality and protection. He describes at some length the reception given him by Rauḥ b. Zinbā', chamberlain of 'Abdalmalik; when he no longer could hide his identity he fled, leaving on his couch a poem in which he takes his host to task for prying into his lineage. A similar reception was given him by Zufar b. al-Ḥāriṯ, the leader of Qais, with similar results. At last he finds security and refuge with some people of Azd, at Rūḏ Maisān, with whom he remains to the end of his days.

The poem in which 'Imrān describes his *ultima thule*, together with the compositions on his experience of the search for an asylum, offers an invaluable insight not only into his own conception of the new genealogy but into the tenacity of the old genealogy among his contemporaries:

124. Ibn Sa'd, VII, 113:7; Aġ., XVI, 152:3 f. (*šā'ir faṣīḥ min šu'arā'i 'š-šurāt*); *ibid.*, l. 1, bottom; Brockelmann in *EI*, *2*, 476.

125. Al-Mubarrad, *Kāmil*, ed. W. Wright (Leipzig, 1864), p. 532:13; see the excerpt of a letter of Ḥajjāj to 'Abdalmalik concerning 'Imrān, Aġ., XVI, 153:1 f.; cf. p. 152:9, bottom.

We have alighted by the grace of God in the best of abodes,
gladdened by the gentility and chasteness of its people . . .

Among them I am secure. How they are unlike the clans
who would come upon me crying: " Art thou of Rabīʿa or
Muḍar?

Or else of the tribe of Qaḥṭān? " ! Stupidity this!
But thus did Rauḥ address me, and thus did his friend
Zufar!

There is none among them except that he would be pleased
with a pedigree
that would make me his kin, however remote! [126]

Yet we are [all] sons of Islam! For Allah is One!
And the best of God's servants is he that's submissive to
God alone.

It is noteworthy that the sentiment expressed in the last couplet moved the scholiast of the poem to cite a parallel sentiment conveyed in a composition of Nahār b. Tausiʿa, who is said to have been the leading Arab poet in Khurāsān. He was a contemporary of ʿImrān, and like him, belonged to Bakr; but apparently he was not a partisan of the Khawārij. The cited verses read:

The usurper of tribal nobility makes gifts to his challenger
so that he connect him with a most excellent pedigree.

[As for me], my forebear is Islam and I have none beside it,
let others boast of descent from Qais or Tamīm.[127]

126. Al-Mubarrad, p. 534:5b; *wa-'in kāna* (supply: *dālika*, i. e., *at-taqrīb*) *ḏā nafr*; it is possible, however, that the subject of *kāna* is the same as in *yusarru*, namely, any of his hosts: *wa-ma minhum* (*'aḥadun*) *illā yusarru*, etc.; in this case, the phrase *wa'in kāna ḏā nafr* would no doubt mean: " however scant he (i. e., his clan) might be "; for the reading *minhum*, see Wright's n. c., *ad loc.*

127. Al-Mubarrad, pp. 533:17; 534:3–6; 538:10–15; on Nahār, see Ibn Qutaiba, *Shiʿr*, p. 342, where the two verses are quoted, in reverse order and

When Mu'āwiya invited to his court the two great savants of his time, Daġfal and Ibn Sharya—both of whom had witnessed the ministry of Mohammed—in order to be instructed in matters of ancient history, he must have been surprised to learn from them that Arab tribal genealogy had now been extended to lead back beyond 'Adnān and Qaḥṭān to Noah and his son Sām, the biblical Shem, while the pedigree of 'Adnān was held now to go back to Noah by the medium of Abraham and Ishmael.[128] Theoretically, this was the most significant concession made by Arabism to the remembrance of Allah in the era of Early Islam. The conception of the new genealogy thus appears to have militated not only against the division of the community of believers into Moslems of more noble and less noble pedigree, as witnessed in the verses of 'Imrān and Nahār, or into Moslems of Arab and non-Arab descent, as demonstrated by the uprising of al-Mukhtār. Obviously, it also militated against the racial particularism that had limited the historical horizon of the converted Arabs to an ultimate hero eponymous of their own Arab blood. By the monotheism of Islam, by the conception of history incessantly stressed in the sermon of Mohammed, their ultimate eponym could be none other than Noah, the forefather of the human race in God's plan and design.

Nor was the work of the new genealogy confined to Arabs. We are told that Daġfal also led the Persian origins back to

with some variants, together with a third verse. In adducing the verses of Nahār, the scholiast—whether al-Mubarrad (d. 998) or his source—cites the same Koranic passages as those upon which Maqrīzī (d. 1442) bases his demonstration of the new genealogy that came into being by the rise of Islam (see above, n. 120), with virtually identical expository remarks. On illegitimate genealogical claims and instances of forged pedigrees, see Goldziher, *1*, 133 ff., 181 ff.

128. *Fihrist*, ed. G. Flügel (Leipzig, 1871), p. 89:15 ff. and ll. 25 ff.; of each, the author says: *'adraka 'n-nabīya wa-lam yasma' minhu*; so also Ibn Qutaiba, *Ma'ārif*, p. 265, and, of Daġfal, Ibn Sa'd, VII, 102:4; on the chain from Ma'add and Adnān to Ishmael and Abraham, see Aġ., I, 13:4 (*'an Daġfal wa-ġairihi*)-9; the reading "'Abīd b. Sharya" (rather than "'Ubaid" and "Shariya") is that of Flügel; see also Ibn Hishām, pp. 3–6; Aġ., I, 12:6 ff., and cf. below n. 129.

Noah, and it seems indeed that he applied his system to the Greeks as well.[129] We learn that a work of Ibn Sharya, which was widely read down to the 10th century, dealt with ancient traditions, early kings of the Arabs and non-Arabs, the cause of the confounding of speech, and the dispersion of the race following the confounding. Mu'āwiya is said to have been so much impressed with the teachings of this great genealogist that he ordered them recorded in a divan and provided that the latter be marked as a work of Ibn Sharya.[130]

Moslem authors of the 'Abbāsid period list an impressive array of genealogists for the era of Early Islam; as might be expected, the listing is headed by Daġfal and Ibn Sharya.[131] Actually, the new, universalistic genealogy, with its biblical-koranic terms of reference, can be shown to have been appropriated by the leading poets of the Umaiyad caliphate, even though it did not lessen their zeal for the old, factional genealogy of clan and tribe. In fact, references to Daġfal occur as early as in the verses of al-Farazdaq (d. 92) and al-Quṭāmī (d. *ca.* 100), who cite his authority in matters of genealogical assessment and ancient history. Although no works of Daġfal are specifically mentioned by the authors just referred to (n. 131), al-Farazdaq speaks of a " volume " (*al-ṣaḥīfa*) of Daġfal in which he had borne testimony to the " nobility " of the poet's ancestry as superior to that of the forebears of Jarīr.[132] Al-Quṭāmī, on the other hand, refers to

129. Hamadāni, ed. M. J. De Goeje (Leiden, 1885), p. 314:15 (*qāla Daġfal kharaja Khurāsān . . . b. Sām b. Nuḥ*); on the chain from Alexander to Isaac, see Ṭabarī, I, 700 f.; and cf. Abū 'Ubaida (?) ad *Naqā'iḍ*, ed A. A. Bevan (Leiden, 1905–12), No. 104:35 (Bevan, p. 995:5): *ya'nī 'anna 'l-'ajam min banī 'Isḥāq b. 'Ibrahīm.*

130. *Fihrist*, p. 89:27 f. (*fa-'amara Mu'āwiya an yudauwan wa-yunsab ilā 'Abīd*; see Flügel, p. 43, n. 11); on the subject of this *dīwān*, see Fihrist, p. 89:26 f.; on its popularity down to the 10th century, cf. Mas'ūdī, IV, 89:6 f.

131. Ibn Qutaiba, *Ma'ārif*, pp. 265 ff.; *Fihrist*, pp. 89 ff.; cf. Wüstenfeld, *Muhammed Ben Habib* (Göttingen, 1850), p. v.

132. *Naqā'iḍ*, No. 39:33–5 (Bevan, p. 189:7 ff.); it is barely possible, but highly improbable, that Farazdaq uses here *al-ṣaḥīfa* in the sense of " oral record."

Dagfal as one of " the two sages " who transmitted the ancient traditions of 'Ad and Jurhum.[133]

In the era of Early Islam, then, the remembrance of Allah endeavors to counteract the tenacity of Arabism by applying a new idea of the past to the issues peculiar to this era. In the sphere of political realities, the effect of such endeavors must be seen to have been negligible or of little avail. But they proved incalculably effective in the realm of the religious yearning, the cultural and intellectual quest, of individuals. The new genealogy forced upon the Moslems of the era a concept of history involving all men, all nations, all times—a concept of world history. The Arabs of the era continued to speak and act in terms Muḍar and Rabī'a, Ma'add and Yemen, 'Adnān and Qaḥṭān, but they learned to think in terms of the world.

To give Islam a basis of reality, its early exponents adjusted it to the age-old principles of Arab society. But to save the Moslem community from reverting wholly to the mores of that society, they anchored the most perilous of its principles, that of clan consciousness and tribal genealogy, in a lineage going back to Creation. And, confined to the sphere of individual piety, the new lineage might have proved strong enough to cancel the last vestige of Arabism. We have met with various protagonists

133. *Dīwān*, No. 11:4:

aḥādīṯa min 'Ādin wa-Jurhuma jammatan
yuṯauwiruhā 'l-'iḍḍān Zaidun wa-Daǵfalu

Many tales about 'Ād and Jurhum
that are recounted by the two sages, Zaid and Daǵfal.

The scholiast points out that *'iḍḍān* means as much as *dāhītān* and that Zaid is none other than Zaid b. al-Kaiyis an-Namarī (cf. Ibn Qutaiba, *Ma'ārif*, p. 266:3 and *Fihrist*, p. 90:1); Goldhizer, *1*, 184, quotes Maidānī (whose *Amṯāl* is not available to me) as saying (reciting?): " Erzählungen von den Geschichten der 'Ād und Ǵurhum, welche die beiden Wundergelehrten Zejd und Daǵfal durchforschen," which sounds like a close paraphrase of the Quṭāmī verse just adduced; in addition, Maidānī is quoted by Goldziher as referring to the two sages by the rare adjective *al-'iḍḍān*; Goldziher adds parenthetically to " Zejd ": b. Ḳejs (*sic*) al-Namarī, and he explains *al-'iḍḍān*: ungefähr " die beiden Teufelskerle."

of the trend toward individual piety, nearly all of them Moslems of pure Arab blood. The imprint they left on the great quest and search that were to engulf the theologians and philosophers of the classical period—mostly Moslems of non-Arab descent—is yet to be fully appraised. They themselves were fully aware of the impact which the new genealogy might have had on the community of believers, an awareness to which they gave expression in utterances such as: "We are [all] sons of Islam. For Allah is One"; and "My forebear is Islam—I have none beside it."

But to the spokesmen of the Arab masses, their tribal leaders, poets, and generals, the new genealogical orientation merely served as a means of maintaining a balance of power between Arabism and Islamism. We recall how Ḥassān b. Ṯābit claimed that a new kind of nobility was added to the old glory of his tribe, the Banū Najjār of Khazraj, by the appearance of Mohammed as the Messenger of Allah, since the Prophet's paternal great-grandmother was a descendant of that tribe. Similar claims, but of much greater consequence, are now raised by poets of Ma'addic descent. When, under the Umaiyads, the old rivalries between Ma'add and Yemen broke forth with unprecedented fanaticism, splitting the entire nation into numerous hostile camps, the northern tribes, the tribes of Ma'add, found that the new genealogy rendered their racial superiority over the tribes of Yemen part of God's plan of salvation: only *they* were linked by an exclusive nexus of blood kinship with Ishmael and Abraham, the founder of monotheism, the true precursor of Mohammed.[134] Hence the poet Jarīr, in exalting the nobility of his Ma'addic kin in terms of their pagan heritage, augments his *mufākhara* by pointing to their new nobility in terms of monotheism:

Our forebear is the "Friend of Allah" (Abraham) . . .
He built the qibla of God for man's guidance,
And made us inherit glory and sovereignty everlasting.[135]

134. On endeavors made by Yemenite genealogists to counterbalance this new claim of Ma'addic superiority, see A. Fischer, "Ḳaḥṭān," *EI*, *2*, 630.

135. *Naqā'iḍ*, No. 104:27–8; cf. *ibid.*, ll. 23–6 as contrasted with ll. 27–34 (Bevan, pp. 993–5).

Similarly, the poet al-Quṭāmī combines his exaltation of the great prowess of Ma'add in the Days of the Arabs with his praise of the new distinction of their pedigree:

> And of us are the prophets . . .
> And, after Allah, Ishmael did establish
> for us rightness when [our] ranks were heightened.[136]

Thus the factional kinship of clan and tribe was polarized with the universal kinship going back to Creation, in order to keep alive old claims of blood superiority and to vindicate old rivalries under the banner and authority of Islam. A prototype of this polarity, it is well to keep in mind, was effected by Mohammed in Medina when he made the pilgrimage rites and the service at the Ka'ba a fundamental tenet of Islam and then postulated these very rites of the pagan Arabs as having been founded by Abraham and Ishmael, thus putting them in a context of monotheistic world history.

V. SCOPE OF INQUIRY

A full, comprehensive study of the idea of history in Early Islam would be obliged not only to look backward to pre-islamic Arabia but also to look forward to the classical period of Islam and, to some extent, even to the postclassical period. Such a procedure would be suggested, first, by the peculiar situation concerning the sources of our knowledge of the pre-islamic and early islamic eras, and second, by the question as to the proper method of bringing those sources to bear on the particular problem of our inquiry. It would thus seem appropriate to conclude the present discussion with a note regarding these matters.

136. *Dīwān*, No. 29:71–3; cf. ll. 54–70, 75–8; this ode—in which Quṭāmī pleads with the Kalb-Quḍā'a to forsake the tribes of Qaḥṭān (ll. 54 ff., 75) and to join those of Ma'add, to whom they had originally belonged (ll. 54, 56, 75)—offers a good illustration of how, down into Islamic times, the *mufākhara* poetry was used for political and strategic purposes; see Barth's Notes on the ode, pp. 48 ff.; cf. also above, pp. 251, 257.

Excepting only the Koran itself, virtually all our knowledge of the initial, formative era of Islam, all information concerning its sociopolitical trends, its literary products and leading personalities, its civil strife and foreign wars, has come to us from sources collected, compiled, and recorded in the *classical* era of Islam, a period of some three hundred years following the rise of the ʿAbbāsid caliphate about A. D. 750. It has been called the period of the renaissance of Islam, its golden age, the prime of its achievements. Indeed, the dramatic contrast between this and the initial era becomes obvious even at a superficial comparison. The community of believers is no longer dominated by native Arabs but by descendants of many different stocks—Arabs, Syrians, Persians, Turks, Hindus, Copts, Berbers, Spaniards—many of whom, or many of whose ancestors, had been converted to Islam not from paganism but from Judaism and Christianity, and many others from Manichaeism, Zoroastrianism, or Buddhism. The gigantic exploits of the armies and generals of the initial era are now superseded by no less gigantic exploits of the spirit and the intellect. Having built a world empire by sheer physical force, Islam now bids fair to conquer the world of ideas by means of pen and ink. And those who wield the pen are for the most part devout Moslems of non-Arab descent; yet in the main, it is they to whose efforts and genius we owe the incomparable literature of classical Arabic prose—a literature that brought to new life and blossom the whole realm of medieval culture, and to a good extent, even presaged the dawn of modern culture: philosophy, philology, theology, mathematics, medicine, astronomy, as well as such peculiarly islamic disciplines as *ḥadīṯ*, *tafsīr*, *fiqh*.

No literary branch of this era, however, is more remarkable for its vastness of volume and monumentality of structure than that of immediate concern to the present inquiry: the branch of historiography with its subsidiary disciplines of genealogy, archeology, and biography. To become cognizant of the enormous task accomplished during the classical era in behalf of early islamic and pre-islamic history, one need only place in juxtaposition the works of Ṭabarī, Balāḏurī, and Mas'ūdī for history proper, those of Ibn Hishām and Ibn Sa'd for biography, the *Mufaḍḍalīyāt*, the *Ḥamāsa*, and the well-nigh inexhaustible *Kitāb al-Aġānī* for political and literary antiquities.

Long after Islam had passed its prime, having spent as it were its creative prowess, there appeared in North Africa a Moslem savant who advanced a new approach to islamic history and indeed to history in general. Although himself the author of a world history in which he follows closely in the footsteps of the great historians of the classical era, he apparently feels dissatisfied with their, and his own, purely factual registration of events and changes of the past without due regard to inner causes and underlying motives. I am referring, of course, to Ibn Khaldūn (d. 1406) and his widely renowned *Muqaddima fi't-ta'rīkh*, in which he undertakes no less a task than that of establishing the interconnection of past events and movements, of defining the principles of historic change and social evolution, and of thus raising the study of history to the level of an exact science. No wonder, therefore, that this work has been hailed as revolutionary and epoch-making by recent historians, philosophers, and sociologists. In fact, no single learned Arabic work has ever received wider attention or greater acclaim from non-Arabists than the *Muqaddima* of Ibn Khaldūn. He has been called " an Oriental Montesquieu," " a Darwinist before Darwin," " a forerunner of the 19th century *Geschichtsphilosophie* "; and his work has been compared with that of Machiavelli, Battista Vico, Hegel, and Herbert Spencer.[137]

It should be obvious that neither the historiography as con-

137. For the more recent literature, cf. N. Schmidt, *Ibn Khaldun*, New York, 1930; E. Rosenthal, *Ibn Khalduns Gedanken über den Staat*, in *Historische Zeitschrift*, Beiheft 25 (1932); and A. Schimmel, *Ausgewählte Abschnitte aus der muqaddima*; cf. F. Rosenthal in *JNES* (1954), pp. 60 ff. In a class by itself is the admirable study by H. Ritter, " Irrational Solidarity Groups," *Oriens*, Vol. *1*, No. 1; it is to be hoped that Professor Ritter's pioneering analysis will stimulate further inquiries (long overdue!) into the inner symptoms of *'aṣabīya* (such as exemplified by several specimens in the course of the preceding discussion; cf. pp. 258 ff.).

ventionalized in the classical era nor the theory of history as advanced by Ibn Khaldūn could have been made to serve as point of departure for an inquiry into the subject as suggested by the present symposium. To be sure, the great historians and archeologists of the ʿAbbāsid period will have to remain our first and last resort: on their staggering collections and compilations we will forever depend for the enormous mass of pertinent data and materials bearing on the early era of Islam and its pagan prehistory. But they themselves make no attempt to analyze those data and materials or to discover their inner coherence and significance, let alone to deal with them in terms of general trends and basic ideas. Ibn Khaldūn, on the other hand, does deal with the laws of historic change and causation, but he fails to bring these laws to bear on his own *Ta'rīkh*, so that it was bound to remain debatable how much of his Geschichtsphilosophie is Geschichte and how much of it is pure Philosophie.

It thus seemed clear that an independent attempt would have to be made if we were to ascertain what ideas and concepts of history or what notions and fancies of the past can be shown to have attended the making of Islam: in its antecedents, its birth, its early vicissitudes. Should such ideas or notions prove discoverable, it was felt, a criterion might be gained by which to determine whether and to what degree the conventional historians of the classical era of Islam reflect the true temper of the formative era, at least in their choice, arrangement, and presentation of materials. By the same token, it seemed, a criterion might perhaps be crystallized to test the extent to which the theory developed by Ibn Khaldūn may be seen to apply to the hard and fast realities of early islamic history.

BIBLIOGRAPHY

(with key to abbreviations)

Aġ: *Kitāb al-Aġānī* of Abu 'l-Faraj al-Iṣbahānī, Vols. 1–11, Cairo, 1927–38; Vols. 12–20, Būlāq, 1285 A. H.; Vol. 21, ed. R. E. Brünnow, Leiden, 1888.

C. Brockelmann, *Geschichte der arabischen Litteratur*, Vol. 1, Weimar, 1898; Vol. 2, Berlin, 1902.

——— *Supplementband* 1, Leiden, 1937; 2, Leiden, 1938.

L. Caetani, *Studi di storia Orientale*, Vol. 3, Milan, 1914.

W. Caskel, "*Aiǰām al-ʿArab*," *Islamica*, Vol. 3, Pt. V, 1930.

A. P. Caussin de Perceval, *Essai sur l'histoire des Arabes*, 3 vols. Paris, 1847–48.

M. De Slane, *Le Diwan d'Amro'lkais*, Paris, 1837.

——— *Les Prolégomènes d'Ibn Khaldoun*, Paris, 1863–68.

C. M. Doughty, *Travels in Arabia Deserta*, 2 vols. London, 1936.

EI: The Encyclopaedia of Islam.

H. O. Fleischer, *Abulfedae historia anteislamica*, Leipzig, 1831.

I. Goldziher, *Muhammedanische Studien*, 2 vols. Halle, 1888–90.

Ḥam: *Ḥamāsa* of Abū Tammām, ed. G. G. Freytag, Bonn, 1828 (see Rückert).

P. K. Hitti, *History of the Arabs*, 3d ed. London, 1946.

Ibn Hishām, *Das Leben Muhammed's nach Muhammed Ibn Ishâq*, ed. F. Wüstenfeld, Göttingen, 1859 (see Weil).

Ibn Khaldūn, *Muqaddima* (see De Slane; Ritter; Schimmel).

Imrulqais, *Dīwān* (see De Slane; Rückert).

G. Jacob, *Altarabisches Beduinenleben*, Berlin, 1897.

A. von Kremer, *Culturgeschichte des Orients*, 2 vols. Vienna, 1875–77.

H. Lammens, *Le Berceau de l'Islam*, Rome, 1914.

C. J. Lyall, *The Dīwāns of ʿAbīd Ibn al-Abraṣ and ʿĀmir Ibn aṭ-Ṭufail*, E. J. W. Gibbs Memorial Trust, Leiden 1913.

——— *The Mufaḍḍaliyāt*, Oxford, 1918.

——— *Translations of Ancient Arabian Poetry*, London, 1930.

Muf: *Mufaḍḍaliyāt* of al-Mufaḍḍal aḍ-Ḍabbī (*see* Lyall).

A. Müller, *Der Islam im Morgen- und Abendland*, 2 vols. Berlin, 1885–87.

R. A. Nicholson, *A Literary History of the Arabs*, London, 1907.

——— *The Idea of Personality in Ṣūfism*, Cambridge, 1923.

T., Nöldeke, *Beiträge zur Kenntniss der Poesie der alten Araber*, Hanover, 1864.

——— *Geschichte der Perser und Araber zur Zeit der Sasaniden*, Leiden, 1879.

——— *Fünf Mo'allaqāt*, in *Sitzungsberichte der Akademie der Wissenschaften*, Vienna, 1899, 1900, 1901.

——— and Schwally, F., *Geschichte des Qorāns*, Leipzig, 1909.

J. Obermann, " Das Problem der Kausalität bei den Arabern " in *Wiener Zeitschrift für die kunde des Morgenlandes*, Vienna, 1917.

——— " Political Theology in Early Islam," *Journal of the American Oriental Society*, Offprint Series, No. 6, New Haven, 1938.

——— " Islamic Origins " in *The Arab Heritage*, ed. N. A. Faris, Princeton, 1944.

H. Ritter, " Irrational Solidarity Groups," *Oriens*, Vol. 1, No. 1, 1948.

F. Rückert, *Hamâsa*, 2 vols. Hanover, 1846–48.

——— *Amrilkais, der Dichter und König*, 2d ed. Hanover, 1924.

E. Sachau, " Einleitung " (prefaced to *Ibn Saad-Biographien*, Vol. 3), Leiden, 1904.

A. Schimmel, *Ausgewählte Abschnitte aus der muqaddima*, Tübingen, 1951.

W. Robertson Smith, *Kinship and Marriage in Early Arabia*, Cambridge, 1885.

A. Sprenger, *Das Leben und die Lehre des Moḥammad*, 3 vols. Berlin, 1861–65.

Al-Wāqidī, *Kitāb al-Maġāzī*, ed. A. Von Kremer, Calcutta, 1856 (see Wellhausen).

G. Weil, *Das Leben Mohammed's* (of Ibn Hishām), 2 vols. Stuttgart, 1864.

J. Wellhausen, *Muhammed in Medina* (paraphrase of Wāqidī's *Maġāzī*), Berlin, 1882.

——— *Reste Arabischen Heidentums*, Berlin, 1887 (2nd ed. Berlin, 1897).

——— *Muhammeds Gemeindeordnung von Medina* in *Skizzen und Vorarbeiten*, IV, pp. 67 ff., Berlin, 1889.

——— *Prolegomena zur ältesten Geschichte des Islam* in *Skizzen und Vorarbeiten*, VI, Berlin, 1889.

——— *Das arabische Reich und sein Sturz*, Berlin, 1902 (Eng. trans., M. G. Weir, *The Arab Kingdom and Its Fall*, Calcutta, 1927).

F. Wüstenfeld, *Genealogische Tabellen der arabischen Stämme und Familien*, Göttingen, 1852.

——— *Register zu den genealogischen Tabellen*, Göttingen, 1853.

——— *Die Geschichtschreiber der Araber und ihre Werke* (*Abhandl. d. Königlichen Ges. d. Wiss. zu Göttingen*, Vols. 28 and 29), Göttingen, 1882.

ZDMG: Zeitschrift der Deutschen Morgenländischen Gesellschaft.

THE TWENTIETH-CENTURY WEST AND THE ANCIENT NEAR EAST

Paul Schubert

THE eight preceding essays are, primarily, the result of long and critical scientific study applied to many minute details and to one staggeringly comprehensive problem. This is as it should be. They also are an expression—at once substantial and modest—of 20th-century Western culture's intense and fateful preoccupation with its own idea of history. Both aspects of the work will be in every reader's mind as they were in every writer's. For this reason a ninth essayist was assigned the task of looking at the ancient Near Eastern idea of history explicitly from the standpoint of our 20th-century idea of history. What is *our* "modern," "Western" idea of history? How does it affect our discovery (or successive rediscoveries) and understanding of ancient Near Eastern ideas of history? And do such discoveries in turn affect our ideas?

This essay attempts to deal with these and similar questions, in part explicitly, in part implicitly, by first examining our own idea of history. To point to the serious difficulties and inescapable ambiguities of this task will be a major aspect of these reflections. But no 20th-century historian who wishes to know what his technical, professional work means in terms of his own life and that of his fellow men wants to evade the issues. Indeed he can hope to solve some of his own difficulties; and somehow he must come to terms with the inescapable and perhaps insoluble ambiguities with which his chosen task confronts him.

This task is in no way eased by the fact that the leading proponents of contemporary philosophies and theologies of history [1]—from Hegel and Marx to Burckhardt and Nietzsche; to Dilthey and Troeltsch; Croce and Collingwood; Barth, Tillich, and Bultmann; Heidegger, Jaspers, and Sartre; Meinecke and

1. For bibliographical references see the footnotes that follow and the bibliographies throughout the volume.

Butterfield; Spengler and Toynbee; Reinhold, Richard Niebuhr, Loewith, and so on—have sometimes failed to gain essential approval even from their most competent admirers and from the most brilliant of their own pupils. No wonder then that quite a few professional historians, philosophers, and theologians go on with their professional routine as though nothing of great importance were happening in the contemporary history of thought and action.

But when we are willing to face our own difficulties, our difficulties in understanding the past also may be eased. Keeping in mind clearly what we do know may help in our learning from the past something worth knowing.

Thus equipped we shall proceed to survey the ancient Near Eastern ideas of history as a whole. Here the task is twofold: to note some of the similarities and contrasts between any Near Eastern and any modern ideas and to offer a genetic reconstruction of the historical fate of all these ideas from the beginning to the end of the ancient Near Eastern cultures, which, for the purposes of this volume, is set with some justification and some inescapable arbitrariness at around A. D. 750.

I. THE TWENTIETH-CENTURY IDEA OF HISTORY

1. OUR HISTORICAL CONSCIOUSNESS

There can be no more convincing argument for the all-pervasiveness of our modern historical consciousness than that we cannot define the meaning of our existence except in terms of the past, present, and future. Aristotle, this relatively late Greek representative of Near Eastern culture, could be satisfied with defining man as a *being in society* (*zoon politikon*). In Aristotle's thought history played no leading role, for community (*polis*) is for him but an actualization of a timeless form. The latter dominates his thought. Modern man can only define himself as a *being in history* (*zoon historikon*), a being with a past, a present, and a future, however difficult it may be to say what past, present, and future are or mean in this connection. It suffices to add here that all schools of contemporary thought share the realization that truth, understanding, and reality have the character of events rather than of things.

We must therefore attempt to give a brief account of the modern idea of history in terms of our historical consciousness. If this concern were nothing more than an abstruse preoccupation of ivory tower thinkers, the matter might be of relatively small importance. Although this essay, too, is somehow moving within the particular limits of academic discussion, it does so only in the conviction that the academic work itself is, from the perspective of the historical consciousness of our age, but a small part, at once glorious and modest, of actual events, deeds, and happenings which are the very stuff of human life on all levels of human societies and in all ages of human history.

a. *18th- to 20th-century Enlightenment.* Faith in the autonomy and all-sufficiency of human reason was not proclaimed for the first time in the 18th century—this had been done by the ancient Greeks—but in that century it became vastly more powerful and successful than ever before in the history of the ancient Near East. This is one factor which accounts for the special character of our idea of history.

The genius of the 18th-century Enlightenment—like every form of ambitious rationalism—was of itself not at all concerned with history. In fact this enlightenment was characterized by an attitude of profound indifference, not to say aversion, to history. Eighteenth-century reason was interested in universally valid truth about reality to be stated in terms of universal, timeless propositions and laws, while history, if it is or was anything, is or was the realm of particulars more than of the universal, of the contingent more than of the necessary, of the false as much as of the true, of evil as much as of good. Thus the irresistible temptation of course arose to despise the past and exalt reason's coming to power. Thus at once, unexpectedly and disconcertingly, began the so-called new, modern, and true history—namely, the beneficent, omnipotent reign of reason, a kind of kingdom of God; reason being God and the kingdom being reasoning people, or the people of reason.

As time went on, reason with all its new-found power and devotees found that unreason was not giving up so readily as it should. Thus the need for a full-fledged rationale of history unexpectedly and unreasonably emerged. The past had been no good, but this very admission could no longer be evaded. There *was* a past. According to A. Comte's rationale, it had been ruled at first by the demons of mythology and somewhat later by the demons of metaphysics. Now the rule of positive reason was beginning, under the authority of the natural and social sciences, called positive as their positive function is to be the directing of human affairs. But the persistence of the demons made necessary a further rationale, the elaboration of a futuristic but still imminent consummation of history within history, which would take place as soon as unreason was completely conquered by reason, as soon as the positive sciences were completely in the saddle. As time went on, the delay of the demons' departure resulted in still vaguer yet perhaps better statements. The advent of the perfect society was pushed into a more distant but still reasonable and definite historical future. Finally there arose in the latter part of the 19th century the nicely modified, well-balanced, and " realistic " faith in a gradual progress within history.

The parallel of this modern development to the modern interpretation of the history of early Christianity is exact and obvious. But it is a real question whether the unadmitted exigencies of this modern dilemma did not *produce* this explanation of that particular piece of ancient Near Eastern history, without fitting too well all decisive, historically knowable facts about early Christianity.

The 18th- to 20th-century Enlightenment, being thus forced into producing a philosophy of history in order to save itself by modifying itself, made its own best possible use of the Christian idea of history [2] which, however poor, was still alive in the 18th century, by turning selected elements of it into arguments for the defense of its own position. Thus, creation became evolution; Jesus Christ became the religious consciousness of mankind —under special conditions favorable to both; the expectation of the end of history, of the coming of the kingdom of God, became in several attractive versions the theory of gradual progress. The end result was a dogmatic, though attenuated and humanized, eschatology.

A further dilemma arising for the believers in the Enlightenment finds its expression in the fact that the simple faith in the autonomy and all-sufficiency of man's reason led by a kind of reaction to thorough despair of ultimate truth, excepting only the dogma of gradual historical progress. In the various types of positivism reason is no longer considered able to solve all rational problems. It is reduced to a magical tool employed for helping along the *élan vital* or inspiring sociologists and other scientists to invent the techniques for running the admittedly irrational human society properly.

May not this be regarded as a somewhat muddled humanization of the Holy Spirit of Christian faith, who was not the truth itself but the true agent for leading men to the truth (the truth in the Christian case being defined in neither rational nor irrational terms but rather in terms of personal relations)?

Thus the valid and the dubious heritage of the 18th century is a first characteristic of 20th-century ideas in general and of the idea of history in particular. The spirit of the Enlightenment lost some of its luster in the confusion of absolute truth (everything is explained or explicable) and of positive reason (only empirically demonstrable truths are true). In both forms lurks the danger of reductionism, the tendency to reduce all experience to rational causes, in opposition to all views which were, or seemed to be, victims of the opposite tendency, namely, to explain and understand everything directly in terms of divine providence,

2. See the references to this process by K. Loewith, *Meaning in History*, pp. 104–44.

miracle, and ready-made, historically handed-down dogma. When it comes to rational explanations, the principle of reductionism and the principle of extravagance are equally dangerous.

b. *Historical Criticism.* This is a second characteristic of our historical consciousness. As such it may even outrank the Enlightenment in importance, if its older age and its new-found vigor are an indication worth pondering and testing. We have seen that it was not *history* as such that was congenial to the Enlightenment but *criticism*, which was eminently so. As *scientific criticism* historical criticism was an indigenous element of the Enlightenment. As *history* it was the living heritage of ancient Near Eastern, Hebrew, Greek, Christian, and Islamic achievements and experiences. Modern historical criticism and our historical consciousness are thus *the* product of the inextricable coexistence of a new spirit with an old and still powerful heritage.

It is sometimes said that this heritage was dormant during the Middle Ages. It is probably true that tradition and consciousness of history acquired a certain rigidity and stability under the heavy hand of medieval institutionalisms, economic, social, religious, political, and intellectual. But seen from a different perspective the Middle Ages mark a society on which the Christian consciousness of history in various forms of Augustinianism has imprinted deep and characteristic marks, notwithstanding some noteworthy anti-Augustinian aspects of the medieval spirit. If medieval theology was less " historically " oriented than Augustine, the vital medieval piety was dominated by the Christian consciousness of history with its undiminished eschatological expectation.

The Renaissance and the Reformation provided not only new (old) materials for the study of history but also fresh perspectives for the growth of historical consciousness and historical understanding. These vital efforts and concerns resulted in the immense amount and the high quality of labor which 17th-century scholarship devoted to the study of history. The modern historian is inclined to limit his appreciation to the great treasures of historical records which that work put at his disposal. He is inclined to forget that 17th-century historians did this " preliminary " labor for the sake of their own vital concern with the meaning of history.

It is the achievement of the 18th and the 19th centuries to have elevated the study of history to a systematic, i. e., scientific study, which we call historical criticism. We must consider briefly its own history in order to appreciate its present status and the effective role it has played in shaping our own historical consciousness.

Historians of the 18th and 19th centuries described the nature of their work with admirable clarity and comprehensiveness. It was divided into two parts: " lower criticism " and " higher criticism." This distinction is still useful since it furnishes the historian with a wholesome reminder that there is a critical, scientific element in every part of his work, from beginning to end.

Lower criticism had the preliminary task of discovering, collecting, describing, purifying, classifying, preserving, and publishing the records and monuments surviving from the past. A great many critical techniques had to be employed and developed to make sure that this work was done scientifically. Thus philology (with all *its* auxiliaries) was the main equipment for the lower criticism of documents which contained writing. Higher criticism meant the critique of the activities, opinions and judgments, decisions and feelings of persons of the past. The criteria for *this* critique were furnished by the positive sciences, which were thought to yield the true insights into human nature and activity.

The reasons for the gradual decline of this distinction in the discussion of the methods of the historian's work are equally instructive, but it is to be noted that no part of lower or higher criticism has lost its importance. Historians, however, have learned that the most important problems of lower criticism cannot be handled, except superficially, until the most important results furnished by higher criticism are brought to bear on them. When, e. g., the critical choice between two or more variants in a given sentence of one of St. Paul's letters has to be made (lower criticism), the historian has to know critically the whole mind of Paul and the way it worked, his style, his vocabulary, etc., in general, and even at the precise moment when he wrote this particular sentence (higher criticism). Since professional historians can do a great deal of useful and relevant work every day, even when they work on hard questions like this one, without troubling too much about their methodological theories, they incline to say less about them. A fairly good and conscientious way of doing that is to emphasize rather the *unity* of all criticism, thus diverting attention from the radical problems posed by both lower and higher criticism.

The second reason for the decline is a dilemma which arose from the practice of higher criticism. The work of several generations of scholars made painfully clear that their ability to make critical judgments about a dead man's train of thought and state of mind at any and every moment of his former life has its limits. The paucity or the unreliability of even critically analyzed records causes serious limitations. Yet they are small compared to the inner limits which are set to the historian's, to any man's, ability to feel himself critically into another person's train of thought or state of mind. It was precisely W. Dilthey,[3] who did more than any other scholar to advance the practice and analysis of empathy (*Einfühlung*), who also realized its limitations. The earlier, more or less rationalistic critique had to be radically recast. Lower and higher criticism have their limits; even empathy has its limits. But Dilthey insisted that within these limits one thing is still possible and necessary: true and adequate understanding of past history. Thus the term *understanding* came to replace, in large part and in general popularity, the inclusive distinction between lower and higher criticism as the best description of both methods and aims of historical research. For the same basic reason "understanding" became a central concern in several types of philosophical thinking.

c. *The Christian Faith.* The changes within "classical"

3. *Gesammelte Werke*; see especially Vols. *1* and *7*.

enlightenment had brought back, as we have seen, the Christian tradition in the form of secularizations by rationalists of several shades. Soon it was to make its reappearance in its own right and power. Kierkegaard, conditioned by his opposition to Hegel, as well as to the Romantic movement in Germany, and inspired by a fresh reading of the New Testament, was the chief of the lonely prophets who in the 19th century heralded the new life of the Christian faith. Kierkegaard stated the case for faith in Christ in terms of radical opposition to Hegel's and every autonomously human idea of history. He took seriously the New Testament proclamation that Jesus Christ was and is and continues to be the end of history: Christ *is* the fullness of time (Gal. 4:4–10) and the fulfillment of the hope of the ages.

In the 20th century Kierkegaard, thanks in part to our historical consciousness, was rediscovered simultaneously by various philosophers and theologians and somewhat later by some historians. However, it would be a mistake to hold Kierkegaard primarily, or even exclusively, responsible for this innermost change in our historical consciousness. Kierkegaard himself was saturated with the Christian idea of history as contained explicitly and implicitly in the setting of his own immediate, pietistic Christian heritage.

d. *Roots of Our Historical Consciousness.* It suffices here simply to point to the fact that the hundreds of millions of people who in several generations make up our Western culture have perhaps not experienced such a profound and explicit change in their consciousness of history, for the reason that they had no professional or academic ax to grind. The idea of history centrally inherent in the Christian faith was, on these deepest levels, secure. At the same time many millions of people could not resist the growing impact of contrary ideas which were at heart rationalistic.

It is at this point that two academic suggestions may make their greatest contribution, because they are directly concerned with the correlation, on inclusive and precise terms, of faith and of technical-scientific criticism in the understanding of history.

H. Butterfield's distinction [4] between, and correlation of, technical and creative understanding of history is useful and promising. It has considerable structural similarity with Richard Niebuhr's analysis of external and internal history.[5] The difference is that Butterfield, as a secular historian and a confessing Christian, emphasizes within his correlation the role of technical (external) understanding, while Niebuhr, as a technical theologian and a confessing Christian, emphasizes the internal (creative) understanding of history.

It is heartening indeed that the recent work of idealists (Croce and Collingwood),[6] of naturalistic process philosophers (Whitehead and Wieman),[7] also shows notable similarity with the concerns of a Butterfield and a Niebuhr.

In this intense search for the meaning of history history seems to "repeat itself." In Greece and Hellenistic Rome also the problem of history was discussed for centuries by men of thought and action and imagination. Even deeper in the history of the ancient Near East, Israel and early Christianity were above all else in their experience concerned with the ways of God, his rule and his grace, in history.

2. SPECIAL ISSUES UNDER DISCUSSION

We attempt to give some indication of what ground has been gained and what issues are still at stake.

a. *R. G. Collingwood and M. Heidegger.*[8] A brief comparison

4. *Christianity and History.*

5. *The Meaning of Revelation.*

6. B. Croce, *Theory and History of Historiography; History as the Story of Liberty*; for R. G. Collingwood, see below, n. 8.

7. A. N. Whitehead, *Process and Reality*; *Adventures of Ideas.* Cf. also W. W. Hammerschmidt, *Whitehead's Philosophy of Time*; H. N. Wieman, *The Source of Human Good.*

8. R. G. Collingwood, *The Idea of History.* The editor's preface to these posthumous essays places Collingwood within the contemporary philosophical scene, and otherwise helps to read Collingwood's important work rightly. For the quotations that follow see Collingwood, pp. xii f., 113–21, 172 f., 175, 227 f., 305, 315–20, 323, 333. M. Heidegger, *Sein und Zeit.*

of these two representative and influential thinkers who differ widely in their approach to the problem of history serves to focus the issues. Collingwood has categorically stated that "history is the only kind of knowledge," and that "philosophy as a separate discipline is liquidated by being converted into history." But throughout his essays in *The Idea of History* he speaks as a philosopher rather than an historian. His controversial concern is to rescue history from the false absolutisms of positivistic, empirical-objective understanding of history. Thus Collingwood without changing his position could also have stated the dogma that philosophy is the only kind of knowledge and that our only knowledge is the knowledge of minds in history. His two most characteristic and supplementary definitions of history confirm this judgment. "History does not presuppose mind; it is the life of mind itself, which is not mind except as far as it both lives in historical process and knows itself as so living." This should be regarded as a purely philosophical judgment. The continuity of Collingwood's philosophy with Hegel's and with more recent process philosophies is also apparent. History does not, at bottom, consist of successive events. Events are only external manifestations of the activity of mind. Therefore, knowledge "has for its proper object thought; not things thought about, but the act of thinking itself."

One is tempted to conclude that the idealistic terminology in Collingwood sometimes borders on idealistic subjectivism. Fundamentally Collingwood is saved from that charge by two factors: his insistence that "the life of the mind" is an historical process and the thesis which dominates all his thought that "historical knowledge . . . is knowledge of the past in the present, the self-knowledge of the historian's own mind as the present revival and reliving of past experiences." Thus objective knowledge is not repudiated but assigned its strictly defined domain. Thus also events as such and chronological successions as such [9] are subordinated to a secondary role, while the primary role in the historical process is assigned to men's actions which are at

9. Collingwood, pp. 117 ff.

bottom actions of the mind. This is not intellectualism of any kind. Although I know of no evidence that Collingwood has read either Kierkegaard or any other existentialist,[10] there is here a clear affinity between Collingwood's insistence on history as self-knowledge of mind and the existentialist insistence on self-understanding. Collingwood's "existentialist" concern is nonetheless impressive for not sharing the terminology and some of the special preoccupations of the formally existentialist schools. He does share with them, negatively, the discriminating skepticism toward speculative epistemology and metaphysics and toward the absolutist tendencies of empirical science; positively, he shares with them the centrality and validity of mind and of human freedom.

In the logic of his position Collingwood could not neglect the eschatological aspect of his understanding of history, but his treatment of it is one of the weaker parts of his work.[11] His eschatology is in terms of progress: "Progress is not a mere fact to be discovered by historical thinking." This erroneous notion is perhaps not sufficiently criticized; yet Collingwood offers no comfort to the believer in a law of progress governing the historical process. That faith "is bred of an unnatural union between man's belief in his own superiority to nature and his belief that he is nothing more than a part of nature. If either belief is true, the other is false: they cannot be combined to produce logical offspring." In this connection Collingwood offers a valuable analysis of decisive differences between the notions of evolution and progress in nature and of progress in history. "The conception of historical process as a mere extension of natural process [must be] denied . . . by any sound theory of history."

The positive statement reads as follows: "It is only through historical thinking [12] that [progress] comes about at all." Colling-

10. Cf. the editor's comment concerning Kierkegaard and Collingwood, *ibid.*, p. xvii.

11. *Ibid.*, pp. 321–35.

12. Note that for Collingwood "historical thinking" always is "the activity of the mind."

wood's "scientific proof" for the proposition that "human activity is free" may not be convincing, but that would not affect its truth or its importance in Collingwood's thought.

Although the "sense of crisis" is as strong in Collingwood as it is explicit in Heidegger, Collingwood, who came from history to philosophy, advanced his upsetting ideas about history by speaking the language and using the logic of traditional philosophies. Heidegger, who came from theology to philosophy, came to feel the crisis so strongly that he became convinced, like so many philosophers before him, of the necessity for constructing a new terminology and a new method for the philosophic enterprise. This formal demand is no doubt an integral part of his thought. The impossibility of translating his re-made German language into intelligible English entitles us to paraphrase him. His thought is significant not because of its great influence in continental Europe but because his radical re-examination of all historical philosophic thought throws sharp light on our historical consciousness. In it many minority voices and partial insights of the 19th century have found a radical analysis and a systematic exposition. It is no accident that one of the most fruitful aspects of his work is the intensive and original interpretation of many philosophers and poets, both ancient and modern.

Heidegger's basic concern [13] is with man's understanding of himself out of and in his *Geschichtlichkeit* (temporality *and* historicity). It is clear that this concern with man's existence in historicity is not unrelated to Collingwood's concern with man, who, as mind, is both the subject and the object of historical activity.

Similarly, Collingwood's conception of history [14] as self-knowledge corresponds closely to Heidegger's central endeavor to lay bare the true and full possibility of man's understanding of himself out of and in his own historicity. "The primary concern of philosophy is not a theory of historical knowledge [15] but the under-

13. In *Sein und Zeit*, as well as in his later works.

14. *Op. cit.*, e. g., pp. 227 f., 315, etc.

15. This negative preamble is, I take it, a protest against empirical historians

standing out of and in its historicity of that which really *is* historically. That which is historically must not be equated with anything that changes in the historical process or in its observation. It is not derived from the latter, but is that which if it were known, makes possible historical science." [16] (This is a free, though I trust faithful, translation of Heidegger's text.) Heidegger is still working on the analysis of this transcendent historicity of man, but he is sure that our modern notions about the historical process are a mixture of truths and falsehoods, a construction by which Western man in the course of history from Plato to Nietzsche has fatefully enslaved himself to his own views of his own world.[17]

Moreover, Heidegger is able to make a judgment about the meaning of the whole of Western history quite similar to judgments which other thinkers have made on grounds which Heidegger and many others consider inadequate. Thus, Spengler's biological and eschatological idea of history is inadequate because of its biological criteria. Heidegger's own idea about the end of Western culture seems to rest on the assurance that he has learned enough about what man as such historically *is* to enable him to predict what is *going to happen to* the men of Western culture. In principle this must be regarded as a legitimate procedure. At any rate it is a procedure not essentially at variance with Hebrew-Jewish-Christian thought during the whole course of its history. Here man was understood as *being* created in the image of God and as *being* under the judgment of God. A notable difference is that the Christian tradition, because of its greater age, wider influence, and deeper perversions, has produced a larger variety of speculations, while in several of its currents of tradition,

and objectifying philosophies of history. As we have seen, it does not in any sense demolish Collingwood's definition of "historical knowledge," or his idea of history as a whole.

16. *Sein und Zeit*, p. 10.

17. From here to the end of Section a I am especially indebted to K. Loewith, *Heidegger*; see especially, pp. 55 ff. Loewith's small book offers a clear exposition, appreciation and critique of Heidegger's philosophical enterprise and its history.

from the beginning to the present day, all eschatological speculation was understood figuratively rather than literally, metaphysically, or historically.[18]

We may note two more points at which Collingwood's and Heidegger's ideas about history are both different and similar. When Collingwood speaks of the mind as the creator of progress, progress is by no means conceived as gradual or assured. Thus Heidegger's eschatological "hope" that the world is racing toward the fulfillment[19] of its true destiny by virtue of a kind of ontic power of salvation is not far removed from Collingwood's eschatology.

Lastly, both agree, with many other philosophies and faiths of the 20th century, on the cardinal point within our historical consciousness that reality and truth are of the nature of events and actions rather than of things.[20]

Our analysis has shown a variety of outlooks, of ways of thinking and speaking in our age; but also it has revealed a remarkable family likeness in common concerns and conclusions regarding the 20th-century idea of history. There is no need to underestimate or overestimate the real dilemmas of thought and action in our age, which many thinkers, both modern and ancient, have analyzed, many poets have sung, and many prophets have answered by their call to salvation.

b. *A Summary of Issues.* For the sake of the subsequent survey of the ancient Near Eastern idea of history it may be helpful to list some of the special issues at stake in present-day research and discussion.

1) It remains to be seen whether philosophy or history or theology will gain supremacy by absorbing the rivals within itself. The fact that all three of them have had an age-long history by no means argues for the supremacy of history as the science of comprehensive understanding. The histories of philosophy, his-

18. See below, pp. 345–51.
19. Loewith, *Heidegger*, pp. 109 ff.
20. *Ibid.*, pp. 66–72; 109 f.

tory, and theology suggest that each of these three disciplines fulfills its own task best by going its own way without losing sight of the courses which the other two take.

2) If there is any certainty at all, it is the validity of the methods of historical criticism as they continue to develop in its practice and self-criticism and through the continuing critiques by philosophy and theology.

3) A problem of seemingly minor significance is the problem of periodization. By what criteria does one periodize, i. e., chronologically define, successive cultures? The modern traditional periodization, e. g., of our own Western history into ancient, medieval, and modern, has long been questioned from several competing points of view. Obviously, one's periodizations depend upon one's eschatology. This is the experience of both ancient and modern thinkers and prophets.

4) The problem of periodization must also be regarded as just one aspect of the problem of time, succession, movement, simultaneity, and eternity. At this point, too, relevant insights have by no means come from ancient to modern times in a line of progress and increasing sophistication.

5) The relation between history and nature is another continuing and major problem. In the 19th century human history was simply looked upon as a short span in the chronological history of the universe of nature. In that situation the only unsolved problem is whether the universe has or has not an historical beginning and an historical end.

In the present discussions the 19th-century form of the question is not ignored, but it is not the center of interest. The present questions are directed rather toward finding valid insights into the undeniable differences between nature and history.

The sketch of our modern idea of history has suggested in several respects our nearness to the experience and thought of the ancient Near Eastern cultures. The chronological proximity and the genetic continuity are perhaps less important than is a more profound nearness, the solidarity of men this side and the other side of the ambiguous barriers of commonsense, physical, astronomical time. This kind of " solidarity," at any rate, is one of the lessons which the study of the ancient ideas of history might teach us.

II. THE ANCIENT NEAR EASTERN IDEA OF HISTORY

Our task now is to bring the analysis of our own idea of history to bear on that of the Near Eastern ideas of history. The eight essays of this volume exhibit both the difficulties and the virtues inherent in successful pioneering work. For the first time the ideas of history in the ancient Near East have been made the special subject of a joint study by eight experts on various Near Eastern cultures.[21] Each author was to concentrate on his respective field of specialization. Each was to pay particular attention to the analysis and interpretation of " indirect " evidence, to clues which are furnished by the ancient records of events, i. e., by the records as such, by poetry, myth, and cult, etc., and by the effort to understand the spirit which found its expression in these data, rather than to pay attention to explicit reflections and speculations. This well-conceived work led to a number of new insights and opened up new perspectives for further research.

1. UNITY AND VARIETY

Of the unity and variety which divide modern and ancient Near Eastern thought we have already spoken. This " unity " in terms of historical understanding has three inseparable aspects: 1) the historical process as such (not objectively knowable as such, since we are never outside but always inside of it); 2) our own critical and imaginative reflections and speculations on our own past; 3) the undeniable aspect (difficult as it is to define) of the basic

21. Attention should be called in this connection to the important volume by H. and H. A. Frankfort, John A. Wilson, and Thorkild Jacobsen, *Before Philosophy*. This work is inclusive in its subject matter and selective with regard to the Near Eastern cultures with which it deals.

sameness of men throughout historical time and in all historical changes of " becoming and passing-away." [22] If an historian seeks for a serious answer to the problem of unity and variety in a given culture or family of cultures (such as the ancient Near Eastern family), he arrives at conclusions which are susceptible of a philosophical critique; for the historian's problem of unity and variety occupies the philosopher as the problem, e. g., of " the one and the many." Certainly the historian's characteristic task in this respect is to base his conclusions on evidence concretely established by his study of knowable, concrete examples of social and personal interactions in a given culture. Even his " final " conclusions concerning both unity and variety will be particular, because he learns that the elements of unity and variety differ from one culture to another. The philosopher, in his own way, will arrive at similar conclusions, if reality for him has the character of events and processes rather than of static things governed by immutable law.

Ever since the historical-critical study of the ancient Near East began in earnest at the start of the 19th century, the evidence available at each stage of research demanded and received interpretations in terms of unity and/or variety. For a long time attention was concentrated chiefly on establishing theses of unity, in preponderantly evolutionary, genetic terms, in the form of continuity between special Near Eastern cultures. Thus, e. g., Hebrew history and religion were explained in terms of " Pan-babylonism," the assertion that Babylonian culture was here the decisive element of unity. Thus, too, the history of early " Near Eastern " Christianity was interpreted as an evolutionary process toward " Hellenization." Thus the Greek culture, in terms not only of variety but of basic contrast, was conceived as the emergence, from within its own " Western " genius, of a culture essentially different from those of the more Eastern and ancient Near Eastern cultures—an interpretation which was in part due to

22. Cf. R. Bultmann, pp. 47–69; see especially, p. 54 for Bultmann's conclusion regarding 3) above, arrived at through his analysis of Dilthey's theory of understanding.

the admiration of the so-called classical Greek culture that had dominated European thought and imagination since the Renaissance. Thus, too, Oriental-Roman Hellenism was explained in terms of unity as a syncretistic historical process, or in terms of variety, as a " failure of nerve " in contrast to the presumable strength of nerve of classical Greek culture.

Judgments of this kind are by no means passé in present scholarship, but technical historical research has assembled sufficient concrete historical evidence to persuade most experts that the elements of unity and variety have to be looked for by historical research at deeper levels, over wider areas, and throughout longer periods within the ancient Near Eastern culture than was heretofore assumed. The older modern judgments are by no means wrong; they were too sweeping in claiming too much for a few pieces of evidence; they were not sweeping enough because of disregard of other available evidence and ignorance of evidence not yet available.

This new depth-dimension in critical-historical work may be usefully illustrated here by the case of two Near Eastern cultures in which the idea of history stood in the center of attention in two very different ways, in the two cultures which, along with early Christianity, have been studied longer and more intensively than the other Near Eastern cultures—Israel and Greece.

Professor Martin Noth, in a brief, notable, and representative article,[23] concludes that " the history of Israel [from its beginnings in the 2d millennium B. C. to the end in Roman times] is linked up with the contemporary history of the Ancient East." Even the Israelite prophet, as the messenger of God, has his clearly discernible prototype outside Israel, in the ancient Near East. " It is manifest therefore that the pattern of the prophet, which for the Old Testament is central, had a pre-history," as the Mari texts analyzed by Noth show.[24] (Noth's complementary thesis, regarding " variety," will be referred to subsequently.[25])

23. Pp. 194–206; see especially, p. 202.

24. *Ibid.*, pp. 195–200.

25. See below, pp. 344 f.

As regards Greece, two general conclusions are gaining ground in present-day historical research. First, the traditional modern view of " classical " Greece as the " ideal " culture lives on with undiminished strength in a different form: classical Greek thought and imagination, in philosophy, sciences, and arts, still distinguish " the West " from " the East." Secondly, these distinct characteristics of " the Greek way of life " the historian can understand, however highly he assesses them, only in the context of Greece's close and long-sustained interactions and unity with the ancient Near Eastern cultures.

The " Hellenistic Orient " and " Oriental Hellenism " (extending in the East from Alexander the Great to medieval and modern Byzantinism, to Islam and the Mohammedan Empire) can be historically understood only on the basis of much intense interaction between Greece and the Near East throughout the preceding two or three millennia. Many of the most enlightened and most typically classical Greeks, from Hecataeus and Herodotus to Photius of medieval Constantinople, had a deeper appreciation of these facts than did some modern philologists and historians.

The well-known Greek literary references to slightly disreputable adventurers, commercial agents and inquisitive sightseers furnish us only a fragmentary knowledge of many more extensive and intensive interactions of the same kind. They also furnish valuables clues pointing to common concerns on many deeper levels of human activity. Technical research, archeological as well as literary, is increasingly providing us with further clues leading to the same conclusion. Our analysis of the Greek idea of history will at least suggest additional evidence.

At any rate it is certain that Greece must also be regarded, historically and phenomenologically, as belonging both to the modern West *and* the ancient Near East. For all these reasons we may profitably deal with the Greek idea of history first.

2. GREECE AND HELLENISM

In Greek poetry, science, philosophy, and historiography the first attempts were made to examine rationally the idea of history.

At the height of their development the Greeks summed up their whole conception of culture and of education [26] in the maxim that the proper study of man is man. It is in their irresistible drive toward this ideal that within the span of three centuries (600–300 B.C.) they developed and transformed, by rational and creative systems of thinking, the mythological, scientific, and cosmological notions of the older Near East. All this they accomplished along with the unsurpassed achievements of their imagination in the arts, from poetry and the theater to painting, architecture, and sculpture.

Since Greek science and philosophy evolved from and revolved around the human experience of being, becoming, and passing away, it was inevitable that the ever changing fortune of men in their histories should become a central concern of their drive for rational understanding. It is high time scholars stopped talking about the absence of concern or even " interest " in history on the part of the Greeks. A cursory reading of the extant works of Greek historians, many of which still occupy a respectable place alongside the best of modern historical works, should be sufficient to prevent such judgments. The statement made by an eminent expert that Plato's *Laws* contain the elements of a philosophy of history [27] need not be modified greatly to describe the total intention of Plato's lifework. His Socratic dialectic and the speculations of his *Republic*, *Phaedo* and *Timaeus* had as their primary motive the realization of the Good in human culture by education, one Greek word (*paideia*) significantly sufficing to denote both the means (education) and the end (culture).

The false judgment is chiefly the consequence of two prior misconceptions. The first is the misunderstanding of the Greek idea that time—and therefore human history—moves in a cycle; that history is the eternal recurrence of the same; more dogmatically, that, as in Stoic speculation, the Great Year represents one full turn of the cycle of cosmic history.[28] However, the very

26. W. W. Jaeger, *Paideia*.
27. Jaeger, III, 219.
28. For a careful analysis of these matters see J. F. Callahan, *Four Views*

philosophers (Plato, Aristotle, and the early Stoics) who developed this theory saw in it no devaluation of or cause for indifference to history. In fact, the explicit and implicit significance of the cyclical idea of history is to give, in terms of rational theory or metaphysical speculation, ultimate, cosmic significance and meaning to the history of the Greek city-state (*polis*) as well as of the Stoic, universal world-state (*cosmopolis*). To Greek philosophical thinking cyclical motion was the *perfect* motion. In other words, the first misconception comes from the modern idea, in which the understanding of history is thought to require the figure of a straight, forward- and upward-moving line in which beginning and end move ever more widely apart.

The second misconception is closely related. It is the reading of the cyclical idea of history into *all* Greek consciousness and theories of history. However, Hesiod's famous " theory " of successive historical world-ages can be no better illuminated by the cyclical idea than Daniel's " Oriental " scheme of four world empires.[29]

A recent book [30] has done much to demolish the modern misunderstanding and exaggeration regarding the Greek cyclical idea of history. The study of the Greek historians [31] helps further to correct the picture. C. N. Cochrane has shown that Thucydides as an historian was as much a part of Ionian and Athenian sophistic enlightenment as was Voltaire of the 18th century's. No wonder that the 19th century, by and large, considered Thucydides the greatest, i. e., the most scientific, of Greek historians. His objectivity, by and large, is admirable, though it is that of the empirical scientist rather than the technical his-

of Time in Ancient Philosophy and V. Goldschmidt, *Le Système stoïcien et l'idée de temps*.

29. See the discussions of both by J. W. Swain, pp. 1–21.

30. B. A. van Groningen, *In the Grip of the Past: Essay on an Aspect of Greek Thought*.

31. See especially, E. Howald, *Vom Geist antiker Geschichtsschreibung*; C. N. Cochrane, *Thucydides*, especially chs. 1 and 2; see also, the brief sketch of the Greek idea of history by the same author in his *Christianity and Classical Culture*, pp. 456–74; H. Holborn, pp. 3–13.

torian. But it is equally significant that the Greeks themselves always valued Herodotus as "the Father of history." He was (and is) boring and entertaining, credulous and critical, traditional and analytic, superficial and profound by turns. In all he has a breadth of vision and a width of interest which will long guarantee him an honorable place in the family of historians.

Only one historian's work from post-Alexander, Stoic days has survived in substantial parts—Polybius' history of the rise of Rome to world power. While Cochrane thinks that in him Greek historiography—and the Greek idea of history—came to an ignominious end, other historians of Greek historians have a high regard for him. So Howald, followed by van Groningen, thinks that Polybius' reliance on *Tyche* in his understanding history is not, as Cochrane thinks, the confession of the bankruptcy of the Greek idea of history (Tyche as arbitrary, irrational accident), but rather (Tyche as "fate," destiny) a useful means to an understanding of world history as a dynamic organism.[32] One cannot but agree that Howald's judgment on this point is a useful means toward understanding the inner motivations and purposes of Polybius as a man and as an historian.

It is true that Polybius is the first "universal" historian of whom we have substantial knowledge. There is fragmentary but sufficient evidence that the early Stoics developed a more or less systematic theory of universal, i. e., of world history,[33] although we need not overlook Herodotus' width and breadth of interest and inquiry as one root of this growth.

It is true also that Polybius works, formally speaking, with the older traditional tools and established standards of Greek historiography. Thus, he wants to tell nothing but the truth and all important truths about the events and actions he describes and interprets. He works with the old theory of the cyclical succession of the forms of constitutions (tyranny, monarchy, democracy, ochlocracy). He also reflects, though rarely, in terms

32. Howald, p. 92 f.

33. Holborn, p. 7. On the beginnings of universal history in Hellenism, see M. Pohlenz, pp. 211–14.

reminiscent of the cyclical idea of history, on the vanity of historical greatness. He also thinks highly of the study of history as the best schooling for the active statesman. However, the attentive reader of Polybius cannot help feeling that the historian's heart is in none of these traditional standards (or clichés) required of the respectable Greek historian. When he *does* occasionally envisage the vanity of historical greatness, he is dejected, although Plato applauded historical greatness without sentimental fear or hope of the future.

Polybius' work is really motivated by four new concerns. First, in calling his history of Rome's beginning rise to power (221–168 B. C.) "pragmatic history" he is constantly calling emphatic attention to "the inner driving power and energy which spurs individuals or groups and reveals itself in facts."[34] For Polybius *pragma* and its many derivatives denote and connote human actions, motivations, and intentions, as well as the events themselves and their meaning. Secondly, what really interests Polybius is not cyclical succession of types of constitutions, but dynamic interactions of acting persons and groups. This most explicit interest determines in fact the literary organization of his monumental work. Thirdly, the beginning extension of Roman power throughout the Eastern Mediterranean is the unifying theme of all these concrete interactions which make his history "universal" history (*oikumenike historia*). It is not universal history in the literal and abstract sense of the word. There can be no universal history for Polybius unless it consists of verifiable, concrete, and particular interactions which have particular, concrete, and historically knowable results. Fourthly, the most radically new note which Polybius strikes is his awareness that something not only important but new is happening.[35]

Finally, when we ask what is the relation of the Greek idea of history to its Near Eastern antecedents, the most important fact leaps to the eye. The Greek theory of cyclical history is a

34. Groningen, p. 28. Cf. A. J. Toynbee, ed. *Greek Historical Thought*, The Library of Greek Thought (London, 1924), p. 24, n. 2.

35. See Pol., I, 3–4.

direct and rational version of the involvement of men and all their actions and experiences in the mysterious, powerful operation of what we call nature—the very experience of involvement which dominated life throughout the ancient Near East and flourished most brilliantly throughout the long and influential histories of Egypt and Mesopotamia. While the Greek effort had "radical" results, its methods were systematic but not radical; the objects and results of Greek scientific and philosophical thinking remained Near Eastern. Ionian Greek scientists and philosophers started with the methods and results of Mesopotamian study of the heavenly bodies (sun, moon, and planets chiefly). Thus astrology was born with astronomy. What preceded both was neither.

The Greeks took perhaps a somewhat more radical step in extending the older methods of external observations and measurements to the study of man himself. As far as the idea of history is concerned, this meant that history could and did become a separate and vigorous, though, fortunately, not an independent, object of study.

3. EGYPT, MESOPOTAMIA, AND PERSIA

Even if the Egyptian and Mesopotamian cultures developed their respective characteristics without decisive interaction, their cultures show a striking family likeness. Persian culture, with its idea of history, shows common features and relationships with Mesopotamia on the one hand and with earlier Israel and later Judaism on the other. Iranian elements were freely taken over into Hebrew-Jewish thought, but lost their Iranian meaning by becoming Israelite. It seems that the dualism and polytheism of Persian religion, as well as its political history, align Persia more decisively with Mesopotamia.

a. *Egypt and Mesopotamia.* These two ancient cultures are textbook examples of the fact that considerable technological and administrative, moral, spiritual, and intellectual complexity, vitality, political power, practical and theoretical sophistication can develop without the kind of a systematically rational and critical spirit that characterized Greece, which never did rate for long as a first-class political power.

Positively speaking, the self-understanding of these cultures was predominantly mythological (expressing itself in imaginative ideas) and cultic (expressing itself in conduct and liturgical practices). Intellectual reflection on human experience and empirical observations of nature are not absent from their mythological self-expression. On the contrary, they are free to express themselves with a minimum of standardized critical restraint. The most important aspect of a predominantly mythological self-understanding is the experience of spontaneous oneness of man with his total environment, social, natural, and temporal.

Therefore it becomes a very real question, as the relevant articles in this volume have shown, whether we can at all speak of an Egyptian or Mesopotamian idea of history, in spite of the fact that we are rightly confident that *we* can understand *their* history of which they who made it had no such understanding.

In short, in a predominantly mythological culture, experience and practice dominate theory; in a scientific culture, theory (including the theory that practice is everything) tends to dominate experience and practice. Thus, if we cannot speak objectively of an Egyptian or Mesopotamian *idea* of history, we can speak of their *sense* of history, which is the sense of the oneness of all reality, a sense which within and against scientifically oriented cultures must take the form of ascetic, world- and self-denying mysticism.

The essays on Egypt and Mesopotamia enable us to see the essential, concrete features of this sense of history. They are kingship and priesthood, both in Egypt and in Mesopotamia. In both cultures these institutions are understood as divine or as divinely directed and authenticated. In these institutions the sense of oneness finds its concrete but universally valid expression. Priesthood is thus closely and inwardly allied to kingship; but they are by no means identical, as they frequently are in more primitive cultures. This " alliance " indicates a more or less unconscious tendency in the direction of diversification and specialization.

The many records, literary and monumental, that have come from Egypt and Mesopotamia, especially the records of royal deeds and the official annals, filled with political *and* religious items, strike the unwary modern beholder as evidence that Egyptians and Mesopotamians were preoccupied as much or more than we are with chronology and succession and even progress. One need not doubt that such notions and such awareness thus *became* a factor in their own sense of history; but essentially, the official annals were the important documents in which kings and priests rendered their responsible account to their deities, or they were accounts in which the will of the deities was communicated to the responsible institutions of kingship and priesthood.

This ancient Near Eastern *sense* of history need not necessarily be regarded as inferior to an explicit *idea* of history, since the former has at least the possible advantage of being one aspect of the all-pervasive sense of the oneness of all reality, a sense which, in the case of Egypt and Mesopotamia, " made history " of considerable and lasting importance.

It is necessary at this point to refer to the critical discussion of myth which occupies so much of modern psychiatry, poetry, philosophy, theology, and historiography. This discussion is equally and inseparably concerned with the discovery of proper categories for the understanding of ancient " mythological " cultures and for modern man's understanding of himself in his world.[36] The views implicit in our essay may be briefly indicated as follows. Myth has not been superseded by science or anything else. Science has abolished many individual myths, just as it continues to abolish many scientific theories of the more recent

36. A discussion particularly useful to students of the ancient Near East is offered by H. and H. A. Frankfort, *op. cit.*, pp. 11–36, under the title " Myth and Reality." A systematic critique of the whole contemporary discussion with discriminating bibliographical references is contained in E. Buess, *Geschichte des mythischen Erkennens.*

past. The final objects and *results* of the sciences, as scientific world views, are also mythological. Mythological "thinking" is distinguished from modern scientific thinking in method more than in result. Every modern scientific world view is merely a quantitative, temporary refinement of ancient cosmological myth. Myth is poetry. Neither is abolished. Myth, poetry, and science become dangerous only when they are perverted into literalistic, metaphysical dogma. It is such dogmas that science supersedes without ever getting ahead of them for long.

All the essays of this volume deal with the idea of history implicit or emerging in cultures in which mythological thinking played a free and sometimes leading role. It is not the least achievement of these essays that they are making a real contribution to the critical understanding of a critically important aspect of the ancient Near Eastern cultures by helping to refine and to redefine the methods and ends of historical research.

b. *Persia.* Plato's messianic dream [37] of the happy, simultaneous advent and co-operation of a good king with a wise lawgiver found something like fulfillment in the co-operation between Zoroaster, Cyrus, and Darius. In the course of a few decades Persia rose from a conglomerate of near-tribal civilizations to a power and culture that dominated or threatened the whole of the Near East. As Persia proved to be the one Near Eastern power which Rome never crushed, and as the Persian adaptation of Mesopotamian kingship lived on in the Byzantinism of many centuries, so the spirit and the letter of Zoroastrianism lived on in Judaism, early Christianity, and Islam; and it inspired many Persian, Roman, and Moslem armies for two millenia.

The reason for this vitality and influence lies in large part in the nature of the Zoroastrian religion. It includes an explicit idea of world history. Human history, it seems, is not looked upon as the sorry battleground of the supernatural conflict between Ahura Mazda and Ahriman; rather it is viewed as the arena in which men, by choosing sides, determine the outcome of this

37. *Laws* II, 657a.

cosmic conflict.[38] The divine agents are no longer limited to official, all-powerful institutions. Zoroastrianism and Hebrew religion, though in decidedly different ways, are the first Near Eastern religions of conversion by choice and decision.

The theology of Zoroastrianism, with its idea of history, is not in terms of correct ritual behavior and submission to the fate decreed by the deities; it is in terms of an historical, human, and divine conflict between Truth and Lie, between Righteousness and Unrighteousness, between Light and Darkness. (All this has made this religion an attractive and dangerous tool in the hands of Politicians who are convinced, in one form or another, of their divine commission.)

Zoroastrianism has often been labeled an ethical dualism in contrast to the cosmological, anthropological, or metaphysical dualisms of the subsequent Hellenistic Age. It is a question worth pondering how useful this distinction is. Although the emphasis may apparently vary, each kind of dualism requires the other. Moreover the most profound dualistic thought always has a monistic base or monistic end or both. Absolute dualism is always a sign of secondary and slackening thought. It leads to the double dogma of eternal salvation and damnation. In it a good myth has become poor metaphysics.

The appreciation of Zoroastrianism in various forms by Greeks and Romans rests on the common concern with Truth and Righteousness in thought, religion, private and public life. For the same reason Zoroastrianism deeply influenced Judaism. It did so all the more easily since Truth and Righteousness were regarded as character traits of Ahura Mazda and of Yahweh. But dualism of any kind never made much headway in Judaism. The apocalyptic-Jewish idea of the two successive world ages—this age and the world to come—is certainly not dualism; it is simply an objectified, secondary elaboration of preexilic prophetic thought in which " past " and " future " were inseparable from the present. In later Jewish thought both ages are under the exclusive sovereignty of one God. Whatever the facts may be

38. So W. B. Henning, especially pp. 45–59.

regarding concrete interactions or their absence at this point between Persian, Jewish and Greek-Hellenistic ideas, it is clear that the concern of Jewish apocalyptic writers with the Two World Ages, of Zoroaster and his disciples with the World Age, and of the Greek-Hellenistic Stoics with the Great (cosmic) Year are but an indication of the great changes that were then beginning to take place in the Near Eastern idea of history. These changes led to results which have not yet lost their efficacy. They will occupy us as we turn to the idea of history in Israel, early Christianity, and early Islam.

4. ISRAEL, EARLY CHRISTIANITY, AND EARLY ISLAM

In the 19th century these three movements which originated in the ancient Near East were called world religions by the scientific students of comparative religions. It proved difficult to justify this label from the standpoint of a science which studies and compares religions, except on the tenuous basis that these religions (like many others) make universal claims, or on the equally tenuous basis that they are still " living." None of the three has conquered or persuaded the world; none even can be said to have a " universal " appeal. The best way scientifically to justify the label is that each has made an impress on the world at large which far exceeds the impress these religions as such—scientifically speaking—are making within the orbit of their own devotees. In other words, the historian of a given set of continuous cultures can, within his sphere, say something scientifically about the " world-wide " significance of each of these religions.

a. *Israel.* When it comes to the idea of history, it must be said that Israel, through its Sacred Scripture as promulgated by the Jews (the Old Testament as promulgated by the Christians), has proved to be the strongest and most influential single force observable by the historian in shaping the idea of history throughout the two millenia of Western history. The specific contribution of the New Testament to this idea of history is, as we shall suggest soon, much more problematical and complex in every respect, even as regards its influence on the modern idea of history.

In many important respects Egyptian, Mesopotamian, Canaanite, and Persian heritage or influence show themselves in the Hebrew-Jewish culture, which became the religious culture par excellence of the ancient Near East. The role of Israelite kings; the religious conception of kingship; Israelite priesthood, cult, and liturgy; the theme of the unity of nature and man; the didactic emphasis on divine law and obedience, exhortation, and practical wisdom; even the role played by the prophets as divine messengers—all these are positive and constitutive aspects of Israelite culture, religion, and thought which came to Israel through its non-Israelite Near Eastern ancestors and neighbors. Yet Israel, which like Greece enjoyed only sporadically a modest kind of political prosperity, broke with the standard Near Eastern idea of history much more radically than did Persia. Although the Persian Empire and Zoroastrian religion criticized and revitalized Semitic culture in a way from without, Israel criticized its own Semitic-Egyptian heritage and environment more radically from within, transforming it into something new, into a religion which from center to periphery gave expression to a clear and magnificent theology of history.

What were the chief aspects of this radical critique and of this radical reconstruction?

The work of critique and reconstruction was not carried out by the Israelite institutions of kingship or priesthood. (The few notable exceptions prove the truth of the judgment.) It was carried on and sustained throughout the many centuries of Hebrew-Jewish history by individuals and groups from all social strata of the "nation." It was consolidated by the postexilic community under the unofficial leadership of prophets, priests, and teachers. The new institutions—synagogue, priests, and rabbis—could consolidate critique and reconstruction because they themselves as institutions had not yet hardened into institutions concerned with the mere maintenance of tradition and special privilege and into thus becoming objects of critique themselves.

In brief, the sense of a historic community rose from the depths of the community itself, through the voices of many prophets and teachers, of whom Moses, long before the great age of the writing prophets, was regarded as the foremost.

It was the work of these speaking and writing prophets—from Hosea and Amos to Isaiah and Jeremiah to Second Isaiah and Malachi—which brought this sense of historic community to its highest expression and to its abiding efficacy.

Their critique is directed at Israel as much as, if not more than, at her neighbors, the great and small powers of the Near East. The criteria for the critique are inherent in the positive content of the faith that there is only one God, the Creator of all that is and of all that comes into being. As Creator and Sovereign of the world God is the chief actor in and Lord of history. As chief actor in history he is the Creator of the world. There is no speculation in Israel as to what God is. Attention is focused on what God does and says through his actions and agents; it is focused on God as acting. Therefore there can be no adequate image of God, and therefore there shall be none. The faith of Israel is the response to God, who acts in the creation of the world and in their history. The qualities of God's action are holiness, power, righteousness, trustworthiness, loving kindness, and mercy. It is these last three that differentiate most sharply the " character " of God from Near Eastern deities; it is these three that deepen or transform the more generally known traits of holiness, power, and righteousness. Thus Israel's response to her God is Israel's trust in, and faithfulness to, God in mercy, loving kindness, and righteousness.

Israel is a special object of God's concern and action; but Israel's privileged position is even more a responsible and a humble one. The prophets deal (this is Noth's second thesis) [39] " with guilt and punishment, reality and unreality, present and future of the Israelite people as chosen by God for a special and

39. Noth, pp. 201–3; see above n. 25.

unique service, the declaration of the great and moving contemporary events in the world as part of a process which, together with the future issue of that process, is willed by God." The prophets " always speak in the name of God who alone disposes of the great powers of world history and whose will all powers and movements of history serve. . . . According to the Bible, God manifests himself in history which is precisely [40] the sphere in which human life on earth is lived, through the agency of characters and phenomena as they occur in history."

In the Second Isaiah the prophetic faith finds its highest expression. Two special emphases of his may be singled out to supplement Noth's characterizations. In Second Isaiah present, past, and future are by no means so sharply defined and separated as they are in the Greek tradition from Plato to Augustine. Perhaps it is worth asking whether Isaiah's more unified sense of historical time may not be as suggestive to the technical philosophers and theologians as are the Greek analyses.

Secondly, Isaiah's main theme, developed in several pointed variations,[41] is the Lordship of the one God in creation and in history. It is the inclusiveness and simplicity of this theme which in each of the variations forces the critique of any notion of God, wherever it is held, that is smaller than this. The critique of Second Isaiah is not confined to this or that institution, this or that nation or group, this or that individual. It is applied to every concrete, historical situation of men, not as a condition for the reconstruction and transformation of men but as a desirable and inescapable part of the transformation.

b. *Early Christianity.* The Old and the New Testaments have this in common: that there is hardly a book in either canon in which the biblical idea of history is not explicitly set forth; that

40. *Ibid.*, p. 203. The original German edition not being available to me, I risk a slight conjecture, suspecting that a German idiom was slightly understated by the translator. The printed text reads " just as in " for " which is precisely." See the reference to the underlying German text, p. 194, n. 1.

41. Isa. 41:1–4, 21–9; 43:9–18; 45:14–23; 46:1–13; 48:1–22.

this idea is at bottom the same, simple, particular, *and* universal; that there is fundamental unity and fundamental variety within and between the testaments. The variety and quality in the Old Testament ranges from the profundity and ambivalence of Second Isaiah and many Psalms to the clichés of the Chronicles and to the chronological and periodizing calculations on the course of history in Daniel and in subsequent apocalytic speculations. But throughout, the sovereignty of God in creation and in history, in judgment and in mercy, is the fundamental theme. In the new Testament the same theme dominates the apocalyptic thought of the Revelation, the " progressive," " modern," Greek and Biblical historiography of Luke-Acts, the simple narratives of revelatory events by Mark and Matthew, the cosmic setting of the fulfillment of all history in the Fourth Gospel, Colossians, and Hebrews; and, not least, the thought of Paul.

Paul's version of the early Christian idea of history, in this context of the whole New Testament, is at once individualistic and inclusive, critical and constructive, analytical and reflective, certain and ambivalent, radical and traditional, attractive and objectionable. For these reasons we may legitimately orient ourselves on Paul for our summary of early Christian thinking.

For the whole New Testament the person and work of Jesus Christ, the Son of God whom the Father sent into the likeness of sinful flesh (Rom. 8:3), who was crucified and raised from the dead (I Cor. 15:3–5), was the fulfillment of history (Gal. 4:4–10; Phil. 2:5–11; Rom. 3:21–6). " When the fullness of time (*τὸ πλήρωμα τοῦ χρόνου*) had come, God sent his Son, born of woman, born under the law . . ." (Gal. 4:4). Whatever the genetic background and the full meaning of the phrase " fullness of time " may be, Paul could have reversed the formulation by saying, " when God sent his Son, the fullness of time had come." This reversion does not change but clarifies Paul's idea of history. Although the phrase " fullness of time " does not, in this precise wording, occur elsewhere in Paul, it furnishes the clue for the discovery of the essential connotations of many similar, equally central statements in his letters and elsewhere in the New Testament.[42] Conversely, such other thematic passages help to establish the normative precision and inclusiveness of Gal. 4:4.

Whether or not this is exegetically the proper appraisal of Gal. 4:4–6, three specific and important aspects of Paul's and of the whole early Christian idea of history here come into focus.

1) The phrase " Christ in the fullness of time," or " the fullness of time in Christ " denotes and connotes for Paul a definite indefiniteness, a deliberate and ultimate ambivalence. Fullness is a new, *the* new quality of time and history; it is also the end of chronological time and history and the end of existentialist time and historicity (*Geschichtlichkeit*): " Therefore, if any one is in Christ, he is a new creation; the old [history] has passed away; behold, the new [history] has come " (II Cor. 5:17).[43] Yet the new creature (creation) continues to live in the old time (II Cor. 10:3). But the old time is unreal; it has lost its power, " for the *shape* (σχῆμα) of this world is passing away " (I Cor. 7:31b). The end of history has come for faith, though it happens to be true that it is not yet perceived by the human eye (II Cor. 5:7 in the context of 4:7–5:10). For Paul, however, faith has all *necessary* knowledge; faith will not, at some future time, be superseded by objective knowledge. The knowledge of faith will become full and perfect (I Cor. 13:8b–10, 12 f.; Phil. 3:10–16). Faith *now* includes hope (Rom. 5:1–5; 8:24–5; I Cor. 13:8–13; Gal. 5:5–6; I Thess. 1:2–3). For Paul there can be no faith without hope; there can be no hope without faith; neither can be without love of God.

The ambivalence as regards Paul's " hope " is as characteristic as is that of " fullness." It *is* present; it is faith reaching into its own, the real future, God's future. Hope is not *any* kind of rational calculation based on scientifically ascertainable con-

42. To give major examples from only one letter, see Rom. 1:1–4; 3:21–6; 5:12–21; 8:1–4, 18–25, 31–9; 9:1–6; 11:25b; 15:8–13.

43. R. S. V. and most modern translations. A good text-critical, syntactical, and exegetical case can be made for translating thus: " The old has passed away, behold it has become new."

tinuities in human history. These have their rightful, limited place, but so far, they too have been "passing away." Such calculations have their rightful place in Paul's idea of history, as is shown by the futuristic aspect of his eschatology. The two most instructive and explicit statements of it are I Thess. 4:13–5:11 and Rom. 8:18–25. However sharply these two passages may differ in language and thought form,[44] they have in common the necessity for speaking and reflecting in futuristic, human terms, because God's future has begun (see also, I Cor. 15:19), but the limits of such speaking, reflecting, and acting are sharply drawn (Rom. 8:24–5 and I Thess. 5:1–11; I Cor. 7:29–31). They have in common the hope which is now, a hope which does not ignore but transcends all human hopes and despairs.[45]

2) The second aspect of Paul's idea of history is what in many modern textbooks of historical method is called the problem of continuity and contingency, or continuity and discontinuity in history. Paul meets this problem analytically and reflectively, staying within and carrying the biblical idea to something like its fulness. The fullness in Christ is not fullness arrived at by adding up a series of events on a straight, upward-slanting line. The fullness of history came through God's free and sovereign, creative and redemptive, particular act of sending his Son "into the likeness of sinful flesh."[46] Continuities and discontinuities in history open to scientific judgment have their place as tentative and indispensable *working* hypotheses (I Cor. 3:21–3, in the context of the whole chapter), but both continuity and contingency have their reliable, first, and ultimate ground in the reliability of God "who was in Christ" (II Cor. 5:19; I Cor. 3:21–3; Rom. 8:31–9).[47] Here again Paul rests with ambi-

44. Rom. 8:18–25 may be regarded as more Hellenizing in both respects, and I Thess. 4:13 ff. as more Judaizing.

45. For a somewhat different view of "fulfillment in Christ" see O. Cullmann, *Christus und die Zeit: Die urchristliche Zeit und Geschichtsauffassung.*

46. Rom. 8:3. Note once more the characteristic ambivalence, necessary to Paul, of this phrase.

47. Rom. 9–11 must be read in this perspective too.

valence, satisfied and assured in the certainty *and* the skepticism inherent in his faith in God who raised Christ from the dead. Here is faith in the reliability, the trustworthiness of God (see also, Rom. 3:3–8); in God's freedom and sovereignty; even in a freedom of man apart from Christ, however man may abuse, pervert, and destroy it (Rom. 1:18; 2:29; 7:1–24); in the freedom of the man in Christ as present *and* future reality (contrast and correlate Rom. 8:14–16 and 8:19–21). For Paul there can be no realized eschatology without futurist eschatology (I Cor. 15:19; Goodspeed's translation); there can be no futurist eschatology without realized eschatology.

Ambivalence also is the final note of his reflections in Christ on the continuity and discontinuity of God's revelation as between the old and the new Covenants (II Cor. 3:4–18). Once more he rests, rejoices, labors, and suffers in holding both to strict continuity and to strict discontinuity (see also, Rom. 9–11; 15:8). Both have their ground in the freedom (discontinuity) and reliability (continuity) of God. What applies to Hebrew history and the history in Christ thus also applies to all history that becomes *our* history in Christ.

It is very strange but inescapable that Paul's faith, theology, and idea of history should encompass other New Testament and patristic expressions of the faith of Christ, even if the latter seldom encompass Paul's. Thus Jesus of Nazareth is the subject of the Synoptic Gospels only because he is first and last their risen Christ, like Paul's. The fact that the Synoptic Gospels have a somewhat more literalistic and futuristic eschatology would not have greatly disturbed Paul. He shares both realized and futurist eschatology with them. That the Fourth Gospel emphasizes realized eschatology more strongly than does Paul does not give the Fourth Gospel, as it stands, a different idea of history, for Paul shares it fully and explicitly.

As Christianity, in the course of a few decades and centuries, expanded to the very corners of the Roman-Hellenistic-Near Eastern world, the expression of its faith expanded from its center to so-called heresies on the left, on the right, and in the middle, thereby illustrating, in a small way, the fullness of the power and wisdom of Christ as the beginning of the new creation, of the new history, and the finiteness of the human mind, including " first of all " of the mind of those who have faith in Christ (Rom. 11:33–6; I Cor. 13:8–13; Phil. 3:7–16).

Leaving the extreme " heretics " aside, Tertullian, with his rigid Montanist, apocalyptic idea of history, was more deeply imbued with Paul's faith, example, and spirit than any church father before Augustine. The politicotheological idea of history so fulsomely advocated by Eusebius of Caesarea and others before and after him found more and better justification in Paul's letters than anywhere else in the New Testament by a somewhat special reading of several carefully selected passages, including the Paulinist Pastorals. The Alexandrian theologians, in their emphasis on both *gnosis* and the history of salvation, followed Paul more than the Fourth Gospel. From the Fourth Gospel via Justin they got the *logos* idea, but they gave it a Paulinist rather than a Johannine interpretation. Augustine's theology of history, in spite of its Christian Platonism and its Platonic analysis of time,[48] comes closer to an appreciation of Paul's own central idea of history than that of subsequent theologies of history. A few interpreters, such as Luther (Augustinian), C. F. Baur[49] (Hegelian), and Kierkegaard (anti-Hegelian), after long periods of ecclesiastic and rationalistic dogmatisms once more got to the heart, each in his own way, of Paul's theology of history.

Since the early 19th century Paul's idea of history has been studied feverishly, with passion, partisanship, sobriety, erudition, and objectivity. As long as we are concerned, like Paul, with understanding ourselves out of and in our historical consciousness we will not neglect the study of Paul's Christological theology of history. In this consciousness we have come to know, as Paul did in his own, that the fullness of wisdom is in the fullness of Christ, in which is revealed the fullness of God in history. We have come to understand, as Paul did, that the fullness of our

48. *Confessions* X–XIII.

49. F. C. Baur, *Paulus der Apostel Jesu Christi.*

understanding of Christ is not to be confused with the fullness of Christ, because our fullness comes from God, from whom and through whom and to whom are all things (Rom. 11:36).

c. *Early Islam.* Not the least significant contribution of this volume is the inclusion of Islam. Even in technical, objective scholarship, there is a tendency to think too exclusively in terms of our Hebrew-Christian and Greco-Roman heritage and to disregard the persisting realities of the Moslem Empire, culture, religion, and idea of history.

If the Hebrew-Jewish religion and Zoroastrianism may be regarded as the first and second instances of " world-wide " conversion religions to emerge from the ancient Near East, Christianity may be regarded as the third, and Islam as the fourth. In the early rise of Islam (A. D. 622–*ca.* 750) we behold once more a development of " revolutionary " rapidity and of " world-wide " consequences.

One of the decisive causes for this rapidity and these enduring consequences is certainly the personality of Mohammed. As a prophet of the ancient Near East he has not only his peers but even his betters; as the founder of a new Near Eastern religion he had no peers, for he proclaimed an idea of history which was *meant* to " make history " and to explain theologically the meaning of history. He " claimed " as a visionary prophet; he proclaimed as the founder of a faith; he commanded and administered the Moslem community as its unrivaled, unchallenged leader. (His authority in Islam exceeds that of his nearest rivals, Moses in Hebrew religion and even in Judaism, and Zoroaster in Zoroastrianism. It is difficult to classify Jesus as founder of a religion.)

The Islamic form of the Near Eastern idea of history is no doubt the product of the dynamic " fusion " of pre-Islamic Arabism with selected, special strains of Judaeo-Christian thought. The fusion is largely the work of Mohammed himself.

The analysis of the pre-Islamic Arab sources and of Mohammed's message and career presented in the eighth essay brings to light the specific and decisive elements of Arabism which went into this highly effective fusion. In our context two of these elements must be briefly considered.

1) The clan consciousness of the pre-Islamic Arab tribes means, at bottom, that there is no consciousness of the individual as an individual, that the consciousness of the " individual " member of the tribe is the consciousness of the unquestioned solidarity of the tribe. Thus the thematic emphasis on genealogy, blood kinship, and blood feuds is an expression of this solidarity in which there is " originally " little if any interest in or consciousness of, the past as different from the present. This is indirectly but clearly indicated by the first efforts after Mohammed's fusion of Arabism with Judaism and Christianity to construct *chronological* genealogies (in contrast to the genealogies of clan solidarity). These first attempts would place the chronological beginnings of the northern and southern Arab tribes in the 3d and 7th centuries B. C., respectively![50] That is to say, around A. D. 660 there was little reliable, chronologically oriented genealogical tradition. We can also conclude that when under Jewish-Christian influence Arabic-Islamic genealogy became more consciously chronological it did not by any means lose the connotation of solidarity. However, this is no longer primary clan solidarity but solidarity of the present with the past. This is a solidarity which also characterizes many postexilic genealogies of Judaism. Under the influence of biblical chronology, chronological sense and sophistication grew rapidly. Islamic genealogies were carried back to Abraham and Ishmael, to Noah, and to Adam and Eve—to the beginning of creation. But Mohammed, not the Second Temple, not Jesus, was the *ultima ratio* of this Arab-Jewish-Christian-Mohammedan genealogy.

2) The jihad (pious effort; war; holy war). Clannish blood feud is the inimical brother of clannish blood kinship. The evidence for its importance in Arabism is overwhelming, as the relevant essay has shown. It is the chief root of the Moslem idea of history that Allah, the sovereign of history, commands his

50. See essay VIII, pp. 244–53.

faithful community to convert the world by " the sword of Islam," by force, by jihad.

The special strains from Judaism and Christianity which entered with Arabism into Islam to produce the Islamic idea of history are the strains of the chronologically historical books of the Hebrew-Christian Bible rather than those of Second Isaiah or of Paul. Support for a theology of history which called for military action and direct exercise of concrete and universal political power could be found, if looked for, in several parts of the Old and New Testaments. They could be found more easily in the histories of biblical believers—in the Jewish movement of the Maccabeeans and the Zealots (also in the Persian-Zoroastrian armies), and in the ecclesiastic, militaristic politics of 5th- and 6th-century Near Eastern, Byzantine Christianity. All these models furnished Mohammed with practical examples, as well as with ready-made exegetical and theological arguments, to support his prophetic vision.

The divine command in Islam for direct military and political implementation of the faith is by no means a form of the idea of history which can be brushed aside by moralistic, logical, or even theological argument. The history of Christianity and of its theologies of history up to the present moment shows that the Moslem question and answer are concerned with a problem which is implicit everywhere in history and in every idea of history.

The historian may say that the strength of the Islamic idea of history shows not so much in the past glories of the Mohammedan Empire of the Eastern and Western Middle Ages as in the common heritage which unites Islam, Judaism, Christianity, and Greek culture. These four have shared for thirteen centuries a dramatic history of vital interactions. They have their living roots in the ancient Near East, and they are vital forces still helping to shape our 20th-century consciousness of history.

BIBLIOGRAPHY

F. C. Baur, *Paulus der Apostel Jesu Christi*, Leipzig, 1866 [2].

T. Boman, *Das hebräische Denken im Vergleich mit dem griechischen*, Göttingen, 1952.

E. Buess, *Geschichte des mythischen Erkennens*, Munich, 1953.

R. Bultmann, " Das Problem der Hermeneutik," *Zeitschrift für Theologie und Kirche*, Vol. *47* (1950) .

——— *Das Urchristentum im Rahmen der antiken Religionen*, Zurich, 1949.

H. Butterfield, *Christianity and History*, London, 1949.

J. F. Callahan, *Four Views of Time in Ancient Philosophy*, Cambridge, 1948.

C. N. Cochrane, *Christianity and Classical Culture*, Oxford, 1940.

——— *Thucydides and the Science of History*, Oxford, 1929.

R. G. Collingwood, *The Idea of History*, ed. T. M. Knox, Oxford, 1946.

B. Croce, *History as the Story of Liberty*, trans. by S. Sprigge, London. 1941.

——— *Theory and History of Historiography* (trans. by D. Rinslie) , Philosophy of the Spirit, Vol. *4*, London, 1921.

O. Cullmann, *Christus und die Zeit: Die urchristliche Zeit und Geschichtsauffassung*, Zurich, 1946 [1]. Trans. F. W. Filson as *Christ and Time*, Philadelphia, 1950.

W. Dilthey, *Gesammelte Werke*, Leipzig, 1923–36, 12 vols.

H. Frankfort, *The Problem of Similarity in Ancient Near Eastern Religions*, Oxford, 1951.

H. and H. A. Frankfort, John A. Wilson, and Thorkild Jacobsen, *Before Philosophy: The Intellectual Adventure of Ancient Man: an Essay on Speculative Thought in the Ancient Near East* (Penguin Books, 1949) , No. A198.

P. Friedlander, *Platon: Band I: Seinswahrheit und Lebenswirklichkeit*, Berlin, 1954.

P. Fuglum, *Edward Gibbon: His View of Life and Conception of History*, Oslo, 1953.

V. Goldschmidt, *Le Système stoïcien et l'idée de temps*, Paris, 1953.

E. R. Goodenough, " Kingship in Early Israel," *Journal of Biblical Literature and Exegesis, 48* (1929) , 169 ff.

——— " The Political Philosophy of Hellenistic Kingship," Yale Classical Studies, *1* (1928) , 51–103.

B. A. van Groningen, *In the Grip of the Past: Essay on an Aspect of Greek Thought*, Leiden, 1953.

W. W. Hammerschmidt, *Whitehead's Philosophy of Time*, New York, 1947.

M. Heidegger, *Sein und Zeit*, Halle, 1927.

W. B. Henning, *Zoroaster: Politician or Witch-Doctor?*, Oxford, 1951.

H. Holborn, " Greek and Modern Concepts of History," *Journal of the History of Ideas*, Vol. *10* (1949).

E. Howald, *Vom Geist antiker Geschichtsschreibung*, Munich, 1944.

W. W. Jaeger, *Paideia: the Ideals of Greek Culture*, Oxford, 1939–45, 3 vols.

W. Kamlah, " Die Verlegenheit dieser Zeit," *Die Sammlung: Zeitschrift für Kultur und Erziehung*, *7* (1952), 1–14.

Karl Loewith, *Heidegger: Denker in dürftiger Zeit*, Stuttgart, 1953.

——— *Meaning in History: the Theological Implications of the Philosophy of History*, Chicago, 1949.

F. Meinecke, *Ranke und Burckhardt*, Berlin, 1948.

H. Richard Niebuhr, *The Meaning of Revelation*, New York, 1941.

M. Noth, " History and the Word of God in the Old Testament," *Bulletin of the John Rylands Library*, *32* (1950), 194–206.

R. B. Onians, *The Origins of European Thought*, 2d ed. Oxford, 1954.

H. Ott, " Neuere Publikationen zum Problem von Geschichte und Geschichtlichkeit," *Theologische Rundschau*, *21* (1953), 63–96.

M. Pohlenz, *Die Stoa: Geschichte einer geistigen Bewegung*, Göttingen, 1948.

G. Schrenk, *Studien zu Paulus*, Zurich, 1954; especially the essay on " Die Geschichtsauffassung des Paulus auf dem Hintergrund seines Zeitalters " (1939), pp. 49–80.

J. W. Swain, " The Theory of the Four Monarchies," *Classical Philology*, *35* (1940), 1–21.

A. N. Whitehead, *Adventures of Ideas*, Cambridge, 1933.

——— *Process and Reality*, Cambridge, 1929.

R. C. Zaehner, *Foolishness to the Greeks*, Oxford, 1953.

INDEXES

ANCIENT EGYPT

ADOBE, 17
Akh-en-Aton, omitted from king lists, 8
Amūn of Thebes, theology of, 24
Amun-ḥotpe, son of Ḥapu, 19, 29; royal decree for mortuary temple foundation, 30–2
Amun-ḥotpe III, 11, 19, 29–32
Annals, Old Kingdom stele of, 4–5, 7, 12, 15
Archaism in art and architecture, 10, 20
Architecture, stone, 17–19
Atūm, 22–3, 24, 28–9
Ay, not given cartouche, 11

CATTLE, as booty, 14; census of, 15
Conquest of southern by northern Egypt, 5, 12–14
Creation myths, 22–5
Crowns of Upper and Lower Egypt, 4, 5, 12–14

"DELIVERANCE OF MANKIND," 25–6
"Demigods," 7
Djoser, step pyramid of, 17–19
Dynasties, numbering of, 4, n. 3

EIGHT, THE, *See* Ogdoad of Tḥōt
Ennead of Heliopolis, 22–3, 28

FARINA, Giulio, 6
"Followers of Horus," 12

GĒB, earth-god, 23
Genealogical lists, 9–11
Genealogy of Memphite priests, 10–11
"Glorified ones," 7
Gods who reigned on earth, 5

ḤAT-ḤOR, 26, temple of, at Sarābīt el Khādim, 16
Ḥat-shepsūt, omitted from king lists, 8, 9
Hattušili, Hittite king, 20
Hierakonpolis, capital of southern "Followers of Horus," 12
Hieratic inscription on stele, 28, 31
History of Egypt. *See* Manetho
Horus, last of the god-kings, 7
Hyksos, 21; in Turin papyrus, 6; omitted from king lists, 8, 9; in genealogy of Memphite priests, 11

IBSCHER, Hugo, 6
Im-ḥotep, architect of step pyramid, 17–19; as son of god Ptaḥ identified with Greek Asklepios, 19
Isis, 23

KARNAK, temple of, 7, 18, 20
Khmūn, theology of, 23–4
Khufu, King, 19
King slaying captive, 13, 16
King lists, 4–12

LEATHER, records on, 16, 28
Leather roll at Berlin, 28–9
Legal documents inscribed in tombs, 21

ANCIENT MESOPOTAMIA

ANCIENT PERSIA

ANCIENT ISRAEL

SUBJECT AND AUTHOR INDEX

INDEX TO BIBLICAL REFERENCES

THE HELLENISTIC ORIENT

Thucydides, 144, 147, 148, 154
Tyrtaeus, 142

UGRAITIC EPIC, 138

XENOPHON, 143, 145, 150

ZENO OF CITIUM, 158
Zeus, 137

EARLIEST CRISTIANITY

ACTS OF THE APOSTLES, 188, 196, 199
Aeon, 176, 179, 181, 183, 186, 188, 189, 193, 194, 197, 198, 204, 206 f., 209, 211 f.
Allegory, 187 f.
Anthropology, 178 f.; *see also* Man
Antioch, 197
Apocalyptic, 184, 189, 192, 194, 203, 207; Jewish, 179 f., 189, 190, 192, 193, 204, 206, 209; Synoptic, 192, 196
Apostolic fathers, 171; *see also* the individual sources
Aramaic, 202
Asia Minor, 196
Assumption of Moses, 179
Augustine, 189, 190, 214

BABYLONIAN CAPTIVITY, 206
Barnabas, Epistle of, 188
Baruch, Apocalypse of, 206

CATHOLICISM, early, 171, 202
Church, 181, 191 f., 197, 200, 209
Clement of Alexandria, 184
Clement of Rome, 201
Colossians, Epistle to the, 200, 207
Cyrill, 177

DEUTERO-ISAIAH, 181
Dualism, 178 f., 204

EGYPT, 197
Enoch, Slavonic, 207
Ephesians, Epistle to the, 200, 207
Ephraim, 177
Eschatology, 177, 179 f., 183, 188, 198, 199, 200, 203, 204, 207, 209; existential eschatology, 190, 204; eschatology and history, 197, 204, 210 f.; eschatological Israel, 185; " realized eschatology," 180
IV Ezra, 206 f.

FORGIVENESS, 180, 182
Freedom, 183, 189, 213

GNOSTICISM, 204, 207; Christian, 178; pre-Christian, 198, 202, 207 ff.
Greece, 196
Greek: allegory, 188 f.; antiquity, 190; idea of history, 172, 206, 209; science, 172; Stoicism, 208; time, 214

HEBREWS, Epistle to the, 197–9, 200, 201
Hermas, Shepherd of, 197, 201
Hippolytus, 177
History, 171 ff., 177, 179 f., 182 f., 184, 188 f., 196, 197, 198, 201, 210, 214; existential category, (189) 190; Greek idea of, 172, 206, 209; *historein*, 171; historical method, 172, 188; historical proof, 195; historicity, ideas of, 171, 180, 198, 205–14; philosophy of, 186, 187, 210;

PATRISTIC CHRISTIANITY

EARLY ISLAM

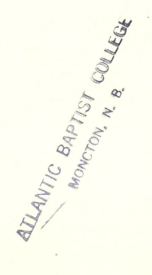